COMPARATIVE
UNION
DEMOCRACY

COMPARATIVE UNION DEMOCRACY

Organisation and Opposition in British and American Unions

J. David Edelstein
Malcolm Warner

Transaction Books
New Brunswick, New Jersey

Library of Congress Catalog Number: 77-80874
0-87855-623-0 (paper)
Printed in the United States of America

Library of Congress Cataloging in Publication Data

Edelstein, J   David, 1918-
  Comparative union democracy.

  Bibliography: p.
  1. Trade-unions—Great Britain.   2. Trade-unions—United States.   3. Democracy. I. Warner, Malcolm, joint author. II. Title.
HD6664,E27 1978   331.88'0941   77-80874
ISBN 0-87855-623-0

Contents

Preface to the Revised Edition

In writing this book we were sustained by a belief in its relevance for the structure and functioning of a democratic socialist society. Indeed, chapters 3 and 11 touch briefly upon this question, but we would like to make the connection between union democracy and democratic socialism more explicit so that the reader may consider some of the broader implications of the book as he or she progresses.

How to establish democratic socialism on a sound basis must remain an open question, since such a society does not exist. It it perhaps the key question of our time, and one not likely to be resolved without active intervention on the basis of some guiding principles. Here we would like to deal with some questions of organizational structure, especially within large work-related organizations or associations of such organizations.

While the organizational foundations for democracy in a large trade union and a democratic socialist society are not quite the same, we think they overlap considerably. This is most obvious if, as we believe, trade unions would still have an important role to play in representing the interests of workers on specific jobs, and in specific occupations and industries. We assume that the division of labor would become less rigid, but not be eliminated. Workers with urgent grievances might justifiably be neither pacified by promises of future remedies, nor appeased by references to the social ownership of the factory or its collective operation by the workers. Nor, to the extent that differences in pay and work-related benefits remain, can we expect workers to regard these as justified, either in general or in their particular instances. Sidney and Beatrice Webb wrote pertinently about this in 1897, in their *Industrial Democracy*. Concerning their version of socialism, based on cooperatives, and municipal and government ownership, they said:

'Experience of all administration on a large scale, whether public or private, indicates how difficult it must always be, in any complicated organisation, for an isolated individual sufferer to obtain redress against the malice, caprice, or simple heedlessness of his official superior [we would add, even if elected by the workers]. Even a whole class or grade of workers would find it practically impossible, without forming some sort of association of its own, to bring its special needs to the notice of public opinion, and press them effectively upon the Parliament of the nation . . . . In short, it is essential that such grade or section of producers should be at least so well organised that . . . it could if need be, as a last resort against bureaucratic stupidity or official oppression, enforce its demands by a concerted abstention from work.'

With unions in a socialist society perhaps expanding their functions to include publicly-financed occupational training, and the operation of safety and work-related welfare programs, as is the case to some extent today in some Western European countries, union democracy should be an important aspect of democracy in society. Finally, although how socialism might be achieved is beyond the scope of this book, unions might play a role (especially democratized unions) in the establishment of democratic socialism, through the struggle for industrial democracy.

Of even greater relevance than the incorporation of trade unions in a democratic socialist system is the similarity in overall skeletal *structure* of unions, and of the probable industrial organization basic to such a society. At the heart of democratic socialism, as we picture it, would be a comprehensive system of industrial democracy—active control over all aspects of work-related life, including the management of industry itself, by workers. Although workers would probably share power, to some extent, with community members and representatives of the public at large, the day-to-day operation of work enterprises would be worker-controlled. The point is that these work enterprises, together with their superstructures of regional and national bodies coordinating them (in some cases loosely) by industry, would have structures—and as we shall show, problems—which parallel those of unions today. Particularly, industrial unions usually established a separate local union for each large or even medium-sized plant (at least in the United States), special coordinating councils to bargain with large multiplant companies, and an overall national (or international) jurisdiction which corresponds roughly with that of a given industry.

Democracy in large work organizations and trade unions would have to overcome similar interrelated *tendencies*: toward top-down hierarchical organization;toward a segmented, relatively isolated organizational life; toward depoliticization and a managerial approach; and, largely as a result of the foregoing, toward low levels of member interest and participation. Such oligarchic tendencies may be facilitated by the perception, justified or not, of a homogeneous membership: the officials would be workers, and hence matters could more safely be left in their hands. Finally, there is the possibility that large work enterprises, as well as unions, might lack the widespread autonomous subassociations (political parties, interest group associations, social clubs, educational societies, etc.) often thought to be the basis for organized opposition in the larger society. The arguments for a pluralist theory of democratic socialism are strong indeed, even though many of the proponents of pluralism have capitalist democracy in mind, and greatly exaggerate the genuineness of its pluralism and its democratic features.

Many of these tendencies or problems would be eased to the extent that work organizations could be integrated into the life of the larger community, but in many cases it may not be initially feasible to substantially blur the boundaries between these two spheres of life. People may still have to travel many miles to work, and spend most of each day performing specialized tasks in the work setting. Furthermore, we believe it is desirable to maintain a high degree of autonomy of worker-controlled enterprises, from the point of view of pluralism in the larger society. 'The community,' in a highly urbanized region, may represent a level of government too far removed from daily life, and in spite of intentions to the contrary, may be too closely linked to the central government. Certainly many strands of socialist thought assume a high degree of self-government in industrial and other functional organizations as the basis for socialism, although such autonomy is presumed to be accompanied by a high degree of cooperation toward social goals.

On the whole, it seems likely that relatively autonomous work enterprises can be much more involving of their members and more politicized than trade unions oriented primarily toward collective bargaining. Nevertheless, the need for high-level coordination of large work enterprises, and the humdrum quality of much of organizational life, would seem to promote tendencies toward oligarchic control not unlike, though weaker than, those in trade unions today. Under somewhat unfavorable conditions, such tendencies might combine with others, of external origin, to threaten the foundations of democracy in the society. It seems safest to proceed on this assumption, and to seek to foster countertendencies. Since this book presents and tests an organizational theory of union democracy, our contribution here is in the sphere of internal, formal organization.

Basically, we show how formal organization itself can at least stimulate close competition for office among full-time officers of relatively equal rank, based preferably on organizational subdivisions with relatively equal numbers of members (and votes), and resolved through a voting system which is not biased in favor of the administration. The power of the administration may also be checked by a number of important power centers (for example, policy-making bodies) near the top of the organization, and by a judicial process outside the administration's control. With a number of relatively equal potential competitors for each level of office, oppositionists might be able to gain an uninvited entry into the officialdom, often with the assistance of factions, and achieve representation for their supporters in the higher councils of the organization.

Thus, on the basis of this organizational framework, the full-time officialdom would be neither monolithic nor secure, and differences with respect to policy would often become electoral issues. A very high level of democracy would require more than this, but such a framework, suitably elaborated, would provide a sound basis for a fairly democratic process under somewhat adverse conditions. How applicable this approach may be to large work enterprises under democratic socialism, or to associations of work enterprises, must depend largely on the inventiveness of those willing to apply it.

We would like to call attention to the sociological radicalism of our general stance in this book: we are profoundly sceptical that effectiveness of opposition, at the level of the national union, is much or consistently affected by such factors as the age or size of a union, the nature of a union's relationship with employers, or the informal social relationships among its members. Instead, we have emphasized the internal, formal organizational features to account for differences in the unions we studied, and shown surprisingly strong relationships between these and the effectiveness of opposition. We completed this study convinced that formal organization contributes even more to democratic decision making than we have been able to show here.

We thank Isidor Wallimann, Barry Glassner, Louis Kriesberg, and Manfred Stanley for helpful reviews of drafts of the new sections in this revised edition. Only we are responsible for the views expressed.

J. David Edelstein
Malcolm Warner

Preface to the First Edition

'No King is as safe in office as a Trade Union Official', one of Shaw's characters remarks in his play *The Apple Cart*. To explore the theme, this book presents and tests an organisational theory of union democracy. The motif of the theory – ways in which internal formal organisation tends to create relatively equal opponents in elections for top leadership posts – is broad enough to be suggestive for many kinds of organisations. However, it applies particularly to the large, well-established, nominally democratic organisations of the labour movement, over eighty of which have been examined in this study. The major theorists of modern organisational democracy, e.g. Robert Michels and later Seymour Martin Lipset, have been concerned with such organisations, following the Webbs.

Strictly speaking, our theory concerns the effectiveness of opposition rather than all aspects of democracy. In most instances we will focus on opposition in elections, in post-war decades, to top union office, and occasionally on the representation of dissidents and on power sharing among organised factions. Democracy and Opposition are interlinked.

Union democracy, we believe, can be achieved only through the continuous self-conscious struggles of numerous union members. We are concerned that union democrats or their friends may find our formal organisational emphasis too aseptic, too far removed from the smell of the day-to-day struggles of rank-and-file workers and their leaders in the workshops. What we are really saying is that, nonetheless, in the long run the outcome of such struggles *is* largely predetermined by the organisation of the union, insofar as these struggles are for control over the union structure. But there is a more positive implication: formal organisation is susceptible to planned change in a democratic direction in the British and American unions, and elsewhere as well. We therefore hope that those working towards more democratic organisations, and more democratic societies, will find the study useful.

This work would have been impossible without the co-operation of many dozens of trade union members, officers and staff too numerous to mention individually. It was funded by a grant from the (American) National Science Foundation.

We are also grateful to the academic institutions, both present and past, in which we respectively worked over the period of the research, for their co-operation. We thank Keith M. Pockross and Boonsanong Punyodyana for their past research assistance, and are deeply indebted to our former research associates, W. F. Cooke and Stanley L. Weir, for their considerable involvement and field-work beyond the call of duty, and for their sophisticated reports and comments, many of which have been incorporated directly or indirectly into this book. We profited from reviews of portions of the manuscript or of preliminary drafts made by Irving Richter, Sidney Sufrin, Bernard Dix, Louis Kriesberg, Allan Mazur, Vinnie P. Morris, William J. Heisler, George S. Aitken, John Child, Raymond Loveridge, L. J. Handy and Donald O. Granberg.

We also benefited from discussions with many colleagues in both countries, particularly Roderick Martin and Jim Mortimer. Ruth R. Greenberg Edelstein provided extensive and valuable suggestions on numerous drafts during the entire study. We thank Peter M. Prowda for, the computer programming. We must in addition thank the Organizational Behaviour Research Group, (Derek Pugh and colleagues), at the London Business School for their direct and indirect assistance, and the (British) Social Science Research Council who supported their research programme.

Finally, we must thank our editor, Victor Thorpe, for his professional skills and critical judgements which have proved so helpful.

Part One

COMPARATIVE AND THEORETICAL FRAMEWORK

Chapter 1

Introduction: The Comparative Approach

THE RELEVANCE OF UNION DEMOCRACY

Union democracy or its absence has become centrally pertinent to democracy in society as unions have expanded their explicitly political functions. In perhaps all advanced countries, the national trade unions and their federations have supported or opposed the incomes policies of their respective governments. These have often found such support useful, however briefly or nominally offered. International confederations of unions have demanded and received union representation on consultative bodies of the European Economic Community, and have demanded Europe-wide legislation to provide for greater worker representation on the boards of directors of all large corporations.

An expansion of democracy to include worker participation in the running of large-scale industry would require democracy in large unions or union-like organisations (see E. Roberts, 1973: 191). Indeed, there is a strong current of opinion in the British labour movement for such participation to be through the unions themselves. Thus the problems of union democracy, and especially of democratic representation, would be transmitted via the unions to work organisations, which in turn are faced with many problems of social policy, obliterating the few remaining distinctions (in the minds of some) between the political and the economic spheres.

The political dynamics of trade unions are hence an integral part of the broader national and international political process. Over one-third of employees in advanced Western countries belong to trade unions, and even more have their wages, benefits and economic security directly affected by agreements between unions and their employers (often the government itself). Probably most union members participate at least occasionally in union activities, at work or elsewhere, and in spite of considerable apathy the unions provide the only organisational participation for a considerable portion of their members (cf. Goldstein, 1952). The unique place of unions in the social system, their membership base and associated resources are often used directly by the official union leadership for explicitly political purposes in the larger society, and indirectly by governments and political parties in alliance with this leadership.

We are aware of the argument that unions need not be internally democratic to represent their members' interests as against those of employers and the state, but whether they indeed do so is problematic and often subject to argument among the members themselves. Such debate is conducted most freely, and is most likely to affect union policy as the membership wishes, where its major vehicle is the competition of would-be leaders for union office. Incumbent and opposition candidates and factions forge as well as express the membership's opinions in the course of the debate, and the policies desired by the majority are more likely to be furthered by democratically elected leaders.

We are concerned in this study with the organisational foundations of democracy in large autonomous national unions – in particular, with those features of union structure and procedure which facilitate democratic competition for top and near-top posts. While there is more to democracy than competition between leaders or would-be leaders, the absence of such a basic aspect of democracy has been all too obvious in probably most of the large national unions in many countries, and some would have it in all.

Most social theorists have, on this basis, argued that oligarchy in large unions is highly likely, offered reasons for this, and let it go at that. Some have redefined or downgraded union democracy, arguing that the membership is not particularly concerned with who runs the union at the top so long as it gets what it wants or can reasonably expect out of the unions. Yet others have debated whether when there is a choice of leaders, there is much to choose between them. But opposition does not depend upon 'the' membership in any simple way. Where little or no electoral *opposition* for top posts manifests itself in a country with democratic norms, we would ordinarily conclude that a union's organisational climate is unfavourable, if not hostile, to democracy.

We began our study with reason to suspect that there was *more* competition than was generally believed for top posts in British and American unions, and that it was worth finding out why *some* unions in each country had more competition than others. We also believed that the general level of electoral opposition was higher in British unions, so that the two countries should be compared. These expectations were fulfilled, as will be seen, in the study of fifty-one American and thirty-one British unions, the backgrounds of which we shall now attempt to describe.

UNIONS AS FORMAL ORGANISATIONS

The large national unions in Britain and the United States are in some respects contrasting counterparts, sociologically, of large business enterprises and large government agencies. Unions, businesses and government agencies are *similar* in that, first, all have fairly clear boundaries which set their major internal operations relatively apart from other organisations and from society at large. Second, there are usually clear lines of authority within these organisations, with higher and lower divisions headed by higher and lower officers. Third, all these organisations have bureaucratic-administrative functions (see Child *et al.*, 1973) and leadership with some degree of expertise, although the unions have this to a lesser degree and in a more political form. Finally, business firms, government agencies and, in practice, unions are highly particularistic, segmented organisations. They have limited goals and can make only limited demands for involvement upon most of their members because they appear irrelevant to most of members' social needs.

These characteristics are generally thought to predispose formally democratic organisations to domination by the few. Control is in the hands of (hierarchically organised) full-time officials who gain political and technical expertise mainly by holding office. Ordinary members, especially workers, have little opportunity to gain such skills in other ways (cf. Beynon, 1973: 187ff.). The external political arena has little opportunity to directly influence organisational politics, and the members generally remain un-involved and apathetic. Thus the tendency towards domination by the few is strong indeed.

The *contrast* between the unions and the other organisations turns on the formally democratic nature of unions: theoretically and legally under their constitutions, all authority derives ultimately from the membership. However, in business firms and government departments the 'members' (employees) are responsible to their supervisors in explicit authority relationships, subject of course to the limitations of legality and relevance to the job. The distinction casts the previously noted 'clear line of authority' within the unions in a different light (see Donaldson and Warner, 1974). Certainly, the general secretary of a union has more authority in mutually relevant spheres than a regional officer, but the latter may be elected by his regional constituency and ordinarily be responsible to it rather than to the general secretary. In some American building trade unions, for example, the authority of the regional officer is ordinarily greater than the president's in matters pertaining to collective bargaining. The locals and the local trade councils seem to be the locus of power. Professor Sidney Sufrin comments that the matter seems to turn on whether the goods are transportable and on the relationships between the local unions and management. A neglect of such downward responsibility, and an exaggerated view of the extent to which the activities of officials can be routinised, have led many organisational theorists to apply the term 'bureaucracy' too imprecisely to unions.[1] Advancement through a competitive electoral process, at least where such exists, also seems inconsistent with the bureaucratic model.[2]

Of course, some unions do indeed resemble corporations somewhat in the appointment rather than the election of most of their full-time officials. We are interested in such *differences* between unions, and in the effects that this and other differences in formal organisation have on competition for top posts.

Some of the features of formal organisation whose effects we will examine seem related to democracy in rather obvious ways: Does a suspended member or lower-ranking officer have the right to appeal over the heads of the body which suspended him? Are policy-making conferences or conventions held annually, or very infrequently? Other features of formal organisation which we thought important for electoral opposition are less obviously related, or even apparently unrelated, to union democracy: Is the top officer elected by the convention, or by the general membership? What percentage of the executive council consists of regionally elected full-time officers? Apart from the specific effects of such organisational features singly, we have tried to judge their cumulative effects.

It is true that competition for high union office must be affected by the nature of a union's relationship with employers, the government and other unions with which it is in competition, by the political culture of the country, and by anything in the social context which may have some effect on a union's internal political process. However, we believe such contextual features to be secondary to internal factors (e.g. the voting system) that *directly* affect the struggle for high union office, which is what we are attempting to explain. This is particularly the case for a study involving Britain and the United States, where union movements and political cultures have much in common, and is why these two countries were chosen as the focal points for our research. Such differences in external relationships or social contexts as do exist are often reflected in the formal union structures themselves. For example, unions which bargain with several industries may have officers elected from such recognised industrial constituencies. And political cultures, such as the American, which favour strong independent powers for their chief executive may foster parallel powers for union top officers.

Democratic rules need not produce effective political opposition, but those who cite absences of the latter in nominally democratic unions often neglect the pitfalls, or structural-procedural inadequacies, in the rules themselves. Union democracy is on the whole a fragile plant requiring favourable conditions to bloom, and the effectiveness of electoral opposition especially may be substantially lowered by any of a number of organisational obstacles. Thus, a really democratic union should have a combination of well-considered organisational features.

BRITISH AND AMERICAN TRADE UNIONS

Organisations and their social settings are never purely abstractions, and while we may generalise about them this is usually safer after placing them in historical and societal perspective. Ultimately, a theory of union democracy should take account of the cross-national differences in industrial relations systems, and other organisational or societal peculiarities which may require qualifications of or changes in the theory itself. We therefore provide some general background to the British and American trade union movements, for the specific period to be covered by this study. Events after this interval are less vitally relevant to the overall test of our organisational theory to be reported later, although they may be alluded to.

The British and American union movements will be placed in perspective, with emphasis on what features characterise the national unions as organisations and may affect their internal political processes. It will be helpful to bear in mind their boundaries, authority, Weberian bureaucratisation and segmental character. These, however, cannot exhaust the circumstances relevant for internal opposition. Apart from internal structure, what are ultimately significant are the permeability of the unions to political issues and influences, and the members' or activists' perception of the importance of the decision-making process.

Although we will discuss later developments in union democracy, by the period when the *formal* sample ends, there were over 10 million British unionists and over 18 million American. (The American total has since moved up to over 21 million, and the British has risen to over eleven) Unionists represented 43 per cent of the British civilian labour force, and 27 per cent of the American. These proportions rise even more if employee associations are added.

There were nineteen unions with 100,000 members or more in Britain and fifty in the United States. These contained 70 per cent of all British unionists and 82 per cent of all American (Bureau of Labor Statistics, 1966: 53). The merger of national unions in both countries, particularly after 1966, has resulted in an even greater concentration of membership than previously. Some of the unions we studied disappeared through mergers in the late 1960s and early 1970s.

The growing proportions of white collar workers, service workers and women in the labour force have had little impact on the absolute size of the manual and low-status non-manual unions we examined during our sampled period, 1949–66. In only a few instances has there been

substantialcompetitionbetween manualand non-manual unions. Nevertheless it is true that some white collar and even professional employees have
been absorbed into primarily blue collar unions.

ORGANISATIONAL HISTORY AND SOCIAL CONTEXT

The histories of British and American unions have been intertwined since
at least the beginning of the nineteenth century, when British immigrants
influenced to some degree the adoption of unionism and collective bargaining in the United States. Later, when 'two of the founders of the American
Federation of Labor, transformed the Cigar Makers International Union
into an effective economic organization by raising dues, centralizing control
over local unions and strikes, and establishing a benefit programme, they
cited the British national unions of the 1860s as their model' (Derber, 1968:
55). We shall see shortly how this model came about.

There have been differences in the historical development of the union
movement as well as striking similarities. Many explanations have been
offered for the greater emphasis of American unions on militant collective
bargaining, with relative stress upon local contracts rather than political
action or industry-wide bargaining. These include: the greater American
geographic spread; ethnic heterogeneity; a fierce localism among American
unionists; the lesser solidarity of the workers as a class due partly to
egalitarianism, individualism and achievement orientation in the culture;
the supposedly greater competitiveness, and the certainly later and more
rapid development, of American industry; and the greater resistance of
American employers to both unionism and collective agreements through
employer federations. It has been further argued that lingering aspects of
pre-capitalist culture explain the greater propensity for group agreements
in Britain, and the willingness of the British working class to assume unpaid
union posts.

However, such explanations of differences between the labour movements are necessarily speculative and subject to argument. Timing is an
extremely important element in social and organisational development, and
it is no doubt misleading at times to cite broad societal differences rather
than specific historical events or contexts. Britain started its take-off into
economic growth prior to the American Revolution. So, while it is possible
to find parallel developments both early and late, the crucial events in the
rise of unions came much earlier in Britain.

The character of a union movement is set by those organisations which
survive, succeed and serve as examples to other organisations. Britain as
well as America saw a great many unions disintegrate after bitter struggles
with employers. The 1829–42 period in Britain culminated in failure, but
it included: bitter strikes, aggressive as well as defensive; several attempts

to form one big union; the formation of a mass Owenite union with utopian economic as well as trade union aims; massive demonstrations and general strikes in some cities; and radical political agitation. The failures, of course, led to disillusion. The successful formation or re-establishment of national unions from 1843 on was based, according to the Webbs' view (1965), on the spread of education among the rank and file and the influence of more practical counsels. However, in addition there was the factor of economic growth:

'From 1850 industrial expansion was for many years both greater and steadier than in any previous period. It is no mere coincidence that these years of prosperity saw the adoption by the Trade Union world of a "New Model" of organization, under which Trade Unionism obtained a financial strength, a trained staff of salaried officers, and a permanence of membership hitherto unknown' (S. and B. Webb, 1965: 180–1; cf. 113–83).

Many of the new unions were craft unions, including the original New Model, the Engineers, whose rules and methods were explicitly emulated. One of the Engineers' innovations was a contribution for insurance and strike allowances (one shilling per week) 'which surpassed the wildest dreams of previous Trade Union organizations' (on this see 1965: 222). Another characteristic was the central executive's absolute power to grant or withhold strike pay (for example, 1965: 221) and thereby control strikes. The new Engineers was a highly centralised union, for its day: 'The great object of the amalgamation was to secure uniformity in trade policy, and to promote the equalization of ... "real wages" throughout the whole country' (on this point, 1965: 221). Its constitution was elaborately worked out, and its system for financial and trade reporting was extremely methodical, due in part to the personality of William Allan, its founder.

'Even today [1894] the Engineers' head office retains throughout the impress of Allan's tireless and methodical industry. Excessive caution, red-tape precision, an almost miserly solicitude for the increase of the society's funds, were among Allan's defects ... at a time when working men "agitators" were universally credited with looseness in money matters and incapacity for strenuous and regular mental effort ...'. (on this see 1965: 234).

Thus the union succeeded and became a model in itself, because it met the needs of its very special period.

The national trade union did not become the secure and predominant form of organisation in the United States until at least the late 1880s. Organisation remained local until the formation of the short-lived National Trade Union in 1834 as an 'association of city associations of [local] unions' (Leiserson, 1961: 92). A similar attempt was made in 1866 with the formation of the National Labor Union, this time with the participation of some well-known existing national craft unions formed in the 1850s and 1860s. Its main objective was the passage of labour legislation rather than collective bargaining, and it soon attempted to turn itself into a labour and reform party. The national unions were dissatisfied and began to withdraw, and the 1873–80 depression decimated most of the other constituent organisations. The total membership of all unions fell from 300,000 in 1873 to under 50,000 in 1878 (Cohen, 1970: 75n.). More national unions were formed from the late 1870s on, but an all-inclusive rival to the national union form arose in the Noble Order of the Knights of Labor, which held its first open convention (it had been a secret society) in 1878 (Leiserson, 1961: 92–8).

'For some years . . . it looked as if the centralized empire of labor about which the Knights dreamed would become reality. Between 1880 and 1886 the membership of the Knights of Labor increased from 28,000 to more than 700,000. It absorbed many national unions and established them as subordinate trade districts, while numerous locals of the craft unions went to it en masse. . . . At the same time, it was attracting every variety of reformist group to its ranks' (Leiserson, 1961: 97).

The Knights of Labor fell into decline after its leadership failed to support the 1 May 1886 general strike for the eight-hour day called by the national unions, on the grounds that it was premature and that a legislative approach was more appropriate. On the appointed day about 350,000 workers in 11,562 establishments struck, with the support of many of the Knights' affiliates, most of its rank-and-file and many varieties of left-wing organisations. The immediate results, at least, were successful and inspiring enough to discredit the Knights.

The story of the Knights shows how different American unionism might have been, not only in social philosophy but also in organisational form. The current American exclusive jurisdiction for any one union at any one workplace outside the building trades, which contrasts with a multi-union jurisdiction in most of British industry, developed as a direct result of the national unions' strained relationships with the Knights of Labor.

At least eleven national unions survived the 1873–80 depression and eight more were formed during the depression. By 1885 there were thirty 'national' unions (some more so in aspiration than in actuality) with a membership of perhaps 125,000. The Knights encouraged the allegiance of the national unions, but also that of their local members separately.

The basic structural unit of the Knights was the district assembly of mixed trades, consistent with its idea of one big union. Ulman (1968: 377) argues that the one big union of skilled and unskilled was not a viable form of organisation at that time:

'The Knights . . . were obliged to gamble that the leveling influence of technological change would be great enough to make membership in the Order a matter of self-interest to the unions' members. The trade union, on the other hand, relying for its strength upon the economic isolation of its membership, was obliged to gamble on the permanence of that isolation. The Knights lost this bet.'

The mixed district assembly could initiate united action by all workers, thus bypassing the national unions. District trade assemblies were also permitted within the Knights, and eventually these were allowed to combine into national trade assemblies, of which there were twenty-two by 1887. Conflicts between the national trade assemblies and national unions were inevitable, since both were competing for members in the same trades or industries.

'The Knights seem usually to have been the aggressors in these conflicts. They did not hesitate to take in rebels and dissenters from a national union and set them up as a trade assembly. In some cases the Knights induced, or tried to induce, trade-union locals to secede from a national union and switch over to the Knights' (Reynolds, 1951: 90; see also 86–91).

The Knights may also have undermined local wages and working conditions, perhaps partly through the use of its general assembly's power to issue travel cards (work permits) (see Ulman, 1968: 350, 359–61, 388). Indeed, the power to issue travel and transfer cards may have contributed to the Knights' rapid expansion in membership.

Thus, 'it was the struggle with the Knights which elevated the principle of exclusive jurisdiction to its position of unchallenged eminence in the American trade union movement' (Ulman, 1968: 405). Perhaps the structure of the economy made exclusive bargaining rights more likely in the United States than in Britain, but the experience of the national unions with the Knights removed an historical option which had remained open until then. According to Ulman (1968: 361–8), an accommodation between national unions was more likely in Britain because of: the greater class consciousness and solidarity of the workers, which discouraged the raiding of membership and the undercutting of standards; the apparently more local nature of British markets, in spite of the smaller size of the country, which made national control by a single union less necessary; and 'the more leisurely pace and less highly competitive nature of capitalist enterprise in Britain' (362). He also points out that until 1917 British law required a two-thirds majority vote of each union to complete an amalgamation. Since the 1950s there has been keen competition in amalgamations and recruiting among the three major British unions. With the establishment of the union contract by the American Federation of Labor in the 1890s as the accepted method of dealing with employers (Reynolds, 1951: 93), and of a more efficient national union organisation as in Britain, the major outlines of American unionism were completed.

Full-time Officials

On the whole, the American labour movement of the 1890s appears similar to the British of the 1850s. National craft unions predominated in both countries, with similar aims, techniques and internal organisation. Among the differences yet to appear were the much larger proportion of paid full-time officials in the United States, the practice of appointing many of these by the top officer or the executive council, and the development of business unionism in all its peculiarly American aspects, including anti-radicalism, corruption and highly paid union officials.

In the periods in question, full-time national staffs appear to have been limited to an ill-paid overworked top officer, possibly with the assistance of one additional officer. In the known American cases, salaries were often paid grudgingly and inconsistently (cf. Ulman, 1968: 217–23).

Currently, the United States is probably unique among advanced societies in the high salaries of its union officials, the extent of reported corruption among them, and the high ratio of full-time officers to union members. An estimate of the latter, in the late 1950s and early 1960s, was 1:300 in the United States, 1:775 in Denmark, 1:900 in Australia and only 1:2,000 in Britain. Sweden and Norway were not very different from Britain, with 1:1,700 and 1:2,200 respectively (Lipset, 1967: 218). The position in Britain is virtually the same today. The percentage of full-time officials who are appointed, rather than elected, is on the whole higher in American manual unions than in British, and such appointment is generally made by the top officer or executive council. Thus, American unions have a greater weight both of locally or regionally elected full-time officials, supposedly responsible to their constituencies, and also of nationally appointed officials, generally responsible to the top officer.

Even in 1973, top union salaries were generally below the middle managerial norm in Britain. The highest known annual salary for a British general secretary of a manual workers' union in 1958 was £2,045, at a time when the average annual earnings of all adult males were £650–750 per year

(Clegg *et al.*, 1961: 56–9). The salaries plus perquisites of several other top officials of large British unions were under £1,300, although those in other unions are not known. Among the highest American salaries in 1962 were $55,000, plus $17,000 in allowances, for the president of the Operating Engineers (a highly paid manual occupation) and $50,000 for the Mine Workers president, while the median income of full-time year-round male craftsmen in 1962 was approximately $6,100 (Bureau of the Census, 1971: 234).

The lowest salaries in 1962 for full-time presidents were between $7,000 and $8,000, with that for the American Communications Association – a fairly large union – among them (cf. Barbash, 1967: 86). It is clear that the salaries of American top officials are relatively higher, particularly in the larger unions, although major differences exist among American unions in this respect. In addition to high salaries, some American presidents had very high accumulations towards retirement and other benefits.

Barbash provides an excellent summary of the administration of American unions in 1960, showing that on the whole the headquarters organisation is not only simple, but also modest. This applies even more to British unions. The basic American situation is probably much the same today, allowing for changes in the value of the dollar. In 1960:

1. Approximately 10 per cent of 250 unions reporting to the Department of Labor had receipts of $5 million or more. The average American unionist belonged to a union with receipts of this order.

2. The six wealthiest unions had assets, excluding welfare and pension reserves, between $111 million and $29 million and four of these six had $55 million or less. (Most of even these unions could probably not have sustained a major strike for more than several months.)

3. 'Most of the staff departments (law, economic research, education, publications, public relations; probably, in the larger unions, also "industrial engineering, international affairs, health insurance and pensions, and investments"), except for a very few large unions . . . are one-man departments.'

4. Apart from the legal department, the professional and technical staffs were unlikely to be influential in deciding strategic policy.

5. 'A 1950 analysis of union expenditures showed organizing used 32·5 per cent, benefits to members 21·9 per cent, administrative expense 14·5 per cent, strike benefits 13·2 per cent, publications . . . 6·1 per cent.' Other

types of expenditure, including donations, legal, conventions, research, education and political activities, accounted for 2 per cent or less each.

6.   The most numerous headquarters staff was for record keeping, which operation probably absorbed most of the administrative expense.

7.   The field staff was stationed at regional headquarters. (Members might, however, be shifted or assigned duties by the national officers.)

8.   The officers at headquarters normally included the president and his assistants (the latter might have no constitutional recognition as officers), the secretary-treasurer, the equivalent of an executive vice-president, and in some cases executive councillors (often called vice-presidents) who might be assigned regional or occupational jurisdictions for bargaining and/or organising. However, the latter might be regionally based, or their responsibilities might be handled by senior staff instead (cf. Barbash, 1967: 185–7).

Indeed, a report in *The Times* Business News of 21 August 1973 pointed out that:

Whereas union officials in Britain, even at the very top, rarely receive much more than £3,000, in America union officers have come to expect payment on a par with that of the presidents of many companies.

Just how well the top United States union bosses do is dramatically illustrated by a recently published survey of union leaders' earnings in 1972. Topping the league, as they do year after year, are two men from the Teamsters Union (lorry drivers), once presided over by Jimmy Hoffa and known for its conservative views and the frequent allegations of scandal against it. Frank Fitzsimmons, its president, receives £50,000 a year and the secretary £40,000, quite apart from expenses and allowances.

But the Teamsters are far from an isolated case. The president of the iron workers was paid £38,000, including expenses, and 10 officials received more than £30,000. Getting more than £20,000 is commonplace; there are 42 officials who receive this.

On the whole, the unions which pay their leaders most are those whose membership get the highest pay, and therefore might have the most to thank their leadership for. But this is not always the case. The miners seem to have suffered badly over the years from the introduction of mechanisation, but this didn't stop their then president, Tony Boyle, paying himself over £39,000 last year before being thrown out of office by a man who promised to cut wages.

There are also unions which make a point of trying not to pay ultra-high salaries; the auto workers (one of the richest) pay their president "only"

£15,000, while the electrical workers restrict their leader to the top pay being received on a union-negotiated contract. Still, since this works out at £9,000 he's not exactly starving.'

The path to top office in British and American manual unions is normally from within the boundaries of the organisation, and usually involves long service in a subordinate capacity. This is less true of British white collar unions, which are more likely to have an appointed general secretary (often chosen from the professional stratum) as the most important officer. The existence of such an opening may be advertised outside the union.

Even in the United States, prominent appointed staff such as legal advisers have been known to compete for, and even win, top office, although this is rare. Ralph Helstein, the president of the United Packinghouse Workers until its amalgamation with the Meat Cutters, was general counsel when he won the presidency of the UPW in 1964 at a turbulent convention (Brody, 1964: 226).

It is not uncommon for the lowest level of appointed field staff, particularly organisers, to be appointed from outside American unions. These are often temporary positions. There is also a tendency to regard the seasoned field representative as having a distinct occupation, and there is some job-hopping across unions. (The Worker Education Local of the American Federation of Teachers maintains a file of such openings, as well as of more 'professional' jobs.) However, a move to a higher office, if possible at all, would usually require the attainment of an elective post. This is no doubt sometimes achieved, but in most blue collar unions such a candidacy would be of doubtful legitimacy even where possible, and an outside origin would handicap a candidate for high national office. However, it is possible that some autocratic regimes bolster themselves by managing to fill some lower-level elective posts with their previously appointed 'organisers', 'representatives' or 'walking delegates'.

The institution of candidacies from the outside, or from among the professional staff, could conceivably promote democracy by politicising a membership and offering members a wider choice. But the introduction of full-time officers under the guidance of the national officers is a threat to democracy, particularly where they are unrestricted as to further progress. In this respect the British and American union movements offer a degree of protective restriction, but the former much more than the latter.

On the whole, the most striking differences between British and American national unions are not to be found in the size of central staffs or their degree of specialisation, nor in the financial resources under their control, although there are indeed differences. The most striking differences, and undoubtedly the most important for democracy, are in the powers of the American president and national officers, constitutionally recognised or otherwise, over the appointment of officials stationed elsewhere, and indeed over much of the organisational machinery.

The Sources of Business Unionism

American business unionism involves an ideology of fighting for more money rather than for social reorganisation, usually through the application of 'business-like' techniques which place a low priority on rank-and-file involvement in the running of the union. By the turn of the century it was becoming associated, in many unions, with an ethic which justified the self-enrichment of union officials through high salaries, and even corrupt practices.

Lipset has argued that the larger full-time union officialdoms and their higher salaries are basically related to the less 'aristocratic' and more 'achievement-oriented' nature of American society. American workers lack 'the kind of class consciousness characteristic of more aristocratic societies' and are oriented towards getting ahead. Furthermore, they have lacked the 'aristocratic' model of *noblesse oblige* (requiring the devotion of time to good works) which historically has been the basis for the European inhibition against employing a large number of officials in voluntary associations. Union officials have come to view their jobs as 'careers' rather than 'callings', in line with the ideology of business unionism.

The greater the rewards associated with their positions, the more motivated are American leaders to hang on to them by undemocratic and even dictatorial means. Since American workers are less deferential, it is argued, their union officials are doubly motivated to suppress opposition. This explanation of European–American differences in union leadership is admittedly based more on a comparison of the societies, and especially their value systems, than on their specific historical developments (cf. Lipset, 1967: 9–12, 212–23).

While such an argument is persuasive on these questions, another authority has shown that the *early* growth of field staff under national office control was intimately related to the extensiveness of the territorial jurisdictions of the national unions. The problem of extensiveness was compounded by the facts that the United States had 'markets [that] were frequently more thoroughly "nationalized", and there was less concentration of industry within limited areas' (Ulman, 1968: 225, see also 212–42).

As a result, many union presidents travelled a great deal during the last century, from the 1860s on, at a time when they alone, or they plus the secretary, were the entire full-time staff. These presidents soon could not perform their constitutional duties and found themselves usually in the field not only organising, but also negotiating with employers and authorising and leading strikes. The presidents eventually received the assistance of field representatives who, in many respects, acted as deputies. Because most early national unions were reluctant to assume a high fixed cost of organising, appointment was made on an *ad hoc* basis by the president and executive board, and the normal process of election by the convention could not be followed. The unintentional effect was, of course, the beginning of a patronage system.

Local unions and city-wide federations also began to employ full-time officials in the late 1880s and early 1890s because, it has been argued, of the savage attacks by employers. Spies wrecked local after local and militant unionists who could be identified were blacklisted. The business agent therefore took on such functions as organising, penalising the employer for infraction of rules, calling strikes and representing the local union in the federation's regional council. With so many functions in the hands of one person who could not easily be intimidated, employers offered bribes and found some takers. This was the more likely because, from the beginning, there was many a business agent with no knowledge of the trade, or of any trade for that matter, who had acquired 'a formidable reputation as a tough guy, and some of it in prison' (Foner, 1964: 138; see also 137–73).

During the 1890s, committees of able-bodied members began to be used to protect picket lines from attacks by strong-arm squads hired by employers. By the late 1890s, these were supplemented in a number of unions, mainly in large cities, by hired thugs paid on a daily basis. By the early 1900s, many local officials used hired thugs to terrorise rebellious members. The large majority of unionists were never directly under such oppression, but those conservative national leaders with racketeer-dominated locals seldom took action against them and remained in power for decades with such local support.

In addition to the American value system, the greater decentralisation of bargaining has facilitated racketeering, militancy and a larger proportion of full-time officials. Racketeering is more likely and less visible where local union leaders deal directly with businessmen; militancy is less likely to be restrained by political considerations or the inability of a section of industry to pay; and strong local organisation can support, or require for effectiveness, a larger full-time staff (Lipset, 1967: 223–6).

Collective Bargaining
The most important differences between British and American collective bargaining, from our point of view, are those which affect internal union processes and union relationships with other organisations.

In the United States, virtually all the manual workers in a given workplace belong to the same union, which is the sole bargaining agent for such employees (although this does not apply to the construction industry nor sometimes to a small number of skilled building maintenance workers in a large industrial plant). Shop stewards, plant grievance committees and negotiating committees are all extensions of the local union, and in a large plant communication normally takes place regularly among these.

The absence of exclusive bargaining jurisdiction for any one union in most of British industry creates a break in the lines of authority and communication between the shop stewards, on the one hand, and both the branch and national organisations on the other. The result is that the shop stewards and 'joint' plant committee in such situations are not responsible to any one union and are in a sense outside them all (see, for example, Beynon, 1973). This is particularly true in the engineering and automotive industries, which employ a considerable portion of the workforce and are organised by several of the unions we have studied.

Parallel to these differences is a variance in the structure of local unions. In the American case there are factory-based locals where factories have a sufficient number of employees. Where they do not, or where the workers are dispersed by the nature of their trade, workers belong to 'amalgamated locals' which still include all the workers of a given employer in the same local union. In Britain many unions have small, geographically based branches even where their members are concentrated into large workplaces. Several have recently considered a move towards factory-based locals.

The anomalous position of British shop stewards (see Evans, 1973: 82ff.) is heightened by the failure until recently of most of their unions to take official note of the existence of shop stewards' committees.[3] Such committees were recognised in the rules of only four of eighteen large unions in the mid 1950s, and in two of these the committees were not mandatory (B. C. Roberts, 1956: 71).

In some British industries, including engineering, union and employer confederations have recognised local shop stewards' committees as representing the union side, but this official status has not simplified the relationship between stewards and their respective unions. (The position was even further complicated by the Industrial Relations Act 1971). Relationships have been even more indirect where, as in the automobile industry, the workplace organisations of large multi-plant employers have become linked by 'combine' committees of stewards formed on their own initiative (cf. Hughes, 1964: 12–27). In such situations unofficial strikes are often called (without the endorsement of union officials), and even strikes in defiance of agreements made by union officials. The latter occur in the United States also, but more covertly, briefly and perhaps less frequently, because American agreements are legally binding, more comprehensive and detailed and typically for two or three years rather than for an indefinite duration, as is often the situation in Britain (cf. Derber, 1968: 56–62). Thus, British rank-and-file leaders are more likely to gain a reputation beyond their immediate environs by militant anti-leadership activity.

American shop stewards are not generally a centre of dissent against either their union leadership or management. Indeed, their power in the American automobile industry was much weakened after the early 1940s as a result of company demands and oligarchic trends in the union. Nevertheless, they remain in constant contact with the ranks and may reflect a widespread dissatisfaction with the paid leadership, where such exists (cf. Barbash, 1967: 48–51; Weir, 1970: 466). On the other hand, the British convenors (heads) of large multi-union plant committees are not always radical, nor even militant. They have been known to make a career of the kind of strong non-ideological personal leadership, known on both sides of the Atlantic, which devotes itself to local issues and capitalises on a reputation for keeping its word to both management and workers. Interestingly, Richter (1973: 70–86) found British stewards to be less political than national union leaders. British as well as American stewards have sometimes been provided with training-course direction by their national unions (rather than by university extension divisions or worker education associations, as is usually the case).

On balance, the often ambiguous and extra-union place of British shop stewards is probably favourable for intra-union electoral opposition. However, certain qualifications must be made. First, it is by no means easy for a stewards' movement to exert direct influence on the politics of a national union, even in Britain where the industrial relations system fosters such movements. Second, the official place of important workshop representatives in their local unions has served, at times, as a springboard for a challenge to the local and national leadership. Third, some British unions have approached exclusive bargaining jurisdictions and have therefore been able to integrate their workplace representatives into their official structure, as in the United States. Finally, employer-recognised British workshop organisation has been weak in some small or medium-sized plants in engineering, absent until very late in our period of study in building trades, and not achieved for seamen (Hughes, 1964: 12–13).

Centralisation of Bargaining

Democracy thrives on interest, controversy and hope. An excessive centralisation of collective bargaining may make it appear to the typical member that participation within the union is ineffective as a means of influencing policy or redressing grievances. While this would detract from a sustained interest in the politics of the national union, desperation might occasionally manifest itself in an electoral revolt. This assumes that the national union itself, rather than the federation or purely political sphere, remains the locus for decision making.

Collective bargaining in Britain is less centralised than in mainland Europe, but more so than in the United States. In 1963, Britain had 450 national agreements in force in both private and public sectors, but some were in rather specialised 'industries' and they were not always intended to be all-inclusive. At one extreme are the railways, with central negotiations predominating; at the other is the building industry, with regional and local deviations permitted and approved by the central body. In engineering and shipbuilding only modifications in basic (actually, minimum) wage rates are negotiated nationally, although these tend to set the pattern for changes in all wage rates in these industries. In recent years there has been a move towards greater bargaining at the workplace in much of British industry. National bargaining has not necessarily meant centralised bargaining.

The American trend since World War II has been towards a centralisation of bargaining, mostly in the form of agreements with large multi-plant employers like General Electric, General Motors and Bell Telephone. Such agreements are called national even where the company has rivals within the same industry, in view of the number of employees involved and the number and geographic spread of its plants. In some fields pattern setting has become the rule, with the union selecting one of several large companies as its initial target, in the expectation that competing companies will make comparable concessions. Union members in related companies may find themselves contributing to strike funds but otherwise being onlookers during major negotiations. Their representatives may, however, have participated in establishing the initial demands and their priority.

There is wide variation from one American union to another in the degree to which rank-and-filers, or local union officials, participate directly in drawing up demands for or monitoring national negotiations. It must not be assumed that a centralisation of bargaining entirely deprives local leaders of their influence. Indeed, a long-term recognised collaboration of local unions dealing with the same employer may provide a forum and an organisational departure from simple hierarchy which may be more difficult for national officials to dominate. The International Union of Electrical Workers, for example, has a 'conference board' of local unions to coordinate bargaining with General Electric. This conference board elects its own chairman and publishes its own newspaper. The Auto Workers, similarly, have had Ford, General Motors, Chrysler and other national committees for bargaining purposes. Nevertheless, the actual negotiating of national agreements is ordinarily done by the national officials who, when pressed, bend in order to retain control.[4] Thus, such democracy, as may be associated with national bargaining is seldom reflected directly in competition for top national posts.

It has been suggested that concentrated ownership in an industry tends to require a union to create a large centralised administration of its own; the latter is, of course, unfavourable for union democracy (Lipset *et al.*, 1956: 414). There is some truth to this, but the relationship between industrial and union centralisation seems to be far from overwhelming in Britain and the United States. This is partly because union centralisation takes place for other reasons as well. The relationship between centralisation of bargaining and union democracy is complicated, in the United States, by the fact that racketeering is more prevalent where bargaining is highly decentralised, as pointed out earlier. Finally, while the centralisation of bargaining may reduce the autonomy of locals and the interest of their membership, it also tends to nationalise issues and possibly to generate dissatisfaction with the leadership. Certainly militant or dissident groups in both countries have succeeded at times in taking factional advantage of such dissatisfaction, to the point of registering impressive electoral challenges to national officials. But the opportunity for electoral success is closely tied to the susceptibility of the organisational machinery to such use.

There is no strong reason to state that the greater centralisation of bargaining in Britain as compared to the United States is a greater or a lesser liability, *in itself*, to democracy. It may be, however, that British centralisation outside the nationalised industries is limited, loose and ineffective enough to stimulate opposition without being as oppressive as the more highly organised American centralisation of bargaining, where such exists.

There are other differences between collective bargaining in the two countries. In most industries in the United States, full-time officers beyond the level of the local union are more likely to assist in the negotiation of local agreements, and these agreements 'must adhere to the standards negotiated in the overall agreement [if any] at the industry or [employer] association level. Furthermore, the local agreements must usually be approved by the national union as must a strike over failure to reach a settlement' (Stieber, 1968: 235; see also 234–8). These American agreements run for fixed periods of time and are legally binding, although some permit strikes under certain conditions. They cover many more issues and 'will usually spell out procedures to be followed in layoffs, transfers and, less frequently, in promotions'. There may also be detailed procedures covering the assignment of overtime, changing incentive standards and, more recently, the introduction of major technological changes. In Britain, these problems are more likely to be left to be dealt with as they arise and 'Inevitably this results in negotiations under adverse conditions which more often end up in unofficial strikes . . .' (Stieber, 1968: 236). Unauthorised strikes are also more common in Britain, it has been argued, because of the much more widespread use of payment-by-results schemes.

American agreements usually include the availability of arbitration by a neutral party as the final step in an orderly grievance procedure, and this also has been credited with reducing unofficial strikes: 20,000 cases go to arbitration each year. Nevertheless, companies have been known to allow vast numbers of cases to go to arbitration – something which most local unions cannot afford for long since they generally pay half the costs of the semi-judicial proceedings. Thus, in the United States one cannot separate the effects of the availability of arbitration from those of the illegality of most strikes during the term of agreement. Stieber 'hazards a guess that something like 25 to 30 per cent of all strikes in the United States are unauthorised . . . and account for perhaps 5 per cent of all man-days lost' (1968: 234–5). In Britain the latter figure was 60 per cent during the period 1960–64.

The percentage of *all* working time lost because of strikes in the United States, however, is more than double that in Britain, in spite of the rather low contribution of unofficial strikes to the total over the period of this study. B. C. Roberts (1959: 95) has noted that 'It is a commonplace for visitors to America from European countries to remark on the apparently much less friendly relations between unions and management in the United States. They are astonished at the virulent criticism that is expressed during industrial disputes, at the apparent readiness of unions and employers to ignore all other interests but their own'. Even today, many employers appear never to have reconciled themselves to the existence of unions, and certainly the past history of industrial relations will continue to affect the future for some time. However, it would be wrong to imply that American industrial conflict is basically irrational; it is undoubtedly based on an aggressive pursuit of the self-interests of the major parties involved, as these interests are perceived.

Some observers of the British scene have noted a drift towards the 'Americanisation' of industrial relations since 1960, in the form of some long-term agreements, productivity bargaining, and a desire in many quarters to move towards a simpler, more official and more integrated system of workshop bargaining (on this last point, see Parker, 1973: 20). The now superseded (Conservative) Industrial Relations Act was intended to encourage exclusive bargaining jurisdictions and to regulate many features of bargaining which had been entirely voluntary, but union opposition to its punitive features had made its applicability erratic and lessened its effect upon the main direction of industrial bargaining. The recent incomes policies of the American Government have been viewed as a convergence from the other direction. Our comparative perspective on such developments, in general but particularly as they have affected intra-union life, indicates that thus far it is too early to judge, except that they have encouraged a higher level of militancy in the British case.

Power, Affiliations and Autonomy
British and American national unions are strong in relation to both their local affiliates and their trade union federations. Members must maintain themselves in good financial standing and branches (locals) usually bargain with at least the general guidance of the national union, although they may maintain considerable autonomy. Virtually no collective bargaining takes place through the American Federation of Labor and Congress of Industrial Organizations (AFL–CIO) or through the British Trades Union Congress (TUC), although the federations in each country have been induced to (or have had to) accept government 'guidelines' or regulation of wages during wartime and, since World War II, in peacetime for limited periods. Most American unions have considerably more power to discipline their locals, to the point of suspending their officers and taking over the locals' administration.

Political Affiliations
The affiliation of a union movement to a particular political party may have various effects on internal union political processes, depending upon whether the party is in the government and especially upon whether it participates in the regulation of wages over an extended period of time. The combination of party affiliation (or a close alliance with a particular party), a centralised federation, and an emphasis on political statesmanship and responsibility rather than collective bargaining would appear to be unfavourable for union democracy. This seems to be the situation in Scandinavia. The previous arguments for the deterrent effects that affiliation to a centralised federation has on opposition apply, but with even greater force when the social democratic parties are in the government. The arguments might not apply if there was a meaningful participation of unionists in the workplace management, linked somehow to the making of national economic policy (e.g. by a labour-dominated government, since this would politicise union affairs), but this situation rarely exists, (we note that the recent Danish case is an exception to the rule). Nevertheless, a prolonged official policy of wage restraint may become an issue in itself, and ultimately generate attempts to change the leadership or, more likely, lead to unauthorised strikes.

Not since the early 1920s, until which time American socialists contributed heavily to intra-union factionalism, have American labour politics had much effect on intra-union opposition. Many radicals participated as individuals in industrial unions of the mid 1930s, but failed to establish a mass base. The several unions which fell, for a time, under the domination of the Communist Party, for example (including the United Electrical Workers and the National Maritime Union), contributed little towards a radicalisation of the working class and were as unreceptive to opposition as most other unions. Certainly by 1949, the beginning of our period of study, American radicalism was weak and ineffective as an opposition force.

Political differences of a more conventional sort have continued to exist within the American labour movement, but their usual manifestation has been in rivalry at the federation level between a few prominent leaders. In 1966 the Auto Workers, under the leadership of Walter Reuther, withdrew from the AFL–CIO, and in 1968 formed the Alliance for Labor Action together with the Teamsters (currently 2 million members). The Rubber Workers and the International Chemical Workers also affiliated. The Alliance had a more activist orientation towards the organisation of un-organised workers and the poor. In the 1972 Presidential election, while the Teamsters supported Nixon, the Republican, and the Auto Workers McGovern, the Democrat, the AFL–CIO as a federation remained neutral. In addition, the Auto Workers and the Teamsters had a more 'dovish' approach to the Vietnam War than the top leadership of the AFL–CIO and especially its head, George Meany. The prospects for a rival federation envisaged by Reuther were never good. The Alliance for Labor Action is now defunct, but the breakaway unions have not yet rejoined the AFL–CIO, maintaining their separate policy stance. According to Richter (1973: 209ff.), the Auto Workers' leadership wished to re-establish its alliance with American blacks and to cement its relationships with unions abroad, both of which aims were hampered by continued membership of the more conservatively led AFL–CIO. At any rate, it was an alliance made from above and did not stimulate opposition within national unions.

Organised labour in the United States was probably never strong enough to set up a separate national party of its own, under a two-party system. Apart from the greater resistance of American employers to unionisation, the labour force in American agriculture has been relatively dispersed and difficult to organise. The American political structure makes a departure from two-party representation difficult because of the direct election of the President and governors, and the primary system which encourages the settling of differences within the two major parties. Lipset has argued that 'if the United States had ever adopted proportional representation or even the second ballot run-off, it would have developed several main parties, "including" a labor party, based on urban workers and perhaps on ethnic minorities outside the South' (1967: 343; cf. 327–65).

Although it appears paradoxical, American workers may have been oriented less towards independent political action than British because male suffrage was won more easily than bargaining rights.[5]

Finally, American workers were less prone to an ideology of the left because of the rapid growth of industry, vast immigration with its resulting ethnic and religious diversity, racial cleavage, possibly sharper differences in life styles and income than among British workers, and the premium placed on success in American society (cf. Wilensky, 1966).

The orientation of American Catholicism was an additional factor. The Catholic Church played an active anti-socialist role in the American Federation of Labor during the first two decades of this century. Karson (1958: 212–84) shows that at least sixty-two presidents of national unions were Catholic during 1906–18 and offers five additional reasons for the weakness of socialism and the absence of a labour party during this century: '(1) The vitality of American capitalism (which was capable of meeting the unions' demands), (2) The middle-class psychology of American workers, (3) The American's faith in individual rights, (4) The conservative features of the American political system, ... (6) The anti-Socialist leadership of Samuel Gompers (head of the AFL)' (286).

We have already mentioned the reaction against the reformist politics of the Knights of Labor, which has also been interpreted as 'the failure of American labor's basic aspiration . . . (during the last sixty or seventy years of the last century) . . . to escape from the wage system into producer's co-operation, for which, under the Knights of Labor, a last but grandiose effort has been made' (Perlman, 1958: vi).

Nevertheless, American labour in the twentieth century has *not* been as unaffected by ideology as many think; its ideology has been egalitarian but not radical. Since the Great Slump, when the older as well as the newly formed industrial unions joined the Roosevelt coalition, industrial unions have adhered for the most part to the social aspects of what became known as 'New Dealism' (although the term is out of style): union security, full employment and social security. Civil rights should be added, but cautiously as issues come closer to home. Since the New Deal, one can hardly find a journal or newspaper of an American industrial union without a display of interest in social legislation at both federal and state levels. Indeed, the display of such interest is often to the point where only a specialist in legislative affairs could possibly follow, let alone act on, the volume of bills, favoured or opposed, already drafted. Many craft unions, on the other hand, have taken a defensive stance on union security, but since the New Deal have largely neglected legislation involving social welfare. At the state level, and fairly recently the national, many craft unions have been as apt to support Republicans as Democrats if it served their purposes.

Richter (1973: 217–25) argues that the British trade union movement, by and large, has had no legislative aims of consequence since 1945 except the preservation of job security and full employment. Even the former has not (until very recently) required political action. Social reform, let alone socialism, has not been an objective, and union-sponsored Members of Parliament have often been ignored by the Engineers and the Transport and General Workers (the two largest unions) and certainly not used to initiate much social welfare legislation. Nevertheless, Richter argues, the fates of the trade union and Labour Party leaders are intertwined, and the function of union political action – and of the Trade Union Group (sponsored MPs) specifically – is ceremonial and symbolic, to assure the loyalty of the membership to the union bureaucracies and Party leaders. This view must be modified in the light of recent union militancy, especially under the leadership of Jack Jones of the TGWU, among others.

Outside of a few localities (e.g. Detroit), American political action has not drawn union activists into any sustained activity which could reflect upon their political life within the unions. The ideology of social welfare, in those unions where it has been most vigorously promoted, has facilitated a dialogue with socialists and a rare flirtation with the idea of independent politics. But the results even there, in terms of factional organisation or ideological controversy, have been negligible. However, the struggle for racial equality has led to the organisation of important black caucuses in some major unions.

Conclusion

British and American national unions are strong, autonomous bodies in relation to their union federations, the government and political parties. They are also strong in relation to their local unions and memberships, but the ability to discipline subsidiary organisational units and members is greater in the American case. On the other hand, British national unions make a greater number of national collective bargaining agreements. The unions are hierarchically organised in both countries, at least in the sense that the relationships among sub-units are reasonably simple and under the control of those with higher constitutional authority. American unions have greater proportions of both national and local full-time officials and also larger staffs of specialists (but these wield little power in their own right). American unions are more bureaucratised, but it is arguable how well the term characterises the essential features of subordinate–superordinate relationships within even American unions.

Union organisation is more complex and less hierarchical in many British unions because of the ambiguous position of workplace representatives in plants where no one union has exclusive bargaining jurisdiction. In the United States, local unions often co-operate to bargain with large multi-plant employers or with regional employers' federations, but this has been less significant for internal opposition. In both countries the nature of hierarchical authority has been modified to the extent that responsibility downwards is more than a legal fiction.

The factors considered thus far suggest a greater possibility for union democracy in Britain, based primarily on the more limited powers of full-time national officers and greater presence of ideological cleavage among activists. However, there are extreme differences between unions within each country in internal organisation and competition for office, and it is with these differences that we were primarily concerned, as we shall later see.[6]

NOTES TO CHAPTER 1

1 Interviews of 175 British first-line full-time union officers, representing thirty-five unions (Industrial Relations Unit, Warwick, *c.* 1971: 1–5), showed that 50 per cent listed negotiations at the workplace as their most time-consuming activity, 19 per cent listed routine office work, 9 per cent preparing material for negotiation and 9 per cent recruitment. (For an analysis of the administrative rationale of trade unions and the degree to which it is interpenetrated by the representative function, see Donaldson and Warner, 1972; Child *et al.*, 1973.)

2 Hall (1972: 76) states that 'it seems impossible to discuss the voluntary organization [which includes the union] from the same perspectives as other organizations' because of qualitative differences, although he nevertheless makes a tentative effort to do so. Stinchcombe (1973: 53) goes so far as to exclude voluntary associations (including unions) from the category of formal organisations because authority – 'the capacity for people to plan the activities of other people' – 'barely exists'. Stinchcombe goes too far, as some union leaders have the constitutional and effective authority to hire hundreds of staff, suspend members and local unions, authorise or fail to authorise strikes, etc. And the negative consequences of leaving a particular union may be greater to a member than those of leaving a particular place of employment.

3 A shop steward is chosen from among the unionists in a plant section to be readily available to deal with their day-to-day disputes with the employer, on the spot if possible. A British plant-wide shop stewards' committee would serve the same function as an American grievance committee, but it might have the additional power to negotiate changes in pay and more basic conditions of employment. In the United States, these can usually be changed only at the expiration of a contract and are negotiated on the union side by a specially elected negotiations committee, rather than by the grievance committee.

4 Local unions may negotiate supplementary clauses to cover local conditions, at about the same time. Great pressure may be exerted on a local union if the final acceptance of a national agreement hinges upon its resolving its own dispute. Since the early 1960s there has been a trend towards the local rejection of proposed national agreements.

5 It could be argued that the American unions have been not less, but differently, oriented towards politics (in contrast to politics through a specifically 'labour' party). This may be true, but the percentage of trade union activists who have been politically interested in recent times seems to be much greater in Britain.

6 The eighty or so organisations were studied *via* a detailed archive and documentary research methodology, plus interviews with officials and experts, and a long structured 'questionnaire' (of over 800 variables) completed for each union *by the investigators themselves*, and designed to bring out such differences. A content analysis of constitutions was the main formal method (see Table 4.3).

Chapter 2

The Nature of Oligarchy

One approach to the question of democracy is by way of its crucial opposite, oligarchy. Ideas about oligarchy have generally been confused or over-
simplified, especially where trade unions are concerned. We will discuss
the meaning of oligarchy and the various forms in which it has existed in
large trade unions. Finally, we will extract some common organisational
features of oligarchic rule as it exists in large unions so that a theory of
organisational democracy can take them into account.

The structure of power in an organisational society includes power relationships within large organisations (see Hall, 1972). Power, income and
social status may vary almost as much within single organisations as within
society as a whole, and they may co-vary even more with the holding of
formal organisational office than with positions within the state. While the
structure and mechanism of power may be almost self-evident in many
admittedly authoritarian organisations, they seem less clear in ostensibly
democratic mass-membership organisations (see Lipset, 1964; Lazarsfeld,
1973: 25–6). First, in such organisations, deviations from equal political
rights and social equality are usually denied, and seldom given formal
recognition. Second, the membership may be recruited from a single
stratum or occupation, especially in trade unions, and there may in fact be
little inequality apart from that associated with organisational office. This
situation is, in many respects, analogous to that in supposedly classless
societies with nationalised economies.

It is ironic that the very factors which make the oligarchic–democratic
continuum especially useful in describing power relationships in large
membership organisations, namely their often fairly homogeneous memberships and formally democratic constitutions, have also often made
agreement difficult on placement along that continuum. The self-perpetuation of union leaders is often tolerated where it would not be in government
(cf. Hayes, 1973) because, after all, whom do the leaders represent if not
the members? And the members could depose them if they really wanted
to. Thus, the one organisation may be called democratic and oligarchic by
different commentators. With such confusion we tend to become unduly
optimistic, pessimistic or indifferent regarding the chances for democracy,
according to political taste.

It is clear that one end of the continuum can be fully defined only in terms of the other: we cannot neglect oligarchy if we wish to understand democracy. It is also evident that sociologists and others have been so absorbed in such questions (see Gouldner, 1971: 299), and in explaining occasional deviations from the 'iron law' of oligarchy, that important differences between oligarchies have been neglected.

While oligarchy is usually defined in terms of the structure of power, democracy is usually considered to be a system for decision-making and its definition is complex and multi-faceted. One simplistic definition of democracy is majority rule with minority rights. An adequate expansion of the concept of *majority rule* in a large organisation or society would take the following points into consideration (see especially Won, 1962: 37–47; Pateman, 1970; E. Roberts, 1973: 191):

— The majority must prevail with respect to both the formation and implementation of *policy*, and the selection of *officers*.
— The membership may act either *directly* in small groups or meetings or through referenda, or *indirectly* through elected representatives.
— On many matters the appropriate majority is a *local*, or at any rate a *subnational* one (although this is also related to minority rights).
— The extent and quality of membership *participation* are relevant (although these are sometimes beyond the control of an organisation).
— The officials must be kept *accountable to the membership*.

All these points assume that the membership is actively involved in discussing and choosing among alternatives, which is inconceivable without minority rights. An adequate expansion of the concept of *minority rights* would take these rights into consideration:
— The right to *oppose* through formal and informal channels is basic to minority rights, as is the right to *organised opposition*.
— Significant political minorities have the right to significant *representation* among the elected decision makers, preferably through the normal operation of the electoral system (such representation should not be taken for granted in organisations).
— The usual *civil rights and liberties* apply to all members or citizens and all are presumed to be politically equal.
— A fair and adequate *appeals system* (due process) should be available for ordinary members, officers and organised collectivities.

This list implies that high degrees of local and individual participation are possible and desirable in the modern world, and that a decision-making system which maximised these as well as the other characteristics above would be the most democratic. We would argue that our implicit definition of democracy is workable, even if normatively and prescriptively motivated. And it is not unique to ourselves. However, since democracy is *multi-dimensional*, no systematic way can be offered to arrive at a general combined measure of the degree of overall democracy. This would be the case even if there were no incompatibilities between some of these elements. The logical argument that insistence on minority rights in the face of majority objection is minority rule and therefore violates the fundamental principle of democracy (see Ranney and Kendall, 1969: 41–63) sets a priority for a special situation but does not solve the aforementioned problem. Nor does it take into consideration the number of issues on which the majority and minority are irreconcilable and the importance of each issue to each group.

To summarise these points in a working definition: Democracy in a large organisation or a society is a decision-making system in which the membership actively participates, directly and indirectly through its representatives, in the making and implementation of policy and in the selection of officials, for all levels, on the basis of political equality and majority rule. Furthermore, the system operates on the basis of the accountability of officials, the legitimacy of opposition, and a due process for the protection of the rights of individuals and minorities. Each aspect of democracy can be achieved to a different degree and there is probably no way to characterise the overall degree of democracy except on the basis of crude judgement. However, these aspects of democracy are probably to some extent mutually interdependent and supporting.

When we say that we have introduced many of these aspects of democracy into our research in order to explain the effectiveness of opposition, we mean specifically that we have tried to find the *empirical* relationships between opposition and such features as: the protection apparently offered by the formal appeals system; the extent to which voting systems seemed likely to represent political minorities at the convention or on the executive board; the apparent accountability of the top officer to the executive board (or vice versa); the absence in the constitution of punitive clauses against factionalists; and the protection of possibly dissident local unions against arbitrary takeovers under the direction of the top officer. If it is indeed shown that such constitutional provisions tend to support closer elections for top posts, there would seem to be an excellent chance that they also tend to act as they are supposed to, i.e. process appeals fairly, represent minorities on decision-making bodies, hold the top officer accountable, etc.!

OLIGARCHY IN ORGANISATIONS

In nominally democratic mass trade unions, the only important basis for internal stratification may be the holding of organisational office, and often only elective office. Nevertheless, it is a commonplace that the top elected leaders in many such organisations are almost invulnerable to opposition, and that by virtue of their office they have power, privileges and often income which, it might be reasonably argued, place them in an exploitative relationship with their own members. Many sociologically oriented writers have employed the term oligarchy to describe the government of such organisations, although in most cases their meaning has been only implicit (see Jenkin, 1968: 283; May, 1965: 417; for modern critiques of the concept).

However, pluralistic theory has led to a neglect of oligarchy and an accomodation to it (see Gouldner, 1971: 299; Pease *et al.*, 1970), and writings of Michels on oligarchy, are now frequently indexed under 'elitism' or 'leadership' (Parry, 1969: 13).

Michels. Michels' opening sentence in his best-known work implies that the two main forms of government are oligarchy and democracy: 'The most restricted form of oligarchy, absolute monarchy, is founded upon the will of a single individual', and he continues shortly thereafter: 'At the antipodes of the monarchical principle, in theory, stands democracy, denying the right of one over others'. But in spite of what seems to be the case, the two principles are 'so elastic that they often come into reciprocal contact' (Michels, 1962: 43; cf. May, 1965: 419).

According to Michels (1962: 43–4), democratic forms actually *veil* the 'tendency towards aristocracy, or rather oligarchy which is inherent in all party organization'. The move in terminology from aristocracy to oligarchy is never well explained, but it is evident that oligarchy is his generic term for oppressive minority rule, and that he is not using 'oligarchy' and 'aristocracy' in their Aristotelian sense.

Michels' basic dichotomy between oligarchy and democracy is also evident in the formulations of his iron law of oligarchy:

'Reduced to its most concise expression, the fundamental sociological law of political parties (the term "political" being here used in its most comprehensive significance) may be formulated in the following terms: It is organisation which gives birth to the dominion of the elected over the electors, of the mandataries over the mandators. Who says organisation, says [tendency towards] oligarchy.[1]

'Every party organization represents an oligarchical power grounded upon a democratic basis. We find everywhere electors and elected. Also we find everywhere that the power of the elected leaders over the electing masses is almost unlimited. The oligarchical structure of the building suffocates the basic democratic principle' (Michels, 1962: 365).

Thus, by oligarchy Michels means undemocratic abuse of power, not simply the existence of organisational leadership. The latter leads to the former, but the distinction is recognised.

Lipset.   Lipset also follows this usage and makes the meaning he attaches to oligarchy virtually explicit:

'At the head of most private organizations stands a small group of men most of whom have held high office in the organization's government for a long time, and whose tenure and control is rarely threatened by a serious organized internal opposition. In such organizations, regardless of whether the membership has a nominal right to control through regular elections or conventions, the real and often permanent power rests with the men who hold the highest positions' (Lipset, *et al.*, 1956: 4–5).

And further on:

'There is no more persuasive illustration of the unanticipated consequence of men's purposeful social actions than the recurrent transformations of nominally democratic private organizations into oligarchies more con-cerned with preserving and enhancing their own power and status than in satisfying the demands and interest of the members' (1956: 8).

Thus, we have a picture of oligarchy as undemocratic control of govern-ment vested in relatively few individuals and exercised in their own interests by virtue of their firm grip on high organisational posts.

DISTINGUISHING ORGANISATIONAL OLIGARCHY FROM DEMOCRACY

According to Friedrich (1930: 464), 'As soon as the opportunity for a choice between at least two alternatives is eliminated, oligarchy is in fact established; and it can be only a question of time until it begins to exhibit the typical tendency of an established oligarchy to contract.' Thus a crude cutting point is established, below which the governments of societies – and, we shall argue, of large-membership organisations as well – are oligarchic.
    A democratic choice in the selection of leaders must be active rather than

passive and, if meaningful, can hardly achieve unanimity or even over-whelming majority with a high degree of regularity. This, of course, implies a view of social reality, which we shall amplify.

In large organisations with a small number of important posts, and especially with one or two recognised top posts in terms of social status and power, there are normally a number of individuals or groups aspiring to control such posts. This potential conflict (competition) normally involves differences in policy to some extent, but questions of personal competence and personal ambition, as well as the antagonisms generated by organisation life, may be sufficient. While such tendencies towards competition may be viewed abstractly, simply as organisational outcomes, there are ordinarily individuals involved who are quite conscious of a desire to achieve a top post, even at the expense of the incumbent(s), however impracticable this may appear at the time.

Given democratic norms and an absence of organisational obstacles, attempts to displace the top leaders will certainly be made. If there is indeed a structured way to compete for top posts, e.g. electoral machinery, this is in fact used. Thus, the absence of regular use of such machinery (and, of course, its absence) is a sign of control over the organisation by a limited number of individuals on a non-competitive basis: in other words, of control by the few, with perhaps a disproportionate weight given to a single individual among them.

It has been suggested that 'The simple fact is that, in the absence of care-fully cultivated unity myths, in the absence of leadership interests in non-competition, and in the absence of the disciplinary weapons provided for the punishment of organised dissent, party organisation [we would say factions] within private associations would be much more common' (Fisher and McConnell, 1954: 142). And further: 'Every organisation, every group of human beings, is rich in conflicts. There are always abundant issues – and real ones. Underlying all of them in an organisation is the fundamental issue of leadership power. Organisation cannot exist without leadership. Where leadership exists, there is an issue of power.' If constitutional checks place limits on the leadership, differences of 'interest, desire and belief' provide the basis for competition (1954: 143).

Perhaps the strongest argument against taking the absence of anti-leadership opposition (or the long-term ineffectiveness of such opposition) as a sign of oligarchy is that the leadership may be the instrument of a consensus-oriented membership, rather than the membership the compliant victim of the leadership. However, the victims of an oligarchy include not simply 'the membership' but other would-be leaders. Second, there are few organisations which, on close inspection, show a truly homogeneous membership, and still fewer if the members' politically relevant points of view are considered.

Last and most important, fundamentally different economic or other differences in interests are unnecessary for factionalism and democracy. Organisational goals are never fully achieved, and if substantially achieved, new problems present themselves. Over a period of time progress must be erratic, often slow, and insufficient in the view of many members. Differences of opinion on tactics and strategy tend to develop and be reflected – perhaps exploited – in struggles for leadership. As in the fairly homogeneous but democratic International Typographical Union in the United States, 'The outs usually make charges of centralization and defend local autonomy; they demand economy and efficiency; they seek greater organizational activity and a more militant leadership' (Fisher and McConnell, 1954: 142).

DISTINGUISHING BETWEEN OLIGARCHIES

The conceptual tools for distinguishing between oligarchic power structures and mechanisms in membership organisations have been largely lacking. Those concepts with some applicability have been developed for organisations in general, and deal with such characteristics as the type of leadership (e.g. bureaucratic or charismatic) and kinds of incentives offered for the compliance of followers (e.g. coercive, remunerative and normative). There are also some general terms available for describing an organisation's power structure (e.g. for distinguishing whether or not those who have power also hold formal office) and how power-holders and sub-collectivities interrelate (see especially Etzioni, 1961: 12, 89–126). But there has been little progress in differentiating among the power structures of membership organisations since Lipset, Trow and Coleman (1956: 3) characterised 'almost all' of them (including trade unions) as one-party oligarchies; nor is it entirely clear what 'party' means in this context.[2] Thus the current situation with respect to membership organisation oligarchy is analogous to the former situation with respect to bureaucracy: 'Since there is only one model of bureaucracy, the tendency is to emphasize similarities, while the differences are seen as "exceptions"' (Etzioni, 1961: xiii). Oligarchies too *have inadvertently been made to appear more homogeneous than can be justified.* As Lipset has pointed out, 'For the most part, Michels' ideas [on oligarchy] have been used for descriptive purposes and for polemics denouncing organizations as undemocratic, rather than for specific analysis of the conditions under which variations in oligarchic patterns occur . . . researchers have usually overlooked the variations in internal political systems among parties and other political groups' (Lipset, 1959: 103–4). Lipset himself and more recent writers have generally been more concerned with democracy than oligarchic distinctions (see Marcus, 1962; Martin, 1968).

We are concerned here with oligarchy in large, stable, nominally demo-cratic national unions with clear boundaries from the rest of society, many full-time officials, fairly simple hierarchical relationships between levels of organisation and of status, and some membership involvement. In prin-ciple, our discussion should apply to membership organisations of other kinds with a similar set of characteristics, but these restrictions narrow the field considerably and probably exclude most political, religious and even professional associations from full applicability. The question of such applicability is also touched upon in Chapter 3.

Models of oligarchy will be presented here which differ in their basic structures and supporting mechanisms and, at a more abstract level, in some common underlying *dimensions*, which we hope will be a logical pre-cursor to the development of our structural theory discussed in Chapter 3. Oligarchies will be distinguished primarily in terms of the membership and location of the oligarchic subgroup, its supporting structures (e.g. political groupings) and their interrelations. Most of the structures will have formal organisational, but not necessarily official, bases. In addition, some of the models include auxiliary norms found in the culture (e.g. collegial leader-ship in the Netherlands) or occupational subculture (e.g. seniority among railwaymen).

Most sociological models are non-mathematical 'pregnant' types: preg-nant, that is, with implicit rather than explicit explanatory power. Models of organisations often select a single dominant theme, e.g. the type of con-trol exercised, which presumably organises or pervades the life of the sys-tem as a whole and by inference helps explain its operation. Multiple-characteristic models are more similar to our own, e.g. the 'democratic' as compared to the 'hierarchical' (the difference is in the separation of powers, method of selecting chief officers, and locus of the veto; see Katz and Kahn, 1966: 211–15). Most such sets of models, and ours as well, could be called typologies instead, since they disappoint the full expectation of the delinea-tion of the relationship (static or dynamic) among the parts of the system. However, our models in particular are explanatory in that they emphasise differences in *who* holds oligarchic power and *how*, the assumption being that such concentrations of power tend to resist dissolution.

The oligarchy models possess, in simplified and exaggerated form, a distillation of features of many unions. They are vignettes, drawn from the literature and unpublished research, with some surplus of detail where this seems important. The models convey overall pictures of idealised oligar-chic systems against which our own theory, and the data later presented, should be set. Their associated characteristics and dimensions, presented separately, make clear the common analytical components. The models include a simple official hierarchy, a one-party system, a federal oligarchy, a collegial oligarchy, two neo-classical oligarchies, two eternally-appointed oligarchies, a summit oligarchy, and a procedural model (discussed separately) called electoral monopoly.

THE DISTINGUISHING FEATURES OF OLIGARCHIC CONTROL

The name of each model indicates its dominant theme – a core aspect of structure around which oligarchic power is organised. However, the models themselves are more complex and more than one of the following core features, plus others, may be present, as will be indicated later.

1 *Simple official hierarchy.* A large staff of hierarchically organised officials, extending down to the local level, is elected or appointed with the consent of a powerful top officer and remains under his control.

2 *Federal oligarchy.* There is a decentralisation of administrative authority to large oligarchically-dominated units of organisation, typically regions, with the top officer retaining his position only with the consent of the collective intermediate leadership. However, the organisation is pseudo-federal rather than federal, since the intermediate units lack complete autonomy.

3 *Collegial oligarchy.* Collegial norms and practices, perhaps with some constitutional support, greatly modify the exercise of power within what formally is a simple hierarchy of oligarchic full-time officials. The top committee rules collectively, lesser officials have some say in the co-optation of new personnel, and there is general restraint in the exercise of personal power.

4 *Summit oligarchy.* A permanent top full-time officer can usually have his way in the making of important organisational policy, entirely on the basis of his prestige, expertise and central position. His power does not rest upon a control over lower officials or over any special political machine, nor does any special group exert control over him.

The four characteristics above all pertain to the structure of power among full-time officials, and are mutually exclusive by definition in their fully-developed forms. The three remaining characteristics involve relationships between full-time officials and others, including non-members of the organisation, and are at least logically (but not necessarily practically) compatible with each other. The logical and hypothesised practical compatibility of the seven dominant characteristics of the models of oligarchy are summarised in Table 2.1.

TABLE 2.1   *The logical and hypothesised practical compatibility of the
dominant characteristics of the models of oligarchy*

0 = incompatible by definition
1 = incompatible in a stable system
2 = of intermediate or doubtful practical compatibility
3 = fully compatible; may co-exist without strain

Characteristics	Characteristics						
	1	2	3	4	5	6	7
1 Simple official hierarchy	—						
2 Federal oligarchy	0	—					
3 Collegial oligarchy	0	0	—				
4 Summit oligarchy	0	0	0	—			
5 One-party system	3	1	1	0	—		
6 Externally-appointed oligarchy	3	1	2	0	3	—	
7 Neo-classical oligarchy	2	3	3	0	,2	1	—

5   *One-party system.*   The only openly-organised internal political party
or politicised faction of any significance, consisting of non-office-holders as
well as full-time union officials, is under the control of the top full-time
officer. The centralisation of the party makes it readily compatible with a
simple official hierarchy, but not with a federal or collegial oligarchy.

6   *Externally-appointed oligarchy.*   An outside organisation covertly or
overtly selects and controls at least the top official, but may intervene in the
selection of those at lower ranks as well. The existence of external control
is fully compatible with a simple official hierarchy and a one-party system.

7   *Neo-classical oligarchy.*   The full-time governing oligarchy is controlled by, and may be a part of, a larger high-status economically-
privileged stratum within the organisation. The concept of a non-governing
oligarchy is discussed below.

Multi-feature Models
The first four characteristics above pertain to the basic structure of the full-
time officialdom itself, and the remaining three to possible auxiliary groups
or mechanisms. An unqualified reference to a model in terms of its basic
structure (a simple official hierarchy, a federal oligarchy, a collegial
oligarchy or a summit oligarchy) implies the self-sufficiency of the full-time
oligarchy – in other words, a single-characteristic model, insofar as the
seven organising themes are concerned. On the other hand, a reference to
a model as a one-party system, an externally-appointed oligarchy or a
neo-classical oligarchy implies a superimposition of such a theme on

a basic structure and hence a multi-feature model. We list below only multi-feature models with fully compatible characteristics, as shown in Table 2.1.

1   *A one-party system model* involves the single party as a political mechanism for the *simple official hierarchy*, both being centralised under the top officer. The full-time officials are the backbone of the party or faction.

2   *An externally-appointed oligarchy* involves the appointment by an outside organisation of the top officer of a *simple official hierarchy* structure, and thus the maintenance of an acceptable internal governing oligarchy.

3   *An externally-appointed one-party system* involves a combination of the features of the two models above, as its name indicates, and hence by definition of a *simple official hierarchy* as well. The dominant internal party is controlled ultimately from outside the organisation, perhaps by an external political party with which the internal party may be co-extensive, with the top officer a leader in both. To the extent that an external party may influence union officials at lower levels against the wishes of the top officer, this is a departure from a simple official hierarchy.

4   *A neo-classical federal oligarchy* involves a federally-structured ruling oligarchy dominated by, or a part of, a larger privileged stratum. This privileged group probably has contact with the full-time officialdom at various points, and thus is especially compatible with either a federal or a collegial oligarchy.

5   *A neo-classical collegial oligarchy* is obviously parallel, and has a similar rationale to that of the neo-classical federal oligarchy.

Governing and Non-governing Oligarchies

It is useful to distinguish more broadly between oligarchs with and without formal office. By a *governing oligarchy* we mean one with formal office. Unqualified references in this book to oligarchy in organisations are to the governing oligarchy. As pointed out earlier, oligarchic status in most unions is held only by virtue of formal office.

By a *non-governing oligarchy* we mean one without formal office, but with either plutocratic power (economic privileges maintained through, or in alliance with, the governing oligarchy) or direct political power (which can exist without economic privilege or office holding, under special circumstances) or *both* plutocratic and political power. It is conceivable that some politically powerful non-governing oligarchs may be non-members of the organisation. Specific forms of non-governing oligarchies are discussed in connection with the neo-classical and externally-appointed models below. Apart from the characterisation of a non-governing oligarchy as a whole as primarily plutocratic or primarily political, individual members of a non-governing oligarchy may vary widely in these respects.

VERTICAL AND HORIZONTAL DIMENSIONS

We have adapted the familiar idea of vertical (hierarchical) and horizontal (non-hierarchical) differentiation in organisations (cf. Hall, 1972: 143–6) to describe the structure of oligarchic power. The *vertical* family of dimensions locates the governing oligarchy and its possible political allies at the various *levels* of organisational *structure* (national, regional, local) and individual *rank* (higher and lower positions, usually among office-holders). The *horizontal* family of dimensions extends from the governing oligarchy to possible members of a non-governing (unofficial) oligarchy at *equivalent levels* (structurally, or in terms of status) on the basis of *unofficial or informal* relationships. A truly horizontal relationship involves collaboration based upon compatible interests and mutual influence. To the extent that non-governing oligarchs impose their political will upon office-holders of even equivalent social status, a diagonal rather than horizontal relationship exists. However, even such a one-sided power relationship is still adequately described as horizontal in structural terms, e.g. as occurring between corresponding local, regional or national-level oligarchs.

The vertical and horizontal dimensions can also be used to describe the *limited* nature of oligarchic power, or a *departure* from the particular oligarchy model in practice. For example, the downward extension of the governing oligarchy among full-time officers may be none at all, in a democratic organisation, or through only the top offices, in the summit oligarchy model. Likewise, the degree of penetration of each level by the oligarchy, e.g. in terms of the percentage of full-time officers controlled by the governing oligarchy, could suggest the degree of oligarchy (or departure from it) in the organisation. The place of the models on some dimensions of oligarchy, and the hypothesised most likely deviation from each model in practice, are shown in Table 2.2. The size of the active directorate, which is one important aspect of the concentration of power, is another important dimension (see Caplow, 1957: 487–8).

A SIMPLE OFFICIAL HIERARCHY

In the simple official hierarchy model the full-time officers collectively, under the direction of the top officer, constitute the sole political machine for the preservation of their offices and power. The main elements of the

TABLE 2.2 *The place of the models on some dimensions of oligarchy*

Models	Dimensions				Hypotheses
	Emphasis on hierarchical relationships	*Primary locus of political power*	*Lowest official in governing oligarchy*	*Lowest status in non-governing oligarchy or party*	*Most likely deviation from model, in practice*
1 Simple official hierarchy	very strong	top officer	local	none	some local officers outside oligarchy
2 Federal oligarchy	weak	regional officers	regional or local	none	a rebellious regional officer
3 Collegial oligarchy	weak to moderate	top committee	local	none	more hierarchical than model
4 Summit oligarchy	none	top officer	top only	none	some top control over lower officers
5 One-party system	very strong	top officer	local	rank-and-filer	partial atrophy of party
6 Externally appointed oligarchy	very strong	superior organisation	local	officer of superior organisation	partial atrophy of external power
7 Externally appointed one-party system	strong	external organisation	local	rank-and-filer in union or external organisation	atrophy of party at lower levels
8 Neo-classical federal oligarchy	weak	regional officers	regional or local	local plutocrat	excessive local autonomy
9 Neo-classical collegial oligarchy	weak to moderate	top committee	local	local plutocrat	some loss of power of full-time officers

model are a powerful top officer and large staff of full-time officials extending downwards to the local level. These officials are largely appointed by and ultimately responsible to the top officer. The top officer delegates power to other important national officials who also work under his direction and who, although for the most part elected, owe their positions to him. Thus, the real power in the national organisation – administrative, judicial, and in effect policy-making through control over the convention – is exercised by a very few top officials. All this is quite compatible with nominal democracy, since some officials are elected at most organisational levels and most powers of the top officer have an explicit constitutional basis (although with his control over the appeals system there is little to prevent his exceeding them). This is not too severe a characterisation of the situation in many large American unions (cf. Taft, 1954).

The machine is not dependent upon a non-governing plutocracy – none exists. The infrequent succession 'crises' are normally weathered without incident, the outgoing chief playing a part in the selection of his successor. But the full facilities of the national union, including the full-time field staff, are available for mobilisation against those oppositionists bold enough to try for elective office. This is seldom necessary, but when it is the full-time officials do not admit to an existence as a collective partisan body. This centralisation of the internal machinery does not, in practice, preclude considerable local autonomy in relationships with employers.

While specific constitutional bases may not be necessary to sustain a regime approaching that of the model (apart perhaps from the power to appoint and assign officials), many opposition-free American unions give their top officers powers that might have been designed towards that end. Officers, members and local unions are often subject to the discipline of the president, with or without his consultation with the executive council. Final appeals are made to the national executive council or the large infrequent convention, both of which the president chairs and dominates. The president appoints chair-persons of conventions committees, including the resolutions committee. His appointed field staff are in some cases eligible to serve as elected delegates from local unions. If the executive council includes rank-and-file members, they may be dependent upon the president for special assignments which permit them time off from regular employment at a *per diem* rate sometimes set by the president himself. Full-time councillors work under the direction of the president. Vacancies on the executive council may be filled for the expiration of the term, which may be years, by the president or remainder of the council. This list of assorted rules is by no means complete. The rules might support any centralised type of oligarchy, including the next to be described.

A ONE-PARTY SYSTEM

Lipset *et al.* (1956: 5) have argued that many oligarchic voluntary organisations 'more closely resemble one-party states in their internal organization than they do democratic societies with organized legitimate opposition and turnover in office. Indeed, the pattern of one-party oligarchy is . . . common in the labor movement', but one gathers that they refer to the office-holders themselves organised hierarchically as a political machine, rather than as a party.

However, one of the characteristics of a political party is, after all, that it addresses itself to the public and appeals for public support, even in one-party states, where the party has not atrophied. But in the previous model of a simple official hierarchy (one of a number of no-party systems) the hegemony of the machine is unquestioned, and the oligarchy had best let sleeping publics lie while concealing its very existence as a collective partisan force.

The key elements distinguishing the one-party system model are politicisation, an open stance of the administration's faction as an internal organised political group, the inclusion of non-office-holders or non-full-time officials in the faction, and – possibly – this broader basis for some factional decision making. The United Auto Workers of America (UAW) has had the essential features of the one-party model, although somewhat softened by some more democratic ones as well (see Stieber, 1962: 67–73, 131–57).

The 800 full-time UAW 'international' and regional representatives (Richter, 1973) appointed or approved (if regional) by the president, with the consent of the executive board, constituted the core of what was called the Reuther caucus until the recent death of the UAW president. Some representatives are assigned full-time to political work. The total number reached 1,000 at one point. Reuther won the presidency with the support of his caucus in 1946, with a bare majority at the UAW convention. The caucus lapsed into disuse for two years after it decisively defeated the opposition caucuses in 1947. It was revived after the 1949 convention, at which some administration proposals were defeated and some Reuther supporters made demands for a greater membership voice in the affairs of the union, although by this time there was no serious opposition from other caucuses.

'With the decline of factionalism and opposition groups, the national caucus has become so large that it is virtually meaningless, except as a symbol of the leadership's recognition of its ties to rank-and-file local union leaders. The national caucus meets only at conventions and any UAW member is welcome to attend. . . . Routine endorsement to . . . [leadership] recommendations is given by the caucus' (Stieber, 1962: 68).

The caucus steering committee, which consists of 200-250 local union leaders selected by regional directors and national officers, is more important. It meets before and generally during the convention to endorse candidates for national office recommended by the leadership, to act as a sounding board for the leadership, and to resolve occasional disagreements within the union's executive board (e.g. on the size of a dues increase). The affiliated regional caucuses serve similar functions, but also select the administration's candidates for regional directorships. There may be elections to such candidacy within the regional caucuses, but caucus discipline is insisted upon in the actual election. These activities are expensive; Stieber has estimated that over $100,000 was contributed by officers and staff members in 1962, exclusive of local caucus funds. Anti-administration caucuses have existed at various times since 1960, but as yet none has seriously threatened the entrenched position of the leading caucus.

The continued existence of the Reuther caucus might have been impossible if the caucus had not been built originally by politicals, and if many of the important leaders had not had political ambitions and hoped that the talented Walter Reuther might lead them into some kind of labour–liberal third-party coalition. To climb this ladder they needed Reuther and the preservation of their team (see also Widdick, 1964: 189).[3] A cult of personality was associated with Reuther, particularly among many in the rank-and-file (but even extending to admirers outside his own union). This is not uncommon in the United States, although perhaps no more than a handful of top union leaders, at most, would be regarded as 'great men' at any one time. Widdick (1964: 80) has remarked that:

'. . . the cult of personality performs a useful function [for an entrenched leadership]. It simplifies the task of the staff man when the ranks are over-awed by the great-man theory, for challenging policy becomes more difficult, or ridiculous. For union officialdom, life is less hazardous when policy is dictated from the top. The staff can avoid any danger of making a wrong guess on policy . . . What has emerged in this social milieu is the counterpart of the corporation organizational life.'

Widdick adds that Reuther in particular 'cannot tolerate any criticism' and 'operates the UAW with an air of infallibility, and with the iron grip of an infallible man' (185–6). With Reuther's death, the future of the caucus remains to be seen.

The single-party system serves a more subtle function for the top leadership, and the top officer in particular: it neutralises potential competitors by offering them a political role, while at the same time binding them to the administration. It solves the general problem of how to combine ambitious and capable men 'into a political machine that can control the union, giving each figure in the machine a post that satisfies his ambitions without letting him gain such a following that he can contest control of the union' (Seidman, *et al.*, 1958: 110).

FEDERAL OLIGARCHY

Oligarchy often parallels formal organisational structure, taking advantage of, or at least adapting itself to, this structure. Just as the simple official hierarchy of most unions lends itself to hierarchical no-party and one-party oligarchies, so does an administratively-decentralised structure with large intermediate units of organisation lend itself to a federal oligarchy.

Michels took note of provincial oligarchies within national political parties, and of the possibility of occasional conflict between a regional and the national chief, the former wanting nothing more than to force his way into the innermost circles, conceivably to the top. Having failed to gain entry into the top ruling circles of the larger oligarchical group, such a regional leader might continue to sulk in a smaller one as a chief regional oligarch (Michels, 1962: 176, 198). In this example, regional autonomy has perforce been recognised by the top leaders as a last resort, but not accepted as a form of rule. A federal oligarchy would go further.

The structural basis for the federal oligarchy is typically a regional division of administrative authority. The central office lacks the staff under its direct control to supervise the activities of regional leaders, or the means to apply sanctions to keep them in line. The central staff is small, regional activities are diffuse and distant, and the boundaries of the major intermediate structures are meaningful politically, functionally or historically. In the simplest case this division of authority is formalised and legitimate – in others it is simply a *modus vivendi* on the basis of the given power relations.

This can be the basis for a collective leadership of regional oligarchs, with a compact among them resulting in the choice of an undisputed top leader who 'takes his' while allowing considerable leeway to his regional chiefs. 'Live and let live' would be the motto within the oligarchy. Or, to each his own territory, with the head oligarch's function being to occupy the top position (which must be occupied by someone) and to mind his own business, closing his eyes to what he had best not know. Daniel J. Tobin, a predecessor of James Hoffa of the American Teamsters' Union, is said to have maintained his top post in this way (cf. Romer, 1962: 28).

The nature of substructural oligarchies is open and can vary from region to region. It could include simple official hierarchies and one-party systems, but if the regional administrations were also decentralised, they would be more likely, on their scale of operation, to be decentralised systems of patronage rather than federal systems paralleling the national. A decentralised patronage system can operate quite efficiently on a small scale without overlooking too many of the more important potential recipients. Relatively minor favours might be sufficient at this level. Patronage is superficially a less political method than many, involving a less obvious exercise of power, and is perhaps therefore less likely to stir up potential political opposition.

Relationships within the top council of the oligarchy are based on approximate equality, since none can impose his will within the jurisdiction of another. The rudiments of democratic decision making exist within this council, but ordinarily without attempt on the part of any to appeal to a wider audience. There is always the possibility, however, that a change in the relationship of forces may undermine the president's power and result in his demise; or that a trend towards the centralisation of the union, perhaps due to national collective bargaining, may elevate the top leader still further at the expense of regional ones. At any rate, there may be a conflict of authority: 'Both Dave Beck and James Hoffa [of the American Teamsters] generated opposition to their programs of centralized bargaining on the part of local and area leaders whom Hoffa styled as "kings of their individual little isolated areas"' (Barbash, 1967: 129).

COLLEGIAL OLIGARCHY

A collective oligarchic leadership may be based on a centralised rather than a federal organisational structure. Collegial oligarchy appears to exist in most Dutch trade unions, based on virtual co-optation as a method of leadership selection, virtual permanence of tenure as long as colleagues are satisfied, and norms associated with the not uncommon practice of collective leadership in Dutch society:

'Collegial decision-making was for many decades customary in the Dutch cabinet. Business organizations also seem able to function effectively under several director-managers with coequal powers. Some European political organizations, especially those of the left, have traditionally entrusted their leadership and administration to a collective secretariat.'

The relationships among the full-time officials are such that:

'. . . no strong man is allowed to achieve a preeminence that would enable him to treat the organization as his personal fief. The ability to work with fellow officers as equals is a fundamental precondition for high union office. With almost no exceptions, strong men like John L. Lewis or Ernest Bevin have not been allowed to rise to the top of Dutch labor organizations. The presidents of the individual unions and of federations . . . are first among equals and no more' (Windmuller, 1969: 220; see also 211–25).

The situation is similar in Swiss unions (Siegenthaler, 1970: 193–4).

The collegial relationship among the full-time officials is self-sustaining because the trial appointments of such prospective officials and their confirmation are made collegially (presumably after consultation with non-full-time officials as well). Aggressive and flamboyant candidates are weeded out by common consent. Nevertheless, there is still a hierarchy among officials, with the members of the leading committee making the appointments and other important decisions. One may speculate that in some unions a pseudo-collegial style conceals something closer to our simple official hierarchy model.

SUMMIT OLIGARCHY

In summit oligarchy, there is an institutionalised permanence for an elected top officer who is the acknowledged or semi-acknowledged political expert, rather than simply an executive secretary. The permanence, security and prestige of the top officer allow him to retain and wield considerable power without a downward-extending mechanism, and without his having or being able to stifle a relatively free competitive process in the election of lower full-time officials and in the discussion of issues. In the latter, his personal view on important matters nevertheless usually prevails. The top post represents the pinnacle of a semi-oligarchic, or semi-democratic, organisational government.

The primary bases of summit oligarchy are the superimposition on an otherwise democratic organisation of a *formally permanent tenure* for all full-time officials, a *formally-recognised seniority* among these and *corresponding norms*, all of which make advancement highly predictable. We know of only one organisation, the British National Union of Railwaymen, which represents this type fairly well. However, with the permanence of top posts and a fair amount of competition in the election of new officers being more the rule than the exception in British unions (see Allen, 1954: 215), this model also sheds some light on other national unions of mixed type.

Constitutional permanence (barring gross incompetence or malfeasance) in summit oligarchy is combined with what in effect is a compact among the full-time officials, apparently including the membership, to live and let live. This tolerance extends to the expression of differences of opinion and to competition for higher posts when openings occur, so long as it is understood that the permanence of officials is not to be undermined.

Some lower full-time officials usually make the attempt to bypass seniority when higher openings occur, but they invariably fail. Advancement by seniority is considered right and proper because it parallels the much-valued place of seniority in occupation (e.g. railroading). More important, the seniority system is ubiquitous by virtue of constitutionally recognised titles. If the constitution recognises two or more permanent assistant general secretaries, the one elected first is titled the senior assistant. Likewise, there would be a senior organiser among a number of organisers.[4] If the senior official at a lower rank is eligible to stand for a vacancy at the next higher rank (i.e. if he is not over-age), he has an overwhelming advantage. Nevertheless, it would be a foolish senior contestant who did not exert himself in the campaign.

The seniority system largely depoliticises the ranks of the permanent officials. First, seniority together with permanence implies a civil service function, which may very well have been intended by the framers of the constitution. Second, the system is politically neutral and fair; even political deviants might have a turn as vacancies occur (although, of course, there are never enough near the top to go around). Third, it is well recognised that a political stance is of little use in winning elections. A less senior candidate runs mostly to keep his name before the electorate, in case the day comes when a recognised senior official is too old or ill to run for a higher post. Fourth, most officials as well as members believe the senior candidate to be most competent. Finally, by accepting their own function as essentially apolitical, officials are implicitly legitimising their own permanent status.

The political neutrality of the selection system may very well result in a new top officer with a different political persuasion. But each neutral succession *may* have been so long in the coming that the successor has been effectively socialised to a common pro-establishment orientation, whether this involves the interest of the full-time officials as a group, a conception of the role of the top officer, or the policy stance of the union. The subsequent role of leader and chief negotiator with employers and government tends to create the same great pressures towards accommodation and organisational conservatism as for the previous leader, especially after many years in office.

The rarified atmosphere in which the top officer exists, from the point of view of the relative absence of a power base, may be compatible with a considerable degree of democracy or of long-term arbitrary rule. On balance, the importance of the top officer plus his permanence seems to favour a limited form of non-punitive oligarchy. His personal inclinations can place an indelible stamp on the nature of decision making during his reign, and in a permanent leader this is oligarchic.

NEO-CLASSICAL OLIGARCHIES

Our two neo-classical oligarchies, the federal and the collegial, have pluto-cratic non-governing oligarchies in control of, or in collaboration with, a governing oligarchy of full-time officials. The special stake of the pluto-crats would in most cases be outside the union, e.g. in maintaining a mono-poly of skills, licences or desirable jobs as against less well-qualified or less entrenched members of their own organisation. Or the dominant privileged stratum might consistently sacrifice the interests of the less privileged in negotiations with employers, to its own advantage. A neo-classical oli-garchy is especially consistent with any decentralised or collective govern-ance structure, as mentioned earlier, and the distinctions between the federal and collegial models will be ignored here.

It has been alleged that the American National Educational Association, which engages in collective bargaining for teachers, was controlled by school superintendents and other supervisory officials who were permitted membership (Callahan, 1966: 32). Also, it has been claimed that the American Medical Association, which is not a union, was similarly con-trolled by highly-paid specialists (Editors of the Yale Law Journal, 1966). Self-employed typographers, plumbers, barbers or even small employers may retain their union cards. Managers of co-operative retail stores are eligible for membership in the British Union of Shop, Distributive and Allied Workers. Many trade unions do not grant full membership rights to apprentices or temporary workers on special permit (the latter may be quite numerous), nor do some to non-whites or women. Such workers have sometimes been segregated into special local unions or sections.

The governing oligarchs would probably have arisen out of the non-governing plutocrats and have similar backgrounds, interests and life styles. Some members of the two oligarchies would undoubtedly mingle during leisure pursuits, while many others would mix at conventions and other meetings. Members of the two groups might thus have reason and occasion to influence each other mutually and painlessly.

In a professional union, high-status members might rotate as lay national officers alongside the permanent executive secretary and his staff, and exert a direct influence on them while remaining available to the pluto-cracy. Generally, a higher-status non-governing oligarchy, while providing a base for those in full-time office, might arise from among the plutocrats, which would be reason enough for the officials to placate them. Where necessary, individual officials might be quietly replaced, or vacancies at all levels filled with those more acceptable to the non-governing oligarchy. Even the top officer might be subject to influence or replacement. Thus, the nature of the leadership could be changed without crisis, or an occasional minor crisis might be tolerated if certain leaders were incorrigible.

EXTERNALLY-APPOINTED OLIGARCHY

Some national unions are formed by other organisations, political or industrial, supposedly democratic or otherwise, with an interim leadership appointed from outside. Such leadership may last for many years and, necessary or not, can hardly be considered democratic from the point of view of internal organisational life. Where the top official is appointed he probably chooses his own staff, and the internal structure approximates a simple official hierarchy. However, the simple fact of external appointment, and therefore of ultimate *control*, is outstanding enough to characterise this as a special form of oligarchy.

The relatively short-lived Steel Workers Organizing Committee (swoc), formed in 1936 in the United States by the Committee for Industrial Organization (cio), is an example. The union, headed by Phil Murray, had organised over 600,000 members and represented even more workers under contract before it finally achieved independent status in 1941. Murray became its first president and in the post-war period arranged for the succession, through uncontested election, of David J. McDonald (Ulman, 1962: 3–39).

In Tanzania, the president of the one-party nation has appointed the heads of the central labour union, which is affiliated with the party (Davies, 1966: 162). There is some doubt as to whether the union may be considered nominally democratic and the first general secretary, appointed in 1964, was concurrently Minister of Labour. To the extent that the party operates inside the union, this would approximate our next model.

EXTERNALLY-APPOINTED ONE-PARTY SYSTEM

External political and religious organisations have sometimes managed to exert oligarchic control over national trade unions, even where the union movement has not been dominated by the government. For a period, the Communist Party of France seemed to control the Confédération Generale des Travailleurs, subjecting its union leaders to the same type of purges as were common in the Party (Lorwin, 1954: 164–7). In the United States, the Communist Party appears to have controlled the Mine, Mill and Smelter Workers, the Marine Cooks and Stewards and other unions at various times between the late 1930s and early 1950s (Ozanne, 1954).

In a fully-developed case, an externally-appointed one-party system would function through an openly-operating internal party, which we shall call a caucus. The caucus would maintain a working relationship with the party (or other external organisation), overtly or covertly, and would include union rank-and-filers as well as full-time officials. The core caucus members at all levels might be in close contact with, and possibly active members of, the party. The top union official would be the head of the caucus, a leading member of the party, and the controller of the centralised union administration characteristic of the simple official hierarchy. Thus, in an extreme case there could be a direct surveillance of union members and officers at all levels, including factory level. None of the models has covered the case of external control by a political party over a full-time officialdom feigning political neutrality.

ELECTORAL MODEL

Any feature of organisation which promotes a monopoly of political power at the national level may be the basis for oligarchy. The executive councils of many American unions are elected simultaneously (usually by the convention) and, apart from a few leading officers, *en bloc* by simple plurality – a voting system which encourages winner-take-all. For example, the relatively democratic American Federation of Teachers uses this system, with the result at its 1972 convention that all twenty of its vice-presidencies as well as the presidency were won by the incumbent Progressive Caucus – in spite of the support for many opposition candidates by about one-third of the delegates.[5] Under such a voting system the leading faction or clique tends to monopolise the commanding heights for the entire period between conventions, which in the United States usually means for a number of years. At the next election disloyal members of the faction, if any, are dropped from the slate.

As a variant of this system, many American unions have nominally district representatives on their executive councils, but these are elected by vote of the convention (or sometimes the membership) as a whole. In the 800,000 of American Carpenters, 'As a result, individual board [council] members who desire to be reelected cannot remain independent of the administration, nor can they take positions in opposition to the administration' (Horowitz, 1962: 35).

Thus, long-term monopolistic domination of all the national offices – oligarchy of some degree – may result from the normal workings of biased electoral *procedures*, in a union with an otherwise only mildly unfavourable climate for democracy. In such a situation, the structural framework for describing the oligarchy would remain, but the explanation for its self-perpetuation would shift towards a somewhat disembodied procedural 'how' and away from 'who' and 'where'.

Electoral systems belong to a category of rules which deserve more attention from sociologists: those which automatically transform information (in this case, votes) into decisions (as to who get elected). The programming inherent in the system may bias the outcome in unrecognised ways. No doubt semi-oligarchic cases of electoral monopoly, and of summit oligarchy, will continue to plague those concerned with organisational democracy with endless debates.

A view of electoral competition in unions or government which has some appeal to the cynical streak in most of us holds that even close competition is a fraud: it takes place between groups which are or aspire to be oligarchic, and hence 'democracy' equals oligopoly, if not oligarchy. To holders of this view it hardly pays to point out that some choice is qualitatively different from none at all (unfortunately, a not unusual situation), and that choices often have demonstrable effects on leadership and policy for some time beyond an election. Admittedly, however, the General and Municipal Workers in the British sample is a likely candidate for oligopoly in spite of some moderately close elections for the top post (see pp. 352–3, 358).[6]

Since continuity in office is the essence of oligarchy, we would ordinarily take notice of changes in the leadership group. An alternation of leaderships based on elections would usually reflect membership opinion to some degree and provide a semi-democratic interlude. On this basis, some electoral monopolies would, in practice, be less undemocratic than others due to differences in their associated organisational features, environments or memberships (especially democratic norms and degree of involvement).

IMPLICATIONS FOR DEMOCRACY

The models are more useful for diagnosis than prognosis. One person may be very ill with a severe attack of what is ordinarily a rather mild disease, while another may be less ill with an arrested case of a serious disease. Diagnoses of their conditions are nevertheless made in terms of the two diseases in question, the evaluation of their general states of health being another matter. Likewise with oligarchies; the structure and functioning of a modified one-party oligarchy – one which in spite of itself exists alongside a rather weak but organised opposition – are still best described under the rubric of one-party system. How democratic or oligarchic such an organisation is can best be answered separately.

Leaving aside summit oligarchy and electoral monopoly, it would be difficult to argue that any one model of oligarchy is noticeably more in the democratic direction than the remainder, even taking into consideration the separate dimensions of democracy mentioned earlier. If one compares the most likely *deviations* from the models shown in Table 2.2, the federal oligarchy stands out in that the rebellious regional officer mentioned might occasionally provide some electoral opposition in a contest for the top post. The deviations of the two neo-classical oligarchies would be in the general direction of decentralisation, but this would probably bring power more directly into the non-governing plutocrats' hands than into those of the general membership.

Equally oligarchic organisations are not necessarily equally oppressive in the exercise of political power. Probably the most centralised models – those having the feature of a simple official hierarchy, with or without a party machine or external appointment – have the greatest potential for the arbitrary exercise of political power against internal dissidents. But persistent exploitation by a plutocracy is also oppressive, in a different and not directly comparable way. This leaves summit oligarchy, electoral monopoly, federal oligarchy and collegial oligarchy probably less oppressive and exploitative than the remaining models, but in practice there must be considerable variability even among unions approximating any one model fairly well.

Some of the models' core features are suggestive for models of democracy. Certainly the federal and collegial oligarchies have analogous democratic forms. Even the simple official hierarchy may have its counterpart in a centralised democracy, although it would seem especially susceptible to oligarchic degeneration. Neo-classical oligarchy, with its reliance on informal relationships between the plutocrats and governing oligarchy, has its counterpart in a competitive 'democracy' for the plutocrats only. However, there seems to be no democratic version of either external appointment or the one-party system. A summit democracy makes no sense at all, but the auxiliary features in the model of permanence, security and political permissiveness for full-time officials seem able to support a certain level of democracy.

Oligarchic occupational membership organisations are basic aspects of the social structure of existing modern societies. Given the present underdevelopment of organisational theory, it would appear most useful to continue with a wholistic approach to their internal dynamics. The development of theoretical models is one strategy, and a further perusal of the comparative literature from various points of view would seem well worthwhile (see Udy, 1965: 702). However, we are much more interested in our models of oligarchy for clues as to what to avoid – i.e. as a guide to a theory of union democracy. From this point of view we can say that a large democratic union would, above all, avoid an undue concentration of power in the hands of the top officer. More specifically, this means having limitations on his control over the other full-time officials, preferably by assigning them independent bases of power and by limiting his arbitrary power to discipline members and local unions. Stated more positively, power should be shared by other powerful officials, by union conferences and by subsidiary bodies. Since the officialdom itself is the key to oligarchy, in most of the models, and in all the more common ones, perhaps all full-time officers should be elected. The electoral system should facilitate rather than obstruct the representation of minorities and election of some dissidents. The structure of the ranks among the officialdom should facilitate competition rather than suggest advancement by seniority. A more systematic and theoretical integration of these and other considerations will be presented in Chapter 3.

NOTES TO CHAPTER 2

1 The original German included 'tendency towards' (see P. J. Cook, 1971: 787).
2 The reference is to 'one group, which controls the administration, usually retains power indefinitely, rarely faces organized opposition, and when faced with such opposition, often resorts to undemocratic procedures to eliminate it. This is especially true for national organizations'.
3 This interpretation is based on a personal communication from Stanley L. Weir. Weir adds that Reuther took over a ready-made caucus built during World War II by the anti-Communist left without the help of the top or secondary leadership of the union. 'Reuther gained the cadre to build a one-party system, or what would become that, out of the aspirations and then the demoralization of the left' (Weir, 1970).
4 In the British Railwaymen, if it should happen that two assistant secretaries are elected simultaneously, the one with more votes receives and retains the senior assistant title. We wish to thank W. F. Cooke for pointing out the special importance of seniority in the railway industry.
5 The problem is exacerbated by the fact that the delegates from New York City, which has approximately one-third of the membership, are elected under a similar system. The same is probably true of other large locals. *The New York Teacher* of 20 May 1973 (p. 13) reports, concerning the local elections: 'With him, Shanker carried the entire Unity Committee slate: eight other officers, 66 [local] executive board members, and 475 delegates to the annual conventions of the American Federation of Teachers and the National Education Association [with which the local is also affiliated].' In practice, there is virtually block voting of the delegates at the national convention. Under this system not only a majority, but also in certain circumstances a minority, of voters in the locals could elect all the national officers. (See M. Harrison, 1960, for a discussion of block voting in the British labour movement.)

   Shanker defeated the incumbent president, David Selden, in 1974. The latter had broken with the leading Progressive caucus, and Shanker received its endorsement, winning by better than six to one (*American Teacher*, September 1974).

   Shanker retained his posts as president of the New York City local and executive vice-president of the New York State United Teachers (with 207,000 of the 425,000 national members; *New York Times*, 21 August 1974), and drew a total tri-level salary of almost $70,000 (*Teacher Forum*, December 1974). See propositions 5, page 70; 16, page 78; and 19, page 79. It is unlikely that he can be displaced from the presidency while he holds the New York office.
6 W. F. Cooke comments on the GMWU: 'Family connections are important, due historically to the fact that District Secretaries—the power in the union—were responsible for staffing their own offices and recruited relatives. The present (now former) General Secretary (the fourth of the union) is the nephew of the second, and son-in-law of the third.'

Chapter 3

An Organisational Theory of Union Democracy

INTRODUCTION

New evidence suggests that the question of union democracy should be reopened, after the long period during which unrelieved pessimism prevailed (cf. Goldstein, 1952). As we shall show, the presidents of five American unions were defeated between 1949 and 1966, and two large British unions have held fairly close elections, for half a century or more, in filling vacancies for top posts.[1] The differences in electoral opposition from one union to another within each country are great enough to warrant an attempt at an explanation.

Most social scientific theories have attempted to explain the general prevalence of oligarchy in large organisations rather than departures from it, as we indicated earlier. Previously we have referred briefly to the environmental approach to union democracy, contrasting it with the internal organisational approach which we prefer. However, we will indicate some of the environmental factors whose relevance we accept, but take for granted, for the unions to which our theory applies. We have argued elsewhere that, as Turner (1962: 232) has said, 'Trade union forms are a product of trade union origins'. Much of current trade union organisation is relatively independent of *current* context, and the effects of context are transmitted largely through its influence on union organisation. The ideas of Lipset and his associates are most relevant where the influence of internal factors on democracy is concerned, and these will also be mentioned.

LIBERAL AND SOCIALIST APPROACHES

The approaches to union democracy in and around the labour movement generally neglect the essence of what we would call organisational structure – the various subdivisions, conferences, committees and posts and how these relate to each other, particularly near the pinnacle of the national organisation. This is not surprising, since the effects of alternative structures in membership organisations have received little attention during the past fifty years from either political or sociological theorists, although early trade unionism was much concerned with ways to keep power in the hands of the rank-and-file.

The civil libertarian approach to union democracy is probably the most common one in the United States. It emphasises the right to criticise and oppose the union officialdom without harassment and, in particular, the right to organise factions and participate in fairly-run elections. The latter involves a reasonable opportunity for candidacy, a properly-supervised ballot and a fair count – a tall order indeed in those unions run by, as some suggest, would-be dictators, strong-arm men and racketeers, let alone common-or-garden varieties of officials anxious to retain power. This is not to say that unionists here and there have not raised some structural demands in their own special situations (e.g. the right to elect their district directors at the regional rather than the national level) but there appear to be few, if any, structural principles advanced for the democratisation of the union movement and, indeed, very few procedural principles as well (e.g. in the area of voting systems) apart from the simplest and least contro-versial. The civil libertarian approach is simply the application of the Bill of Rights to trade unions and hence is a lowest common denominator for assorted American liberals and radicals. It has been said, with unions in mind, that 'freedom of association includes the right to organize at all times about any question, including opposition to incumbent leadership' (Spinrad, 1970: 280). Spinrad here also points out that free expression and association in a union can be blocked by such things as a lack of information before meetings, the inability to get on the agenda and the exclusion of opposition views from the union press. Therefore, mechanisms for free association and expression are required. We will discuss civil liber-ties later in connection with the powers of national officers and the appeals system.

A number of strands of socialist, anarchist and syndicalist thought have contributed to a *neglect* (and often disparagement) of national level de-mocracy and representative government in general. Their positive ideas have included an emphasis on direct action, shop-floor democracy and masses in motion, while their negative ideas have included a disparage-ment of 'parliamentarism', national officials, and even (in some cases) the unions themselves as inevitably the instruments of capitalism. The Australian branch of the Industrial Workers of the World, a syndicalist organisation, proclaimed in 1914 that it 'stands for straight-out direct action principles, unhampered by plausible theories of parliamentarians, whether revolutionary or otherwise' (quoted in Renshaw, 1968: 229). Perhaps even today sections of the British labour movement, which had its own syndicalists, resonate to such ideas, as do sections of the American 'new left'.

Karl Marx had little to say about the structure of a socialist state except to imply that its central assembly should be, like the Paris Commune of 1871, 'a working, not a parliamentary body, executive and legislative at the same time' (1940: 57) with its delegates elected by district assemblies and subject to formal instructions and recall at any time. In addition, officials were to work for working-men's wages and their terms of office were to be short, judges were to be elected, and the standing army and police were to be abolished as special forces (57–8). Lenin took a similar but nebulous view in his oft-cited *State and Revolution*, written shortly before the Russian Revolution, but he was no more specific than Marx concerning the form that a socialist state might take. Indeed, he made a virtue of this: 'There is no trace of Utopianism in Marx, in the sense of inventing or imagining a "new" society. No, he studies, as a process of natural history, the *birth* of the new society *from* the old [emphasis in original]' (1932: 42; 36–65). Lenin argues for 'centralism' (a unitary state) as against federalism, in agreement with Marx and Engels, still taking the Commune as a model. He quotes Marx concerning 'the few but important functions which still would remain for a central government' (Lenin, 1932: 44; see also 45–6, 54–62). No undemocratic interpretation seems warranted, in spite of the meaning given some years later to 'democratic centralism' as the guiding principle for political life within the Communist parties (i.e. the illegitimacy of organised freely-operating internal factions). Such a stance, in favour of relying on history for organisational forms, has pervaded Leninist, Trotskyist and most derivative movements to this day and probably made them uncongenial to system making and theory for national organisational democracy of any type.[2]

The rapid degeneration of the Russian Revolution left the Communists in Russia and abroad in no position to elaborate schemes for representative democracy. It was not long before Zinoviev, speaking for the Communist International, was mocking 'bourgeois democracy' in terms which could only cast aspersions upon any form of representative democracy. At any rate, the institution of the one-party system in Russia left Communists abroad unwilling to formulate any general theories of organisational democracy, although Communists have at times advocated such reforms as the abolition of permanent posts, as in the British Miners.

The reaction against Stalinism, and against what for a time was the state-socialist ideology of much of European social democracy, led to a renewed emphasis on workshop democracy by the socialist left. The workers' councils, established briefly in the mid 1950s during the Hungarian and Polish revolts, were hailed by many as the basis for democratic socialism. Lenin's original idea that everyone, and therefore no one, was to become a 'bureaucrat' (1932: 92) had always had some support on the far non-Communist left, and this idea was strengthened by the developments in Eastern Europe, including the Yugoslavian workers' councils (see Vanek, 1972, on the latter). The idea of delegates electing delegates to the eventual summit of the state remained, by and large implicitly or with little elaboration, as the conceptual model for the socialist state, and has partly been incorporated into the new Yugoslav constitution of 1974. In short, the view of socialism in these quarters was about the same as the Bolsheviks' view *before* the Russian Revolution and little different from that of Marx (the main difference from Marx being in that the workshop rather than the local community was the primary original constituency). How could a programme for organisational democracy arise from those whom so much of the history of oligarchy had passed by? Or from those who concluded that representative, as opposed to direct, democracy itself was the thing at fault?

There are also views on the far democratic left which argue that any genuine democracy, in unions or elsewhere, is likely to emerge only as the outcome of a popularly-based struggle which bursts the bounds of organisations (and society) as we know them. The emphasis is therefore on stimulating such struggles, educating towards this end, and/or building the organisation which will eventually educate and lead. The resulting union democracy, if indeed it took this form, would be transitional to some larger social reconstruction. One gathers that such union democracy would be short-lived, as either a stepping stone or a heroic defeat, so that the details of its structure would be unimportant beyond the level of direct local participation. Unions and all limited-purpose organisations tend to be conservative and therefore, it has been argued, revolutionists should adopt an agnostic view as to whether or not a mass movement of workers should move through or bypass the unions.[3]

A more extreme view would explicitly reject the reformation of unions in favour of concentrating on workers' problems in the factory: 'We have no illusions that the unions can be transformed, "democratised," restored to the rank and file or converted into instruments of "encroaching workers control".' However, 'some of the lower levels of union organisations can sometimes be used as channels of communication and rank and file organisation' (Fore, 1970: 16).

André Gorz, a contemporary widely-translated French left-wing socialist, provides an additional reason for emphasising direct and local democracy, in unions as well as the state (1973: 98–107): the failure of representative government, especially in the absence of mass democratic parties. Such parties are necessary to establish global *social* objectives in place of the existing privatised goals of alienated individuals, especially (but not exclusively) under capitalism:

'A parliament can have true representative value and reflect the popular mind only if it is composed of mass parties deriving their authority from collective action and continuous public debate on policy; and if those parties have a comprehensive view of society . . . The popular will can find itself only in parties such as this, not in ballot boxes or in elected assemblies where a miscellany of separate individual purposes are mechanically added together' (104).

What is needed, therefore, is the creation of socialist parties which will remove the political battle 'to the places where people work and live together' (106), preferably on the basis of demands transitional to socialism. However, in developing 'socialist' nations he favours internal democracy within 'the' party, along with autonomy for trade unions and the administration of society (197–8, 207–14). In a chapter titled 'Unions and Politics' there is not a word on trade union government which goes beyond direct democracy, but quite a bit disparaging representative democracy which 'has always been, and must necessarily be, a mythical substitute of government by the people' (75). Gorz's views seem to be continental in that they reflect the domination of the French and Italian unions of that time (1966) by single political parties – Communist, Socialist or Catholic as the case may be (hence parties must therefore become revitalised if the unions are to be) – and philosophically French (Rousseauian) in his rejection of representative government (although one sometimes wonders if he can be taken literally). There is a hint of Rousseauian philosophy in that he seems to see democracy as the expression of the general will – democratic parties and unions being 'groupings . . . whose activities are sustained by the formulation *in common* of a common project embracing the entirety of their *common* existence [emphasis added]', this proceeding from direct participatory democracy (101). This sounds much like Rousseau (1962, 193–4), but Rousseau also said: 'If then, the general will is to be truly expressed, it is essential that there be no subsidiary groups within the State, and that each citizen voice his own opinion and nothing but his own opinion' (194). This could help explain Gorz's neglect (perhaps absence) of a consideration of organised factions in parties and unions. Nevertheless, he states his case in general terms, and it qualifies him to join the chorus of others neglecting or rejecting the question of democracy in existing national unions.

Since the early 1960s, a section of the British left has linked workers' control of industry with trade union democracy in a manner congenial to a discussion of overall reorganisation of both industry and the unions. *Tribune*, a left-Labour weekly, has always been available for occasional critical letters from readers on questions of democracy in unions, the Cooperative movement and the Labour Party. (The weaker and more fragmented nature of the American labour and socialist left has meant the lack of a particular likely place either to express or to find such views.) In 1963 the new *Voice of the Unions*, under the editorship of Walter Kendall, made in its programme an explicit link between workers' control of industry, union democracy and socialism. Its approach differs from that of shop-floor democracy pure and simple in that it proposes or encourages integrative schemes for control over specific industries, and it takes the unions as its major arena for the furtherance of its ideas. Its strategy has been the promotion of congenial left-wing movements in the unions, for the purpose of winning union office as well as of general education. (See Chapter 9 on the British Engineers.)

The Labour Party itself, in the mid 1960s, platonically proposed a step towards workers' control of production *through the unions* at shop-floor level, and the Trades Union Congress has recently favoured *union*-nominated representation on the boards of corporations with more than 200 employees (in contrast to 'worker' representation on the continent). In view of such developments, thoughts such as these cannot help but occur to a fair number of workers: 'Industrial democracy means workers' control of their industry. Surely a prerequisite for this must be members' control of their union' (letter to *Tribune*, 11 July 1969).

It would be going too far to say that any particular organisational theory of union democracy lies behind the proposals of *Voice of the Unions* and associated individuals writing elsewhere (see Fletcher, 1970: 73–85), but there is clearly a tendency to go beyond civil rights and liberties (although the right to organise factions, in the American sense, has been avoided). Trade union officers should be elected, not appointed, and be subject to periodic re-election. Rank-and-filers should have a significant say in and perhaps dominate the various committees. Workers should no doubt have the last say on agreements with employers. If there is a central concept, it is rank-and-file control. Perhaps this could be the core of a structural theory. It is, of course, not the function of an agitational tabloid to present abstract formulations which cover all circumstances.

MICHELS ON COMPETITION AND DECENTRALISATION

Since the theory of democracy presented here rests largely on the possibilities for regional autonomy and competition among full-time officers, Michels' views are briefly presented for relevant contrast.

According to Michels the ideas of decentralisation and of revolt against the supreme authority of the central executive make continuous progress in the labour movement, because of ineradicable differences of environment, but are of little significance for democracy. He disparaged several features: the motives of the provincial leaders, which were to resist subordinating themselves to the national leaders and to 'find the most effective means of forcing their way into the circle of the chiefs' (1962: 176); the

relationship of these leaders to the masses, who were not ripe for independence; the nature of the provincial regimes, which were oligarchic; the
probability of the leaders' defeating the national oligarchy decisively, which
was very low indeed; and the profit for democracy of such a victory which,
were it to be achieved, would be practically nil. In all this there is a com-
pelling mix of theory and evidence, value judgement and mood. Let us
disabuse ourselves of the latter two and pay further attention to the
decentralising tendencies which Michels recognised.

LIPSET ON FORMAL AND INFORMAL UNION ORGANISATION

Lipset's ideas on union democracy are closely tied to his study (Lipset *et al.*,
1956), of the International Typographical Union (ITU), which is generally accepted as democratic even by most confirmed sceptics. This union
had regularly close elections and occasional defeats in contests for the
presidency and other offices, and two stable internal political parties
sustaining this competition. Our own study confirms the uniqueness of this
two-party system[4] and the exceptionally close elections, although no president has been defeated since 1944.

The reasons offered for democracy in the ITU fall into three classes: first,
historical developments, with the evolution of the two-party system from
early secret societies being largely fortuitous and unlikely elsewhere;
second, informal organisational factors, especially the close association of
printers with each other and their tendency to form extra-union groups
due to their hours of work, the homogeneity of the membership, and its
tendency towards ideological splits due to its relatively high but ambivalent
social status (neither middle-class nor typically working-class); and third,
structural and procedural aspects of organisation (less often cited, apart
from the two-party system which had no constitutional basis) including
the relative autonomy of local unions and the use of referenda to elect
officers and decide officers' salaries.

To expand upon the informal factors: the high status of printers nar-
rowed the status gap between the leaders and members, and facilitated the
establishment of a tradition for defeated national officers returning to the
shop. It also seems to have led to a tendency to develop a separate identity
from blue collar workers, but printers were marginal individuals in the
sense that they were not quite able to become the peers of white collar
workers. Being squeezed between two groups they were forced to interact
with one another. Printers' marginality also led to a propensity for left–
right ideological split, which helped sustain internal factionalism. In addition, the craft nature of printing gave printers a ground of common interest.

The informal social relationships among printers were facilitated by the
fact that almost half of them worked nights and so had less opportunity to

interact with their families and workers in other occupations. In addition, the pace of night work was more relaxed, giving more opportunity to socialise on the job.

Such factors contributed to the development of an occupational community: 'In this community, various circumstances had resulted in the creation of a large number of community institutions – newspapers, clubs and sports organizations – which served to link printers with the political institutions of the community – the union and its parties – and to train men in the skills of politics, creating a regular system of communications among members of the group.' Lipset's view was that his analysis of the basis for democracy was close to that of de Tocqueville. He thought that 'the organizations of the occupational community broke up the mass-and-leader relationship which exists in most trade unions' (Lipset, 1964: 104–5).

Thus, the essence of Lipset's analysis of trade union oligarchy and democracy is this: 'the average large trade union contains only one formal organization, the union apparatus itself, and a mass of individual members. There are no atonomous suborganizations which can function as centers of opposition or as independent sources of organizational communication . . . [within the unions] the members are usually unable to act collectively in dealing with their leaders' (Lipset *et al.*, 1956: 77). It is true that union organisation at the shop level (which in large shops in some unions may be co-extensive with the union branch) *may* be able to operate as a politically significant group. However, 'In most one-party unions the only means of communication among shops or with the union administration is through the bureaucracy of the organization itself. A shop group is also usually dependent on the officers of the union for support against the employer and thus ordinarily cannot constitute a basis for organized opposition' (78). We should add that local union officers wishing to rise in the union hierarchy may be dependent upon the leaders for doing so, and that the typical 'one-party union' would be in our terminology a no-party union (see Chapter 2). Therefore, Lipset's emphasis is on informal rather than formal organisation.

The stable internal formal organisational factors which Lipset singles out as favouring democracy in unions (414–17) are local autonomy, less centralised and bureaucratised administration, constitutional protection for the rights of political opposition, and in general a 'distribution of power in the union [which] makes it impossible for the incumbent leadership to destroy the opposition without destroying or seriously weakening the union' (416). It seems that the latter might include formal or informal factors, but Lipset seems to have little expectation that these formal factors, or even all the ones mentioned above, would lead to a two-party system or many significant deviations from oligarchy in trade unions. A number of writers (e.g. Sayles and Strauss, 1967: 166) have interpreted Lipset *et al*, as saying that union democracy requires a two-party system and that the 'institutionalization of opposition' means a party system by definition. We think this is going too far, but it is easy to see how they got this impression.

A Contrast: Lipset's Theory and Ours

In contrast to an emphasis on informal organisation – i.e. on bypassing the formal structure – the theory to be proposed suggests an organisation in which the formal status system and formal substructures allow or even promote a high level of competition for office. In other words, autonomous suborganisation would be a part of the formal structure, to a greater degree than Lipset thought possible. In addition, the formal organisation might be complex and untidy enough to represent a significant departure from the typically simple hierarchical arrangement which facilitates a downward exercise of power.

COOK ON UNION DEMOCRACY

Alice H. Cook's (1963) model for union democracy was developed in the course of her study of four large (over 25,000 members) multi-shop local unions with only very tenuous and seldom used ties to their national unions. The model is presented as applicable to national as well as large local unions, although occasionally its suggested 'workable instruments meshed to operate as a balanced whole' (221) seem to be more pertinent to the local level. It deals primarily with formal internal structures and procedures. Cook approaches union democracy with the belief that the elements underlying public democratic government are generally applicable (except a party system), including 'a system of checks and balances between the functional branches of government' (219). She organises her presentation under five major headings: the separation of powers; the autonomy of intermediate bodies; the judicial system; election; and the rights of members. The first two are more original and fully developed and will be discussed here.

Although the model is prescription rather than theory, and a multi-faceted democracy is the aim, its most unifying notion seems to be the division of powers. The latter is relevant in several relationships: between the executive, legislative and judicial branches of government; between the executive council and full-time officers, where the distinction is valid; between rank-and-filers and full-time officers generally; between various levels of officers; and between the various levels of organisation.

The most novel proposals for trade union government are offered as an antidote to the usual weakness of the legislature (the convention) in relation to the executive branch. The legislature should have its own executive council, which is entirely separate from the executive branch, chiefly to plan its agendas. This applies to district as well as national legislatures. The legislature also needs a rationally-elaborated structure of standing committees, oriented to serving legislative purposes and not, as ordinarily, to simply 'carry[ing] out some part of the union program under the supervision of the executive officers' (227). Public hearings to develop policy, and hear criticisms of the executives, would be a natural procedural extension of the committee system. The committees should also have the power to hear officers. The meetings of the legislature itself should be conducted so as to make it possible to expose officers of any rank to direct questioning and criticism. So far as we know, only professional associations among national membership organisations even begin to approach the implementation of this set of proposals, and even then this is in a spirit which seldom confronts the question of real power.

Among other proposals which relate to the division of power are: the inclusion of some rank-and-filers in the 'cabinet' of the executive officers (the usual executive council), as suggested by Sidney and Beatrice Webb; the election at the district, rather than national, level of full-time officials servicing the districts; 'a provision guarding the superiority of the union's government over its collective bargaining apparatus' (225), since the officers in charge ordinarily accumulate powers not covered in the constitution; and the establishment of intermediate bodies which share in the collective bargaining power and function, or in other significant functions.

These suggestions are related to our propositions under local autonomy and distribution of powers later in this chapter.

THE SCOPE OF THE THEORY

The theme of the theory – ways in which structure tends to create equal competitors for leadership – is broad enough for it to be suggestive for many kinds of organisations. However, it applies particularly to large, formally democratic organisations which have clear boundaries from the rest of society, insulated internal status systems (which exclude many sources of competition) and the basic minima of democratic potential, stability in relationship to the external world and cohesiveness (which allow the competition-stimulating features to make a difference without their threatening the organisation's existence).

The most important minimal aspects of formal democracy, or democratic potential, include the filling of at least some important posts through elections, an electorate which is separate and apart from the competitors for office themselves, active or potentially active local rank-and-file leaders, enough members who care what happens nationally, no great shortage of aspirants to national office, and democratic internal norms.

The above are probably characteristic of most well-established unions (as well as professional associations) which are independent of the state machinery, unaffiliated to ideologically narrow political parties and oriented to collective bargaining. A brief contrast of such bargaining unions with political parties and revolutionary unions will provide a better appreciation for the scope and foundation of the theory.

Bargaining unions have some short-term goals on which both a leadership and an opposition might agree, and a reasonable load of non-partisan internal administration or routine activity which facilitates their co-existence. However, in revolutionary unions or ideologically narrow parties the content of daily activities might be propagandistic and involve the same programmatic issues as those under internal dispute. If organisational structure did tend to create competition for office, splits or defections might result or differences might be voluntarily suppressed in the interests of unity. Coser (1964: 206–8) points out that in closely-knit groups there is a tendency to suppress hostile feelings, but if conflict breaks out it may be intense; this applies particularly to groups engaged in external conflict. Thus, in such highly-politicised organisations, a sustained high level of effectiveness of opposition without extreme crises would seem to require a strong, articulated position for inclusiveness and tolerance in order to minimise divisiveness, and perhaps some special provision for the representation of minorities in decision making.

Large parties with a good deal of political power under a two-party system overlap the community and state, and offer numerous ways to build reputations and various enclaves for opposition in regional and even national government. Thus, opposition is less dependent upon special internal organisational forms. (This point is developed in Schlesinger, 1965: 773–4). In a sense, there are distinctive state and local party systems in the United States.

The problem, of competition for national leadership positions in such large parties, is complicated by the fact that there may be both parliamentary (public office holding) and associational (internal) leaders. Indeed, it has been suggested that domination by the former may not require a bureaucracy, an oligarchy or even a cohesive national leadership (see Schlesinger, 1965: 767–8). Nevertheless, parliamentary leadership tends to develop around key persons to some extent committed to specific policies, and it is reasonable to ask how the formal organisation of the party affects the success of opposition – at the parliamentary level if need be. But, since the parliamentary system as a whole (especially the electoral system) determines the composition of the party's parliamentary contingent, a theory based only on internal structure could hardly pay high dividends.

The European social-democratic parties seem to be similar to bargaining unions in having clearly-defined memberships, some degree of isolation from the political community, democratic norms, an expectation of some political heterogeneity, an internal status system requiring long service and step-by-step advancement, and a certain amount of discipline on the part of members (see Duverger, 1963: 63–79, 160–74, 177–9, 190–7). Actually, the European social-democratic parties seem to have some characteristics both of small sectarian parties (e.g. in the tightness with which factions within them discipline members) and of broad parties in two-party systems (in the independence of parliamentary leaders), although the situation has varied from time to time and from country to country. The theory should apply, but whether an adequate range of its variables will be found for testing is another question.

EFFECTIVENESS OF OPPOSITION

It has already been implied that the effectiveness of opposition for high office may be manifest in the closeness of votes or frequency of defeat of incumbents. However, the concept is broader and includes any manifestation of the degree to which factional groupings or individuals achieve office through uphill electoral struggle. This may also be manifest in a top leadership with mixed and competing political tendencies (see Lipset, 1956: 51), in the frequency with which one dominant political tendency replaces another, in the number of times candidates are defeated for a particular office before achieving it, and in the frequency with which candidates defeat others of equal or higher official position when no incumbent is involved. (The candidate with the highest status would ordinarily represent the administration.)

Fairly effective opposition for the top post could hardly be maintained regularly, in most organisations, without similar or higher levels of effectiveness for intermediate posts. Even typically close votes for a top post in perhaps widely-spaced succession crises, considered alone, suggest the presence of other criteria in the interim. However, the absence of close competition for the top post provides a poorer indication of the competition for the second-ranking and lower posts. At the time of a second-ranking officer's election the voters may expect the winner eventually to take over the top post. This does not necessarily preclude close elections for the lower post. The use of the multiple criteria at all levels would provide a more complete picture, and it suggests an additional criterion by which unions may be compared: the highest rank in the hierarchy at which some given average level of effectiveness of opposition is achieved, e.g. a specific degree of closeness of elections.

The propositions to be presented were framed with special reference to the average closeness of elections for top-post vacancies or – since unions differ in the variability of this closeness – to the percentage of elections reaching a given level of closeness. The other criteria (excepting an alternation of national power) would be expected to be fairly highly correlated with the central criterion, but only in the long run. The defeat of top incumbents in particular would be rare in most unions, and hence was expected to prove less sensitive as a measure of differences among unions than one based on the closeness of elections.

Most of the propositions assume some minimum levels of variables which occur in other propositions, e.g. some reasonable opportunity to achieve nomination.

Should a union which generally fills vacancies at all important levels through close elections be regarded as democratic, if the top officer is rarely defeated or is formally elected 'permanently' (as in most British unions)? Such a union is non-oligarchic in that no one group controls advancement in the hierarchy, but the answer should clearly take into consideration the associated organisational features, such as those discussed below, on which the close elections may rest.

The proportion of the membership voting in elections has been neglected in this chapter. The extent of such participation is relevant to union democracy, but within very broad limits we believe that it does not, in itself, have great bearing on the closeness of elections. B. C. Roberts (1956: 234–5) has shown that in Britain the greatest single determinant of the proportion voting is the place or manner of balloting, e.g. at the workplace or at a distant union hall (see pp. 114, 274–6, in our later chapters).

THE NOTION OF EQUALITY

Close elections are, by definition, those in which a loser runs neck-and-neck with a winner in terms of numbers of votes. The basic notion of this theory is that close elections are most likely to result from competition among contenders of *equal* status, power and reputation, which is resolved by an electorate formally subdivided into potential supporters (e.g. regions) of *equal* electoral strength, under voting systems which ameliorate rather than exaggerate any structurally-produced inequalities.

The *number* of potential competitors and supporting subdivisions must also be considered, since these affect the availability of candidates at any given time, the probability of finding two or more who are equally matched, the opportunity for coalitions, and the distribution of votes.

There are, however, at the *national* level structural subdivisions other than territorial and industrial-occupational sections, and if these were thrown behind one of the competitors there might be gross imbalance in electoral strength. Equality at the national level implies, in part, the existence of more than one significant power centre – such as the presidency, executive council and national convention – and a lessening of the inequality between these national centres on the one hand, and the territorial and industrial subdivisions on the other, means a greater amount of regional or industrial *autonomy*. National power centres may also be *internally* divided. Where the top officers are concerned this would mean the existence of two (or more) officers of equal status (e.g. a president and a general secretary) who might exert downward influence in different directions.

To sum up this far: the basic notion centres on equality and how formal structure and procedures may produce it. The variables are the number and equality of potential contenders and substructural supporters, the distribution of powers, and the ground rules for electoral struggle. The latter will be discussed separately.

STRUCTURAL MODELS

The structural variables suggest two contrasting models for the production of close votes: the countervailing-powers model, in which the potential and actual contestants are few and equally powerful; and the random model, in which they are numerous and equally powerless. While the models are secondary to the propositions and do not fully represent them, they are presented first with a few pictorial flourishes so that the direction of the argument can be appreciated more easily and certain qualifications can be made.

Countervailing-powers model. In this model the contending forces are equal in status or size, few and powerful, with independent, impregnable and institutionalised bases of support. The contenders would probably be regions or regional officers, but several nationally-elected vice-presidents of equal status and secure position (perhaps permanent officers) might play analogous roles. Long-range differences of interest, policy or ambition exist, and no pre-election arrangement could satisfy all. The logic of bloc making would counteract somewhat the tendency towards close votes (especially if there was an odd number of contestants), but this would be ameliorated by free campaigning among the electorate which would have less to gain from blocs than those making them. Similarly, when two or more important posts fell vacant at about the same time, so that the spoils could be divided, elections would usually be contested even when defeat seemed assured, since they offer an opportunity to build reputations at no cost.

Bloc making, or simply dependence upon a few important decision-makers, would make the closeness of vacant-post elections variable and imperfect, and occasionally would result in the defeat of incumbents. Multiple criteria for the effectiveness of opposition would be particularly necessary for unions approaching the structure of the countervailing-powers model.

To simplify matters, variability has been neglected in the structural propositions which follow.

Random model.   Here there is little differentiation in internal structure, apart (perhaps) from numerous small branches or local leaders with little power or attention outside their own spheres. With few restrictions on nomination, the result would be numerous candidates with probably little basis for distinguishing their merits (especially in a vote by the general membership) and a diffuse anarchic competition.

A postal vote in a large professional association may serve as an example, particularly where there are constitutional provisions limiting the stay in office or there is a rapid turnover of top leaders due to their primary interest in their occupation. The competition would be 'random' in both the nomination of particular candidates, i.e. unpredictable structurally and unbiased politically, and the irrelevant choices made by most individual voters.

The model is especially applicable when no incumbents are present to dominate the scene. The advantage for the incumbent could be superimposed on an otherwise equal distribution of electoral support, making his victory almost certain. However, in practice one of the other candidates might have an advantage in some other respect. Some controversy might be superimposed on the system without eliminating fairly close elections.

THE HIERARCHY OF OFFICIALS

All the following propositions pertain especially to the average closeness of elections for top-post vacancies. However, they also pertain, without specific reference, to other high posts, periodic elections and other indications of effective opposition in elections.

Let us consider the contenders for office and their supporters as individuals, temporarily neglecting their structural affiliations and support. The place of these individuals (if any) in the hierarchy of officials clearly affects their capacity to influence votes. The overall nature of the hierarchy largely determines the usual path from low to high office, and encourages or discourages a long-term effort for advancement through electoral means.

The propositions immediately below apply especially when the offices referred to are full-time. ⅄

Equality of status.   As developed in the discussion of the basic notion:

1   *A hierarchical structure which provides two or more offices of the same rank at each level, including the top, is favourable to the production of*

close electoral contests. The job titles at each level need not be identical, provided the positions are considered to be equally relevant to the next higher post and have equal control over resources which may influence elections. The optimum number at the second rank – a particularly sensitive level – would be more than two, but not so many as to substantially reduce the status of the individual posts below that of the top post, a point related to the next variable.

Status gaps between adjacent levels.   Very small status differentials make it appear reasonable for even third-rank officers to compete for a top vacancy and for second-rank officers to compete against their chiefs. On the other hand, an extreme status differential might allow a powerful chief officer more leeway in grooming his successor. Thus:

2   *Narrower status gaps between adjacent high offices tend to result in closer elections.*

A full-time rather than a rank-and-file executive council might place a greater number of potentially successful candidates within range of the top office, if the councillors have independent bases of support, as in the British Engineers. Many writers and trade unionists have viewed an all rank-and-file executive as more democratic, but in practice such a council seems to be easily manipulated by top officers and provides little competition for the top post. Rank-and-filers might be brought into the picture in other ways, such as frequent conventions, national meetings of shop stewards, a larger general council to which the executive council would be responsible, the reservation of some seats for rank-and-filers on the executive council – or in all of these ways.

Number of elected levels.   With a given status gap between rank-and-file members and the top officer, the greater the number of levels of elective office the smaller the status gaps between adjacent levels. Therefore:

3   *A greater number of levels of elected officers is favourable for close elections, but not to the point where there remains an inadequate number of potential competitors at each level.*

Proportion of full-time officials elected.   If appointed officials are controlled by the national officers, they may act as virtually full-time campaigners for an administration's candidates. They themselves would be in an extremely weak position as candidates in opposition to their supervisors. Most appointed officials have channelled their energies into non-electoral paths for advancement. Thus:

4   *A higher proportion of elected full-time officials tends to produce closer elections.*

REGIONAL SUBSTRUCTURES

The nomination or endorsement of candidates for national posts, by regional and local unions or their officers through either official or un-official channels, is quite common. There is a good deal of self-interest and parochialism in the desire of members and officers for direct representation in the higher councils, or for the presence there of 'friends'. Ordinarily most voters probably follow the recommendations of their regional or local leaders, and often they have little basis for doing otherwise.

The propositions closely parallel those on the status hierarchy, with a region's voting strength replacing a status's vote-getting capacity. They also apply roughly to occupational substructures which do not overlap the regions in membership. In addition, one would have to assume an equal possibility for mobilising the various occupations for participation in elec-tions (if members voted directly), and no special affinity of one occupational substructure for another (unless the combination was considered to be the unit).

5   *Elections tend to be contested more closely where the major formal regional units are less unequal in their available voting strengths.* The same degree of relative inequality of leading units has a greater potential for reducing the closeness of elections where the leading units control a larger portion of the total vote. Conceivably there might be no regions, or they might be unimportant, in which case the proposition would pertain to the local unions. Some locals are city-wide and quite large.

6   *A greater number of fairly large regional units is conducive to close elections.*[5] The effect of only a few such units has been discussed pre-viously under 'countervailing-powers model'. For a union of a given size, an increase in the number of regions can only be at the expense of their average size. Some minimum size is necessary to maintain regional autonomy (as against the national officers) and to capture the attention of members in other regions.

Local Autonomy and Distribution of Powers
The previous propositions on the equality of substructures make little sense

without some degree of local autonomy and of limitation or distribution of national power.

Extent of local autonomy.   Autonomy may be found at any level below the national and pertains to independence in such diverse matters as collective bargaining, finances, internal administration and political activities.

7   *Organisations with a greater local autonomy of any type, and with a greater overall autonomy at all subnational levels, tend to have closer elections.*

Location of formal control over full-time officials.   The only reliable basis for effective opposition in most unions is competition among full-time officers. The greatest threat to the free expression of electoral competition lies in control over officials by a national administration. Therefore:

8   *The greater the proportion of full-time officials elected or appointed by, and under the control of, meaningful structural subdivisions, the greater the success of opposition in elections to high office.*

Intermediate structural shields.   Under favourable conditions, the local unions themselves may have considerable autonomy. Since in some unions the regions have only advisory functions – the locals being serviced directly by nationally-elected or appointed officials – the question arises as to the optimum locus of the autonomy. Regional autonomy seems favourable to close national elections even at the expense of local autonomy. Regional officials with administrative or executive functions would promote intra-regional communication, build their own reputations, and be in a position to filter or criticise communications from the national office. For these reasons they would be less dependent upon the national officials for assistance in achieving national office. Thus:

9   *A structural shield, in the form of an important intermediate level of organisation between the national and local, is favourable for close elections.*

National power centres.   National committees or conferences may increase local autonomy by counterbalancing the power of the chief officers. The same applies to an independent appeal court. However, there is a more direct relationship to autonomy in the representation of regional or occu-pational substructures on national bodies, which can veto officials' deci-sions. Such bodies may, also, generate controversy within themselves, depending partly upon the opportunities for political as well as substructural representation (to be discussed later), and this may be considered an aspect of their independent power. Therefore:

10   *The greater the independent power exercised by national committees and conferences, the less the probability of the domination of an organisation by a single tendency, and the closer the elections.*

Conventions exercise more power if they function as policy-making groups rather than as showcase meetings. Small size, frequent meetings and adequate time for deliberations would tend to increase their power. As James Madison has argued, concerning an increase in the size of a legislative assembly beyond a number sufficient for its basic purposes: 'The countenance of the government may become more democratic, but the soul that animates it will be more oligarchic. The machine will be enlarged, but the fewer, and often the more secret, will be the springs by which its motions are directed' (1961: 360–1).

NOTIONS OF EQUALITY THROUGH VOTING SYSTEMS

Voting systems may be considered in terms of who makes the decision, under what electoral systems, and under what related rules. The previous structural notions and propositions are applicable when the 'who' includes the representatives of substructures at meetings, usually conventions, and/ or when each substructure must cast its entire voting strength *en bloc* behind one of the candidates, perhaps after a vote of its members or delegates.

A transfer of the structural principles to the floor of a convention requires these assumptions:

a   The degree to which convention delegates vote independently of the wishes of national officials is directly related to: (*a*) the overall degree of substructural autonomy; and (*b*) the degree to which the delegates, in their usual year-round roles, are subject to substructural rather than national control.
b   The closeness of elections for the delegates themselves is influenced by structural factors within their constituencies, similar to those already discussed for the election of officers, particularly when the constituencies are large and structurally complex.
c   Closer elections for delegates tend to result in closer elections of national officers by the convention, since the body of delegates tends to be more heterogeneous politically and the close competition is often a politicising influence.

Certain additional and somewhat unrelated notions are required for a reasonably comprehensive set of structural–procedural propositions. These notions include the following:

d Electoral systems which are more favourable to minorities, or to initially weaker tendencies, tend to result in closer elections.
e Different voting systems and different ways of formalising electoral constituencies are differentially biased with respect to factional tendencies (and therefore, if used simultaneously, may generate competition).

ELECTORAL MODELS

Electoral models for really effective opposition make sense only if one assumes a possible, but imperfect, structural base. The pure random model would profit little from an electoral system favourable to opposition, except when incumbents were involved. Realistically, voting systems often significantly affect the probability of close elections.

Two-party system model. This model provides a self-adjusting mechanism for the production of close votes. Both parties opportunistically attempt to adjust their programmes to attract a sufficient number of independents, or marginal supporters of the other party, to obtain a majority of the vote (see Downs, 1957: 135–7, 297). The two-party system is compatible with the countervailing-powers model when the electorate is not unduly affected by the sometimes unequal structural pressures generated by the countervailing powers. While a two-party system would probably not have explicit constitutional support, it might nevertheless be institutionalised, as in the ITU. While other close approximations to it seem unlikely, it is included here to facilitate appreciation for the next model, and for completeness.

Homeostatic electoral model. What the two-party system accomplishes through the opportunistic adjustment of programmes can also be done through formal electoral means. Basically, this model provides for the progressive elimination of all but the leading candidates, either by preliminary elections (elimination balloting) or by the transfer of votes in the counting process. When there are numerous candidates, the selection of the two highest to proceed to a final ballot may easily result in one or both final candidates representing organised minorities. If only one such candidate belongs to a distinct, but unpopular, minority he may be overwhelmingly defeated. For this reason, a transferable vote system should yield closer elections.

This elimination permits the pooling of the votes of weaker tendencies and makes agreements among these profitable (especially under transfer systems), thereby usually producing closer elections than would otherwise be the case. It is possible to combine transferable votes with the election of several representatives simultaneously, with a majority of votes being required for each candidate. In principle this system could produce the same results as the winner-take-all system described under electoral mono-poly in Chapter 2, if factional lines were firmly drawn. However, the pro-cess of listing preferences would seem to give *some* encouragement to deviations from a slate, where individual voters were casting the ballots.

Progressive elimination encourages numerous candidacies (since there is less fear of splitting the anti-administration forces) and allows the selec-tion of the (usually two) leading candidates on the basis of programme, personal characteristics, or whatever is most warranted by the given state of politicisation or divisions within the electorate. Close votes would be maintained during periods of quiescence by the selection of program-matically similar finalists. Thus, there is an inherent mechanism for making the most equal division possible.

VOTING SYSTEMS AND PROCEDURES

While the ultimate electorate is theoretically the eligible membership, the deciding votes for officers may occur at meetings of widely-differing size, composition and manner of election, as well as through direct ballot of the membership. The next four propositions, and one other, concern dif-ferences in the composition of the body of convention delegates and in how they are elected and how they vote.

Proportion of full-time convention delegates.   Some union constitutions permit and others prohibit the election of full-time delegates to national conventions. Certainly the presence of many full-time officials as voting delegates would deter close competition if their posts were due to appoint-ment by a national administration. On the other hand, full-time regionally-elected officials may be the most logical and effective competitors for national office, and their presence at a convention would facilitate their building national reputations (and probably promote the interests and maintain the autonomy of their regions). The next propositions follow from this reasoning:

11   *The smaller the proportion of nationally-appointed or controlled officials as convention delegates, the closer the elections.* Even the presence or participation of national or nationally-controlled officials as *ex officio* delegates without vote or as visitors, may pro-vide an administration with a claque and with an opportunity to

dominate the debate, to conduct informal caucus work, and to intimidate the other delegates psychologically or through threat of reprisals.

12   *The greater the degree of local control over regionally-assigned full-time officials, and of local autonomy in general, the greater the proportion of such officials that may be tolerated as delegates with little or no decrement in the closeness of elections at conventions.*

13   *The presence as delegates of a small-to-moderate proportion of locally or regionally-controlled full-time officials is the optimum condition for close elections.* Displacement of rank-and-file delegates beyond a certain point would decrease political diversity and interfere with feedback to the membership. Feedback on the national political situation, and on the performance of the full-time delegates, would be favourable for both competition and democracy.

Number and size of branches in delegates' constituencies. Lipset *et al.* (1956: 364–82) found opposition support in the Typographical Union to be greater in the larger locals, for both local and national office. They explained this as due to the larger locals' greater effective autonomy, their better communications with those engaged in extra-local politics, and less disruption of inter-personal relationships with opposition (see also Faunce, 1962). It is also reasonable to assume that with larger size there is a greater possibility of finding qualified opposition leaders. These considerations would tend to affect the political process in the organisation generally, the elections of convention delegates, and competition for office at the convention itself.

There are some special obstacles to the injection of the competitive struggle for national posts into elections for convention delegates. Local members frequently regard the occasion as an opportunity to reward their local leaders for services rendered throughout the year. When this factor is not operative the usual competitive advantages of incumbents apply, with the additional one in this case of their being (or seeming) better able to represent the local union at the convention in its special grievances or problems. The question of whom the prospective delegates might support for national office at the convention might be ignored or considered secondary (especially with inadequate information), to the probable advantage of an entrenched national leadership, if such existed. (Indeed, in many cases nominations for national office are made only at the convention, so that opposition candidates, if any, would not be known in advance. This is relevant to the discussion of the referendum *v.* the convention below.)

This weakness and apparent irrelevance of opposition would tend to be counteracted by the structurally-articulated heterogeneity of *multi-branch* constituencies for the election of delegates. These are fairly common in Britain, organised on a regional basis. The branches or their leaders would tend to compete against each other, the closeness of the elections being affected by such organisational factors as the equality of branch voting strengths and the voting systems. There would be strong motivation for inter-branch communications, to campaign and to make electoral agreements. (For example, in the British Railwaymen's elections to conference, branches often advertise in the *Railway Review*: 'Vote for X. If you can't give him your first choice, give him your second.') Political issues would be more likely to be raised, including national ones, and if the national leadership could not remain neutral in the internal struggle it might generate opposition to itself. Thus:

14   *Elections at conventions tend to be closer when delegates are elected from larger constituencies*, in the sense of a greater number of members and/or branches per constituency. However, beyond a certain size the closeness of national elections might decline under voting systems unfavourable to dispersed minorities (e.g. those which encourage winner-take-all victories of slates in the simultaneous election of several delegates). This point is amplified immediately below.

The referendum v. the convention.   In a typical confrontation, between a national administration and an electorally weaker and less well-organised minority tendency, an election by national referendum would avoid most of the above disadvantages for opposition of the single-branch delegacy. A referendum would make it unnecessary for a minority to find candidates for its slate in each branch, centre attention on national issues, permit a more direct flow of communication to the membership (perhaps with the assistance of news media), require less campaign funds and machinery, and make national opposition compatible with sending possibly pro-administration local leaders to the convention.[6] The use of multi-branch constituencies for the election of convention delegates would tend to lessen, but not eliminate, the relative advantages of the referendum for close elections.

The premium placed upon a direct flow of communications to the membership in a referendum, and upon organising voters in the bailiwick of hostile local officials if possible, would tend to promote factional organisation and politicise the membership. Arguing against a proposed constitutional amendment to elect the president of the American Federation of Teachers by referendum rather than convention, it was stated:

'Where the elected leadership of a local opposed him, a candidate would have every reason to enter that local and seek to organize potential supporters.

'Electing the AFT president by referendum would cause the intrusion of national politics into local affairs. It would force a local's leadership to ignore problems of direct concern to their members – in order to turn back these challenges to its leadership and authority' ('information on the Second AFT Referendum Ballot', official AFT flyer enclosed with ballot, 1973).

The other arguments offered in this flyer against electing the president by referendum included: the high cost of mounting a campaign to the entire electorate; the inability of challengers to match the mobility and 'exposure' of the incumbent; the necessarily inferior information possessed by individual voters as compared to delegates; and the divisiveness if the president and vice-presidents were to be chosen from different slates, since the latter are elected at the convention. In the AFT each presidential candidate normally receives a full page for an election address in the union's monthly newspaper, which is mailed to each member. In practice, delegations from larger locals arrive at the convention committed to a slate or candidate, and cast what are virtually block votes (see our discussion of electoral monopoly in Chapter 2). A meaningful campaign at the AFT convention would therefore be unrealistic except in unusual cases. This would probably be true at most times in most well-established unions.

In the turbulent days of a new and still-democratic union, the still-volatile secondary leaders at the convention might represent more of a threat to the national administration than the membership, and the top leadership would be more secure if elected by referendum. (For example, a former president and founder of a Congress of Industrial Organizations union, when asked why the referendum was instituted, said: 'The advantage of the referendum is that it is so seldom used.' As it turned out, he miscalculated.) There are also circumstances where some dissatisfied national leaders or a rank-and-file opposition might run a candidate against the top incumbent at a convention, but fail to do so in a referendum because a candidate of national stature is lacking. Nevertheless, *ordinarily*, in oligarchic unions with *some* elbow room for potential opposition, the opportunity to bypass all administration-dominated structures by taking the vote directly to the members would result in more electoral success for an opposition. In the 1957 presidential referendum in the American Steelworkers, a rank-and-file oppositionist received over 40 per cent of the vote, while the incumbent 'was endorsed for the nomination by 1,905 locals, as against only ninety-one for Mr. Rarick. The union president also has the solid backing of all the organization's twenty-nine district directors' (*New York*

Times, 10 February 1957). The president of the American International Union of Electrical Workers was able to control almost completely the opposition at the 1964 convention, just ninety days before his defeat in a referendum. But let us return to some basic reasons for the convention's inferiority, even in the absence of some of the cruder forms of oligarchic control.

The strength of dispersed minorities may be mechanically dissipated in elections by convention. (Most minorities intent on winning national elections would tend to become dispersed as they extended their influence.) It is well known that small differences in the popular vote for parties are usually exaggerated in the composition of parliaments elected by majority or plurality vote, and moderate differences often overwhelm the minority (see Lakeman and Lambert, 1959: 25–49).

In addition, as Taft (1954: 36) has pointed out, 'frequently canvasses of strength are made before the actual election and potential candidates withdraw when they find defeat inevitable or likely'. Taft probably had the convention in mind. In our study we found two elections at American conventions in which the challenger withdrew while the count was in progress. Thus, the convention system tends to discourage the use of electoral machinery.

The basic principle is that dispersed minorities are less likely to dominate a majority decision in separate 'samples' of voters *as these increase in size.* The sample in a referendum would include only one individual, whose decision would contribute directly, without diminution, to the final vote. In election by convention the 'sample' would be the constituency, and if delegates from the same constituency were required to vote *en bloc*, there would be additional 'samples' among the delegates which would further wash out the strength of a minority. Minorities would suffer similarly where national delegates were elected by regional conventions or committees. Thus:

15   *With an intermediate degree of structural–procedural bias against anti-administration forces, the referendum is more favourable for close national elections than the convention,* there being little or no difference when the situation is extremely favourable or unfavourable to opposition.[7]

16   *The greater the extent to which convention systems interfere with proportional representation for weaker tendencies, or insist upon delegations voting* en bloc, *the more unfavourable convention systems are for effective opposition.* The appointment of an officer by a small executive committee would be particularly unfavourable for close elections, because dispersed minorities would usually be under-

represented and the inter-personal situation would deter a formal expression of opposition.

Ease of nomination. The frequency and extent of use of the electoral machinery tend to establish (as well as result from) the legitimacy of opposition, and to foster internal communication and knowledge of the candidates. In some unions where nomination for top office is extremely easy, e.g. where any of 2,000 branches may nominate, candidates enter elections with sure knowledge of defeat in order to become known. In other unions, to achieve nomination is as strenuous as to win a major election, since prior endorsement by a large region is required. Such obstacles may impose severe limitations on opposition, as may a nomination process which bars certain types of members, imposes difficult personal requirements, or allows the administration great leeway in determining eligibility. Bearing in mind that ease of nomination beyond a certain point may decrease the closeness of elections (especially under plurality systems):

17   *The more restrictive the rules for nomination, and specifically the greater the proportion of potential nominators required for candidacy, the less frequent and extensive the use of the electoral machinery, and the less effective the opposition for national office.*

Frequency of elections. Since the frequency of use of the electoral machinery can be no greater than the frequency of elections:

18   *The more frequent the vacancies and periodic elections for top and near-top posts (the vacancies being of greater importance), the closer the elections.* The frequency of vacancies is due to both formal reasons (e.g. rules for compulsory retirement) and informal reasons.

Opportunity to pool minority votes. Electoral systems which allow the pooling of opposition votes reduce the probability that numerous candidacies may be to the advantage of an administration, and tend to produce closer elections for the reasons given in our previous discussion of the homeostatic electoral model. In addition, a knowledge of the preliminary votes or counts may enable a loser to better direct his campaigns or make coalitions in subsequent elections, or it may encourage his efforts if he did better initially than finally.

19   *Any method of casting or counting votes which permits a combination of the supporters of oppositionists or minor candidates, or of their votes, tends to lead to closer elections than a plurality (relative majority) system.*

Different voting systems within the same union.   The electorate voting at branch meetings is often quite different in social status, and in the degree of union activity and political involvement, from the members voting in a general postal ballot. Different electoral systems are also differentially biased, especially in the degree to which they favour compromise candidates or can be dominated by strong minorities, usually but not always the leadership. A heterogeneity of voting systems for national officers and/or national power centres may heighten the general level of controversy in the union. Thus:

20   *The use of a greater number of voting systems for national representatives tends to heighten controversy among them and ultimately to be reflected in closer elections.* However, the effect of some systems much more unfavourable to effective opposition than others might not be compensated for by the effect of heterogeneity.

NON-HIERARCHICAL STRUCTURAL RELATIONSHIPS AND
OVERLAPPING MEMBERSHIPS

While territorial divisions in the formal structure usually fit neatly into a hierarchical system, this is often less true of industrial or occupational divisions. For example, all local unions which negotiate with a large national corporation may band together in establishing a 'conference board' for the exchange of information, mutual assistance and, ultimately, joint bargaining. Such an organisation may have a newspaper and a chairperson. The latter, usually full-time, may be elected by the local unions concerned or appointed by the national executive council, perhaps from among its own members.

An industrial structure may also fit neatly into a simple hierarchical structure if regional associations are absent. A left-wing critic of the administration of the British Electrical Trades Union has argued: 'In 1965 the existing area committees of the union were abolished. They were organized on a cross-industry regional basis and were the organising base for the rank and file. They provided large scale contact between members in different industries.' Without cross-industry regional committees there is 'no contact between members in different industries below national conference level' (Industrial Correspondent, *7 Days*, 27 October 1971).

Thus a local union may have multiple affiliations and be subject to a variety of influences. In this case, inter-local communication would be promoted and an arena provided for the building of national (if limited) reputations. These effects would be limited to the extent that the suborganisation could be controlled from above and that a segmentation of the union's life took place through a neglect of territorial associations.

The above reasoning applies also to the situation in which individual members belong both to heterogeneous branches and to occupationally relevant subassociations, as in a union of teachers or doctors where occupational specialisations find formal internal expression. To sum up:

21   *Effective opposition is promoted by the existence of parallel formal structures, especially territorial and industrial-occupational structures, when the memberships of these overlap and retain an interest in both.* The absence of an institutionalised relationship between such parallel structures might promote opposition, but so might their formal representation on national committees.

RELATIVE IMPORTANCE OF THE VARIABLES

Since the organisational variables interact, the question of their relative importance is complex. To simplify matters, two related questions will be asked and then answered, although more on the basis of judgement than of logic. First, if all variables but one were quite favourable for successful opposition, the lack of which one (apart from a reasonable opportunity to nominate, which is obvious) would most seriously decrease the closeness of elections for the top post?

Purely internal affairs ordinarily seem to provide a psychologically insufficient basis for the politicisation of a union membership. The union fulfils a limited function, and the range of policy options is or appears to be narrow in view of the union's limited power and its place in the social system. Stable parties are unlikely to exist in these circumstances, except perhaps as reflections of deep political divisions within the working class itself. Factions tend to come and go or, if they persist over longer periods, to approximate cliques rather than parties. The members are more often interested in the 'qualifications' of candidates, including their experience, than in programmatic differences. And if in such circumstances there happens to be only one vice-president, and he is in effect the sole apprentice for the presidency, who could be better qualified? Thus, the existence of a clear and 'logical' line of succession would substantially reduce the closeness of the typical election during the succession crisis for the top office. In other words, the absence of two or more offices of similar or identical rank at each level near the top of the hierarchy would most seriously interfere with the closeness of competition.

Second, in an otherwise unfavourable situation, what would result at least in more election-fights and the occasional registering of effective protests? Probably a suitable voting system would, if there were no great fear of reprisal by the administration. Ease of nomination and a reasonably fair count would be basic, and elimination or preferential balloting in combination with the referendum would allow oppositionists to take their case to the membership with the optimum chance for a good showing. Freedom from fear of reprisal might be based on some internal or external (perhaps government) court of appeal, on concern for elementary democratic rights among both members and leaders, or on the protection of candidates by local or regional unions.

RELEVANCE FOR SOCIETIES

This organisational theory of democracy may apply to whole societies that are diagnostically similar to unions in their lack of widespread autonomous associations, or in their apparent homogeneity and state of depoliticisation in which administrative problems take precedence over ideology.

The first part of the diagnosis may apply to developing societies with still largely traditional populations, which have been recognised as a 'poor social base for modern forms of political life requiring extensive autonomous organization of an electorate' (Stinchcombe, 1965: 145). Presumably semi-autonomous communities and federally-organised regions with representatives in a national assembly might, under a sympathetic leadership, sustain electoral competition for top or near-top posts. As in the case of unions, organisational heterogeneity would be an asset in the form of overlapping electorates, different voting systems for different offices, and perhaps some parallel structures in no clear hierarchical relationship – if these could be devised (e.g. combinations of communities for self-help on common problems). But it can hardly be said that such a system would be self-sustaining in the modern world.

The second half of the diagnosis, depoliticisation as a result of apparent homogeneity and a precedence of administration over ideology or interest-group politics, might apply in a new socialist, state socialist or managerial society. An actual or incipient stratification system might not be recognised in a supposedly one-class society. With no attempt at repression whatsoever, the lines between trade unions and the state might become blurred, which might also be the case for other associations. If such a social system were initiated under democratic auspices, the survival of democratic opposition might depend upon its early refuge within a comprehensive but heterogeneous and decentralised government with representative systems favourable to minorities. The election of at least some important officials by national referendum would bypass the numerous union-like substructures, raise general political questions, and promote competition for office both nationally and within substructures.

CONCLUDING REMARKS

A theoretical system should be evaluated in the light of the claims made for it. We have presented organisational characteristics which should tend to counteract the depressing effect on competition for office of the usual top-down hierarchical structure in large unions with many full-time officials. The structures and procedures mentioned in the theoretical statements may be viewed as providing the basis for creating opposition and perhaps, under favourable conditions, for stimulating it. As our discussion of the referendum *v.* the convention shows, there are undoubtedly circumstances where the reverse of our predictions would occur. We are thinking in terms of the long haul under somewhat unfavourable conditions for union democracy, and not in terms of the time of an 'uprising' by the rank-and-file or its shop-floor leaders. The 'masses' have never remained in revolt indefinitely, and while they may some day gain a victory which establishes a new and higher social basis for their democratic participation, even then democrats had better provide a basic framework resistant to oligarchic tendencies and supportive of opposition in somewhat adverse circumstances.

If we had been thinking in terms of a very high order of stable national democracy, rather than in terms of the fairly democratic as against the highly oligarchic, we would have included more on communications and supplementary forms of organisation such as shop stewards' councils, and strengthened conventions as suggested by Alice Cook. However, it is unrealistic to base a theory of effective opposition on such reforms while full-time officials are mostly appointed, the convention meets infrequently, and the succession to the top office is virtually prearranged. This does not mean that the demands for national stewards' councils and a powerful representative convention should not be raised, or that one should not think about aspects of union organisation which we have neglected.

NOTES TO CHAPTER 3

1 For studies of smaller democratic unions see Pearlin and Richards, 1960 (the American Actors' Equity) and Wootton, 1961 (the British Draughtsmen).
2 For example, note the flavour of an interesting, somewhat speculative but nevertheless anti-system-making article on 'Democracy Under Socialism' (Coben, 1953), as may be gathered from the following comments. Concerning rank-and-file committees as the basic political unit, Coben says that under socialism 'No one "invented" this idea . . . History has shown . . .'. Concerning the possibility that existing government institutions may be democratised, he says perhaps, but 'We do not believe it useful for socialists to fix a programme or a blueprint on this point; the people will decide . . .', and 'it is not in the field of governmental *forms* [emphasis in original] that the main problem lies. It is a question of fusing political democracy with economic democracy.' Social ownership by co-operatives, local communities and 'free collectives' are considered along with workers' committees, but national government is neglected.
3 See Council of Ruskin College, 1968, for the expression of such a view in 1919. It still has currency, and at times its pragmatism might gain a ready acceptance among workers not particularly enamoured of their unions.

4 The Israeli Histadrut has a multi-party system based on proportional representation, but is more akin to a federation than a national union.
5 Rousseau preferred 'no subsidiary groups within a State' for a true expression
   of the general will, but added: 'where subsidiary groups do exist their numbers
   should be made as large as possible, and none should be more powerful than
   its fellows' (Rousseau, 1962: 194).
6 For an elaboration of these points see Edelstein, 1960. In addition, Lipset *et al.*
   (1956: 397) express the view that even in the ITU, which once used the convention for the election of officers, this system was 'more easily controllable by
   the administration' than the referendum.
7 We would argue that elections by referendum would usually be closer even
   where some 'hanky-panky' existed in the ballot counting. The possibility of an
   incumbent top officer being defeated is another matter; a reasonably fair count
   is of critical importance, whether assured by the union itself or by the opportunity to appeal to the courts or a government administrative agency. The
   accuracy of the count at a convention is ordinarily less in question.

Part Two
OVERALL FINDINGS

Chapter 4

Overall British–American Differences in Organisation and Opposition

The major objectives here are to convey an overall picture of the extent of electoral opposition for top posts in British and American unions in the period studied and to report some outstanding differences between the two countries in specific organisational features relevant to our theory of union democracy. Many of the specific measures of opposition or organisation described here will be used again, in Chapters 5 and 6, to test the theory within each country separately. Most of the organisational differences might be expected to generate more opposition in Britain than in the United States, and indeed we found a striking difference, in favour of Britain, in the success of opposition in filling top and next-to-top vacancies.

THE UNIONS STUDIED

The British 'sample' included twenty-nine national unions which were overwhelmingly blue collar in composition, and two in which low-status white collar plus blue collar workers were in the majority. An attempt was made to include all such unions which had 14,500 or more members in 1952 and which, in addition, used the referendum to elect their top officer, or (in the case of three unions) the block votes of their branch memberships. The three otherwise appropriate unions which used the convention (conference) to elect their top officer were excluded, since they were too few for a meaningful comparison with those using the referendum. Three other unions had to be excluded because of insufficient data.[1] All the unions in the sample organised throughout England and Wales, the overwhelming majority in Scotland as well, and many in Northern (and Southern) Ireland also.[2] All were affiliated to the Trades Union Congress, but to our knowledge none was excluded for lack of such affiliation. Thus, the sample included thirty-one of thirty-four British unions of the size and type studied (see Table 4.1).

The American 'sample' was similar in that it included forty-seven unions with more than regional scope and primarily blue collar composition, and four in which low-status white collar or these plus blue collar, workers were in the majority for approximately the same period. The minimum size for selection was 50,000 in 1954. As both the convention and the referendum are commonly used in the United States for the election of top union officers, a mixed sample totalling fifty-one unions (thirty-five using the convention) was used (see Table 4.2). Independent unions as well as those affiliated to the AFL or CIO were included, but three unions expelled (1956–7) from the subsequently-merged federation because of alleged racketeer control were excluded. Disregarding the latter, the American sample

TABLE 4.1   *British unions included in the study*

Union	Number of members in 1952[a] ('000)
Transport and General Workers' Union	1,285
National Union of General and Municipal Workers	809
Amalgamated Engineering Union	756
National Union of Mineworkers	613
National Union of Railwaymen	396
Union of Shop, Distributive and Allied Workers	348
Electrical Trades Union	198
Amalgamated Society of Woodworkers	196
National Union of Agricultural Workers	135
National Union of Printing, Bookbinding and Paperworkers	135
National Union of Tailors and Garment Workers	132
Amalgamated Union of Building Trade Workers	90
National Union of Boot and Shoe Operatives	84
United Society of Boilermakers	83
Amalgamated Union of Foundry Workers	76
National Union of Furniture Trades Operatives	75
National Society of Painters	73
Associated Society of Locomotive Engineers and Firemen	69
National Union of Seamen	60
National Union of Vehicle Builders	55
Plumbing Trades' Union	54
Confederation of Health Service Employees	53
Typographical Association	49
National Union of Sheet Metal Workers	39
National Society of Operative Printers and Assistants	37
Amalgamated Union of Operative Bakers	28
Shipconstructors' and Shipwrights' Association	23
Fire Brigades Union	20
United Patternmakers Association	16
National Association of Operative Plasterers	16
Heating and Domestic Engineers	15

[a] The means and standard deviations reported elsewhere in this chapter are based on 1957 or, in a small number of cases, the midpoint of the years during 1949–66 in which the union's structure was judged stable.

Source: Allen 1954: 74ff; used to select the sample.

TABLE 4.2   *American unions included in the study*

Union	Number of members in 1954[a] ('000)
United Automobile Workers (CIO)	1,239
International Brotherhood of Teamsters	1,231
United Steelworkers of America	1,194
International Association of Machinists	864
United Brotherhood of Carpenters	804
International Brotherhood of Electrical Workers (AFL)	630
International Ladies' Garment Workers	441
International Hod Carriers' Union	433
Hotel and Restaurant Employees	413
Amalgamated Clothing Workers	385
International Union of Electrical Workers (CIO)	362
Amalgamated Meat Cutters	335
United Mine Workers	301[b]
Communications Workers of America (CIO)	300
Brotherhood of Railway Clerks	294
Textile Workers' Union of America (CIO)	293
Retail Clerks' International Association	265
United Association of Plumbers	241
Brotherhood of Painters	220
Brotherhood of Maintenance of Way Employees	219
Building Service Employees	207
Brotherhood of Railroad Trainmen	204
International Union of Operating Engineers	200
Street, Electric Railway and Motor Coach Employees	190
United Rubber Workers	175
Brotherhood of Railway Carmen	170
International Brotherhood of Boilermakers	150
Pulp, Sulphite and Paper Mill Workers (AFL)	150
Bricklayers, Masons and Plasterers	147
International Association of Iron Workers	139
United Packinghouse Workers (CIO)	133[b]
International Woodworkers of America	105
National Association of Letter Carriers (AFL)	103
International Union of Mine, Mill and Smelter Workers	100
United Electrical, Radio and Machine Workers (Industrial)	100[b]
International Printing Pressmen's Union	99
International Typographical Union	96
American Federation of State, County and Municipal Employees	96
Brotherhood of Locomotive Firemen and Enginemen	95
International Chemical Workers (AFL)	90
Transport Workers' Union of America (CIO)	90
International Association of Fire Fighters	85
Utility Workers' Union (CIO)	81
International Longshoremen's Association	65
International Longshoremen's and Warehousemen's Union	65
International Molders and Foundry Workers	65
United Brewery Workers	62

TABLE 4.2 (*continued*)

	Number of members in 1954[a] ('000)
International Brotherhood of Bookbinders	54
Upholsterers' International Union	53
Glass Bottle Blowers' Association (AFL)	51
United Furniture Workers	50

[a] Average dues-paying membership for 1954.
[b] Estimated from other union sources; not in *Directory*.
Source: *Directory of National and International Labor Unions in the United States, 1955*; used to select the sample.

included fifty-one of fifty-eight apparently eligible unions. Seven eligible unions were not included because of lack of information (although on further investigation some might not have qualified); five of these were the Firemen and Oilers, the Papermakers, the Plasterers, the Sheet Metal Workers and the United Shoe Workers. A sixth union, the Oil, Chemical and Atomic Workers, was formed by an amalgamation in 1954 and was excluded for this reason, although later information suggests a possible reconsideration. Finally, the Retail, Wholesale and Department Store Union should probably have been included. (The Barbers included too high a proportion of proprietors. The Marine and Shipbuilding Workers shrank to only 22,000 members by 1965. The Bakery and Confectionery Workers, the Laundry Workers and the smaller Auto Workers (AFL) were expelled from the AFL–CIO because of racketeer control. The United Textile Workers (AFL) was not formed until 1952, as a split-off from another union. The Alliance of Independent Telephone Unions did not seem to qualify as a national union. The National Federation of Federal Employees, and the Retail, Wholesale and Department Store Union were considered primarily white collar, although marginally so. The remaining unions with 50,000 or more included primarily medium- or high-status white collar workers.)

While the British sample was selected on the basis of a much lower minimum size, the means in the two countries were not that different: 203,000 members in Britain (computed on the basis of 1957)[3] and 268,000 in the United States (in 1954). The differences were also small for the mean number of local unions: 807 in Britain and 841 in the United States.

The unions dominated by nominally white collar workers were included to increase the size of the samples. Low-level white collar status probably has little effect, in itself, on competition for top union posts. Certainly typographers, who are blue collar, are of higher status than most retail clerks in our sample. As has been said concerning the American Retail Clerks International Association, 'Properly speaking, one does not deal here with a craft union of white-collar employees [the old image of the RCIA], but, increasingly, with an industrial union of workers who are located mid-way between the white- and blue-collar type of job' (Harrington, 1962: 6). The same could be said, with even greater weight, of the social status of the Letter Carriers (many of whom collect and deliver mail by truck), the only other union in the American sample considered entirely white collar (Solomon and Burns, 1963). At any rate, in the American sample there was a very weak inverse relationship between the percentage of white collar and mean closeness of periodic elections to top posts during 1949–66 ($r = -\cdot10$).[4] The two British unions in the sample classified as having a majority of white collar workers (Bain, 1970: 200ff.), the Shop, Distributive and Allied Workers (73 per cent in 1964) and the Health Service Employees (62 per cent), together averaged a slightly *lower* mean closeness in elections to fill top vacancies than did the British sample as a whole.[5] Since their top posts were permanent, they did not contribute towards the periodic mean.

PESSIMISM CONCERNING COMPETITIVE SUCCESSION

We stated earlier that the existence of a clear and 'logical' line of succession would tend substantially to reduce the closeness of the typical election during the succession crisis for top office. Indeed, in an otherwise favourable situation, we viewed such a line of succession as probably the greatest single obstacle to close elections. The accession to top office of British assistant general secretaries, and American vice-presidents, is commonplace and has given rise to considerable pessimism regarding the state of union democracy in both countries. V. L. Allen has argued that: 'In most cases the position of assistant general secretary is treated as a stepping-stone to the chief position in a union and is regarded as such by ordinary members' (Allen, 1954: 206). This is, of course, often true, but Allen's demonstration of a preponderance of victories of assistant general secretaries for top posts in British unions probably created a false impression of the overall competitive picture.

There are a number of considerations which may make his statistics regarding victories for assistant top officers misleading:

1 An assistant top officer may be too old to qualify for nomination, under the rules, particularly in Britain, or he may not wish to compete for personal reasons, e.g. ill-health. One should, therefore, also consider top-post elections in which no assistant top officers competed.
2 There may be two or more assistant general secretaries with equal formal standing, and these may compete against each other.
3 The job title of the second-ranking full-time office is not exclusively 'assistant general secretary', even in Britain, nor is the top office exclusively the 'general secretary' (B. C. Roberts, 1956: 263ff.).

4   As Allen himself shows, assistant general secretaries are sometimes defeated for top posts. Allen cites six such instances among twenty-five elections in which such officers competed (Allen, 1954: 203–4), a proportion which is more than negligible.
5   There may be no full-time next-to-top officer at the national level, especially in smaller unions but even in some larger ones.

DEFEATS OF CANDIDATES OF EQUAL OR HIGHER STANDING

The existence of two or more next-to-top officers might be reflected in competition among them to fill top vacancies. In Britain the mean number of second-ranking posts during 1949–66, based on an analysis of constitutional powers, was slightly more than two (a mean of 2·1, with a standard deviation of 2·3), while in the American unions the mean was a little more than one second-ranking officer (a mean of 1·2, with a standard deviation of 0·5).[6] There was a total of eight British unions with two or more next-to-top officers, all considered, throughout 1949–66. Six of these eight unions had three or more.[7]

In view of the number of next-to-top officers, both constitutionally and in practice, and the various considerations cited above, it seemed possible that British top vacancies were often filled by candidates defeating others of equal or higher standing. To test the extent to which this was true, each British succession crisis was examined to determine whether or not the winner defeated at least one other candidate of equal or higher rank, based on our analysis of the status hierarchy, all things considered. Then, for each union, the percentage was computed of succession crises involving the defeat of at least one candidate whose standing was equal to or higher than the winner's. Since the 1949–66 period involved no more than a few vacancies for most unions, data were included *before 1949* where the basic rules, structure and method of electing the top officer had remained substantially the same. Union histories from 1928 or earlier were examined for twenty-three of the unions. There were also six unions, of the thirty-one studied, for which the initial date was between 1940 and 1949.

The mean of all the British percentages of defeats of equal-or-higher-status candidates was computed and found to be 40 per cent (with a standard deviation of 34 per cent). Only eight of the thirty-one unions had no such defeats of equal-or-higher-status candidates. This is particularly impressive since twenty-five of the thirty-one had five or fewer vacancies. Elections to fill top vacancies which did not involve the defeat of an equal-or-higher-status candidate did not necessarily represent a victory for a next-to-top officer. A third-ranking officer might have won over a candidate of still lower rank.

While these figures tell us something about how high office is achieved in Britain, we need further information before we can say that winning over equals or superiors is associated with close elections in filling top vacancies. Conceivably, an oligarchic union administration could throw its support to one among a number of relatively high-status aspiring successors, with a resulting overwhelming electoral victory for the candidate of its choice.[8] To test the possibility that winning over equals or superiors was indeed associated with close elections, the mean closeness of all such elections was computed for each union over the same period of time (i.e. using the very same elections). A moderately high correlation was found between the two measures of competition ($r = \cdot 64$, $N = 31$),[9] considering the fact that most unions had *no more than a few* vacancies, and hence the means were therefore subject to *chance* influences. Thus, elections tended to be closer where they were contested by equals, or where candidates of higher status were defeated. There were twice as many defeats of equals as of superiors, but the latter were spread over just more than half the thirty-one unions.

There is additional information on the filling of British top vacancies which sheds light on the nature of the competitive struggle. We shall in fact also see that losing candidates in the Engineers and the Mineworkers often tried again in later elections, and won. For the entire sample, the mean percentage of top-post winners *previously defeated* for the top post was 22 per cent over the more extended period of time just described. Eighteen of the thirty-one unions had such previous defeats, and in twelve unions one-third or more of their top-vacancies winners had been defeated previously. The correlation between the percentage of previous defeats and the mean closeness of succession crisis elections during the same period may be described as modest ($r = \cdot 36$). There is a similar relationship between previous defeats and the mean closeness of periodic top-post elections ($r = \cdot 39$, $N = 17$). Running in union elections is an acceptable way of becoming known to the membership in British unions, and defeats, up to a point, do not outweigh this advantage in later elections.

Although one would expect that the gaining of the top post after previous defeats would be related to the defeats of one or more candidates of equal or higher standing, the relationship between these two measures was negligible ($r = \cdot 05$). The use of electoral systems for the top office which, in our judgement, offered greater chances for minority candidates (especially, the opportunity to pool minority votes if no one candidate had a majority) was modestly associated with previous defeats for the top post ($r = \cdot 28$). We thought that electoral systems offering greater chances for minorities would encourage a greater number of candidacies, and that this, by increasing the number of defeated candidates, would increase the likelihood that one or more of them might eventually gain top office. The mean number of candidates for top vacancies was indeed related to the percentage of previous defeats to some extent ($r = \cdot 29$), but, oddly, the number of candidates had a negligible relationship to our ranking of the electoral system's opportunities for opposition candidates. We will discuss this number of candidates again shortly.

It appears that, on the whole, there is a good deal of struggle involved in the filling of top vacancies in Britain. This is evident, thus far, in who competes against whom in terms of status, in the efforts of the same candidates in two or more top-post elections, and in the relationship of both of these to the closeness of elections. We do not have comparable data on the United States but, as we shall show, the level of opposition in filling top vacancies here was probably too low to have made such an analysis worthwhile.

THE EXTENT OF MIXED LEADERSHIP

One possible measure of the success of opposition is the percentage of the study period in which leadership was mixed, at executive council level or higher. We were able to estimate this for 29 British unions, for the period 1949-66. Specifically, we used as a guide the presence on the executive council, or among still higher officials (who are not always voting members of the executive council), of one or more recognised dissidents or supporters of minority groupings. The British mean percentage was 48·9, with a standard deviation of 49·4. From this we can infer that some unions had a much more consistent presence of oppositionists at executive council level or higher, but we have not found evidence that these represented open internal factions. This result must be interpreted cautiously because the presence of *only one* Communist member on the executive council, over the whole period studied, would produce the figure of 100 per cent of the period. The finding of mixed leadership applies to the Engineers and the Mineworkers, since 1949 and probably throughout their entire history. We also tried to see if the dominant leadership changed hands to another leadership in opposition to it. We were unable to find such shifts for the unions in the British sample over the period 1949-66, except in the Electrical Trades Union.

We do not have comparable figures on mixed leadership in the American sample, but the mean of 48·9 per cent of the 1949-66 period could not possibly be approached. The reasons for our making this statement will become clear after we have reported the closeness of elections in both countries and, later, described the prevalent American method of electing executive council members.

THE CLOSENESS OF ELECTIONS IN SUCCESSION CRISES

We shall now take a broad look at the level and extent of electoral opposition in the filling of top vacancies. Knowledge of the path upwards to top office can only supplement information on how closely contested the final elections actually were. As in the later discussion of the Mineworkers and the Engineers, the measure of the closeness of an election was the number of votes for the runner-up per 100 for the winner. A runner-up percentage of zero would indicate either a negligible number of votes for the runner-up or an uncontested election. For each union, the *means* of the runner-up per- centages for top-vacancies elections, and then for other kinds of elections, were taken as the key measures of electoral opposition. For a comparison of British and American unions, the mean of these measures was computed separately for top vacancies and for other types of elections, for each country. The measure was adapted for defeats of incumbents (see 273f).

In Britain, the means of closeness of the top and next-to-top vacant-post elections during 1949–66[10] were 53·9 per cent and 69·5 per cent respectively, and in the United States were 10·3 per cent and 14·8 per cent respectively. These figures are even more unfavourable to the American unions than they appear, since only thirty-one of the fifty-one American unions had top-post vacancies during this period, as compared to thirty of the thirty-one British unions. We regard this absence of turnover as a poor sign for competition, in the long run, in unions not contributing towards this mean. The standard deviation of the British runner-up percentages for top vacancies was 22·4, indicating a strong minority of unions with a fairly high *mean* closeness of such elections. Of course, even a union with an average degree of mean closeness had *variability* around its own mean (if it had more than one vacancy), and hence had some elections closer than its mean. There was a mean of 2·0 top vacancies among the thirty British unions (with a standard deviation of 1·0).

If we examine the British unions over the longest period through which their structures and procedures remained basically the same, we find that twenty-nine of the thirty-one unions had more than one vacancy.[11] In fact, nine of the twenty-nine unions had *at least half* of their top vacancies filled by elections with runner-up percentages of 70 or more. As will be shown later, the more recent period is even more favourable for opposition in Britain.

Apart from overall findings of this sort, there are the ambiguous cases where there is comparatively little competition for top posts, but considerably more for the second-ranking posts from which the winner often moves up. The first point is that, because of the late age in Britain of achieving full-time office *and* the usually quite strict rules for retirement at a fixed age, the time interval between assumption of a second-ranking office and assumption of the top office is often relatively small. Second, the undoubted advantage for the second-ranking officer in later top-post elections is, in British unions, often *politically neutral*; it may benefit even a supporter of another political point of view.

The findings were similarly favourable to Britain where percentages of contested elections were concerned. In the United States during 1949–66, only 60 per cent of the sample had *any* contested elections of any kind for top *or* second-ranking posts, as compared with 100 per cent in Britain. The mean percentage of top vacancies contested was 94 per cent in Britain.[12]

PERIODIC ELECTIONS

There are two major kinds of measures of competition in periodic elections for top or next-to-top offices: the closeness of such elections and the frequency of defeats.

Only sixteen of the British unions required periodic re-election of their top and next-to-top officers. The means of closeness of such elections were only 14·4 per cent and 17·9 per cent respectively, but nevertheless were closer than the 8·5 per cent and 6·4 per cent respectively for the American unions during 1949–66.

There was only *one* British union among the sixteen with periodic elections in which a top officer (and in this union a next-to-top officer as well) was defeated during 1949–66. This was through the intervention of the courts in what turned out to be a major case of fraud by the incumbent administration. The union involved was the Electrical Trades Union, which had a Communist-dominated leadership at that time. There was another union with next-to-top defeats, the Engineers, but the defeats in this case might be regarded simply as the more extreme instances of occasionally close elections.

In the United States there were defeats of top officers in five of the fifty-one unions, with two defeats in one of these, and defeats of full-time next-to-top officers in five others. Of the five American unions with top defeats, two had these prior to the passing of the Landrum–Griffin Act 1959, as did four of the five unions with next-to-top defeats. However, one defeat of a top officer, in the International Union of Electrical, Radio and Machine Workers, resulted from the Secretary of Labor intervening on a suspicion of fraud and took place only after a recount of the ballot papers. The Secretary of Labor, who has the sole power under the Landrum–Griffin Act to intervene in cases of suspected fraud in union elections, has, generally chosen to ignore the appeals of aggrieved candidates.

The defeats of the American next-to-top officers should not be taken entirely at face value: in four instances they occurred after opposition to the president by the next-to-top officer. Nevertheless, this may be taken, relatively, as a sign of opposition.

Thus, the percentages of the British and American samples with defeats of either top *or* next-to-top full-time national officers were 12·5 per cent and 19·6 per cent respectively. (If we include the British unions with permanent posts as well, the percentage of unions with such officers removed, defeated or dismissed becomes only 6·5 per cent in Britain, as compared to 19·6 per cent in America.) The British figure, based on only sixteen unions with periodic elections, is less reliable, in view of the limited time span. The point may be put more strongly concerning the fifty-one American unions: in the eighteen-year period, approximately one out of five unions had a defeat of a top or next-to-top officer. This is undoubtedly more effective opposition than most writers on trade union affairs would have expected.

However, in five British unions, all of which filled permanent top posts by election, the second-ranking posts were filled by appointment rather than election. There were also two unions, the Mineworkers and the Bakers, in which there were no formally full-time second-ranking posts at the national level. Thus, there *could* not have been a defeat or removal of any elected full-time next-to-top national officer in seven of the thirty-one British unions.

UNION SIZE AND OPPOSITION

It is, of course, possible to argue that the British and American samples are not comparable because eight British unions with 15,000 to 39,000 members, all below the 50,000 American minimum, were included. It is true that the two British unions with defeats were the third- and seventh-largest. However, among the American unions there was a close-to-zero correlation between the number of members and the occurrence of defeats of top or next-to-top officers (biserial $r = -·02$), and all six correlations between electoral opposition (for filled and unfilled top and second-ranking posts) and size were low, but in favour of the *smaller* unions (see Table 5.3). In Britain, the correlations between size and the closeness of vacant-post elections was negligible, but among the sixteen unions holding periodic elections there was, indeed, a moderately strong, positive correlation between size and the closeness of elections (·53 for top periodic elections and ·56 for next-to-top). Among those British unions electing for life, there was some tendency for the smaller unions to fill top vacancies with closer elections ($r = -·20$).

Thus, the extremely large British–American differences in the closeness of vacant-post elections, in favour of Britain, cannot be explained on the basis of the inclusion of the eight smaller British unions. Nor is it reasonable to invoke size to explain the greater proportion of American defeats, particularly since, on the whole, British periodic elections were contested more regularly and (on average) more closely. Size is inconsistently related to opposition, and the greater opposition in periodic elections among the larger British periodic unions is best explained on some basis other than size itself.

Certainly our data on effectiveness of opposition offer no support for the common notion that larger national unions tend to be more oligarchic. If we turn to the infrequency of national conventions, another variable which has been taken to indicate centralisation, loss of membership control and, hence, oligarchy, we are forced to a similar conclusion. In our British sample, the time between regular conventions was *shorter* in the *larger* unions ($r = -·20$) and in the unions with more locals ($r = -·13$). These relationships were in the *opposite direction* in the American sample ($r = ·20$ and $r = ·18$ respectively), as previous research has shown. Such relationships among American unions become much more pronounced as one adds the entire size range, particularly unions under 29,000. The British relationships in the opposite direction would also hold for the full size range, but would be much weaker than the American, especially if one excludes British unions holding annual meetings of members rather than delegate conferences (see Edelstein and Ruppel, 1970; Marcus, 1966). No national unions are intentionally excluded from these studies.

LONG-TERM TREND IN OPPOSITION

It is possible that there may have been a revival of opposition in American unions in the 1950s and 1960s, but the level of opposition appears to be far below that at the beginning of this century (see Taft, 1954: 41). In Britain, we have objective evidence of a moderate *rise* in the success of opposition over a period of thirty-five years or more.

The data were treated as follows. There was a total of thirteen unions whose structure we judged stable, where the interval between the earliest and latest vacant-post elections (to 1966) was *at least thirty-five years*. The mean year of these elections was computed for each union, and the mean year of the means was found to be 1915. A correlation was computed, within each of these thirteen unions, between the dates of vacant-post elections and the corresponding closeness of elections. Only two of these unions had as few as three top vacancies, and the remaining had five or more. We found that eight of the correlation coefficients were positive and five negative, indicating more unions with trends towards an increase than a decline in electoral competition. The mean product-moment coefficient was ·22, and positive.

Examining all twenty-one unions with three or more top vacancies, we found that sixteen correlations of the date of election with closeness are positive and only five negative. The coefficients for the five largest unions are positive. An examination of the twenty-one unions with three or more next-to-top vacancies (not necessarily the same unions), over roughly comparable periods, gave almost identical results: seventeen unions with positive correlations, and four with negative. *Thus, there is evidence of an overall, moderately long-term trend towards closer competition in elections to top posts, and next-to-top as well.*

Finally, it is possible to compare the mean closeness of elections during 1949–66 with those of the longer periods of organisational stability (*including* 1949–66). For top-post vacancies, the means for the longer periods were 47·9 votes for the runner-up per 100 for the winner, as compared with 53·9 for 1949–66. The corresponding means for next-to-top posts were 64·8 and 69·5 respectively, showing closer elections in the 1949–66 period for both posts.

OVERALL ORGANISATIONAL DIFFERENCES

Much of the basic information gathered on the American unions pertained to national officers: their number, composition, powers and manner of election. The American national convention is closely tied in with the manner of election of officers, since most of the latter are chosen there. We have information on the size and frequency of national conventions, as well as on the composition of their delegations and their governing rules. National officers and the convention usually play a role in disciplinary and appeals systems, which we have also covered. Finally, there is basic information on the hierarchical structure of the officialdom and organisational subdivisions, plus some incidental data to be cited later.

Similar data were gathered on the British unions, and the means and variability within the two countries are compared in Table 4.3. In our view, the outstanding organisational differences are more favourable to electoral opposition in Britain.

THE TOP OFFICE, ITS POWERS AND SUCCESSION

We shall first examine some of the differences in British and American union organisation which pertain to the nature of the top office and the rules governing succession. These differences are clearly reflected in the constitutions of the unions.

The top officer in American unions is generally more powerful than his British equivalent, constitutionally and in practice. In five of the British sample, power is constitutionally divided between two approximately equal

TABLE 4.3 The means of the American and British independent (predictor) variables (and correlations with number of members)

Measure	United States (N = 51)			Britain (N = 31)		
	Mean	Stand. dev.	Corr. with no. of membs.	Mean	Stand. dev.	Corr. with no. of membs.
Highest appeal on trusteeship (executive council, etc.)[a]	4·8	1·30	·08	n.a.	n.a.	n.a.[b]
Highest appeal on suspension, removal of subsidiary officer[a]	4·7	0·99	·26	5·9(29)	1·65	·16(29)
Absence of full-time officers from final appeal body for member or officer[a]	2·0	0·40	·05	2·6	0·56	·03
Highest appeal body for a member[a]	3·8	0·76	·02	3·8	1·20	·02
No. of members ('000)	267·6	293·12	—	203·4	308·23	—
No. of local unions (branches)	840·6	772·84	·45	807·1	1057·71	·78
No. of voting convention delegates (median, in practice)	885·8	701·46	·69	187·8(28)	191·12	·54(28)
No. of levels of hierarchical geographic organisation	2·8	0·73	·48	3·6	0·66	·19
Highest 'weight' of electoral system for top office[a]	8·0	3·01	·10	10·2	5·35	·13
'Weight' of electoral system for executive council[a]	7·7	3·03	·09	10·6	3·97	·11
No. of next-to-top posts (constitution)	1·2	0·47	·19	2·1	2·34	·44
No. of next-to-top posts, all considered	1·2	0·48	·28	2·1	2·08	·30
% of executive council elected by national referendum	19·9	39·49	·03	23·2	37·03	·23
% of executive council elected by convention as a whole	62·4	46·01	·10	3·6	15·89	·11
Top officer elected by referendum[a]	1·6	0·92	·12	n.a.	n.a.	n.a.
% of executive council necessarily subdivisionally-elected or appointed full-time officers	12·0	28·28	·17	10·5	27·32	·23
Time between regular conventions (months)	35·5	16·36	·20	25·8	26·69	·20
Term of office for top post (months)	38·8	14·24	·23	n.a.	n.a.	n.a.
% of total convention votes from largest region	11·0	12·43	·04	n.a.	n.a.	n.a.
No. of levels of elected, necessarily full-time national officers	3·3	0·99	·04	2·5	0·98	·19
No. of levels of elected, necessarily or permissibly full-time national officers	4·2	1·55	·15	2·7	1·17	·11
% of executive council necessarily subdivisionally-elected rank-and-filers	1·7	11·90	·08	42·2	46·79	·02
% of executive council elected by convention as a whole, with referendum for majority if necessary	0·4	2·80	·08	0·0	—	n.a.
Absence of automatic succession in casual vacancy of top post[a]	4·8	4·11	·45	n.a.	n.a.	n.a.
% of convention delegates required for roll-call vote	32·4	17·81	·10	n.a.	n.a.	n.a.
Size of executive council	13·0	7·13	·20	15·8	9·90	·43
% of executive council necessarily nationally-elected or appointed full-time officers	44·9	39·80	·07	15·5	31·89	·14
% of executive council appointed by national officers or executive council	1·0	4·17	·07	0·7	4·06	·08
Absence of 'blanket clause' to discipline a member[a]	2·0	1·18	·26	n.a.	n.a.	n.a.
Absence of single 'logical successor', all considered[a]	2·2	1·52	·01	n.a.	n.a.	n.a.
Top officer formally under direction of executive council[a]	2·0	0·60	·04	2·8	0·40	·29

[a] The measure is based on a ranking of a number of descriptive categories. The higher numbers are considered to be more favourable to electoral opposition.
[b] The measure was not applicable, the information was unavailable, or a somewhat different measure was used in Britain.

top officers: a president and a general secretary (most British presidents are part-time). In *none* of the fifty-one American unions is this the case, although in one union there is another officer with a salary equal to the top officer's.

Many American unions specifically give their president the power to appoint subordinate officials as well as office staff. In others he has the power to appoint, subject to approval by the executive council. According to one study, fifty-one of 115 American unions in the immediate post-war period gave their presidents 'considerable power', which included the right to appoint organisers (Taft, 1948: 459ff.). At least twenty-one of these unions are in our American sample. In contrast, in only one British union in the sample (the Seamen) does the top officer have any constitutional power to appoint subordinate officials on his own initiative; in many cases it is not even clear from the rules that he has the right to hire and fire clerical staff at the head office.

At least constitutionally, the large majority of British top officers in our sample work under the direction of their executive councils, while the typical American president does so only to some extent, according to our analysis of the unions' constitutions. Many American presidents also have the power to suspend other elected officers, including those elected locally, and to suspend all rights of local unions and individual members (Leiserson, 1961: 237).

Succession

The American president's power to appoint high-ranking officers often gives him the constitutional power, in the case of a vacancy, to appoint the officer who would serve the remainder of his term, even if he (the president) retired. This is the more possible since the timing of his retirement may be at his own discretion. A survey of American union presidents in 1966 showed a quarter of the seventy-five respondents to be sixty-five or older, although in recent years several American unions have adopted rules for the compulsory retirement of officers (Friedman, 1969: 21, 31). A study of 111 American unions in 1958 found constitutional requirements for retirement 'rare', and in some cases subject to exceptions made by the executive council (Cohany and Phillips, 1958: 5). All but one of the British sample had a mandatory retirement age, generally sixty-five.

The filling of unscheduled vacancies in the top post often plays a key role in the continuity of an administration's power. In the large majority of our American unions, either the executive council appoints a successor until the expiration of the term of office, or a specified national officer takes over for this period. In eight of the fifty-one American unions, the constitution clearly designates a specific officer, usually a first or executive vice-president, as the new president (as distinct from acting president).[13] Since the mean term of office is over three years, the new or acting president may be very well entrenched by the time of the next presidential election.

In Britain, the death or retirement of a top officer is normally followed, within a few months, by a new election. Only six of the fifty-one American unions require such a special election. The British practice seems related, where the top post is permanent, to the fact that there is no unexpired term of office to fill. But even in the sixteen British unions studied which elect periodically there is generally no fixed term of office linked to the calendar. In other words, *length* of office is generally not linked to specific *dates*. To put it another way, it is generally not the practice to hold a number of elections to full-time national office at the same specified time. This is facilitated by the fact that British elections to top office are generally by referendum rather than convention, and were entirely so in the unions selected for study. However, in addition one may suspect that the indefiniteness of dates of British Parliamentary elections, and the practice of holding by-elections, may have served as models for union practice.

The *number of next-to-top* officers is related to the question of succession in that equal second-ranking officers may compete against each other, as in the Engineers. There are two closely-related indicators of the number of next-to-top officers: the *mean* number, taking possible variabilities into account, based purely on an analysis of *constitutional* powers; and the *minimum* number, taking into consideration our evaluation of *actual practice* in the union. The correlations between the two measures were high in both countries (·88 in the United States and ·82 in Britain). The mean number of next-to-top officers on *both* measures was 1·2 in the United States and 2·1 in Britain. However, the much higher British mean is due more to the presence of some unions with three or more next-to-top officers than to the proportion of unions with more than one. In Britain, 'all considered', there were only eight unions (26 per cent) with more than one second-ranking officer during the entire 1949–66 period,[14] while in the United States there were nine (18 per cent). In the United States only one union had as many as three officers at the second rank, while in Britain seven unions had three or more and five unions had between five and nine.

Other things being equal, a number of next-to-top posts greater than two makes the actual availability of more than one candidate for a top vacancy still more likely. After all, some next-to-top officials may be beyond the age where they are permitted to run (especially in Britain), others may be in ill-health, and still others may consider themselves personally bound or politically allied to other second-ranking officers.

Even where two or more officers just below the top are equal, one may stand out by virtue of title or duties as the 'logical' successor to the top officer. For example, in an American union there may be a first vice-president and a secretary-treasurer of equal powers and status, but the vice-president may substitute for the president in his absence. Even apart from actual duties, the title of vice-president suggests a particular suitability for the top post, just as in Britain the title assistant general secretary suggests a readiness to assume the secretaryship. The more frequent absence of a single logical successor in the American sample reflects, largely, the fact that the line of progression is frequently through a secretary-treasurer who is clearly second-ranking and in line for the top post, but not 'logically' so. This explains, among the American unions, the absence of a relationship between the minimum number of next-to-top posts and the absence of a single logical successor ($r = \cdot05$), whereas in Britain the relationship was strong, as expected ($r = \cdot74$, $N = 30$).

There is a further complexity in that some American secretary-treasurers, while clearly their union's next-to-top officers, are regarded as essentially technical non-political office-holders, and they may even regard themselves as such. At any rate, the secretary-treasurers may, in some unions, survive a number of presidents with different views and fail to compete when openings for the presidency occur. The tendency for the secretary-treasurer to be a technician appears to be related to his constitutionally-prescribed duties, but a formal analysis has not been made in this respect. The fact that the American second-ranking officer may not be in line for the presidency tends to make the number of next-to-top officers of less value in predicting top-post competition. A recent study of over 100 American unions showed that the previous position of 16 per cent of presidents had been secretary, while that of 56 per cent had been vice-president. However, the sample included unions with 6,000 members and unions of this size may not have had full-time secretaries. In the same sample, the last position of 46 per cent of secretaries had been vice-president, while only 0·5 per cent of vice-presidents had been secretary. Even considering the fact that multiple vice-presidencies are common, it appears that the secretaryship is a higher-ranking office (see Friedman, 1969: 28).

THE NATIONAL CONVENTION

The union convention is frequently a court of appeals, a rules revision conference, and, in the United States, a nominating convention, as well as a legislative body. A large convention may also be 'a pageant, a reward for drudgery back home in the local union, and an operation in public relations' (Barbash, 1967: 76–7). In most of its serious functions the convention has the potential to act as a counterweight to the presidency and executive council, thus deterring the growth of arbitrary power and, possibly, serving as an arena in which opposition forces can express themselves and opposition candidates become known. The convention, of course, assumes a special importance in unions, where it elects the top officer and executive council.

There is little doubt that the American convention is less democratic than the British, even apart from the specific data to be cited here. In the United States, convention committees 'are usually appointed by the president, but in a few unions they are designated by the executive board and in a few elected by the convention' (Barbash, 1967: 79). These normally include the credentials committee and resolutions committee, the latter often having the power to make conflicting resolutions 'composite' for presentation to the convention. In British unions, the committees are less likely to be appointed by the top officer, and resolutions by branches or subdivisions must often be considered as submitted unless the consent of the originators is obtained.

Furthermore, the numerous field staff appointed by national officers in the United States often have the right to be elected as local delegates, and in some unions they appear as voting delegates in not inconsiderable numbers. In other unions, the numerous appointed staff attend as visitors or participate without vote by virtue of their official status, and their presence is no doubt useful to the administration. Neutrality of appointed staff is seldom permitted where the administration's life is at stake.

The functioning of American union convention committees and the role of officials in them has been described thus:

'When opposition groups are well organized and act in the open, they are commonly given representation, though they may be kept off key committees. But in unions with a closely knit officialdom (e.g. Carpenters, Miners, Steelworkers, Teamsters, and the garment organizations) the same persons head the main committees in successive conventions to make sure that nothing untoward happens. These are general officers or paid staff representatives, and care is taken to name committee members who are considered "safe". On all important matters, the committees report what has been previously approved by the officials, and the convention rarely changes or rejects the recommendations' (Leiserson, 1961: 187; see also 127–8).

Number of Delegates

Probably the most striking difference between American and British union conventions lies in the number of delegates. The mean numbers of voting delegates in our samples were 886 in the United States and 188 in Britain. Although the correlation between number of members and number of delegates was high in the United States ($r = \cdot69$) and moderately high in Britain ($r = \cdot54$, $N = 28$), the difference in the number of delegates is only partly due to the inclusion of British unions with under 50,000 members.

(It should be recalled that the mean differences in size and number of local unions were not drastically different.) The greater part of the difference in the mean number of delegates is attributable to the use of district rather than local union representation at many British conventions. Our second-largest British union, the Engineers, had only fifty-two voting delegates on this basis, and the Railwaymen, with 396,000 members, had only seventy-seven. It has been shown that thirteen of the largest twenty-one British unions, all with 75,000 or more members, used subdivisional representation (i.e. geographic or occupational–industrial rather than local union representation) at their conference. This is almost unknown in the United States, except as a supplement to local union representation (Edelstein and Ruppel, 1970).

Frequency
British unions with subdivisional representation hold their conferences more frequently than those with local union representation, and this is particularly true among the larger unions. This is a partial, although secondary, explanation for the greater frequency of conventions in the British sample as compared to the American, the mean intervals between conventions being approximately two and three years respectively. In the few British unions without constitutionally-required regular conventions, we arbitrarily assigned ten years. The absence of required regular conventions was associated with the conventions having only advisory functions, in some instances. The unions were the Shipwrights, the Painters, the Woodworkers, and, for part of the period, the Boilermakers (see Allen, 1954). A greater number of members was associated with more frequent conventions in Britain but with less frequent conventions in the United States. Thus, the very large British unions met even more frequently, as compared to the American, than the overall means of the samples indicate.

We have assumed that the convention can be a more effective working body when it is smaller, and when it has accumulated less business since the last meeting. A monster convention in an arena the size of a football field requires half a dozen or more microphones, all under the push-button control of the chair, and it can ill afford to challenge the chair's judgement of ayes and noes on too many occasions (at least, so the chair would argue). On the whole, an ineffective convention is one more easily manipulated by the administration, in terms of both what is done at the convention and what is left undone (and therefore left to the judgement of the executive). But, of course, when officers are elected only at the convention, infrequent conventions mean infrequent elections, and this in itself has been hypothesised as unfavourable for electoral opposition. Our British unions have no advantage in this respect, however, since almost half elect permanently and the remainder elect for terms of three to six years. The American mean term of office was a little more than three years; a maximum of five was set by the Landrum–Griffin Act, but five was seldom exceeded even before it.

Roll-call Votes

Roll-call votes or 'card votes' (based perhaps on differentially-assigned numbers of votes) in convention decision making are more accurate alternatives than hand or voice votes. The common conscious or unconscious bias of chair-persons was already suggested and, given the varied acoustics and vantage points in a large hall, even trusting delegates may often want an exact count on important questions. Both the need for a roll-call vote and the mechanical difficulties in its execution are, of course, greater in the American sample, which has conventions several times larger, on the average.

Apart from smaller size, British trade union practice more often includes the mandating of delegates, often in blocks representing regions or other subdivisions. The delegates themselves may have been elected and mandated at subdivisional conferences, as in the Mineworkers, and block voting at conferences may be traditional or required. Conference resolutions must often, perhaps usually, be presented well in advance, and in many unions these would routinely be submitted to all branches or regions for discussion prior to the conference. In some British trade unions card votes are therefore routine on all questions discussed in advance, while in others a fairly small proportion of delegates may obtain a card vote on request. We have not gathered data on roll-call votes in the British sample, but are sure that the British practice at conventions is such as to make a roll-call or card vote generally easier to obtain, if indeed it must be demanded at all.

In the American sample, twenty-one unions (41 per cent) either had no constitutional provisions for a roll-call vote or required half the convention to demand one. On the other hand, in one-third of the sample a roll-call vote could be obtained by one-fifth or fewer of the delegates (or locals). The mean requirement to obtain a roll-call vote was slightly under one-third of the convention, for the American sample. Oddly, there was a negligible relationship between the size of the convention and the requirements for a roll-call vote ($r = \cdot08$).[15]

THE NATIONAL EXECUTIVE COUNCIL

To the various defects of the convention as a democratic instrument, particularly in the United States, must be added the usual absence of a secret ballot in elections conducted there. An earlier study showed that, of 137 unions nominating and electing the top officer at conventions, only eighteen had constitutional provisions specifically providing for a decision by secret ballot. The writers comment: 'Since union constitutions generally state that the president is to preside over all international conventions, it might be disadvantageous, in certain circumstances, for some local union delegates to cast their votes against the incumbent president – unless they could do so by secret ballot' (Bambrick and Haas, 1955: 73).

Apart from the absence of a secret ballot, the problem of electoral opposition is compounded by the fact that the presidential election is usually followed immediately by the election of the other national officers: unions which elect their presidents at the convention are much more likely to elect larger proportions of their executive councils by vote of *the convention as a whole* (biserial $r = .65$). This applies more strongly to the second-ranking officer. This means that the high-ranking officers from among whom the potentially successful opponent of the president would be likely to come, would face re-election immediately after the opportunity to compete for the presidency, if it were indeed possible for them to be nominated for two posts. Opposition of this type would not be taken lightly, and even in a democratic union the circulation of 'slates' of administration candidates would make any representation for an opposition unlikely in an election by the convention as a whole, short of a system of proportional representation.

The proportions of the executive council elected by the convention as a whole, in the American and British samples, were surprisingly different: 62 per cent in the United States and 4 per cent in Britain. Differences were also large in the percentage of the council required to be subdivisionally-elected rank-and-filers: 2 per cent in the United States and 42 per cent in Britain. This reflects not only the greater prevalence of subdivisional election in Britain, but also the explicit requirement that candidates for the executive council should hold no full-time posts. A mean 45 per cent of American executive councillors were required to be nationally elected (by convention or referendum) or appointed full-time officers, as compared to 16 per cent in Britain (1 per cent or less were nationally appointed in each country). However, particularly in the United States, some nationally-elected councillors would in practice be, and remain, full-time regional officials.[16]

According to our theory, the greater the proportion of full-time officials elected or appointed by, and under the control of, meaningful structural subdivisions, the greater the success of opposition in elections to high office. As applied to the executive council, the most favourable condition for opposition would be a high percentage of subdivisionally-elected full-time officers. Both the British and American samples had low proportions of such officials on their executive councils (10·5 per cent and 12 per cent respectively).

Although rank-and-file executive councils are, in our view, generally incapable of controlling their top officers effectively and are seldom the direct source of opposition in top-post elections, the common subdivisional election of rank-and-filers, as in Britain, seems more favourable for democracy than election by the convention as a whole.

VOTING SYSTEMS

While the substantially greater British closeness of elections for top vacancies may be due to the use of the referendum, it is *not* due to a greater prevalence of voting systems demanding a majority. Some form of voting to insure against a plurality victory, in the case of three or more top-post candidates, was used by 63 per cent of the American sample, as compared to 65 per cent of the British.[17] American unions using the referendum were less likely than those using the convention to employ systems ensuring a majority; only six of the sixteen referendum unions did so, and in three of these the first ballot was at the convention itself. In this perspective, there were very few American unions (six of fifty-one) meeting the more favourable standard of majority system plus referendum employed by most of the British sample (twenty of thirty-one).[18]

A majority of the British sample (seventeen of thirty-one) used the second-ballot (run-off) system, in most such cases balloting the membership twice. Membership-wide primaries in top-office elections are extremely rare in the United States: only one union of 111 studied in 1958 was found to have a preliminary ballot of the membership (Cohany and Phillips, 1958: 8). Such preliminary membership ballots afford an opposition candidate a greater opportunity to campaign and become known. In contrast, most American unions which elect the top officer by convention also nominate at the same convention, in most cases probably minutes before voting. Indeed, at least eighty of eighty-six American unions which elect by convention have been shown to nominate also at the convention (Cohany and Phillips, 1958: 6). Failure to obtain a majority on the first ballot could hardly be expected to delay the outcome by more than a day.

The Mineworkers, the Railwaymen, and two other British unions in the sample used preferential voting by transferable votes, sometimes called the alternative vote in Britain. The effect of this system is equivalent to eliminating candidates one by one until some candidate has a majority, as is sometimes done at conventions. Four unions in the American sample used such systems for presidential elections at conventions, and one apparently had the requirement of elimination balloting by referenda.

DISCIPLINE AND APPEALS

'Blanket Clauses'

The 1953 constitution of the Glass Bottle Blowers' Association provides that the president 'shall have the power to suspend any Local Union Officer or member of the Association for any violation of its laws or insubordination of any lawful command of himself, and shall immediately report the same to the trade' (p. 15). To preclude any doubt as to the meaning of the above, the constitution adds a little later that the president 'is authorized to suspend the card and membership of any member who is working against the welfare of the . . . Association in the interests of any group or organization detrimental to the . . . Association, or for creating dissension among members, or among Local Unions, . . . etc.' (p. 16). He is also authorised to remove or suspend any 'representative' for somewhat less broad reasons (although representatives would also be members), and to fill such a vacant position by the appointment of another. After more along similar lines, it is stated that 'Nothing in this Constitution shall be construed to conflict with this Article' (p. 18).

We found that 46 per cent of the American sample's constitutions had a 'blanket clause' stating that a member may be disciplined for any act unbecoming to a union member or contrary to the interests of the union, and that another 22 per cent implied this possibility. Such provisions would be rare in Britain. In the United States they have, of course, often been applied to critics of the leadership.

Trusteeship

Most American union constitutions provide for the national union's 'trusteeship' over local or subordinate bodies, in addition to its universal power to suspend locals or revoke their charters. Trusteeship appears to be absent from the British union movement, as is indeed the concept itself. It involves the authority of the national union to discipline a local or subordinate body 'by appointing a trustee (or receiver, supervisor, administrator or representative) to assume control over its affairs'. A 1959 study of 114 American unions found trusteeship positions in sixty-seven of their constitutions (Cohany and Phillips, 1959: 1–2). Even where such provisions are absent, a blanket clause plus the power of appointment may serve the same purpose. In the sixty-seven unions with trusteeship provisions, the trusteeship could be initiated by the president in twenty-four unions, the governing council in sixteen, and either of these in eight. Only twelve of the sixty-seven constitutions placed limits on the duration of trusteeships, although since 1959 the duration is subject to law (which is not always enforced) (Cohany and Phillips, 1959: 17). Only seven of the sixty-seven unions required hearings before a trusteeship could be established, and twenty-nine had no provisions specifically relating to hearings on the matter of trusteeship.

In 1958, before the passage of the Landrum–Griffin Act, twelve locals of the Operating Engineers representing 20 per cent of the membership were under trusteeship, seven of them for ten years or more. The Teamsters had 13 per cent of all locals under trusteeship, some for more than fifteen years. These unions, as well as the Miners (cited later) are in the American sample. Such trusteeships are related to the control of the national convention: 'Frequently the trustee appoints the delegates of the local union under his control. Since the general president will name a trustee friendly to himself, the trustee may be expected to follow the president's suggestions in choosing delegates, and the delegates themselves will not be blind to their dependence upon the president's good will' (Cox, 1959: 78–9).

The Appeals System

Many union constitutions are complex documents on matters of appeal from disciplinary decisions, with different procedures regarding ordinary members, officers and local unions. At the national level in both countries, the executive council is apt to be the initial court of appeal, although it is often also a trial body. The court of final appeal is typically the national convention.

We compared the British and American samples on the final court of appeals for a suspended or removed subsidiary officer, using a nine-point category scale running from the top officer or his appointees, through the convention or bodies elected by it, and a referendum, to an extra-union 'public review board'. The simplest way to express the British–American difference on this scale is in terms of the most typical category (which was also the mean). In Britain, the final appeal was to a convention (or body elected by it) at which full-time national officials were explicitly barred from voting. In the United States the body was similar, except that no such bar existed. There was, of course, variability around these mean categories in both countries. The absence of difference between the British and American means for the 'highest appeal body for a member', shown in Table 4.3, is due to the crudeness of the scale: the distinction was not made between lay and other types of convention delegates.

A simpler scale dealt only with the presence of full-time officers on the appeal body: 'An aggrieved member or officer might take his final appeal (short of a referendum) to a body which consisted of full-time officers (1) fully; (2) partially or permissively; (3) not at all'. Both the mean and 84 per cent of the American sample fell at the mid-point of the scale, while most of the British sample excluded full-time officers from the final appeal body.

Clegg has argued, from his observation of British rank-and-file executive

councils, that although these are unable effectively to direct full-time officials, they tend to be independent and act more fairly than full-time
officials *vis-à-vis* disciplinary actions of lower bodies and in taking disciplinary action themselves (Clegg, 1959: 134). The place and manner of election of such lay officials cannot be neglected, of course – we would have
less confidence in rank-and-filers elected partly by vote of permanent
officials at American conventions.

LEVELS OF OFFICERS AND GEOGRAPHIC ORGANISATION

The greater number of levels of elected, necessarily full-time national
officers in the United States (a mean of 3·3, as compared to 2·5 in Britain)
is probably due, largely, to the American secretary-treasurer's special role.
Although we suggested that a greater number of levels of elected officers
is favourable for close elections, this was qualified by 'but not to the point
where there remains an inadequate number of potential competitors at
each level'. Thus, to the extent that the American secretary-treasurer is
clearly in line for the presidency, the mean figures above are not favourable
to closer elections in the United States. To the extent that the secretary-
treasurer is not in the line of succession, the means exaggerate the apparent
American advantage for competitive succession.

When the permissibly, as well as necessarily, full-time levels of national
officials were considered, almost an additional level was added to the
previously-cited American mean (3·3 levels rose to 4·2), but the effect on
the British mean was small (raising it from 2·5 levels to 2·7). This reflects
the fact that probably most American executive councils include part-time
members who may be (and often are) full-time subdivisional officers. This
in itself is a favourable condition for opposition. The mean number of
levels of *geographic* organisation falling into a simple hierarchical relationship were 2·8 levels in the United States and 3·6 in Britain.

One-third of the American sample lacked a purely geographic structural
shield in a direct hierarchical line between the local and national levels.
As we have pointed out, this may make the locals more dependent upon
their national officers, and deprive the union of an important layer of
potentially independent officials. However, we lack systematic information
on the existence of occupational–industrial intermediate organisation in
the United States which might compensate for a lack of intermediate
geographic organisation. It is also conceivable that some regional co-
operation took place outside the usual chain of command. We have such
information for Britain, but not for the United States.

SIZE AS RELATED TO OTHER ORGANISATIONAL VARIABLES

Very few of the organisational variables are consistently and sizeably related to the number of members, apart from the number of locals and the number of delegates. The number of hierarchical levels is moderately related to union size in the United States ($r = \cdot48$) and to the size of the executive council, especially in Britain ($r = \cdot43$). Larger unions are less likely to have automatic succession in the United States ($r = \cdot45$), but such succession is absent in Britain, of course. The number of next-to-top posts tends to be greater with larger size in Britain ($r = \cdot44$, based on constitutional powers), but is somewhat related to smaller size in the United States. There is some tendency in both countries for the larger unions to have a greater proportion of the executive council consisting of full-time subdivisional officers. We shall see shortly, in considering the American factor analysis, that only the number of organisational levels was grouped with numbers of members, locals and delegates. We shall also see that size has no consistent relationship to the success of electoral opposition (cf. the Aston research which emphasises the size variable, as applied to trade unions and voluntary associations; see Donaldson and Warner, 1974). Structural variables, as used in our study, seem, however, to predict internal (political) performance (i.e. opposition), reasonably well.

CONCLUSIONS: BRITISH–AMERICAN DIFFERENCES

In both countries, opposition in important elections has been found to be more frequent and successful than many observers would have thought possible in trade unions. In the British unions, this is the case especially with respect to competition for top vacancies, and in the American unions with respect to the defeat of top and next-to-top officers. The overwhelmingly closer British elections for top vacancies seem related to and explained by the more favourable organisational situation in British unions. This is obviously true in the area of democratic rights and procedures, which includes the appeals system and limitations on the powers of both the top and other national officers. The latter is also reflected in the more democratic nature of British conventions, but there are also less obvious structural features which favour the British convention.

In matters directly affecting the succession, the situation is also more favourable in Britain: the succession is seldom automatic or as much under the control of the executive council, and the number of potential competitors at the second rank appears to be greater. The greater use in Britain of the referendum for electing the top office appears favourable also, especially in view of the administration's advantages at American conventions. The much greater prevalence of subdivisionally-elected executive councillors in Britain is favourable for minority representation and opposition, as also is the apparently greater prevalence of an intermediate level of organisation shielding the local union.

Indeed, the only factor we have measured favouring opposition in the United States is the greater number of levels of full-time national officers – a variable whose meaning is somewhat contingent upon the number at each rank, and which is clouded by the special and/or inconsistent place of the American secretary-treasurer in the hierarchy.

In view of the overwhelming weight of factors favourable to electoral opposition in British unions, it is puzzling that the British periodic elections are not much closer than the American, and that top officers are more rarely defeated in Britain than in the United States.[19] This appears to us to be related to the absence of openly-functioning factions in British unions. which we shall discuss again later.

NOTES TO CHAPTER 4

1 The National Society of Metal Mechanics (33,000), the Amalgamated Society of Woodcutting Machinists (31,000) and the Constructional Engineering Union (20,000) were excluded for lack of data. Also excluded were five unions of appropriate size and composition which appointed their top officers by action of an executive council or its equivalent, and one union which elected by vote of branches, each branch having one vote. Two additional unions which elected by convention are not mentioned above because they appeared to us to be essentially regional (the Card, Blowing and Ring Room Operatives, and the Cotton Spinners and Twiners). See also Table 6.2.
2 British-based unions had 40,000 members in the Irish Republic in 1960 and 55,000 in 1970. There were twenty-four such unions in 1970, some probably not in our sample. (See Irish Congress of Trade Unions, *Trade Union Information*, June 1971, pp. 2ff.)
3 This was closer to the mid-point of the 1949–66 period.
4 The inclusion of the American white collar unions had no systematic effect other than to provide the advantages to be expected with larger sample size.
5 Bain shows 25,000 white collar workers in the Health Service Employees in 1948, and 40,000 in 1964; we estimate the proportion in 1949 at slightly more than one-half. The only other union in the British sample with a considerable number of white collar workers is the Operative Printers and Assistants, with 26 per cent in 1964 and about one-fifth earlier. The mean closeness of elections for top-post vacancies during 1949–67 in the Shopworkers was 28·4 per cent, and in the Health Service Employees was 72·3 per cent. The mean of these two is 50·4 per cent as compared to 53·9 per cent for the sample as a whole.
6 These figures were only slightly different when 'everything' was considered: salary, power, prestige, titles suggesting a logical succession, and evidence as to whether officers would not run for each others' posts.
7 The Engineers had 9; General and Municipal Workers, 5; Printing, Bookbinding and Paperworkers, 6; Boilermakers, 6; Seamen, 3; Furniture Trade Operatives, 2; and Operative Printers and Assistants, 3. In addition, the Vehicle Builders had 2 for most of the period (1952–66). The correlation with number of members was ·30 ($N = 30$).

8 We are indebted to Roderick Martin for pointing out this possibility.

9 Correlation coefficients may vary from 1·00 (a perfect positive relationship), through ·00 (no relationship) to −1·00 (a perfect inverse relationship). Conceptually, a correlation (Pearson product-moment, as used here) of ·64 may be interpreted as follows: 41 per cent (·64 × ·64 × 100) of the variability in one variable is associated with (possibly, explainable by) variability in the other.

10 Actually, for British top-post vacancies only, the period covered was extended to 1967 rather than 1966 in order to make the means more reliable. However, all the thirty British unions with such vacancies also had vacancies during 1949–66. The several British unions with two top officers could have had vacancies in both posts, as was the case in the Engineers and the Mineworkers.

11 All thirty-one British unions had vacancies in this longer period, the mean number of vacancies being 3·2, with a standard deviation of 1·8. The advantages of the probably more reliable means in 'the' longer period must be weighed against the disadvantages of (*a*) differences in the lengths of such periods among British unions (due in part to amalgamations and important rules changes), and (*b*) the greater number of *minor rules changes*, which created problems of description and measurement. An example of the latter would be the change from part-time to full-time posts among some national officials.

12 All references to means, here and elsewhere, are to the means of measures describing each union separately. In no case have we pooled all elections without regard for the unions in which they were held.

13 Cohany and Phillips's study (1958) of 111 American unions with 10,000 or more members showed that twenty-eight unions had automatic assumption of the top office by another officer in the case of a vacancy and sixty-four had their vacancies filled by the executive council or governing body.

14 In addition, the Vehicle Builders had two next-to-top officers during 1952–66.

15 The correlation with union size was ·10, and with the number of locals −·15.

16 Full-time regional officials are normally elected to the council of the British Mineworkers, along with rank-and-filers, but they are regionally, not nationally, elected to the council.

17 Two of the British unions with a plurality system (see p. 161), actually used a preliminary ballot, but then sent *three* rather than two candidates to the final vote, thus defeating the usual purpose of the second ballot.

18 It should be remembered, however, that three otherwise acceptable convention unions were excluded from the British sample.

19 It should also be noted that the average voting turn-out was higher than most commentators have supposed, for the period studied. The mean for the 25 British unions for which we have full data was 36·4 per cent, with a standard deviation of 17·9 per cent which is higher than the turnout for many British local elections and comparable to the 38 per cent turnout in post-Watergate off-year Congressional and gubernatorial elections in 1974 in the United States (see the *New York Times* editorial, 18 November 1974). Certainly the latter turnout is exceeded by that in some American unions which use the referendum for the election of top officers, when elections are contested (see also pp. 274–6). There was a weak relationship between voting turn-out and electoral opposition. The median % voting correlated r = ·15 (N = 15), with the mean runner-up % for top vacancies, in the British periodic sample, over 1949–66.

Chapter 5

Organisation and Opposition in the United States

The primary objective here is to test our organisational theory of union democracy in the United States. This will be followed by a similar test, in Chapter 6, in Britain.

A PERSPECTIVE ON THE RESEARCH

It will be recalled that our organisational hypotheses flow from the notion of equality. Close elections are most likely to result from competition among contenders of *equal* status, power and reputation, resolved by an electorate formally subdivided into potential supporters, such as regions, of *equal* electoral strength, and under voting systems which ameliorate rather than exaggerate any structurally-produced inequalities. Electoral opposition would also be more likely given the existence of one or more significant centres of independent national power in addition to that of the top officer, in the form of a convention (or conference), an executive council or an appeal court. Constitutional protection for democratic rights would also facilitate opposition.

One implication of our organisational approach is that we take the *specifics* of union structure and procedure seriously, as likely to prove related to differences in the closeness of elections. Even where a number of organisational features could be placed under a broader, theoretically relevant concept, we were reluctant prematurely to lose their uniqueness by pooling them to form combined measures. For example, we utilised measures of the voting system for both the top office *and* the executive council, although these systems were usually the same and the measures correlated highly (·91). As it turned out, both of these, jointly, along with other variables, contributed towards an understanding of why some American unions had closer elections than others. We reasoned that voting systems are not simply indicators of a concept, but rather are themselves the operative variables. This is not to deny that a conceptualisation of 'voting system' and its varieties is required. Thus, our research orientation is somewhat different from that in the case where indicators are developed as signs of some underlying attitudes, norms, behaviour tendencies, or qualities of interaction. (We are not, in principle, against the formation of combined measures, even where operative variables are concerned.) Two further deterrents to combination were the facts that we studied only dozens rather than hundreds of national unions, and thus had only a weak empirical basis for demonstrating an essential similarity of effects, and that illogical, fortuitous relationships occurred among many of our organisational variables (these will be described later).

The theory's numerous explanatory variables, as well as our reluctance to combine their measures, dictated the use of many predictors *simultaneously* in the analysis of the American results. With the American sample, which was larger than the British, we could afford to use thirty-one predictors simultaneously. Both the theory and this method of analysis (multiple regression) had certain consequences for how the usefulness of the theory could be judged, particularly for the American unions. Because it was impractical to separate out the independent effects of each predictor among so many variables, for conceptual as well as statistical reasons, we looked primarily at: (*a*) the *total predictive power* of the organisational variables as a set; (*b*) the *directions* of the effects of the separate variables in the set on the success of opposition (as hypothesised, or otherwise); and (*c*) the *relative importance* of the explanatory variables, insofar as this could be judged. An auxiliary statistical technique, factor analysis, was used in the American analysis to provide insight into the *interrelationships among the predictors themselves*, which are discussed below. The smaller number of British unions, which varied from thirty-one available for some measures of electoral opposition to only sixteen for others (some unions did not hold periodic elections), made simultaneous use of all important predictors impossible, for statistical reasons. We therefore looked at the relationships between individual predictors and measures of opposition separately, with the consequence that the step from statistical findings to explanation depended even more upon judgement.

The Relationships Among Explanatory Variables

Unions formed during the same historical period in the same country tend to retain similar clusters of characteristics. Thus, particularly for Britain, as we have already noted, union forms are a product of their origins (Turner, 1962: 232). There are at least two important consequences of this. First, since much of the historically relevant social context for the formation of union organisation no longer exists, current formal organisation is *relatively independent*, in its particulars, of current context.

Second, there is a complex but only coincidental (non-causal) set of relationships among many of the structural and procedural variables. Precisely because these relationships are 'non-logical', they may even be in opposite directions in the two countries. For example, the frequency of union conventions, which we hypothesise as being positively related to the success of electoral opposition, is greater among *larger* British unions but among *smaller* American ones. We do not believe that size (number of members) is a directly operative variable where opposition is concerned. However, there are more important, apparently coincidental interrelationships, particularly among the predictor variables for the British unions. Such interrelationships, coincidental or otherwise, present a problem in disentangling the relative contributions of simultaneously-used predictors. The difficulty is unavoidable, as it lies as much in the complexity of the situation as in the limitations of statistical techniques.

First, the fortuitous and illogical, yet often strong, interrelationships among our predictors suggest that we should be especially wary of 'controlling', statistically, independent variables in order to determine the 'independent' effects of the variables singly. By holding some variables 'constant', statistically, we may be 'washing out' the effects of the very variable whose effect we wish to understand. Second, the size of the 'independent' effect on opposition – that remaining after the effects of other predictors have supposedly been removed – may be trivial in comparison with the effect it may exert *in common* with other predictors. The accuracy of an estimate of the net relationship between an independent (predictor) and a dependent variable decreases to the extent that the independent variable itself can be estimated from the other independent variables present. Where partial correlation coefficients or related indicators of net relationships are concerned, these are typically notoriously affected by errors of measurement when more than three or four predictors are used simultaneously (see Ezekiel and Fox, 1959: 261; Peters and van Voorhees, 1940: 245). Furthermore, while errors of measurement tend to reduce simple correlation coefficients, they may either increase or decrease the magnitude of a partial correlation, and even result in a reversal of the direction of relationship (see Lord, 1963).

Contingent Variables
The effects of even relatively 'directly' acting organisational variables are contingent upon the presence or absence of other variables. We mentioned earlier that great obstacles to being nominated for a top post would make other variables virtually irrelevant for opposition. However, there are more complex kinds of contingencies. For example, a great number of elected levels of national officials lessens the status gap between adjacent levels, which presumably increases the competition among full-time officials; but, with a given number of such officials, a greater number of levels may reduce the number *per level* to just one, which would be an unfavourable situation for close competition. Thus the significance for opposition of the

number of levels of elected national officials is much more contingent than the significance of the number of next-to-top officers, which can be interpreted in its own right with less qualification.

The variables describing the national executive councils illustrate another kind of contingency. An executive council has been described in terms of several somewhat overlapping characteristics at once. A high proportion of regionally-elected rank-and-filers would be favourable for opposition *as compared* to a high proportion of appointed executive councillors, but unfavourable, we hypothesise, *as compared* to a high proportion of regionally-elected full-time councillors (who could compete more successfully for the top office). Thus, the separate relationships with opposition should be interpreted cautiously, and in the light of what is prevalent in the particular country.

Our results will be most reliable and easily interpretable where: the outcomes based on variables used in combination are consistent with those based on the explanatory variables separately; the meaning and effects of the more powerful predictors are less contingent upon the other variables present; and similar results are found in both countries.

As the next sections are rather technical in nature, the non-specialist reader may wish to advance to the conclusions at the end of this chapter (pp. 143–7).

THE AMERICAN FACTOR ANALYSES

While it may be useful to employ thirty-one predictors simultaneously, it is virtually impossible to think about them separately when they are complexly related to each other. It would be simpler to think about the possible effects of these thirty-one variables if they fell into a much smaller number of clusters. For example, the four items on the appeals system did in fact correlate well with each other and poorly with other items, and since they had much in common by way of content our conceptual problem was much simplified. On the other hand, knowledge of even a conceptually heterogeneous cluster is a forewarning that disparate forces may somehow be acting in concert, or that the apparent effects of some variables in the cluster may be attributable to others.

We have used the statistical technique of factor analysis to shed light on the complex interrelationships among our predictor variables. The following illustration of its application to eth complex area of human personality conveys its essential meaning and utility:

'. . . suppose that we wanted to describe an individual's personality as completely as possible by means of test scores. If we wanted to be sure to omit no aspect of his personality, we should probably have to give him several hundred tests. We should find so many of these tests intercorrelated that we would realize that we had duplicated our efforts perhaps several times over. By studying those intercorrelations we would find that we could let single tests represent groups of tests in such a way that coverage of traits is not sacrificed. Where each test serves thus for a cluster of tests, we may say that we have an underlying factor. The task of describing the individual is then greatly simplified by having one test do the work of several. Where the factor can be given psychological definition and meaning, we also have a new powerful concept not only for descriptive purposes but also for thinking about human nature' (Guilford, 1954: 470–1).

In our case we were less interested in *omitting* 'tests' than in simply becoming aware of their interrelationships and – as in the example – being able to conceptualise a smaller number of meaningful underlying factors where possible. The type of factor analysis we used yielded entirely uncorrelated (orthogonal) factors. Thus, each factor might be thought of as operating independently of all others. For example, if we discovered an appeals system factor and an electoral systems factor (as we did), we would know that – as defined by our statistical technique – these factors would affect the closeness of elections independently of each other and of all the other factors.

The results of the factor analysis of American organisational variables are shown in Table 5.1. The number in each cell under 'factors' (the factor loading) shows the correlation between the hypothetical derived factor (shown at the top) and the organisational measure (item) in question (shown on the left). Variables in the same factor have been placed adjacent to each other, for convenience. Correlation coefficients of ·50 or more are underlined. The numbers in the column on the extreme right, under 'communalities', show the extent to which all the factors, jointly, are associated with each organisational characteristic. For example, the first number, ·76, indicates that 76 per cent of the variability among unions in the 'highest appeal on trusteeship' item is associated with the twelve factors, taken jointly. (see pp. 124-5 for the interpretation of correlation coefficients.)

Factor I, 'appeals system'.   Each of the first four items deals with the *appeals* system and has a high loading on Factor I. The correlations are $-·75$, $-·89$, $-·61$ and $-·89$; the signs are of no significance except that they are all in the same *direction*, as they should be considering the content of the items. Since no organisational variables other than appeals items have a high loading on Factor I, we may conceptualise it as '*the* appeals factor'. The following describes some of the other factors.

Factor II, 'size and complexity'.   This includes the number of members, local unions and convention delegates, plus the number of levels of

TABLE 5.1 *Principal axes factor analysis of American independent variables, varimax rotation (51 unions)*

Measure	I	II	III	IV	V	VI	VII	VIII	IX	X	XI	XII	Communalities
63 Highest appeal on trusteeship (executive council etc.)	-75	-09	09	00	08	-10	-26	-06	-26	15	-01	02	·76
64 Highest appeal on suspension, removal of subordinate officer	-89	-15	-02	13	18	-14	-02	-01	00	-08	-01	-06	·89
65 Absence of full-time officers from final appeal body for member or officer	-61	20	06	24	-33	33	-23	-05	12	03	17	05	·79
66 Highest appeal body for member	-89	06	07	05	11	02	-12	-06	09	-10	-09	00	·85
46 No. of members	08	85	-03	-18	02	00	-01	-08	-04	31	07	09	·88
47 No. of local unions	-18	57	-15	-25	-02	-36	17	-05	-09	-06	-33	00	·73
61 No. of voting convention delegates	00	80	-03	-07	-05	-18	31	-06	00	-14	-05	-05	·81
54 No. of levels of hierarchical geographic organisation	08	73	17	20	20	08	-04	07	-04	-24	-01	19	·75
78 Highest 'weight' of electoral system for executive council	-06	08	-93	08	-08	06	-08	-13	-04	-04	-10	05	·92
79 'Weight' of electoral system for top office	05	-09	-94	10	-02	-02	08	-08	-04	02	-09	-02	·92
48 No. of next-to-top posts (constitution)	-12	-06	-05	90	-11	-04	03	14	00	-03	03	-04	·87
51 No. of next-to-top posts, all considered	-15	-09	-15	88	-04	-07	-09	04	02	-13	-03	-02	·87
75 % of executive council elected by national referendum	-08	-06	12	-13	88	09	00	-11	07	12	-16	06	·88
76 % of executive council elected by convention as a whole	-12	-11	-22	-10	-79	42	11	07	-05	-09	-10	-06	·92
95 Top officer elected by referendum	-13	14	-13	-13	87	06	-10	13	-14	-06	16	-05	·91
73 % of executive council necessarily subdivisionally-elected or appointed full-time officers[a]	-04	17	-04	-04	03	-82	-08	03	-06	-04	16	-17	·77
60 Time between regular conventions	30	22	-05	-08	-11	17	78	-22	02	-02	-15	07	·88
82 Term of office for top post	25	18	08	-09	-08	11	84	-21	03	-04	-06	-02	·89

Variable													h^2
62 % of total convention votes from largest region	·00	·13	·29	-·14	·00	·28	-·64	-·19	·01	-·24	·11	-·33	·82
52 No. of levels of elected, necessarily full-time national officers	-·19	·06	-·10	-·17	-·04	·09	·16	-·78	·03	-·20	-·03	-·03	·76
53 No. of levels of elected, permissibly full-time national officers	-·04	·02	-·26	-·16	·08	-·04	·11	-·77	-·07	·03	·05	-·07	·71
74 % of executive council necessarily subdivisionally-elected rank-and-filers	-·18	-·01	-·23	-·33	·00	·07	·07	·61	·06	-·30	·12	-·19	·72
77 % of executive council elected by convention as a whole, with referendum for majority if necessary	-·04	-·04	-·09	-·07	·05	·17	-·23	-·10	-·81	-·16	·07	-·09	·81
49 Absence of 'apprenticeship' title to top office[b]	-·02	·06	·22	·09	-·16	-·12	·21	·00	-·64	·35	-·04	-·10	·69
92 Absence of automatic succession in casual vacancy of top post	·01	·19	·01	-·21	·02	-·13	·07	·08	-·06	·84	-·07	·02	·83
81 % of convention delegates required for roll-call vote	·04	·05	-·24	·07	·41	·25	·05	-·08	·17	·58	-·08	·00	·67
71 Size of executive council	·13	·31	·20	·19	·20	-·23	-·18	·18	-·26	-·10	·61	-·10	·80
72 % of executive council necessarily nationally-elected or appointed full-time officers	-·16	-·03	·05	-·33	·15	·14	·09	-·32	·11	·13	-·67	·03	·76
80 % of executive council appointed by national officers or executive council	-·11	-·21	·13	-·21	·09	-·01	-·03	-·20	·13	-·04	·70	-·07	·68
67 Absence of 'blanket cause' to discipline members	-·07	-·19	·01	-·06	-·07	-·13	-·19	-·08	-·05	-·02	-·04	-·81	·82
50 Absence of single 'logical successor'	-·23	·00	-·04	-·04	-·09	-·42	-·35	-·32	-·06	·00	-·30	-·53	·85
70 Top officer formally under direction of executive council	-·03	-·10	·20	·00	-·23	·13	-·31	-·14	·45	·11	·43	-·05	·64
% variance accounted for by each factor	13·6	10·8	9·7	8·2	7·0	5·4	5·4	4·9	4·8	4·2	3·6	3·3	
Cumulative % of variance accounted for	13·6	24·4	34·1	42·3	49·3	54·7	60·1	65·0	69·7	73·9	77·5	80·8	(80·8)

[a] This measure was missing for one union, the International Chemical Workers, at the time the factor analysis was completed.
[b] This measure was improperly applied and was subsequently dropped from the American analysis.

hierarchical geographic organisation. The correlation of the latter with the number of members was ·48 in the United States but only ·19 in Britain, suggesting caution concerning the general utility of this and other conceptualisations, in spite of the fact that it is sociologically tempting to group complexity with size. Actually, this grouping is heterogeneous insofar as our theory is concerned: larger conventions are presumably weaker instruments for membership control, but a greater number of hierarchical geographic levels (certainly more than two) is favourable for opposition, assuming their officers are elected.

All the items in Factor II correlate positively with the salary of the top officer and with the number of national officers receiving salaries of $15,000 or more. The correlations were highest with the number of convention delegates, being ·45 with salary and ·66 with the number of such national officers.[1]

Factor III, 'electoral systems'.   The two such items are similar in content and highly correlated (*r* = ·91).[2]

Factor IV, 'number of next-to-top posts'.   These two items are also similar and highly correlated (*r* = ·88).

Factor V, 'referendum v. convention'.   This factor makes sense on the American scene, where both methods of selecting officers are widely used. One item deals with the election of the top officer by referendum and another with the executive council (the latter in percentage terms). The third item is the percentage of the executive council elected by the convention *as a whole*. This also has a moderate loading (·42) on the *next* factor.

Factor VI, 'subdivisional full-time officers'.   The single item with a high loading on this factor deals with the composition of the executive council, and the factor name indicates its content. However, there is also a moderate loading (·42) on the percentage of the executive council elected by the convention as a whole (in Factor V), without reference to whether or not such officials are full-time.

Factor VII, 'heterogeneous'.   Two of the three items with high loadings deal with the frequencies of conventions and top-post elections. However, a third, the percentage of the total convention votes held by delegates from the largest region, is not only unrelated in content but correlated with the other two in the 'wrong' direction, considering our hypotheses. Of the American sample, 14 per cent had one-fourth or more of all convention votes concentrated into their largest region – an unfavourable circumstance for close elections by convention, or even by referendum. Longer terms of office (and less frequent conventions) should therefore have been positively related to larger regions (since both are unfavourable), but the factor loadings show that this was not the case. However, we believe it is possible that there may have been a curvilinear relationship. Very small percentages of votes allocated to the largest regions may be an unfavourable condition for opposition, particularly if the *absolute size* is also small, since regional power and autonomy would tend to be weak. Of the American sample, 46 per cent had under 5 per cent of convention votes assigned to their largest region. The mean was 11 per cent.

Factors VIII to XII. The remaining factors are heterogeneous in both content and the signs of their factor loadings, considering our hypotheses. One item – the top officer being formally under the direction of the executive council – could not be placed under any single factor. Another rather important item, the absence of a single 'logical successor', has a loading of ·53 on Factor XII, but it also has appreciable loadings on other factors.

We are indeed fortunate that the first six factors make conceptual sense, apart from the qualification concerning 'complexity' in Factor II. These factors account for 55 per cent of the variance of all items taken together. The remaining factors, while they do *not* make sense conceptually, nevertheless have high loadings on clearly-defined sets of items. Knowing which items cluster together will help us interpret the American findings.

A Factor Analysis Including Electoral Opposition
A rather similar factor analysis was performed including, in addition, the mean closeness of periodic top elections. The objective was to see whether the factor loadings on electoral opposition were consistent with our theory, and whether a small number of factors might carry the major burden of a possible explanation for opposition.[3] This preliminary analysis carried with it the danger of spuriousness, to the extent that the electoral opposition measure itself might dominate any factors.

We were fortunate in that there was only one factor which had a high loading ($-$·66) on the electoral opposition measure, and in that several organisational measures also contributed substantially to the formation of this factor. In addition, there were only two other factors with loadings on electoral opposition as high as ·21 (the same on each). Spuriousness could not have been the only important reason for such loadings.

The effect of including the electoral opposition measure was to cause a regrouping of the leading measures of the original Factors IV, VI and VII, together with a lesser item from Factor XII, along with electoral opposition itself. These were the more than negligible components of this factor:

Measure	Factor loading	Direction consistent with expectations?
Absence of a single logical successor	$-\cdot75$	yes
Mean closeness of periodic top elections	$-\cdot66$	—
Term of office for top post	$\cdot51$	yes
Time between regular conventions	$\cdot46$	yes
% of executive council necessarily subdivisionally-elected or appointed full-time officers	$-\cdot32$	yes
No. of next-to-top officers (constitution)	$\cdot30$	no

Looking now at this major factor, we see that the four organisational measures with the heaviest loadings, but not the fifth, had directions consistent with the hypotheses, with the absence of a single logical successor being the most important feature of organisation. However, the latter had loadings of ·30 or higher on five of the original factors, so the simplicity achieved here is somewhat illusory.

One of the two factors on which the closeness of elections loaded ·21 was dominated by the two electoral systems items (the original Factor III). Finally, the other factor was dominated by the three major items of the original Factor V, the referendum *v.* the convention. The directions of all of these loadings were consistent with each other and with that of electoral opposition, based on the theory.

To sum up then, *the closeness of periodic top elections is primarily associated in the directions expected with the absence of a single logical successor and with the frequency of elections and of conventions.* It is also associated as expected with the subdivisional election or appointment of full-time executive councillors, with the electoral system and with the use of the referendum. The only relationship opposite in direction to our predictions was that with the number of next-to-top officers, based on the constitution. We shall find that these results will be largely substantiated by an examination of the simple correlations with a number of electoral opposition measures, and by a multiple regression analysis.

THE AMERICAN FINDINGS: PREDICTORS IN COMBINATION

A multiple correlation coefficient may be interpreted in the same way as a simple correlation coefficient. For example, either a simple r of ·50 or a multiple R of ·50 means that 25 per cent of the variance in the closeness of union elections is associated with differences in the organisational characteristic(s) concerned. However, the degree of association in the multiple *R* is always *maximised* by weighting each predictor, positively or negatively, so as to show the *best possible* prediction of the dependent variable. The *R* can go only up, never down, as new predictors are added. Thus, even random relationships between an added predictor and the other variables already utilised tend to increase the *R*. The greater the number of predictors used, the greater the degree to which fortuitous relationships will exaggerate the apparent predictability of the dependent variable. While the *R* may be taken at face value as showing the degree of relationship between the predictor variables collectively and the predicted variable *in the particular set of unions*, with a small sample a statistical adjustment should be made to 'shrink' the *R* to an estimate of its true value in the theoretical population from which the sample was drawn (to be discussed shortly). We will therefore usually report multiple correlation coefficients and similar shrunken coefficients (*R*s and shrunken *R*s).

The shrinkage of *R*s will be based on the number of predictors *tried* – i.e. given the *opportunity* to contribute towards increasing the *R* – even though the increase due to some predictors may have been virtually nil (such 'predictors' perhaps may have failed to enter the regression analysis). In most cases this shrunken *R* will be *too conservative* an estimate of relationship, since two or more of the predictors are often similar in content and correlate highly with each other (they may approach being the same variable).[4]

Predicting the Closeness of American Periodic Top-Post Elections
The thirty-one organisational variables shown in Table 4.3 were used jointly to determine their degree of association with the mean closeness of periodic top-post elections in the American unions (see Table 5.2). The computer programme employed selected the predictors one by one, adding each to the previous set until the increase in the unshrunken correlation coefficient became marginal.[5] A total of twenty-five predictors was selected,[6] yielding a raw (unshrunken) multiple correlation coefficient of ·876. The conservative shrunken *R*, reduced on the basis of all thirty-one predictors tried, was ·646. This is a rather high degree of association of the predictor variables with a dependent variable as fluctuating as the closeness of union elections, even the mean closeness of several elections for each union. It is unusual, in sociological research, to find more than several variables in combination adding anything appreciable to prediction. The organisational variables were utilised in the predictive (regression) equation in directions generally consistent with the hypotheses (see Table 5.2). For example, the first item selected, the time between regular conventions (their *in*frequency), should be inversely related to the closeness of elections. The negative sign

TABLE 5.2 *Predicting the mean closeness of periodic elections for the top posts of fifty-one American unions, 1949–66: regression analysis trying thirty-one predictors*

No. of predictors (and step)	Variable added (and simple r)	Predicted direction of assn. (*confirmed)	t for regression coefficient (22nd step)	Factor no.	Shrunken R (based on entering variables)
1	Time between regular conventions (−·33)	−*	−3·208	VII	·33
2	% of total convention votes from largest region (−·16)	−*	−2·217	VII	·42
3	% of executive council elected by convention as a whole with referendum for majority if necessary (·30)	+*	2·063	IX	·50
4	No. of next-to-top posts (constitution) (−·11)	+*	2·510^b	IV	·53
5	No. of levels elected, necessarily full-time national officials (·09)	+*	4·796	VIII	·55
6	% of convention delegates required for roll-call vote (−·05)	−*	−3·627	X	·56
7	Top officer elected by referendum (·24)	+*	2·870	V	·58
8	Absence of automatic succession in casual vacancy of top post (·11)	+*	2·310	X	·59
9	Highest appeal body for member (·09)	+^{a}	−2·882	I	·60
10	Highest appeal for suspended, removed subordinate officer (·23)	+*	3·250	I	·61
11	Highest 'weight' of electoral system for executive council (·19)	+*	3·022	III	·63
12	No. of levels elected, permissibly full-time national officials (·04)	+^{a}	−3·084	VIII	·65
13	No. of next-to-top posts, all considered (·04)	+	−2·742	IV	·66
14	'Weight' of electoral system for top office (·22)	+^{a}	−2.054	III	·67
15	Absence of full-time officers from final appeal body (member or officer) (−·15)	+^{a}	−1·815	I	·68
16	Absence of 'blanket cause' to discipline member (·04)	+	−0·960	XII	·68
17	No. of levels hierarchical geographic organisation (−·13)	+	−2·509	II	·69
18	% of executive council appointed by national officers or executive council (−·01)	−*	−2·572	XI	·70
19	Top officer formally under direction of executive council (−·12)	+*	2·088	several	·71
20	Size of executive council (·16)	none	2·321	XI	·73
21	% of executive council necessarily nationally-elected or appointed full-time officers (·02)	−^{a}	1·641	XI	·74
22	Highest appeal on trusteeship (·19)	+^{a}	−1·386	I	·75

^{a} The predictor with the highest *t* representing this factor has the predicted sign.
^{b} This is the only *t* which reversed its original sign, after the introduction of further variables.

of the *t* (−3·208), as well as of the simple correlation (*r* = −·33), indicates that this inverse association apparently exists. Seven of the first eight predictors selected to maximise prediction operated in the expected directions, as did nine of the first eleven.[7]

There was a high probability that the directions of the 'independent' contributions of most predictors represented the directions they would have in a hypothetical larger population of unions. A *t* as large as 2·05 would occur by chance in only five samplings out of 100, and a *t* of 2·76 in only one out of 100. Although we have almost complete samples of American and British unions of the types and sizes in question, the logical construct of a universe of possibilities still seems useful (see Hagood, 1973, for a discussion of this).

It is a well-known phenomenon of multiple regression that highly-correlated predictors often assume opposite signs (i.e. appear to predict in opposite directions) when used simultaneously. In our analysis this was likely to occur *within factors*, and in such cases the direction of the variable with the highest *t* within each factor (and the highest beta) can be accepted with the greatest certainty as representing the effect of that variable, and perhaps that of the factor as a whole.

A focus on the six factors with the highest *t*s (2·870 or higher for the top variable within the factor) shows that all six operated as expected. Of the remaining five factors which entered the regression, three functioned contrary to expectation, first entering the predictive equation at the 4th, 16th and 17th steps. The only variable which represented several factors, the formal functioning of the top officer under the direction of the executive council, was associated with closer elections as expected (*t* = 2·088), in spite of a low negative correlation (*r* = −·12) with the dependent variable. Finally, while Factor VI did not enter the regression, the single item with a high loading on it had simple correlations with the measures of electoral opposition generally consistent with its hypothesised effect. This item, the percentage of the executive council that was necessarily subdivisionally-elected or appointed full-time officers, will be discussed later.

On the whole, substantial support to our theoretical approach is offered by the size of the very conservative shrunken *R* (·646), and by the functioning as expected of the six variables representing the six factors apparently contributing the most to the regression. The latter (abstracted from Table 5.2), are as follows, in the order of the statistical significance of their unique contributions to the predictive equation (the lowest *t* = 2·063):

1 The number of levels of elected, necessarily full-time national officials (Factor VIII).
2 The percentage of convention delegates required to approve a roll-call vote (Factor X). Lower percentages were favourable for opposition.

3   The nature of the highest appeal available to a suspended or removed subordinate officer (Factor I).
4   The time interval between regular conventions (Factor VII). Shorter intervals were favourable for opposition.
5   The highest 'weight' of the electoral system for choosing the executive council, according to our ranking on a favourableness-to-opposition scale (Factor III).
6   The election of the top officer by referendum (Factor V).

These variables representing factors also functioned as predicted':

7   The percentage of the executive council appointed by national officers or the executive council (Factor XI). A higher percentage was unfavourable to opposition.
8   The percentage of the executive council elected by the convention as a whole, with a referendum to obtain an absolute majority, if necessary (Factor IX).

Discussion of Contrary Findings
We shall concentrate on the three variables representing the three factors which did not yield the expected results.

The absence of a blanket clause to discipline a member (Factor XII) entered the regression at the 16th step, and one could have the least confidence in the direction of its independent contribution ($t = -·960$). The weight of this contribution is also small. The hypothesis in question is that the effectiveness of competition for high office is facilitated where there is greater limitation on national power and, more specifically, freedom from fear of reprisal. It should be noted that all four items on the appeals system (in a different factor), also relevant to this hypothesis, entered the regression, with the leading item functioning as expected.

An examination of the correlations between the blanket clause item and six measures of electoral opposition for top or next-to-top posts shows five of the six to be in the predicted direction but all correlations are very low (the highest is ·11). At any rate, the item is of little importance in 'predicting' the closeness of periodic elections; it raised the shrunken R less than half a point when it entered the regression.

The number of next-to-top posts (Factor IV) is of greater importance, both conceptually and in terms of its more prominent place in the multiple regression. It is relevant to the hypothesis that electoral opposition is favoured by a hierarchical structure which provides two or more offices of the same rank at each level. Where the number of next-to-top posts under the constitution entered the regression, at the 4th step, it did so in a direction opposite to that predicted. It subsequently reversed its direction when the number of next-to-top posts, all considered, entered with an even greater weight and a negative sign.

The overall picture of the correlations of both the next-to-top items with six measures of electoral opposition shows a mixed set of very low correlations, with one exception. This is with the defeat of top or next-to-top officers (·17 for the 'constitution' item and ·23 for the 'all considered' item).

Our previous discussion of the number of next-to-top officers showed that the role of the American secretary-treasurer was often such as to preclude this officer from competing for the presidency. With only nine unions in the American sample having more than one next-to-top officer, all considered, and only one union having as many as three, it is possible that the measure was largely irrelevant for testing the hypothesis in question, which assumed that second-ranking officers were generally in the line of succession. The negative input into the regression analysis may be due to correlations with other predictors: the number of next-to-top officers under the constitution correlated between ·22 and ·27 with five predictors in other factors, and ·14 or higher with seven more.

The number of levels of clearly hierarchical geographic organisation (Factor II) also functioned in a direction opposite to that predicted ($t = -2·509$; the simple correlation was $-·13$). The existence of a structural shield, in the form of an important intermediate level of organisation between the national and local, was thought to be favourable for electoral opposition. Approximately one-third of the American sample lacked such a shield, at least in the form specified, although we have no information for American unions on either occupational subdivisions, or intermediate geographic organisation falling *outside* a clear-cut hierarchical relationship. The simplest explanation for our contrary finding is that American top officers can often control the selection and retention of regional officers, thus transforming intermediate organisation from a shield into an instrument for the retention of power. We shall see that this is not the case in Britain.

Predicting the Percentage of Top Defeats
The analysis to predict the closeness of top periodic elections was paralleled by an analysis to predict the percentage of top defeats, using the same thirty-one predictors. The correlation between these two measures of opposition was only ·46, so that similar findings were by no means assured. There were only five unions with defeats of top officers, including one union with two defeats (the International Chemical Workers).[8] For these five unions, the percentages of all periodic top elections involving defeats ranged from 11 to 25 per cent. Given the undoubtedly lower reliability of

this dependent variable, the shrunken multiple correlation of ·56 on the basis of all thirty-one predictors tried was unexpectedly high (the raw R was ·853).

On the whole, the regression analysis for the prediction of top American defeats is similar to, and even more consistent with our theory than, that for the closeness of periodic top elections, although with somewhat lower levels of probability for the directions of effect. Of the eleven factors which entered the regression by the 22nd step, at which the operation stopped, only one variable which best represented its factor functioned contrary to our hypothesis: again, the number of next-to-top officers, all considered. The placement of the top officer under the direction of the executive council, which had loadings on several factors, also functioned in the predicted direction. This time even the number of levels of hierarchical geographic organisation was associated with electoral opposition, as predicted ($t = 1 \cdot 564$).

The most important difference in this defeats analysis was in the prominent role played by *the size of the executive council*, which assumed the role of chief representative of Factor XI ($t = 2 \cdot 941$), displacing the percentage of the executive council nationally appointed. Larger councils were associated with defeats, although we had no hypothesis concerning this variable.

Three other variables assumed more important roles. First, the absence of a 'blanket clause' to discipline members was displaced as the chief representative of Factor XII by *the absence of a single logical successor, all considered*. The latter was positively associated with defeats ($t = 1 \cdot 760$). Second, *the percentage of the executive council required to be subdivisionally-elected or appointed rank-and-filers* became the chief representative of Factor VIII ($t = 2 \cdot 324$), displacing the number of levels of elected, necessarily full-time national officials. It also was associated with defeats, in the expected direction. The same applies to *the absence of automatic succession*, in Factor X, which displaced the percentage of the convention required for a roll-call vote. Nevertheless, four of the five most important factors in this analysis were among the six most important in predicting the closeness of periodic top-post elections.

While the results of this analysis of defeats support our theory, we have more confidence in the stronger and more statistically significant (if more complex) relationships in the closeness of periodic top-elections analysis. We shall see later that the size of the executive council has an inconsistent relationship to various measures of opposition, although it is more in the positive direction in the United States.

A Technical Explanation of the Success with Thirty-one Predictors
On the face of it, it is surprising that such a large set of quite modest and

weak simple correlations with the dependent variable should produce such a high multiple correlation after shrinkage. The reasons for the high multiple are, essentially:

1 The clearly-delineated factor structure and the low intercorrelations between the leading representatives of the factors, which avoided a duplication of their effects.
2 The 'illogical' relationships within some of the factors, considering the directions of the relationships with the closeness of elections. The first two steps in Table 5.2 are an example of this. While both of these Factor VII variables correlated in the same direction with the closeness of elections, as expected, they correlated negatively with each other ($-\cdot35$). This is an ideal situation for predictors in combination yielding substantially higher correlations than singly. Analogous situations existed for Factors X and XI.
3 The usefulness of many of the distinctions between measures that were similar but not identical in content, sometimes even in spite of high correlations between them. The voting system for the top office, and the most favourable voting system for the executive council ($r = \cdot91$), are an example. We take this to be a vindication of our attention to organisational specifics.

A Repetition with One Variable per Factor
To provide information on the relative utility of the predictors when others highly associated with them were removed (thus reducing multi-collinearity), the analysis for the closeness of periodic top elections was repeated with each factor represented by only one of its constituents.

The fifty-one-union factor analysis was used to select the items, which were then used to predict electoral opposition among the American unions after the five low-level 'white collar' unions had been excluded. The use here of this particular set of forty-six unions, rather than the entire fifty-one, is simply a matter of the availability of the completed analysis. Other regressions done with and without the five white collar unions showed only marginally different results.

The organisational characteristic with the highest factor loading was taken to represent nine of the factors, but in the case of Factors V and XI the item with the highest loading was passed over in favour of the characteristic which was more directly related to the top office (V) or not very rare in the sample (XI). The factor loadings on these were only slightly lower. The variable with the highest loading on Factor IX disappeared (had zero variance) in the sample of forty-six unions, leaving only a measure which was ultimately discarded and did not play a prominent role in the regression. Thus Factor IX is not reported here. The number of members represented Factor II, but there was no hypothesis associated with it and it played a negligible role in the regression.

One important byproduct of this analysis is the finding that the single representatives of the factors, used in combination, do not begin to approach the degree of association of the thirty-one independent variables with the closeness of periodic top elections. The estimated R shrunken on the basis of the twelve predictors tried was only ·46, as compared to ·65 for all thirty-one organisational predictors (the equivalent raw R was ·62 as compared to ·88).[9]

Another finding is the virtual absence of multi-collinearity in this analysis (the sum of the squared betas was only marginally larger than R^2), indicating the independence from each other of the leading representatives of the factors. In these circumstances their regression weights (betas) could be taken to indicate their relative importance.[10]

With all the factor representatives forced into the regression so that their relative weights could be compared, it was found that the following six contributed the most, all in the expected directions:

— The term of office for the top post (beta $= -·304$).
— The 'weight' of the electoral system for the top office (·249).
— The number of levels of elected, necessarily full-time national officers (·167).
— The percentage of the executive council who are necessarily subdivisionally-elected or appointed full-time officers (·158).
— The election of the top officer by referendum (·150).
— The absence of automatic succession in the event of a casual vacancy for the top post (·110).

All the above factors also functioned in the hypothesised directions in the thirty-one predictor regression, and indeed *five* of them were *among the top six* in that analysis, in terms of the statistical significance of the direction of their effect (and their apparent weight).

Three of the four remaining items were not associated with the closeness of top periodic elections in the expected directions:

— The number of next-to-top posts, under the constitution (beta $= -·095$, contrary to expectation).
— The percentage of the executive council which is necessarily nationally-elected or appointed full-time officers (·084, contrary to expectation for the United States, since national election was usually by the convention as a whole).
— The nature of the highest appeal body on the suspension or removal of a subsidiary officer (·077, as expected).

— The absence of a 'blanket clause' to discipline a member ($-$·063, contrary to expectation).

Thus, this supplementary analysis confirmed our interpretation of the analysis using thirty-one predictors, regarding direction of the effects, opposite to expectations, of both the number of next-to-top officers and the absence of a 'blanket clause'. The effect of the percentage of the executive council who must be nationally-chosen full-time officers was also not as expected, but in the overall regression we ignored this finding because two other items within the same factor had higher weights. However, none of the directions of association satisfied the usual criterion for statistical significance (the highest $t = 1$·750, and t for the executive council item $=$ ·463).

The term of the top office is by far the most important predictor of the closeness of periodic top elections, according to this analysis. This finding was similar to others using the same twelve items for the prediction of: (*a*) the defeat of a top *or* a next-to-top officer; (*b*) the mean of the two highest periodic next-to-top elections (in both analyses the term of top office had the highest weight); and (*c*) the mean closeness of elections for vacant top posts ($N = 29$), the only other analysis tried with the factor subset of predictors. It should be noted that the term of office correlates highly with the time between regular conventions ($r = $·89), as might be expected since most top officers are elected at conventions.

Predicting the Closeness of American Periodic Next-to-Top Elections

The correlation of the mean closeness of periodic top-post elections with a similar measure for next-to-top posts was ·74, supporting our expectations and leading us to expect similar results in a test of the theory on elections to second-ranking positions.

The effectiveness of prediction of the closeness of periodic next-to-top elections was, however, less than that of periodic top elections. A raw R of ·81 was found, shrunken to ·39 on the basis of the thirty-one predictors tried. The directions of the independent effects of the predictors were consistent with the hypotheses for variables representing seven of nine factors entering the 25-step regression (where the variables first entered), and also for the one several-factor item. In addition, three factors were represented by variables which had no hypotheses associated with them. One of these was the only measure ultimately discarded because of inconsistent application, and it did not enter other regressions.

The two departures from the expected direction of effect were the number of levels of hierarchical geographic organisation, as in the prediction of the top periodic means, and the absence of full-time officers from the highest appeal body for a member or subordinate officer, which previously was not the chief item representing its factor in the top periodic regression (and which therefore could not be evaluated). The number of next-to-top posts under the constitution did act as predicted, contrary to its previous role. On the whole, the various multiple regression analyses and the factor analysis including top periodic elections are mutually supporting.

THE AMERICAN SIMPLE CORRELATIONS, AS A SET

A supplementary approach to evaluating the degree to which our hypotheses are supported is through an examination of the sizes and directions of *all* the simple correlations of the structural–procedural variables with the outcomes of elections. If a preponderant number of predictions are in the *expected* direction, this is at least a hopeful sign. Furthermore, since there are six variables, four of them measures of entirely different kinds of elections, it becomes possible to determine which organisational variables are the most *consistent* in predicting electoral outcomes. However, one must be cautious in one's judgement concerning any particular independent variable, since most of the simple correlations are low.

Relationships Among the American Dependent Variables
The six dependent variables were based on two kinds of elections, periodic and vacant-post, for two levels of office, top and next-to-top. Thus there are four non-overlapping measures of electoral opposition, in the sense that none of the elections contributing towards one measure also contributes towards another. There are, in addition, two measures of electoral opposition which apply to elections for both posts, considered together: the occurrence or non-occurrence of (*a*) defeats, for either office, and (*b*) contested periodic or vacant-post elections, for either office. There were vacancies in the top and next-to-top posts in only thirty-one and forty of the American unions respectively, so simple correlations with these are not based on the full sample of fifty-one.

Most of the fifteen simple correlations between pairs of measures of electoral opposition were only moderate in size, ten *r*s falling between ·39 and ·56 (see Table 5.3). There was a negligible relationship between the presence or absence of any defeats, and the closeness of elections to fill top vacancies ($r = $ ·07). The two highest correlations were between the closeness of periodic next-to-top elections, on the one hand, and the closeness of top periodic and top vacant-post elections on the other ($r = $ ·74 and $r = $ ·70 respectively). Finally, there was a correlation of ·61 between the closeness of elections to fill next-to-top vacancies and the presence or absence of any contested elections.

The relationships among the dependent variables were low enough, on the whole, to make it difficult for a predictor to relate to all six, simultaneously, in the expected direotion. It was found that thirteen of the twenty-eight independent variables concerning which there were predictions did in fact relate to all six electoral outcomes as expected, and that another six predictors related to five of the six dependent variables as predicted.[11] At least one completely successful predictor appeared in nine of the twelve factor sets.

Focusing now on the separate electoral outcomes, we find that:

— The closeness of top periodic elections related in the predicted direction to twenty-two (79 per cent) of the twenty-eight predictors.
— The closeness of periodic next-to-top elections related as predicted to twenty-one (75 per cent).
—The occurrence of any defeats related as predicted to twenty-four (86 per cent).
— The occurrence of any contested elections related as predicted to twenty-two (79 per cent).
— The closeness of elections to fill top vacancies, which occurred in only thirty-one unions, related as predicted to nineteen of twenty-six predictors (73 per cent).
— The closeness of elections to fill next-to-top vacancies, which occurred in only forty unions, related as predicted to twenty-one of twenty-seven predictors (78 per cent).

The most successful predictors, taking both consistency and degrees of relationship into consideration, were the closely-related time between regular conventions and term of office for the top post. The six simple correlations for the former were between $-\cdot26$ and $-\cdot38$, and for the latter were between $-\cdot24$ and $-\cdot36$. The third item in this factor (VII), the percentage of convention votes allotted to the largest region, correlated in the expected direction with all six cases, but at lower levels (between $-\cdot05$ and $-\cdot16$).

Three of the four appeals items of Factor I were entirely consistent in their directions of association with the dependent variables, top correlations being $\cdot36$, $\cdot32$ and $\cdot23$. The two closely-related electoral systems items of Factor III were also consistent, with top correlations of $\cdot22$ and $\cdot25$. The election of the top officer by referendum was entirely consistent with the directions of relationship found, with three correlations between $\cdot21$ and $\cdot29$. The remaining two items of Factor V, the percentage of the executive council elected by the convention as a whole and that elected by national referendum, correlated with only five out of six in the directions predicted, but had top correlations of $-.37$ and $.39$. The absence of a logical successor correlated between $\cdot19$ and $\cdot30$ in the anticipated direction with the six measures of electoral opposition, and the absence of a blanket

TABLE 5.3 *The simple correlations for the American unions of the independent variables with six measures of effectiveness of opposition (and equivalent British correlations where available), based on 1949–66*[a]

Measures	Country or subgroup	Mean closeness of elections for top vacancies (u.s.:N=31; u.k.:N periodic=15 permanent=15 total=30)	Mean closeness of elections for next-to-top vacancies (u.s.:N=40; u.k.:N periodic=15 total=23)	Mean closeness of periodic top elections (u.s.:N=51; u.k.:N periodic=16)	Mean closeness of periodic next-to-top elections (u.s.:N=51; u.k.:N periodic=16)	Any defeats of top or next-to-top incumbents? (u.s.:N=51)	Any top or next-to-top contests? (u.s.:N=51)	Predicted direction
Dependent variables								
Mean closeness of elections for top vacancies	u.s.	—	·56 (29)	·45 (31)	·70 (31)	·07 (31)	·41 (31)	+
	u.k. per.	—	·54 (14)	·12 (15)	·10 (15)			+
	u.k. total	—	·44 (22)					+
Mean closeness of elections for next-to-top vacancies	u.s.	·56 (29)	—	·49 (40)	·52 (40)	·06 (40)	·61 (40)	+
	u.k. per.	·54 (14)	—	-·28 (15)	-·30 (15)			+
	u.k. total	·44 (22)	—					+
Mean closeness of periodic top elections	u.s.	·45	·49	—	·74	·48	·46	++
	u.k. per.	·12	-·28	—	·52			++
Mean closeness of periodic next-to-top elections	u.s.	·70	·52	·74	—	·39	·40	++
	u.k. per.	·10	-·30	·52	—			++
Any defeats of top or next-to-top incumbents?	u.s.	·07	·06	·48	·39	—	·41	+
Any top or next-to-top contests?	u.s.	·41	·61	·46	·40	·41	—	+

Independent variables

Highest appeal on trusteeship							
u.s.	·24	·36	·19	·16	·12	·17	+
Highest appeal body on suspension or removal of subordinate officer							
u.s.	·06	·32	·23	·10	·11	·18	++
u.k. per.	-·13	-·61	·41	·29			++
	(14)	(14)	(15)	(15)			
u.k. perm.	-·18						+
	(14)						
u.k. total	-·15	-·51					+
	(28)	(22)					
Absence of full-time officers from final appeal body (short of a national referendum) for a member or officer							
u.s.	-·24	·10	-·15	-·17	·05	·22	+++
u.k. per.	·44	·47	·21	·25			+++
u.k. perm.	-·12						++
u.k. total	·18	·34					++
Highest appeal body for a member (short of a national referendum)							
u.s.	·08	·23	·09	·01	·02	·16	++++
u.k. per.	·54	·38	·15	·09			++++
u.k. perm.	+·11						++
u.k. total	·37	·41					+
No. of members							
u.s.	-·19	-·09	-·05	-·14	-·02	-·16	none
u.k. per.	·24	·03	·53	·56			none
u.k. perm.	-·20	·04					none
u.k. total	-·02						none
No. of local unions							
u.s.	-·22	-·07	·04	-·05	-·06	-·09	none
u.k. per.	·13	·08	·45	·56			none
u.k. perm.	-·16						none
u.k. total	-·04	-·01					none
Median no. of voting convention delegates, in practice							
u.s.	-·25	-·11	-·04	-·12	-·08	-·05	—
u.k. per.	-·25	-·11	-·02	-·07			—
	(14)	(14)	(15)	(15)			
u.k. perm.	-·11						—
	(14)						
u.k. total	n.a.	n.a.					—

Measures	Country or subgroup	Mean closeness of elections for top vacancies	Mean closeness of elections for next-to-top vacancies	Mean closeness of periodic top elections	Mean closeness of periodic next-to-top elections	Any defeats of top or next-to-top incumbents?	Any top or next-to-top contests?	Predicted direction
No. of levels of clearly hierarchical geographic organisation	u.s.	−·39	−·22	−·13	−·25	·11	−·07	+
	u.k. per.	·53	·03	·63	·39			+
	u.k. perm.	−·26						+
	u.k. total	−·08	−·04					+
Highest 'weight' of electoral system for executive council	u.s.	·10	·14	·19	·22	·13	·13	+
	u.k. per.	−·09	−·39	·13	·48			+
	u.k. perm.	−·05						+
	u.k. total	−·02	−·33					+
'Weight' of electoral system for top office	u.s.	·10	·12	·22	·25	·14	·06	+
	u.k. per.	·03	·04	−·08	·24			+
	u.k. perm.	−·18						+
	u.k. total	−·13	·03					+
No. of next-to-top posts under constitution	u.s.	−·12	−·01	−·11	−·06	·17	−·005	+
	u.k. per.	·13	−·07	·30	·35			+
	u.k. total	n.a.	−·05					+
No. of next-to-top posts, all considered	u.s.	−·09	−·03	−·04	−·003	·23	·06	+
	u.k. per.	·17	−·05	·16	·30			+
	u.k. total	n.a.	−·10					+
% of executive council elected by national referendum	u.s.	·39	·23	·07	·21	−·23	·12	+[b]
	u.k. per.	−·28	−·23	−·11	·12			−[b]
	u.k. perm.	−·002						−[b]
	u.k. total	−·16	−·07					−[b]
% of executive council elected by convention as a whole	u.s.	−·22	−·37	−·19	−·16	·01	−·27	−
	u.k. perm.	·30	−·07					−
	u.k. total	·24						−
Top officer elected by referendum	u.s.	·29	·09	·24	·18	·10	·21	+

% of executive council necessarily subdivisionally-elected or appointed full-time officers	U.S.	·04	·26	·16	·08	·12	·10	+
	U.K. per.	·39	·03	·47	·23			+
	U.K. perm.	·13	–·09					+
	U.K. total	·23						+
Time between regular conventions	U.S.	–·29	–·32	–·33	–·26	–·38	–·31	–
	U.K. per.	–·18	–·17	–·11	·23			–
	U.K. perm.	·11	–·05					–
	U.K. total	–·01						–
Term of office for top post	U.S.	–·24	–·34	–·28	–·29	–·36	–·28	–
% of total convention votes from largest region	U.S.	–·05	–·16	–·16	–·11	–·09	–·05	–
No. of levels of elected, necessarily full-time national officers	U.S.	·07	–·03	·09	·19	–·05	–·16	+
	U.K. per.	·18	–·10	·52	·25			+
	U.K. perm.	–·15	·01					+
	U.K. total	–·05						+
No. of levels of elected, necessarily or permissibly full-time national officers	U.S.	·02	·09	·04	·18	·04	–·01	+
	U.K. per.	·01	–·03	·38	·11			+
	U.K. perm.	–·17	·13					+
	U.K. total	–·13						+
% of executive council necessarily subdivisionally-elected or appointed rank-and-filers	U.S.	—	—	·11	·11	·29	·12	+[c]
	U.K. per.	·21	·07	–·06	–·04			–[c]
	U.K. perm.	–·36	–·04					–[c]
	U.K. total	–·09						–[c]
% of executive council elected by convention, with referendum for majority if necessary	U.S.	—	–·11	·30	·01	·29	·12	+
Absence of automatic succession in casual vacancy of top post	U.S.	–·08	·18	·11	·09	·12	·24	+

Measures	Country or subgroup	Mean closeness of elections for top vacancies	Mean closeness of elections for next-to-top vacancies	Mean closeness of periodic top elections	Mean closeness of periodic next-to-top elections	Any defeats of top or next-to-top incumbents?	Any top or next-to-top contests?	Predicted direction
% of convention delegates required for roll-call vote	u.s.	·21	·19	−·05	·14	−·14	·15	—
Size of executive council	u.s.	−·19	·07	·16	−·04	·24	·16	none
	u.k. per.	−·28	·52	−·41	−·46			none
	u.k. perm.	−·21						none
	u.k. total	−·01	·44					none
% of executive council necessarily nationally-elected or appointed full-time officers	u.s.	·22	−·05	·02	·14	−·15	−·03	—
	u.k. per.	−·49	−·49	−·13	−·07			—
	u.k. perm.	−·05						—
	u.k. total	−·30	−·40					—
% of executive council appointed by national officers or executive council	u.s.	−·02	−·15	−·01	−·12	−·12	·01	—
	u.k. perm.	−·26	n.a.					—
	u.k. total	−·17						—
Absence of 'blanket clause' to discipline member	u.s.	−·07	−·05	·04	·09	−·11	·03	++
	u.k. perm.	·25 (13)						++
	u.k. total	·20 (28)	n.a.					+
Absence of single 'logical' successor, all considered	u.s.	·19	·30	·19	·19	·19	·26	++
	u.k. per.	·64	·43	−·16	−·10			+++
	u.k. perm.	·65 (14)						++
	u.k. total	·61 (29)	·24					+
Top officer formally under direction of executive council	u.s.	·01	·06	−·12	−·01	−·17	·20	+++
	u.k. per.	·14	·33	−·51	−·05			+++
	u.k. perm.	·14						+
	u.k. total	·15	·37					+++

Other variables								
No. of elections to fill top vacancies	U.S. per.	−·10	·02	−·04	·06	−·23	·09	+
	U.K. per.	·23	·01	·55	·45			+
	U.K. perm.	−·32						+
	U.K. total	−·07	−·22					+
No. of elections to fill next-to-top vacancies	U.S.	−·01	·16	·14	·10	·03	·15	+
No. of top periodic elections	U.S.	·23	·35	·21	·20	·33	·24	+
	U.K. per.	·19	·48	·18	·07			+
Top officer's salary, 1963[d]	U.S.	−·28	−·43	−·20	−·28	−·22	−·23	−
Ratio of top to next highest salary[d]	U.S.	−·02	−·09	−·04	−·11	−·02	−·01	−
No. of national officers with $15,000 or higher salary[d]	U.S.	−·26	−·16	−·04	−·04	−·08	−·24	−
No. of locals under trusteeship, September 1959	U.S.	−·13	−·10	−·10	−·14	−·08	−·09	−
% white collar, 1961[e]	U.S.	−·15	−·24	−·10	−·09	−·08	−·21	none
Power of top officer to fill temporary vacancies at executive council or higher levels	U.S.	−·21	−·30	−·11	−·16	−·11	−·24	−

[a] 1949–67 for British top vacancies.

[b] The American and British directions differ because the predominant contrast in the United States is between a national referendum and election by the convention as a whole, while in Britain it is between a national referendum and subdivisional election.

[c] The predominant American contrast is between subdivisional and national selection, while in Britain it is between the selection of rank-and-filers and of full-time officers, both subdivisionally elected.

[d] Or closest available year. Salary correlated ·44 with number of members.

[e] Based on Solomon and Burns, 1963.

clause, also in Factor XII, had very low correlations but with five out of six in the direction predicted. Also fully consistent in direction with the hypotheses were the two items pertaining to the percentage of the executive council subdivisionally chosen. In one case, those subdivisionally chosen were required to be elected rank-and-filers (in Factor VIII; maximum $r = \cdot 29$); in the other, they were required to be elected or appointed full-time officers (the only item in Factor VI; maximum $r = \cdot 26$).

The number of voting convention delegates functioned as expected, with a maximum correlation of $-\cdot 25$. The other three items in the size and complexity factor (II) also produced generally negative correlations, in spite of the facts that there were no hypotheses concerning the number of members or of local unions, and that positive signs were expected rather than the five negative obtained for the number of levels of hierarchical geographic organisation (maximum $r = -\cdot 39$). Indeed, the functioning of this four-item factor was such as to support conventional sociological wisdom regarding the anti-democratic tendencies in large organisations with a relatively simple hierarchical structure. It will be recalled that the number of levels of hierarchical geographic organisation played a moderately important but unpredicted role in the regression analysis for the closeness of periodic top elections, but that the other variables in its factor were of little or no importance. It will be shown later that size and complexity play a very different role in Britain.

The number of levels of elected, necessarily full-time national officers had no overall direction, but the number of levels of permissibly full-time national officers had five out of six correlations in the predicted direction, the highest being $\cdot 18$. These rather poor results are surprising in view of the fact that the former variable made the most statistically significant independent contribution to the regression, using thirty-one predictors, for the closeness of periodic top elections, in the expected direction.

The absence of automatic succession was moderately successful (five out of six, maximum $r = \cdot 24$), as was the percentage of the executive council elected by convention, with a referendum if necessary for an absolute majority (four out of five, maximum $r = \cdot 30$).

The results were mixed or basically in contradiction to the predictions for: the two variables regarding the number of next-to-top officers; the percentage of convention delegates required for a roll-call vote; the percentage of the executive council nationally appointed; and the percentage of the executive council necessarily nationally-elected or appointed full-time officers.

Looking at both the results above and those for the regression analysis, using thirty-one predictors, for the closeness of periodic top elections, we may say that the following important predictors have the strongest joint support:

— The time between regular conventions.
— The nature of the highest appeal available to a suspended or removed subordinate officer.
— The nature of the most favourable electoral system used to elect executive councillors.
— The election of the top officer by referendum.

The last three, and in a sense all, have to do with the democratic process rather than organisational structure. The most clearly disconfirmed variables were:

— The number of next-to-top officers.
— The number of levels of clearly hierarchical geographic organisation.

We explained earlier that, in the United States, the practice of appointing officials probably changed the significance of the number of geographic levels, and that a next-to-top officer was often not in the line of succession to the top post. On the whole, we take the evidence of the multiple regression analysis rather than that of the simple correlations, where these are contradictory. This is so not only because multiple regression can deal with complexities of interrelationship, but also because the very low correlations between some of the measures of opposition indicate that the relationships indeed have somewhat different causes. In the multiple regression, we have focused on the periodic elections to the top post because this post is the most important, and because too few American unions had top vacancies during 1949–66 to provide us with an adequate sample for testing hypotheses.

CONCLUSIONS

Our theory of union democracy was tested on fifty-one American manual and low-level white collar unions. A systematic examination was made of the simple relationships between each of twenty-eight relevant variables, plus three others for which there were no hypotheses, and six measures of electoral opposition. The latter involved periodic and vacant-post elections to top and next-to-top office. One crude indication of whether our expectations were fulfilled for any particular predictor variable was whether at least five of the six relationships with measures of opposition were in the expected direction, provided, of course, that the size of the possible sixth contrary relationship did not outweigh the others. Four of the six measures of opposition were logically independent of each other, in the sense that they dealt with different offices or different kinds of elections, so no great consistency was to be expected on the basis of chance.

A more valuable but complex kind of analysis (multiple regression) involved the use of all thirty-one predictor variables simultaneously, to test the overall predictive power of the set and to gain some insight into their interrelationships and relative importance. To help interpret this overall prediction, a further study was made (through factor analysis) of the interrelationships among the predictors themselves. Vacancy elections were ignored in these more complex analyses because many of the unions had no vacancies for top or next-to-top posts during 1949–66. Most attention was given to the closeness of periodic elections to top office, but some was also given to periodic elections to next-to-top office, and to the percentage of top defeats.

None of the simple relationships between separate predictor variables and particular measures of opposition was strong, but the directions of relationship with the closeness of periodic top elections were as predicted for twenty-two of twenty-eight (79 per cent) of the variables relevant to the hypotheses. The figure was twenty-four of twenty-eight (86 per cent) for the defeat of a top *or* a next-to-top officer. Thirteen of the twenty-eight predictors related to all their electoral outcomes as expected, and another six related as expected to all but one indicator of opposition (see Table 5.3).[12]

In the more complex analyses, the thirty-one variables tried simultaneously were surprisingly successful in predicting the closeness of periodic top elections, considering the at-best modest relationships between the predictors separately and this measure of opposition. By a very conservative estimate, 42 per cent of the variability in the closeness of top periodic elections is associated with, and presumably attributable to, the thirty-one organisational predictors as a set. Fortunately, the size of the union and the number of local unions, for which measures there were no hypothesised directions of association, did *not* contribute towards the prediction. The size of the executive council, for which there was also no hypothesised direction, contributed only modestly, but larger councils were associated more strongly with the percentage of top defeats. The role of the executive council should be reconsidered; three American unions had fewer than five executive councillors.

The evidence from the more complex analyses was such that it could reasonably be said that certain leading variables affected opposition as predicted. However, there were others which were demonstrably important, but whose role (direction of effect) was less certain because of the complexity of the interrelationships among the predictors themselves. For such variables, it was useful to look also at the simple relationships with the six measures of opposition.

The following variables functioned in the directions hypothesised, *as confirmed by the complex analyses* (multiple regression and factor analyses) *and by the respective sets of simple relationships* (+ indicates an hypothesised direct relationship; — indicates an hypothesised inverse relationship; * indicates stronger simple relationships and/or a more important contribution in combination with other variables):

— *The absence of automatic succession in the case of a casual vacancy in the top post (+) (Hypothesis 1).
— *The absence of a single logical successor, all considered (+) (H. 1).
— *The number of levels of elected, permissibly full-time national officers (+) (H. 3).
— *The percentage of the votes at the convention held by delegates of the largest major region (−) (H. 5).
— *The time between regular conventions (−) (H. 10 and 18).
— The percentage of the executive council necessarily *subdivisionally*-elected or appointed full-time officers (+) (H. 8, and H. 19 in the United States).[13]
— *The highest appeal body on the suspension or removal of a subordinate officer (+) (H. 10 and civil liberties).
— The highest appeal body for a member (+) (H. 10 and civil liberties).
— *The election of the top officer by referendum (+) (H. 15).
— *The term of office for the top post (−) (H. 18).
— *The favourableness to opposition of the electoral system for the top post (+) (H. 19, and secondarily, H. 15).[14]
— *The electoral system most favourable to opposition used in electing executive councillors (+) (H. 19 and, secondarily, H. 15).[13]
— *The percentage of the executive council elected by the convention, with a *referendum* for an *absolute majority*, if necessary (+) (H. 19 and 15).
— The percentage of the executive council necessarily *subdivisionally*-elected or appointed rank-and-filers (+) (H. 19, in the United States, and H. 8 by extension).

The true relationship between two variables may be obscured by the effects of other variables. In many instances the complex analyses were capable of shedding light on the true relationships between the predictors and the measures of opposition. The *complex analyses alone* showed the following variables to be functioning in the directions hypothesised, in spite of the fact that the sets of simple relationships offered no support:

— *The number of levels of elected, necessarily full-time national officers (+) (H. 3).
— The percentage of the executive council appointed by the national officers or executive council itself (−) (H. 4 applies, although it is phrased in terms of full-time officials).
— The formal direction of the top officer by the executive council (+) (H. 10).

— *The percentage of convention delegates required for a roll-call vote (−) (H. 10).

The following variables functioned as expected *on the basis of their sets of relationships* with the measures of opposition, but played no role, a negligible role or an uninterpretable role in the complex analyses:

— *The highest appeal on 'trusteeship' over a local union or subdivision (+) (H. 10 and civil liberties).
— The number of voting convention delegates, in practice (−) (H. 10; it is assumed that larger conventions have less independent power).
— The percentage of the executive council elected by national referendum (+ in the United States) (H. 15).
— *The percentage of the executive council elected by the convention as a whole (−) (H. 19).

The following variables also functioned as expected, but were not tried in the complex analyses (see also Table 5.3, page 141):

—*The top officer's salary (−) (H. 2)
— The ratio of the top salary to the next highest salary (−) (H. 2).
— The power of the top officer to fill temporary vacancies in the executive council or at higher levels (−) (H. 10 and 4).
— The number of elections to fill next-to-top vacancies (+) (H. 18).

The following variable played a useful role in the more complex analyses, but the direction of its effect could not be interpreted (because of its subsidiary role) and the set of simple relationships provided no consistent clue:

—The percentage of the executive council necessarily *nationally*-elected or appointed full-time officers (−) (H. 8, also H. 19 in the United States).

The following variables functioned in a manner to *disconfirm the hypotheses*:

— The number of next-to-top posts, based on the constitution (+) (H. 1). A similar variable, based on 'all considered', was also disconfirmed. However, the number of next-to-top posts under the constitution did function in the expected direction in the complex analysis predicting the closeness of periodic *next-to-top* elections. Rather few American unions had more than one next-to-top officer and, with the secretary-treasurer often being out of the line of succession, this measure may have been inappropriate for the United States. A related variable did function as expected: the number of logical successors, all considered.

— The number of levels of hierarchical geographic organisation (+) (H. 9). Disconfirmation may be due to the fact that, in the United States, full-time officers at intermediate levels are often nationally appointed.
— The absence of full-time officers from the final appeal body, short of a referendum, for a member or officer (+) (H. 10 and civil liberties). The evidence is somewhat ambiguous concerning this variable. Three other appeals variables functioned as expected.
— The absence of a 'blanket clause' to discipline a member (+) (civil liberties). The level of probability associated with this disconfirmation was one of the lowest in the complex analyses.

The only unequivocal disconfirmation of our hypotheses, for American unions, pertains to the number of levels of hierarchical geographic organisation, which in fact was associated with less effective electoral opposition. Another aspect of vertical differentiation, the number of levels of elected full-time national officers, was associated with *closer* elections. We suspect that the effect of the number of hierarchical geographic levels is contingent upon whether or not the important posts at intermediate levels are elected, or upon whether the union is democratic or undemocratic in other respects. The British findings will shed light on this question.

Portrait of The Democratic American Union: An Organisational Design

To sum up, the outlines of the portrait which emerges most strongly from the foregoing show a more than usually democratic American union which holds its conventions and important elections frequently, the latter under voting systems which give the opposition a good chance to register its strength, and to take its case directly to the membership through referendum elections. There is no single 'logical' successor to the top post, and there are a number of levels of elected national officers, at least one regionally based, from which opposition candidates occasionally come. Some of the cruder violations of civil liberties and local autonomy are curbed by a constitutionally-prescribed appeals process which ultimately removes the power of decision from the national officers. There are also some suggestions that the size and power of the major regions are less unbalanced than in most unions, and that the independent power of the convention is somewhat greater. While the potential for such a delineation was limited in advance by the kinds of things that interested us and the kinds of information that could be obtained, the synthesis itself is based on our findings.

Some of these questions will be discussed again after the British findings are presented. The general reader may wish to take his chances on the next chapter in its entirety, since it involves less technical material, or he may turn to its conclusions (pp. 181–6).

NOTES TO CHAPTER 5

1 Data were based on the files of the Bureau of Labor-Management Reports for 1963. Where necessary an earlier year was taken, but not one prior to 1961. The correlations with the number of members were both ·44; with the number of locals, ·25 and ·36 respectively; with the number of organisational levels, ·24 and ·33 respectively.

2 The correlation of ·91 is not directly provided by Table 5.1, but a high correlation may be inferred from the very high loadings of Factor III on the two electoral systems measures (·93 and ·94 respectively).

3 This analysis happened to exclude the five unions with large numbers of low-level white collar workers, described earlier. It is an acceptable substitute for a similar analysis with the fifty-one unions. The factor analyses with forty-six unions, *excluding* the current dependent variable, yielded factors identical, in their leading items, to the original Factors I to VII, and XII. Two variables dropped out of the analysis because there were no differences on them among the remaining forty-six unions. One of these was the leading item in Factor IX, and the other was the third-leading item in Factor VIII.

4 The logic for shrinking R according to the number of predictors tried is, simply, that the ten best predictors from among a randomly-selected group of 1,000 are likely to yield higher correlations (singly and collectively) than the ten best from among fifteen (see McNemar, 1949: 162). Some would no doubt consider correction for the number tried to be over-cautious. The formula for shrinkage is:

$$R \text{ shrunken} = \sqrt{1 - [(1-R^2)(n-1)/(n-k)]}$$

where n = the number in the sample, and k = the number of predictors (see Theil, 1971: 178). Theil also provides a way to compute the total multi-collinearity effect (pp. 179–81) but no procedure to adjust the shrunken Rs accordingly. Without such an adjustment the shrunken Rs are too conservative.

5 Unless otherwise noted, the constant to limit the number of entering variables was ·005, meaning that each new variable had to increase the total of the unexplained variance (R^2) in the dependent variable by at least half of 1 per cent. No doubt the raw R (and hence the shrunken R based on all the variables tried) would have been somewhat larger if a smaller constant had been used. The computer programme used was the IBM Scientific Subroutine Package, subroutine STPRG, as modified by Peter M. Prowda. The subroutine performs a stepwise multiple regression analysis.

6 Table 5.2 shows the 22nd step, not the 25th, because the *t*s and the shrunken Rs, on the basis of the variables entering the regression, declined after the 22nd step.

7 Although Table 5.2 shows the first eight selections to be in the expected directions, the fourth variable originally entered with the opposite sign. Its sign was reversed when a highly-correlated variable entered at the 13th step, the two variables assuming opposite signs.

8 The International Typographical Union, which had by far the highest mean closeness of periodic top elections, was not among those with defeats.

9 The ·46 was an estimate, based on N = 51 and the contribution of the 'true' representative of Factor IX (see Table 5·1, footnote *b*).

10 With negligible multi-collinearity, the betas approach the size of the simple correlation coefficients.

11 The direction of even the slightest relationship with a dependent variable was noted.

12 Because some unions had no top or next-to-top vacancies, for one predictor the confirmation was based on four out of four relationships, and for another on four out of five.

13 Hypothesis 19 is involved because the election of executive councils in the United States is usually by vote of the convention as a whole, on a winner-take-all basis (simultaneous election under a plurality system).

14 Although systems were ranked primarily according to their strictly formal characteristics (e.g. plurality, run-off election for a majority, etc.), the use of a system in a referendum was ranked somewhat above its use at a convention.

Chapter 6

Organisation and Opposition in Britain

INTRODUCTION

The testing of the organisational hypotheses on the British unions followed a different strategy, basically because of the smaller sample – thirty-one unions as compared to fifty-one American – and the availability of much fuller information. Emphasis was placed on the directions and size of the simple correlations between the predictors and the measures of electoral opposition, rather than on the complex analyses performed on the American data using all the predictors simultaneously. Factor analysis was literally impossible for statistical reasons: there were too few British unions in relation to the number of variables examined.

Certain of the specific organisational variables tested in the United States were either absent or so rare in Britain that they disappeared from the analysis: constitutional provisions for automatic succession to the top post in the case of a casual vacancy; trusteeships over local unions; blanket clauses for disciplining members; and, of course, the election of top officers by convention, since the few unions using this technique were excluded from the sample. Nevertheless, twenty of the twenty-eight specific variables associated with hypotheses were also employed in the British analysis, in two instances with different predicted directions because of the different practices prevailing in Britain.

The election to permanent top posts in fifteen of the British sample reduced the number which could be compared to the American on the closeness of periodic elections for the top post, which was the most important American measure of opposition. Furthermore, these permanent-post unions were in many respects different enough from those electing periodically to warrant treatment as a distinct British sub-sample.

PERMANENT-POST AND PERIODIC SUB-SAMPLES

The sixteen unions electing their top officers periodically were, in a number of ways, more similar to the American sample than those electing to permanent top posts. All the periodic unions had full-time next-to-top national officers who were also elected periodically, but next-to-top officers were *appointed* permanently by the executive council in five of the permanent-post unions. This was the case in the Transport and General Workers, the General and Municipal Workers, the Shop, Distributive and Allied Workers (these three being the only general unions in the sample), the Agricultural Workers, and the Seamen. Furthermore, three of these had considerable numbers of their executive councillors appointed by the executive council or some section of it (ten in the General and Municipal Workers and eleven in the Seamen) and/or by subdivisional committees (thirteen in the Transport and General Workers and fourteen in the General and Municipal Workers).

The second-ranking officers in the General and Municipal Workers were ten full-time district secretaries who were appointed by district committees, subject to the approval of the national executive council. Five of them sat on the national executive council, and all sat on the larger general council, which we have taken to be the 'executive council' because of its executive powers. The Seamen's executive council, comprising forty-eight members, appointed the three assistant general secretaries, the national organiser and seven district secretaries, all of whom sat on the council.

Also included among the permanent-post unions were two with no constitutionally full-time second-ranking position at the national level: the Mineworkers, and the Bakers until 1964 (when the presidency became full-time). Whether such a situation is favourable for democracy is difficult to say without taking into consideration the power, autonomy and visibility of the second-ranking full-time officials. Finally, the number of permanent-post unions with elections to fill next-to-top vacancies was reduced by one more, to seven, because no such vacancy occurred in one union.

There are other differences between the permanent-post and periodic unions, associated with the periods of formation and the organisational characteristics continued from those times. Thirteen of the sixteen periodic unions had been in continuous existence as more than local trade societies since before 1889 (a landmark year in British trade union history), whereas this was the case with only seven of the fifteen permanent-post unions. It is recognised in Britain that the older, craft or ex-craft unions have usually retained their original periodic elections, while unions formed later – more often single-industry and general unions – are more likely to have begun with, and retained, full-time permanent posts. Thus, the periodic group contained twelve craft or ex-craft unions, while the permanent-post group contained only five.[1]

The permanence of top posts was *not* associated with less effectively-contested top vacant-post elections: on the whole, the permanent-post unions held slightly closer elections (biserial $r = \cdot11$, $N = 30$). Since the fifteen permanent-post unions included the five with the negative features described above, it is even more doubtful that permanence *in itself*, under British conditions, tends to depress competition for top vacancies. But it must be noted that elected national next-to-top full-time officers and probably all other full-time officials are *also* permanent in these unions, and that these are overwhelmingly the major candidates in top-post elections. Thus, given the prevalence of referendum elections, the security of their positions, and the legitimacy of electoral contests in British unions, full-time officers seem to have little hesitation in competing for the top post. This is especially true in the Mineworkers.

PERMANENT *v.* PERIODIC: DIFFERENT MEANINGS OF SIMPLE GEOGRAPHIC HIERARCHY

Those permanent-post unions with a greater number of levels of simple hierarchical geographic organisation were more likely to have a greater number of levels of nationally-appointed full-time officials ($r = \cdot33$) and fewer levels of elected full-time national officers ($r = -\cdot16$). Precisely the opposite relationships existed in the periodic group ($r = -\cdot45$ and $r = \cdot57$ respectively). (All appointments in the periodic group were made below the level of the executive council.) Thus, levels of geographic organisation were associated with characteristics hypothesised as unfavourable to opposition in the permanent-post group, but as favourable to opposition in the periodic group.

Perhaps due to the relationships just cited, an inverse relationship was found among the permanent-post unions between the number of levels of simple geographic hierarchy and the closeness of elections to fill top vacancies ($r = -\cdot26$). On the other hand, the relationship among the periodic group was as predicted and much stronger ($r = \cdot53$). The correlations with the means of periodic top and next-to-top closeness were $\cdot63$ and $\cdot39$, also as predicted, but the correlation with next-to-top vacancies was negligible.

We shall see later that additional complexity variables, and many other kinds of variables, relate as expected to the closeness of elections in the periodic group, but not in the permanent-post group. While there is no single explanation for this, the colouration of some of the contingent variables by their association with the appointment of national officers in the permanent-post group, and the heterogeneous nature of that group, are certainly involved.

RELATIONSHIPS AMONG MEASURES OF OPPOSITION IN BRITAIN

It will be difficult to show consistent support for hypotheses with respect to all four major measures of electoral opposition; these intercorrelate at best only moderately, and at worst negatively (see Table 5.3). One surprising finding is the lack of a relationship, even a negative relationship, between the closeness of periodic elections and the closeness of elections to fill vacancies for the *same* posts. Thus, for the top post this correlation was only ·12, and for the next-to-top it was negative, —·30. When pre-1949 elections were added to the data (see page 99), the correlation for the top post was raised to ·30, while that for the next-to-top became only slightly less negative, —·23 ($N = 17$ in each case).

These very low and negative correlations of periodic elections with vacant-post elections were apparently not due primarily to the unreliability of the means of closeness of elections: the correlations were moderate for elections of the *same type*. That between the means of closeness of periodic top and periodic next-to-top elections was ·52 ($N = 16$). The correlation between the vacant top and vacant next-to-top means of closeness, excluding the unions electing permanently, was ·54 ($N = 14$).[2]

The low correlations between periodic and vacant-post elections are largely due to the fact that in some unions the electoral machinery against top and next-to-top incumbents was totally neglected for periodic elections, while vacancies were contested at least as strongly as in most of the other periodic unions. In seven of the sixteen periodic unions there was no competition whatsoever against the incumbent top officer during 1949–66 (in six unions there were three or more such opportunities), and in five of these seven there was *also* no competition against incumbent *next*-to-top officers (see Table 6.1).

The National Society of Operative Printers and Assistants exemplifies the consistent avoidance of opposition to incumbents, combined with close elections to fill vacancies. Between 1918 and 1965, up to an amalgamation now dissolved, general secretaries ran for re-election on fifteen separate occasions (five during 1949–65), in each case unopposed. The number of next-to-top posts varied during 1918–65, but there was a total of twenty-four periodic elections for these posts (thirteen during 1949–66), all uncontested. Nevertheless, the union's single vacancy for the top post during 1949–65 was won by a left-of-centre candidate, with a runner-up percentage of 85·4, which was much higher than the mean closeness for the British sample. All four vacant-post elections for the second-ranking posts since 1949 were also contested, with a mean runner-up percentage of 69·1, which was virtually the same as the British mean for such elections. (During 1918–48 there were five next-to-top vacancies, of which only two were contested.)

In a country where most full-time union officials are elected permanently, it may be tempting to ascribe the absence of competition against highly-placed incumbents simply to its illegitimacy. This would be unwarranted. In the Operative Printers and Assistants, George Isaacs, the leader from

TABLE 6.1   *The mean closeness of elections in British unions electing top and next-to-top officers periodically, 1949–66[a]*
(*votes for the runner-up per 100 for the winner*)

Union	Rank in size	Top vacant-post	n	Top periodic	n	Next-to-top vacant-post	n	Next-to-top periodic	n
Engineers	1	75·5	5	43·2	8	66·8	20	58·3	35
Electrical Trades	2	42·8	2	49·6	5	48·6	2	44·9	1[b]
Woodworkers	3	16·3	1	13·2	5	61·2	11	16·1	29
Building Trade	4	73·6	3	17·7	5	86·2	2	24·0	2
Boot and Shoe	5	27·2	3	0·0	8	78·2	4	0·0	4
Boilermakers	6	57·6	2	0·0	3	62·1	9	16·3	15
Foundry	7	67·0	3	49·4	3	67·3	3	8·2	3
Furniture Trade	8	—	0	0·0	3	79·0	1	0·0	5
Vehicle Builders	9	61·0	2	11·5	4	82·4	4	8·6	6
Plumbing Trades	10	57·6	2	0·0	2	—	0	48·6	2
Sheet Metal	11	31·7	2	0·0	3	63·6	1	0·0	3
Operative Printers	12	85·4	1	0·0	5	69·1	4	0·0	13
Shipconstructors	13	27·9	2	13·3	2	26·6	1	0·0	3
Fire Brigades	14	69·0	1	0·0	5	81·8	1	0·0	5
Patternmakers	15	47·5	1	11·3	3	58·4	2	32·7	3
Heating Engineers	16	31·6	1	21·8	2	36·3	2	43·5	2
MEAN		51·4		14·4		64·5		18·8	

[a] Through 1967 for top vacancies. In a few instances the period is somewhat shorter due to a change in rules. Where there were two top officers, or two or more next-to-top, all such elections are included. Such elections were conducted separately for each post.
[b] The 1960 election of this type was cancelled.

1909 to 1948, was described thus: '. . . like all powerful figures he wanted things his own way and was prepared to use tough methods with a tough membership. He built around him a group of men whose names occur and re-occur in the history of the union as his loyal supporters' (Moran, 1964: 48). Members of the Communist Party and Minority Movement were apparently barred from office by the 1932 conference. Lord Briginshaw, who won the general secretaryship in 1951, was disqualified for this or other reasons in 1936 or earlier (see NATSOPA *Journal*, August 1936) and applied for the removal of the disqualification in 1947.

In practice, although not by rule, there has been a general prohibition on printed campaign literature, and the Operative Printers and Assistants itself has not circulated election addresses or biographies of candidates. However, there appear to have been no sanctions imposed for the circulation of literature, perhaps because violations have not occurred. Although this is a matter of judgement, the rules appear by implication to empower the national officials to suppress campaign literature deemed slanderous or derogatory to the union or its officials. In these circumstances a campaign against a leading incumbent may appear so difficult as to be

TABLE 6.2   *The mean closeness of elections in British unions electing top officers permanently, 1949–66[a]*
(*votes for the runner-up per 100 for the winner*)

Union	Rank in size	Top vacant-post	n	Next-to-top vacant-post	n	Comment on next-to-top post
Transport and General	1	34·5	2	—		appointed
General and Municipal [c]	2	67·6	1	—		appointed, and not full-time at national level
Mineworkers	3	70·8	4	—		not full-time at national level
Railwaymen	4	17·8	2	81·5	5	
Shop, Distributive [c]	5	28·4	2	—		appointed
Agricultural	6	73·3	1	—		appointed
Printing, Bookbinding	7	93·7	1	93·3	2	
Tailors and Garment Workers	8	77·6	1	94·9	1	
Painters	9	55·6	1	68·9	2	
Locomotive Engineers [c]	10	18·7	3	65·4	3	
Seamen	11	33·9	2	—		appointed
Health Service	12	72·3	3	52·9	3	
Typographical	13	63·7	2	75·1	3	
Bakers	14	83·0	1	—		not full-time at national level[b]
Plasterers	15	54·0	1	98·9	1	
MEAN		56·3		78·9		

[a] See footnote [a] to Table 6.1.
[b] The presidency became full-time in 1964.
[c] Election by branch block vote.

hardly worth the effort, but no doubt the absence of a precedent for opposition to a leading officer is itself an obstacle to its being tried. Things must appear (and be) easier with the incumbent out of the picture. While this may be termed illegitimacy of opposition to incumbents, it nevertheless rests upon more than self-sustaining informal norms.

The question of the representativeness of the 'mean' runner-up percentage for top vacancies is raised, in the case of the Operative Printers and Assistants, since it is based on only the single vacancy. Unfortunately, there is little more to go on (other than next-to-top vacancies) because George Isaacs, the general secretary who took office in 1909, remained until he retired in 1948 aged sixty-five. The only two vacant-post elections after 1909 took place a mere few years apart, in 1948 and 1951 (the secretary elected in 1948 had to retire because of ill-health), and were of roughly comparable closeness.

The Operative Printers and Assistants is similar to much of the British sample in its small number of top vacancies: twelve of the thirty unions with top vacancies had only one, while only seven unions had three or more during 1949–67. Thus, the unreliability of the means for vacant-post elections must have contributed to the low correlations with the means for periodic elections. Such relationships as exist between our organisational variables and electoral opposition should be easier to demonstrate for the more numerous periodic elections.

Finally, it should be noted that all the seven unions without contests against top incumbents during 1949–66 had between 84,000 and 20,000 members. The three very much larger periodic unions – the Engineers, the Electrical Trades Union, and the Woodworkers – were not among them.

THE FREQUENCY OF ELECTIONS AND CONVENTIONS

Since all the unions in the British sample used the referendum to elect top officers, there was a less obvious relationship than in the United States between the frequency of regular conventions and the number of top periodic elections during 1949–66. Nevertheless, there was a low to moderate association between them ($r = \cdot25$, $N = 16$). (In the one or two instances where the rules did not set the interval between conventions, the actual interval was taken.)

The Number of Elections

The correlation between the number of top vacancies and the number of top periodic elections was $\cdot49$ ($N = 16$), due in part to the fact that the four periodic unions with two top officers (to be discussed shortly) had greater numbers of both kinds of elections. A greater number of top vacancies also reflected a later age of achieving the top post, which is probably related in turn to a longer and more competitive promotion ladder. Thus, the number of top vacancies may be a partially dependent variable, in contrast to the more constitutionally-determined frequency of periodic elections.

The frequencies of both kinds of top-post elections were related, as hypothesised, to the four measures of electoral opposition in the periodic group (see Table 5.3). The number of vacancies, which had a greater overall success, correlated $\cdot55$ with the closeness of periodic top elections and $\cdot45$ with the closeness of periodic next-to-top elections. The number of periodic elections correlated $\cdot48$ with the closeness of elections to fill next-to-top vacancies. However, the number of top vacancies correlated negatively ($r = -\cdot32$) with the closeness of top-vacancy elections in the permanent-post group.

Conventions

The frequency of regular conventions had mixed directions of association with the closeness of elections in the periodic group, and the fairly low correlations had only a slight preponderance in support of the hypothesis (see Table 5.3). The correlation with permanent top vacancies was low and opposite in direction to that predicted.

The periodic unions which met more frequently in convention also tended to meet for a greater number of days ($r = \cdot36$) (the permanent-post $r = -\cdot04$). The mean number of convention days *per year* during 1949–66 was associated in the expected direction with all four measures of the closeness of elections among the periodic unions. The correlations with the closeness of top and next-to-top periodic elections were $\cdot58$ and $\cdot37$ respectively, and with the corresponding vacancy elections were $\cdot25$ and $\cdot22$ respectively. The correlation with permanent-post top-vacancy elections was markedly negative ($-\cdot67$), due largely to the fact that the two railway unions, which met annually, had the longest conventions but the least close elections.[3]

Thus, the time spent in regular conventions during 1949–66 is associated as expected with electoral competition among the periodic, but not the permanent-post, unions.[4]

THE APPEALS SYSTEM

Information on three of the original American appeals variables is available for Britain, but there is much additional information. Two of the three available original appeals items were successful in the prediction of electoral competition among the British periodic unions, but none was successful for the unions electing permanently (disregarding one low positive correlation).

The Level of Appeal for Subordinate Officers
The unsuccessful item nevertheless provided a useful description of the British sample, and in a collapsed version was the basis for another, successful, measure. It dealt with the highest level of appeal provided for local or regional officers subject to possible suspension or expulsion, as ranked along this nine-point scale:

1 The top officers or their appointees.
2 The executive council or its appointees.
3 A general executive council which includes the executive council.
4 A general executive council which excludes the executive council.
5 The convention, or an appeals committee elected by the convention.
6 The same as 5, but with full-time national officials barred from voting at the convention except in the case of a tie.
7 A special appeals board elected by referendum, nationally or sub-divisionally.

8   A direct national referendum on the appeal itself.
9   Arbitration (see below) or a public review board (consisting of non-members of the union).

Arbitration and public review board were ranked as somewhat more favourable to an appellant than a national referendum, because they could presumably be more readily called upon. Appeals to national referenda would probably be extremely rare.

Nine of the periodic, but only two of the permanent-post, unions fell at points 7, 8 or 9 of the scale (a special appeals board elected by referendum, or better). On the other hand, subordinate officers of all but two periodic unions and one permanent-post union could appeal at least as far as the convention (one case missing in each group).

The Foundry Workers, in the periodic group, provided for the settlement of appeals by arbitration, with one arbitrator chosen by the appellant, one chosen by the union, and a third agreed upon by the first two. The arbitrators could have been members of any unions affiliated to the Trades Union Congress (1964 Rules). The Patternmakers, also a periodic union, provided for arbitration in special circumstances, with a final vote of the membership where there was a division of opinion within or between appeals bodies. Allen found provisions for the arbitration of appeals in *eight* out of 127 British unions (1954: 170).

The results for this scale of appeal by a subordinate officer were inconsistent, with only the periodic elections being in the expected direction (·41 and ·29 respectively for the top and next-to-top mean closeness of elections; $N = 15$). The negative correlation with the mean closeness of next-to-top vacant-post elections among the periodic unions was one of the highest found in this study, $- ·61$ ($N = 14$).[5]

Appeals for a Member, Short of a National Referendum
It could be argued that carrying an appeal through to a national referendum would be even less feasible for an ordinary member than for an officer. We therefore re-scaled the previous item by recording the highest level to which an ordinary member might take an appeal, *short* of a national referendum. We also simplified the scale by collapsing the two general executive council alternatives (3 and 4), and the two alternatives relating to the convention (5 and 6), which made it possible (as it turned out) to categorise the constitutions of the complete British sample. Ignoring the referendum as an appeals mechanism meant taking the next-to-highest levels of appeal for one permanent-post union and five periodic unions (four of the latter being reduced to the level of the executive council).[6]

The correlations of this appeals scale for a member with the closeness of elections were all positive (see Table 5.3), being ·54 and ·38 for elections for top and next-to-top vacancies respectively among the periodic unions. Given the reasons for the use of this six-point scale, it seems reasonable to accept its findings rather than those of the nine-point scale which included the national referendum.

A number of quite different appeals procedures assured that full-time officers would be barred from the highest appeals bodies. These included appeals to necessarily rank-and-file executive councils, to conventions and to appeal courts. In our sample it appeared that officers could participate directly in arbitration procedures.

The scale utilised provided that 'An aggrieved member or officer might take his final appeal, short of a national referendum, to a body which consisted of full-time officers (1) fully; (2) partially or permissibly; (3) not at all' (our own questionnaire). If the level was different for officers and members, preference was to be given to the higher choice.[7] The correlations with the closeness of elections were all positive in the periodic group between ·47 and ·21.

Other Appeals Provisions
An appeals system as a whole is necessarily complex, and applicable to members, officers and local unions. There are the matters of original juris-diction (e.g. does only the local or regional union have the right to initiate the expulsion of a member?), of intermediate levels of appeal, and of the level, composition and manner of selection of the final appeal body, as mentioned above. In all, we applied thirteen different measures to the four measures of electoral opposition for the periodic group, which yielded a total of fifty-two separate simple correlations. Forty-four correlations were based on complete data, and eight lacked data on only one union.

On the whole, the findings for the periodic unions support the notion that an appeals system may protect oppositionists by limiting the powers of the top officers. Almost half of the fifty-two correlations (twenty-four) were ·20 or higher in the expected direction, but only six were that high in the direction opposite to prediction. Indeed, four of the six negative correlations of −·20 or higher were with the closeness of elections for next-to-top vacancies, which correlated negatively with the closeness of next-to-top periodic elections, as previously reported.

The individual appeals items were mostly inconsistent in direction from one measure of opposition to another, undoubtedly due, to some extent, to the less global and more trivial content of the separate items. To assess the usefulness of the appeals items in combination, a total appeals score was computed for each union, using the unweighted sum of the scales for the ten items for which we had complete information. The correlation with the closeness of top periodic elections was ·25 ($N = 16$), and that with the closeness of top vacant-post elections in the entire sample was the same

($N = 30$). Other correlations with the total appeals score were not computed, but the correlation with the closeness of top vacant-post elections among the periodic unions separately would have been much higher.[8]

Finally, ratings on a nine-point scale of the constitutionally-provided judicial process as a whole, from the point of view of providing a fair trial, correlated ·28 and ·45 respectively with the closeness of top and next-to-top periodic elections, and ·35 and ·06 respectively with the closeness of top and next-to-top vacant-post elections, among the periodic unions. The correlation with top vacant-post elections among the permanent-post unions was −·15 ($N = 14$). Thus, mutually-supporting findings were obtained for the British sample from an overview of the correlations of appeals items considered singly, and from correlations with the sums of such items and with overall ratings of the judicial process.

Among the periodic unions, more equitable appeals procedures were associated with closer top and next-to-top periodic elections, and with close top vacant-post elections. However, there was no consistent relationship between the appeals system and the closeness of elections to next-to-top vacancies.

Among the permanent-post unions there was a fairly consistent finding of low negative correlations between appeals measures and the closeness of top vacant-post elections. However, there were unusually close associations in the permanent-post (but not the periodic) group between appeals items and conceptually-unrelated variables which were relevant, according to our theory, to electoral opposition. For example, the highest level of appeal for a member correlated −·76 with the number of second-ranking officers under the rules, and −·63 with the absence of logical successors to the top post, all considered. On the other hand, it also had a strong negative association, −·74, with the number of executive councillors appointed (sub-divisionally or nationally) rather than elected. Such associations also existed, to a lesser degree, for some of the other appeals items. While these conceptually-unrelated variables were themselves at most only moderately associated with the closeness of permanent-post top elections, the highest correlation being ·28, it is inadvisable to accept at face value the low negative correlations between appeals items and the closeness of permanent-post elections.

THE ELECTORAL SYSTEM

Only two British unions which elected their full-time officers periodically failed to use either a second ballot or (in two instances) an even more sophisticated system for the election of the top officer. After our analysis was completed we discovered that the Woodworkers and the Furniture

Trade Operatives, with a strange logic, sent the *three* highest candidates for full-time office to a second ballot if none among four or more had a majority. Had we classified these two unions as having a plurality system, our not very impressive findings for the electoral system would have been somewhat strengthened (see Table 5.3), although not enough to match the moderate success in the American unions.

In the electoral system scale used for both the top office and the executive council, the lowest weight was given to national appointment and the next lowest to subdivisional appointment by a committee (not a convention) with fewer than twenty-six members. This was followed, in order, by sub-divisional appointment by a larger committee, election by plurality, election by second ballot (as in the Engineers), and election by the alternative vote (as in the Mineworkers) or the equivalent multi-step elimination balloting. Proportional representation was at the top of the scale, but was inapplic-able to executive council elections in our sample. There were also minor intermediate steps between the above, giving some preference to the referendum over branch block voting, and to both of these over voting at conventions. Finally, the filling of posts singly was given preference over filling two or more at a time, other things being equal, since (apart from proportional representation) the latter promotes winner-take-all. Thus, the weighted scale basically ranked the well-known formal electoral systems, with minor adjustments for how these were employed.

For the periodic unions, the correlations between the electoral system for the top office and the closeness of elections were negligible (from ·04 to − ·08), except for periodic elections to next-to-top office (·24). An applica-tion of the scale to the most favourable of the electoral systems used to select executive councillors correlated ·48 with the closeness of periodic elections to next-to-top posts, but − ·39 with that of elections to fill next-to-top vacancies. (The correlation between the two electoral system scales was ·59.) Our theory was given more support by the correlations of these elec-toral system measures with the means of closeness of elections in the periodic group from pre-1949 to 1966. The most favourable system for the executive council correlated ·34 with the closeness of top vacant-post elections, ·33 with that of top periodic elections, ·45 with that of next-to-top periodic elections, and − ·14 with that of next-to-top vacant-post elections.

Finally, the weighted average of the electoral system for the entire execu-tive council – a more sophisticated measure than the single most favourable system – was employed. The variability of this measure was much greater than that of the others, since many unions which assured an absolute majority in elections for top posts did not do so for councillors. This measure correlated ·20 with the closeness of top vacant-post elections, ·31 with that of next-to-top periodic elections, almost zero with that of top periodic elections, and $-\cdot14$ with that of next-to-top vacant-post elections. On the whole, the findings for the periodic group tended to support the idea that the method of electing the executive council is related, in the expected way, to the closeness of elections for still higher posts. However, the findings for vacant next-to-top posts again tended to undermine this support.

All three of the electoral system variables correlated negatively with the closeness of elections for permanent top posts, the largest such correlation $(-\cdot28)$ being with the most sophisticated measure: the weighted average for the council as a whole. This was so in spite of the facts that this variable could take account of the appointment of some councillors, and that the percentage of the council that was nationally appointed correlated negatively $(-\cdot26)$, as expected, with the closeness of top vacant-post elections. The Railwaymen, with by far the highest weighted average measure for the electoral system (the alternative vote for all), had the *lowest* mean for top vacancies (a runner-up percentage of $17\cdot8$). The Locomotive Engineers, with the third-highest weight, had the next-to-lowest runner-up percentage $(18\cdot7)$. The previously-cited value placed on seniority in the railway unions, plus a clear line for succession, took precedence over the electoral system in its effect on top-post elections.

THE EXECUTIVE COUNCIL

The key general variables used to describe executive councils were size, composition and formal manner of selection. The measures of composition included rank-and-file *v.* full-time officer status, and the representation of subdivisions *v.* national election.

Executive councillors should be in a good position to compete for the top post, in favourable circumstances. Such circumstances would include: a relatively autonomous subdivisional constituency, to avoid domination by the administration; high status and a prominent position for councillors; and great collective power relative to that of the top officer (to be discussed later). One variable, the percentage of the council required to be subdivisionally-elected or appointed full-time officers, takes account of the autonomy and status considerations, the latter particularly when the council is small. Table 6.3 shows that the four periodic unions with full-time subdivisionally-elected executive councils did indeed have generally closer elections than those with councils of other compositions. The correlations of this variable (in terms of the percentage of the executive council) with the closeness of top and next-to-top periodic elections were $\cdot47$ and $\cdot23$ respectively, and $\cdot39$ and $\cdot03$ respectively for vacant-post elections, in the expected directions. The correlation with the closeness of elections to fill top permanent-post vacancies was only $\cdot13$, but only the General

TABLE 6.3 *The composition of executive councils[a] among the British unions electing periodically to top and next-to-top posts, as related to the closeness of elections*

Predominant composition (and %)	No. of unions	Mean rank of union size	Mean size of executive council	Closeness of elections				Mean weight of electoral system for executive council
				Mean top vacant-post	Mean top periodic	Mean next-to-top vacant-post	Mean next-to-top periodic	
Subdivisionally-elected full-time officers (Engineers 93%, Boilermakers 83%, Foundry 100%, Plumbers 71%)	4	6·0 (1-10)	6·5 (5-8)	64·4 (58-76)	23·2 (0-50)	65·4 (62-67) (N = 3)	32·9 (8-58)	13·5 (12-18)
Subdivisionally-elected, permissibly full-time in a *lower* office (Sheet Metal 94%, Boot and Shoe 81%) *Note:* Full-time district officers eligible in Sheet Metal: 50% est. in practice. Full-time branch officers eligible in Boot and Shoe: 75% est. in practice.	2	8·0 (5-11)	16·0 (16-16)	29·5 (27-32)	0·0 (0-0)	70·9 (64-78)	0·0 (0-0)	8·0 (4-12)
Subdivisionally-elected, necessarily rank-and-file (Electrical 93%, Vehicle Builders 100%, Furniture 100%, Printers 95%, Fire Brigades 95%, Heating Engineers 90%, Patternmakers 84%) *Note:* Fire Brigades, Furniture Trade and Engineers elected top officer by plurality.	7	10·9 (2-16)	13·7 (6-20)	56·2 (32-86) (N = 6)	13·4 (0-50)	55·0 (9-83)	18·5 (0-45)	9·4 (5-18)
Nominated from subdivisions, elected by national ballot (Necessarily full-time: Woodworkers 100%, Shipconstructors 71%. Necessarily rank-and-file: Building Trades 91%) *Note:* Woodworkers elected top officer by plurality. Building Trades had much closer elections to vacancies than the other two unions.	3	6·7 (3-13)	8·7 (5-14)	39·3 (16-74)	14·7 (13-18)	58·0 (27-86)	13·4 (0-24)	8·0 (6-12)

[a] All voting members, including one who votes only in the case of a tie. All were elected except one subdivisionally-'appointed' councillor in the Fire Brigades union.

and Municipal Workers had any constitutional requirements for sub-divisionally-chosen full-time officers (42 per cent of its council).

The four periodic unions with full-time subdivisionally-elected executive councils, as a group, also had smaller executive councils (from five to eight voting members), were chosen by electoral systems more favourable to minorities (at least the second-ballot system by referendum vote), and tended to be larger unions, although the overlap in size with the other groups shown in Table 6.3 was great.

The directions of correlation with the size of the executive council were mixed: −·41 and −·46 for the closeness of periodic elections, but ·28 and ·52 for that of vacant-post elections. The direction of this association was negative for the permanent-post group ($r = -·21$). Clearly, the size of a council should be regarded as a secondary and contingent variable on logical as well as empirical grounds.

The four groups of periodic unions shown in Table 6.3 are arranged in the hypothesised descending order of favourability for electoral competition.[9] The actual order of the groups, in terms of an overall view of the closeness of elections, is such that the two unions with subdivisionally-elected, permissibly full-time executive councils should have been placed last.

On the whole, there is support for the view that full-time subdivisionally-based executive councils, elected under systems more favourable for electoral opposition, are favourable for opposition in elections to top and second-ranking posts. We may speculate that some proportion of elected rank-and-file executive councillors *in addition* might be an asset to democracy, but we have no evidence in this respect.[10]

TOP AND NEXT-TO-TOP OFFICERS

Next-to-top officers are ordinarily even more likely than mere executive councillors to try for the top post, and if there are two or more they may compete against each other. Of course, executive councillors may themselves be next-to-top officers. A greater number of both top and next-to-top officers also increases the possibility of divided power among the high officials and, of course, results in more frequent elections – both of which are considered favourable for opposition.

There were four periodic unions with two approximately equal top officers: the Engineers, the Electrical Workers, the Boot and Shoe Workers, and – from 1952 – the Building Trade Workers. Among the permanent-post unions, only the Mineworkers had two top officers for 1949–66.[11] The correlations of the percentage of the period 1949–66 with two approximately equal top officers were ·45 and ·39 respectively with the closeness of top and next-to-top periodic elections, ·07 and ·17 respectively with that of top and next-to-top vacant-post elections, and ·14 with that of top permanent-post elections.

There was only one union in the British sample, the Boilermakers, where the second-ranking full-time officer under the constitution (the assistant general secretary) differed from those designated by us as the actual next-to-top officers (the six full-time executive councillors). The essentially technical and administrative nature of the assistant general secretary's work has been officially, but not constitutionally, recognised by the Boilermakers, and the assistant secretaries have not competed for the top post (see Allen, 1954: 206).[12] The other periodic unions with more than one full-time next-to-top officer were the Engineers (nine), the Woodworkers (six), the Vehicle Builders (a mean of 1·8 for 1949–66), the Furniture Trade Operatives (two), and the Operative Printers (three). The correlations within the periodic group for the number of elected full-time next-to-top national officers, all considered, were ·17 and ·16 respectively with the closeness of top vacant-post and periodic elections, and ·05 and ·30 respectively with that of next-to-top vacant-post and periodic elections, all in the expected direction.

As has already been reported, not all the permanent-post unions had elected second-ranking full-time officers at national level. None of those that did had more than one such officer. The three permanent-post unions *without* full-time next-to-top officers (elected *or* appointed) who had primarily national responsibilities (see Table 6.2) tended to have closer elections for the top post (biserial $r = ·37$). This supports the notion that the absence of a nationally-placed contender for a top post is more favourable for opposition than the presence of one, given the existence of important subdivisional organisation and officials.

It was also hypothesised that unions without an *apprenticeship title*, assistant general secretary *or* vice-president, for a *full-time* officer, would offer to second-ranking officers less assurance of a progression to top office. There were four permanent-post unions without such titles for full-time officers (the three shown in Table 6.2 plus the Printing and Bookbinding union). The biserial correlation with the closeness of elections to permanent top posts was ·65, in the expected direction. There were no periodic unions without such titles.[13]

A more complete picture of the formally-encouraged promotion path to top office would include a simultaneous consideration of: whether there was more than one next-to-top post; any apparent special suitability for the top office in terms of job titles and constitutionally-prescribed duties; and the number of top posts. This was of even greater importance in view of the low inverse relationship between the percentage of the period 1949–66 with more than one next-to-top office, all considered,[14] and the similar percentage for the top office ($r = -·15$). This problem was anticipated,

and the following scale concerning '*logical successors*', based on constitutionally-prescribed duties (e.g. substituting for a top officer) as well as titles,
was employed (inapplicable categories omitted, i.e. point two):

1   There is only one logical successor (eleven periodic unions, including
    three with two top officers).
3   There are no logical successors. The placement of this category, which
    applied only to the permanent-post group, was based on the judgement
    that a structured competitive field, with two or more logical successors
    for a top post, was even more likely to lead to effective opposition. The
    absence of a constitutionally logical successor would not preclude a
    particular single 'non-logical', but hierarchically superior, officer from
    having an advantage in competition for the top post. However, this
    a priori judgement may have been mistaken, and the validity of the
    scale for the permanent-post group is somewhat in doubt.
4   There are at least two logical successors for one top post (four unions:
    the Boilermakers,[15] the Vehicle Builders, the Furniture Trades (which
    had no top vacancy), and the Operative Printers).
5   Each of two top posts has more than one logical successor (one union:
    the Engineers).

It should be noted that a union could have one assistant general secretary
and several full-time executive councillors, all of approximately equal rank,
but constitutionally only one logical successor. This was the case in the
Woodworkers.

In the periodic group, the constitutionally-based logical successor scale
correlated ·55 and ·24 respectively with the closeness of elections to fill top
and next-to-top vacancies. The correlations with that of top and next-to-top
periodic elections were negligible (·01 and ·10 respectively), as was the
correlation with that of elections for top permanent posts (·08). The same
scale categories were then applied, with atypical latitude for judgement in
this case, to the total structure and *actual practice* in the unions, rather than
to their rules. We knew the previous posts of top officers, in most instances
since the 1920s. For example, in a small union the full-time officer of the
London district might in practice have·been the 'logical' successor to the
top post. Thus, observed regularities in the position immediately preceding
the top post, in the path towards its attainment, were allowed to influence
the choice of scale category. The correlation with the similar scale based
on the rules was ·84 in the periodic group, but only ·31 ($N = 14$) in the
permanent-post group. As might have been expected, the correlations with
the closeness of top and next-to-top vacant-post elections were even higher:
·64 and ·43 respectively in the periodic group. The negligible correlations
with the closeness of top and next-to-top periodic elections became some-

what negative: —·16 and —·10 respectively. The correlation with the close-ness of elections to fill permanent top vacancies was ·65 ($N = 14$). Some of the permanent-post unions with no constitutionally logical successors obviously had some consistency in their paths to top office.

The high correlation for the periodic unions between the constitution-based logical successor scale and our wholistic judgement on the same scale indicates, although crudely, that the succession paths in these unions are in fact constitutionally-determined in fairly obvious ways.

The post of full-time president in the unions with two top posts deve-loped from an earlier part-time status. A total of six periodic unions still had part-time titular heads, usually presidents, under their constitutions. In addition, the chairman of the rank-and-file executive council of the Furniture Trades was apparently the union's titular head.

In Britain, election by conference is probably the most common method of choosing part-time presidents. As an alternative to a full-time presi-dency, a part-time titular headship should be associated with less effective opposition. However, a *supplementary* rank-and-file presidency alongside the general secretaryship may provide an alternative path to relatively high full-time office, bypassing some of the lower full-time ranks and occa-sionally facilitating a good try for the top post. The following scale was used to indicate the constitutional existence and rank of a part-time titular head:

1 There is *no* such titular head (nine periodic unions).
2 There is such a titular head, below the level of the second-ranking full-time officers (five periodic unions: Sheet Metal, Furniture Trades, Operative Printers, Heating Engineers, and Patternmakers).
3 There is such a titular head, at the level of the second-ranking full-time officers (two periodic unions: Vehicle Builders, and Fire Brigades).

The correlations of this scale with the closeness of top and next-to-top vacant-post elections were ·20 and ·31 respectively, in the predicted direc-tion, and with that of the corresponding periodic elections were —·38 and —·34 respectively. It will be recalled that there were low correlations of the existence of two top posts with the closeness of vacant-post elections, but moderate correlations of it with that of periodic elections (·45 and ·39 respectively for top and next-to-top elections). The titular head scale's necessarily negative correlation with the existence of two top posts (—·46 among the periodic unions) partly accounts for its negative correlations with the closeness of periodic elections. A negative correlation between two predictors sometimes makes them more effective in conjunction with each other. The shrunken multiple correlation coefficient for the closeness of next-to-top vacant-post elections rose to ·41 (·47 before shrinkage), using as predictors both the titular head scale *and* the percentage of 1949–66 with two top posts.

As a set, the top and next-to-top officer variables support the notion that electoral competition is facilitated by divided power among top officials, more equal status among national officers near the top, and the absence of a single logical successor. This is largely true for the unions electing permanently, as well as for those electing periodically, on variables which take into consideration the heterogeneous characteristics of the permanent-post group at the second-ranking level of office.

THE POWER AND STATUS OF TOP OFFICERS

We have already noted the more limited range of constitutional differences in Britain in the extent to which top officers worked under the direction of their executive councils. A three-point scale indicating that the top officer worked under the direction of the executive council, did so 'to some extent', or did not do so has a sample mean of 2·8, with the entire British sample lying in the first two categories. The inconsistent relationships of this constitutional scale to electoral opposition in Britain, including a negative correlation (−·51) with the closeness of top periodic elections (see Table 5.3), should be discounted in favour of findings on more sophisticated scales, which were available for the British analysis.

One such scale provided eight alternative categories, *four* of them actually applicable to the periodic group, in answer to this question: 'Does the executive council, or any section of it, under the *rules*, have the power to suspend or remove the top officer, temporarily or otherwise? Or does the top officer have the power to remove any or all council members?' The following categories were found to be applicable to the periodic unions:

8   The executive council can suspend the top officer, for any reason it sees fit (eight periodic unions).
7   The executive council can suspend the top officer for incompetence or for not fulfilling his duties satisfactorily (six periodic unions).
5   Neither side has the power to suspend (each is protected from the other) (the Woodworkers).
3   The rules are silent on this question (the Shipconstructors, but our rater's additional forced choice, not utilised, was that neither had the power to suspend).

The directions of all correlations with the scale were as expected. Among the periodic group, they were ·47 and ·67 respectively with the closeness of top and next-to-top vacant-post elections, and ·08 and ·12 respectively for the corresponding periodic elections. The correlation with the closeness of elections to fill top permanent-post vacancies was ·21 ($N = 14$). Neither side had the power to suspend in four of the permanent-post unions, and in two the rules were silent. In none of the British sample (with one case missing) did a top officer have any power to suspend an executive councillor.

Another indicator of the relative power of the top officer is his right (or lack thereof) to a vote in the executive council's deliberations. This was shown along a three-point scale: a top officer votes:

3   In *no* circumstances.
2   Only in the case of a tie.
1   With full voting rights.

The correlation of this scale with the power-to-suspend scale was ·35.

The mean right-to-vote scale value for the British sample was 2·6 (with a standard deviation of 0·75). The limitation on the top officer's voting rights correlated ·21 and ·34 respectively with the closeness of top and next-to-top vacant-post elections, and ·10 and −·16 respectively for the corresponding periodic elections. It correlated ·16 with the closeness of elections to fill top permanent-post vacancies. On the whole, these results point in the same direction as the power-to-suspend scale.

It occurred to us that the above scales might reflect a more general concern for due process and democratic procedures, and indeed this appears to be the case among the periodic unions. The power-to-suspend scale correlated positively and moderately with two appeals items: the absence of full-time officers from the final appeal body (·54), and the scale for the nature of the highest appeals body for a member (·33). It correlated ·62 with the percentage of convention delegates who, in practice, were rank-and-filers (undoubtedly due primarily to constitutional requirements), and ·40 with the percentage of the executive council required to be sub-divisionally-chosen rank-and-filers. Oddly, the power-to-suspend scale had an unusually high correlation (·81, $N = 15$), also among the periodic unions, with a scale indicating how ballots were conducted in referenda or branch votes: a four-point scale, ranging from secret ballots *or* signed ballot papers (the latter being an insurance against fraud)[16] to a show of hands at a meeting.[17]

ORGANISATIONAL COMPLEXITY AND SIZE

Students of organisations have often forgotten the crucial difference between essentially bureaucratic organisations and semi-democratic membership organisations: the latter are not hierarchically organised from the top down, to the extent that they are democratic. Structural complexity, in the form of the number of hierarchically-organised levels of organisation

TABLE 6.4 *Intercorrelations for permanent-post unions among organisational complexity variables, size and closeness of elections (N = 15)[a]*

	2	3	4	5	6	7	8	9
1 No. of levels of nationally-appointed full-time officers	·33	·54	−·43	−·44	−·64	·29	·49	−·21
2 No. of levels of hierarchical geographic organisation		·18	−·16	·07	−·20	−·27	·20	−·26
3 No. of levels of non-geographic organisation outside a simple hierarchical structure (e.g. overlapping 2)			·07	−·08	−·06	−·04	·66	−·23
4 No. of levels of elected, necessarily full-time national officers				·65	·89	−·39	−·22	−·15
5 No. of elected, necessarily full-time national officers					·70	−·29	−·13	−·51
6 No. of levels of elected full-time or permissibly full-time officers at and higher than major regions (and major branches, if any)[a]						−·35	−·11	−·06
7 Estimated percentage of branches with full-time officers							−·11	−·15
8 No. of members								−·20
9 Closeness of elections to fill top vacancies								

[a] The equivalent of regions.

TABLE 6.5 *Intercorrelations for unions electing periodically among organisational complexity variables, size and closeness of elections (N = 16)*

	2	3	4	5	6	7	8	9[a]	10[a]	11	12
1 No. of levels of nationally-appointed full-time officers	-·45	·02	-·36	-·21	-·05	·32	-·13	·03	·09	-·29	-·24
2 No. of levels of hierarchical geographic organisation		·55	·57	·69	·41	-·41	·47	·53	·03	·63	·39
3 No. of levels of non-geographic organisation outside a simple hierarchical structure (e.g. overlapping 2)			·57	·44	·53	-·21	·23	·69	·34	·44	-·07
4 No. of levels of elected, necessarily full-time national officers				·57	·64	-·04	·07	·18	-·10	·52	·25
5 No. of elected, necessarily full-time national officers					·63	-·16	·71	·22	-·14	·60	·40
6 No. of levels of elected full-time or permissibly full-time officers at and higher than major regions (and major branches, if any)						·12	·53	·40	·10	·41	·38
7 Estimated percentage of branches with full-time officers							-·11	-·26	·33	-·32	-·36
8 No. of members								·24	·03	·53	·56
9 Closeness of elections to fill top vacancies									·54[b]	·12	·10
10 Closeness of elections to fill next-to-top vacancies										-·28	-·30
11 Closeness of top periodic elections											·52
12 Closeness of next-to-top periodic elections											

[a] N = 15.   [b] N = 14.

and of officials, especially, is therefore very much a contingent variable.[18] Given some subdivisional autonomy and control from below, the top officials may be faced with an organisation which resists their will, and in particular with a promotion path largely outside their control. Given, on the other hand, a downward control through the appointment of many lower officials from above, complexity tends to become a shield for oligarchy and a mechanism which can be controlled only from above. The dictum that, 'Regardless of the form, high degrees of complexity introduce coordination, control, and communication problems for the organization' (Hall, 1972: 170) may apply in the latter case, but not redound to the benefit of democracy.

Of course, such an approach to complexity and democracy can be no more than a general guide. Our own work focuses on aspects of complexity thought to be related to subdivisional autonomy, the promotion path and electoral opposition (see Tables 6.4 and 6.5).

Permanent-Post Unions

All the eight size and complexity variables shown in Table 6.4 correlate negatively with the closeness of elections to top permanent posts. There is a clear cluster of variables which correlate positively with the number of levels of nationally-appointed full-time officers, and with each other. These include: the number of levels of hierarchical geographic organisation; the number of levels of non-geographic organisation (primarily occupational, but also possibly including youth or women's sections) which do *not* fall within a simple hierarchical structure (i.e. which overlap geographic organisation); and the number of members. The correlations of the variables with the number of levels of appointed full-time officers ranged from ·33 to ·54, and certainly this is part of the explanation for their negative correlations with the closeness of elections to top permanent posts, which ranged from −·20 to −·26. We shall see that these relationships do not hold for the periodic group.

The fairly high correlation between the number of levels or types of non-geographic organisation outside a simple hierarchical structure, and union size (·66), reflects the trade-group structure of the large general unions. Size also correlated ·49 with the number of levels of nationally-appointed full-time officials. However, it would be unwarranted to attribute entirely to the general unions the negative associations between the complexity variables above and the closeness of elections: we know that the appointment of officials took place in much smaller unions as well, and the correlation between size and the closeness of elections is relatively low (−·20).

The three variables pertaining to the number, and number of levels, of elected, full-time or permissibly full-time, national or regional-or-higher officials (see Table 6.4) also correlate positively with each other, but negatively with union size (from −·11 to −·22) and negatively with the closeness of top-post elections (from −·06 to −·51). There is an apparent paradox in that the number of *elected*, necessarily full-time national officers, which correlated negatively (−·51) with the closeness of elections, was negatively associated (−·44) with the number of levels of nationally-*appointed* full-time officers. These correlations are attributable almost entirely to the Railwaymen and the Locomotive Engineers, which had the two largest numbers of elected full-time national officials in the permanent-post group (twenty-one and ten respectively)[19] and no nationally-appointed officials whatsoever. (Only six of the fifteen permanent-post unions, but twelve of the sixteen periodic unions, had no nationally-appointed full-time officers.) These two unions also had by far the two lowest mean runner-up percentages for top office in the permanent-post group, for reasons suggested earlier.

The estimated percentage of branches with full-time officers was expected to correlate positively with the closeness of elections to top office, since larger and stronger branches (which could afford such officials) could display more independence from national officers, and their officials would be better placed to compete for still higher posts. We learned, however, that a considerable number of our British unions insisted on a rank-and-file status for officials just beyond the branch level and also for such positions as convention delegate and executive councillor. Thus, a full-time branch officer's post was sometimes a 'dead-end', as we found in the South Wales area of the Mineworkers. This may contribute towards an explanation of the essentially negative association between the percentage of branches with full-time officers and the closeness of elections in both British subsamples. However, the positive association of this variable with the number of levels of nationally-appointed full-time officers in both periodic and permanent-post unions (·32 and ·29 respectively) points towards a mixed explanation of our findings.

Finally, in the periodic group the percentage of branches with full-time officers correlates −·41 with the number of levels of hierarchical geographic organisation, a variable found to be favourable for opposition. It may be that smaller branches, which do not require full-time officers, tend to be co-ordinated by an extra level of geographic organisation, as in the rather numerous districts of the Engineers. Thus, we have no basis for drawing any general conclusions here.

Periodic Unions
The complexity variables are among those most highly associated with the closeness of elections in the periodic unions. The correlations are, on the whole, in the hypothesised directions, except that of the percentage of branches with full-time officers. Disregarding the latter, the six variables

pertaining to the number of levels of organisation or officials, or the number of officials (variables 1–6 in Table 6.5), have mean correlations of ·48 with the closeness of top periodic elections and ·34 with that of top vacant-post elections. The means based on a transformation of r to Fisher's z were only slightly higher, ·49 and ·36 respectively (see Peters and van Voorhis, 1940: 155–7). Five of the twelve correlations are between ·52 and ·69, and the direction of only one negligible correlation is opposite to the prediction. One would have thought this degree of consistency to be difficult to achieve, given the very weak association between the closeness of top vacant-post and top periodic elections ($r = ·12$).

The mean correlation of the six complexity variables with next-to-top periodic elections is ·27, only one negligible correlation being in the 'wrong' direction. The closeness of elections to fill next-to-top vacancies is, with one exception, only weakly, and in three instances negatively, associated with each of the variables.

Before further discussing the significance of these findings, two sets of interrelationships should be noted. First, there are moderate to high inter-correlations among five of the six successful complexity variables, from ·44 to ·69. (The excluded variable is the number of levels of nationally-appointed full-time officers.) Second, three of these five also correlate about as highly with union size, which itself correlates as highly with the closeness of periodic elections. The question arises, therefore, of the extent to which the association between complexity and the closeness of elections in the periodic group may simply reflect a common association with union size.

It is certain that size is *not* the least common denominator in some of these findings (cf. Child *et al.*, 1973; Donaldson and Warner, 1974); it correlates only ·07 with the number of levels of elected, necessarily full-time national officers, but the latter correlates ·52 and ·25 respectively with the closeness of top and next-to-top periodic elections. Furthermore, size correlates only ·23 with the number of levels or types of non-geographic organisation overlapping a simple geographic structure, but the latter correlates ·69 with the closeness of top vacant-post elections. (Five periodic unions had such non-geographic organisation.)

One significant aspect of the number of levels of hierarchical geographic organisation is the structure it tends to impose on the progression to high office, especially where posts are overwhelmingly elective. The promotion path may be lengthened even more, and additional conspicuous potential full-time competitors provided, where there are a number of levels of elected full-time officers at the national level. The longer the progression, the narrower the status gap between adjacent levels of officers. But, of course, the circumstances are even more favourable for electoral opposition where there are a number of full-time elected officials at each level. Other things being equal, a greater *number* of full-time national officers is necessarily associated with a greater number of them *per level*. Thus far, information on the latter point has been missing. The number of elected full-time national officers correlates ·60 with the closeness of top periodic elections. Controlling statistically for the number of levels of such national officers (i.e. holding the number of levels 'constant'), the partial correlation of the total number of such national officials with the closeness of top periodic elections is ·43. Thus, it appears that more officials per level favours opposition.

We are now in a better position to appreciate the effects of union size on electoral competition among the periodic unions. Size correlates ·71 with the number of elected, necessarily full-time national officers, but it correlates only ·07 with the number of levels of such officers. Thus, the *larger* unions have *more such elected officers per level*. We also know that size correlates ·77 with the number of next-to-top officers, all considered, among the periodic group, thus confirming this deduction for the next-to-top level.

We may also speculate that the usual tendency of small groups to suppress overt competition among their members operates when there are too few full-time national officers. Such competition would be particularly unacceptable when directed against an incumbent. Perhaps this helps to explain the complete consistency with which five of the relatively small unions avoided competition in top or next-to-top periodic elections during 1949–66. They had a median of four elected full-time national officers (two, three, four, five and eight), as compared to a median of seven (and a range of from two to fourteen) for the remaining periodic unions. The two unions with the largest numbers of such officers were the Engineers (fourteen) and the Foundry Workers (eleven).

Geographic Departures from Simple Hierarchy
Departures from simple hierarchical geographic organisation may take place in the form of geographic as well as occupational subdivisions, e.g. with optional regional groupings of branches outside the usual authority structure (as in the Shop Workers) or with an autonomous section (e.g. the Engineers' former Australian affiliate). The correlations of the presence of such geographic departures with the closeness of elections are similar to those of the other complexity items: negative for top permanent-post vacancy elections (biserial $r = -\cdot56$), and positive within the periodic group (·56 and ·16 respectively for top vacant-post and periodic elections, and ·08 and ·20 respectively for the corresponding next-to-top elections). These results should be received cautiously, since only two permanent-post unions and two periodic had such geographic departures from hierarchical structure.

Conclusions

The British findings show that union size is only weakly or inconsistently associated with certain aspects of organisational complexity, most importantly the number of levels of elected, necessarily full-time national officers. They also show that certain complexity variables are inconsistently associated with each other; in particular, the number of levels of hierarchical geographic organisation is associated positively with the number of levels of nationally-appointed full-time officers in the permanent-post group, but negatively with this same variable in the periodic group. Insofar as the effects of complexity on electoral opposition are concerned, it is suggested that complexity is a contingent variable. To over-simplify somewhat, a greater vertical differentiation, in the form of levels of organisation and levels and numbers of full-time elected officials, is favourable for democracy if the overall organisational context is favourable to democracy in other respects – especially, if restrictions are placed on the powers of appointment for the leading national officers. In a generally unfavourable context such vertical differentiation is, in itself, an added detriment. Some other complexity variables are considered below in connection with the organisation of conventions.

CONVENTION DELEGATES

Convention Size

We hypothesised that the independent power of small conventions would be greater as against that of the top officer and other national officers. However, none of the British samples reached the American mean of 886 voting convention delegates, and only two approached it: the Transport and General Workers (750), and the Shop and Distributive Workers (775), both of which are general unions in the permanent-post group. The largest number of voting delegates in the remaining permanent-post unions was 360, and the largest number in the periodic group was 330. The basic reason for the smaller number of delegates in the British unions is the prevalence of district (and/or occupational) representation, rather than branch. District representation may be considered to be a form of vertical differentiation.

The Transport and General Workers would have had thousands of delegates on the basis of branch representation. All of the American sample used branch (local) representation, supplemented in some instances by a small number of delegates representing other subdivisions. Branch representation at conventions was used by only five of the British permanent-post group, and by only four of the periodic. Largely as a result of district representation, there were 100 or fewer delegates in four of the permanent-post unions, and in eight of the periodic. The number of delegates is associated with the number of members in the permanent-post group ($r = \cdot 59$, $N = 14$), but not in the periodic group ($r = -\cdot 08$, $N = 15$). Adequate data were *not* available for the Painters (permanent-post). The Patternmakers (periodic) did not institute conventions until 1963.

The absence of very large conventions in Britain tends to limit the possibilities for finding close associations between the number of delegates and the closeness of elections. Although all such correlations were in the expected direction, except that for next-to-top vacant-post elections in the periodic group, all were negligible except that for top vacant-post elections in this same group ($-\cdot 25$, $N = 14$) (see Table 5.3). These findings are similar to those for the American unions.

District v. Branch Representation
We hypothesised that elections at conventions tend to be closer when delegates are elected from larger constituencies, in the sense of a greater number of members and/or of branches per constituency. Although top and next-to-top full-time officers were not elected by convention in Britain, multi-branch constituencies were thought to be favourable for politicisation and competition generally. The four periodic unions which used branch representation included three (the Boot and Shoe Workers, the Fire Brigades, and the Furniture Trades) of the five with entirely-uncontested periodic elections during 1949–66. The fourth union was the Heating Engineers. Although the Fire Brigades elected within 162 areas, we judged these to be the equivalent of local unions on the basis of their small size (a mean of approximately 150 members), control over local finances, and initiation of resolutions to conferences. The mean closeness of top vacant-post elections for these unions with branch representation was also noticeably below that for the remainder of the periodic sample, but there was a reversal for next-to-top elections.

The findings for the five permanent-post unions with branch representation at the convention were decidedly in the opposite direction to prediction. The unions with branch representation had a mean runner-up percentage of 67·1 for top vacant-post elections (the mean for the permanent-post subsample was 56·3). Only one of the five, the Shop and Distributive Workers, had any nationally-appointed executive councillors or full-time next-to-top officers, but this is not enough, in itself, to account for the opposite findings. The other permanent-post unions were the Printing and Bookbinding Workers, the Tailors, the Health Service Employees, and the Typographical Association. The extremely weak electoral opposition in the two railway unions, which used district representation, is again part of the explanation. We do know, from a previous study of seventy-seven British unions of all types (Edelstein and Ruppel, 1970), that district representation was more common among the larger unions and that it was associated with more frequent conventions at all size intervals. Insofar as convention frequency facilitates democracy, there is some indirect support for the notion that district representation is favourable for opposition.

Numbers of Branches and Members per Constituency

More sophisticated indicators of larger and more complex constituencies for the election of convention delegates were available and are related as anticipated to electoral opposition. In the periodic group, the mean number of *branches* (locals) per constituency correlates ·39 and ·38 respectively with the closeness of top vacant-post and periodic elections, and ·11 and ·48 respectively for the corresponding next-to-top elections ($N = 13$ for vacant-post elections, $N = 14$ for periodic elections). The correlation with the closeness of elections to permanent top posts is ·18 ($N = 14$). The methods of choosing delegates in multi-branch constituencies included election by referendum and by district-wide conventions, and selection by relatively small district committees. The number of branches per constituency correlates ·89 with union size in the periodic group, and ·44 in the permanent-post group.

The mean number of *members* per constituency in the periodic group correlates ·80 with the mean number of branches, and its correlations with the closeness of elections are appreciable but somewhat lower, being ·26 and ·33 respectively for top vacant-post and periodic elections, and ·10 and ·39 respectively for the corresponding next-to-top elections ($N = 14$ for vacant-post elections, $N = 15$ for periodic elections). Data were not available for the permanent-post unions. The greater importance of the number of branches is consistent with the structural emphasis of our theory of opposition.

Occupational–Industrial Representation

Although we defined 'district' representation at the convention so as to include any type of supra-branch subdivisional representation, the formal representation of occupational or industrial groups was, on the whole, associated with less effective electoral opposition. The percentage of delegates representing such groups has moderately negative correlations with the closeness of next-to-top vacant-post and periodic elections in the periodic group ($-·36$ for each), and with that of top permanent-post elections as well ($-·34$, $N = 14$). The correlations with the closeness of the periodic group's top elections are positive, but much lower (·15 and ·13 respectively for vacant-post and periodic elections).

A related variable, the percentage of the *executive council* representing specific categories of members (by occupation, industry, skill, corporation, sex, etc.), has mixed directions of association with the closeness of elections in the periodic group (all *r*s in the ·30s), and a correlation of $-·54$ with that of top permanent-post elections. Our finding was similar to that of Marcus (1966) in his study of American unions, in that permanent-post unions with a greater percentage of subgroup representation tended to hold their regular conventions more frequently ($r = \cdot33$). The correlation among the periodic unions is negligible ($\cdot05$). For the entire British sample it is $\cdot18$ ($N = 31$). We doubt that these positive associations reflect anything of general importance. A mean of 14 per cent of British executive councillors represented specific categories of members (the standard deviation was 27 per cent). We assume that in most cases such representation, whether at conventions or at executive councils, is a *substitute* for geographic representation and hence does not involve the overlapping membership which, we have suggested, undermines official hierarchies and is conducive to electoral opposition. Our findings suggest that occupational representation does not, in itself, facilitate opposition. Carried to an extreme, we suspect that it would undermine opposition through electoral channels by solidarising subgroups and their respective leaders, and by encouraging either apathy or compromise (and, rarely, break-aways), depending upon the relationship of forces (see Lipset, 1956: 307).

The Status of Voting Delegates

We hypothesised that the smaller the proportion of nationally-appointed or controlled officials as convention delegates, the closer the elections. This should apply even when top officials are elected by referendum.

Eight periodic unions which held conventions had only one national official, not necessarily full-time, with voting rights at the convention on an *ex officio* basis, in most instances only to break a tie vote. Another four denied voting rights to any national officer, in any circumstances. The remaining three had between five and eight national officers with *ex officio* voting rights: in the Shipconstructors, eight full-time national officers had almost one-third of the total of twenty-five votes at the convention; and in the Boilermakers and the Boot and Shoe Operatives, national officers had 6 and 3 per cent of the votes respectively.

The percentage of the convention votes allotted constitutionally to national officers correlates negatively, as expected, with all the measures of electoral opposition: $-\cdot26$ and $-\cdot38$ respectively with the closeness of top and next-to-top vacant-post elections in the periodic group ($N = 14$); $-\cdot24$ and $-\cdot32$ respectively for the corresponding periodic elections ($N = 15$); and $-\cdot20$ with the closeness of top permanent-post elections ($N = 14$).

British unions which did not provide *ex officio* delegate status, with votes, to national officers may nevertheless have permitted full-time local or divisional officers to compete for the position of convention delegate. These two non-rank-and-file variables correlate $\cdot22$ ($N = 15$) in the periodic

group. The percentage of rank-and-file voting delegates, in practice, correlates $-\cdot70$ ($N = 15$) with the number of national officers with votes among
the periodic unions, and $-\cdot80$ ($N = 13$) among the permanent-post unions.
Four periodic unions had between one-fifth and one-third of their convention delegates with full-time status, in practice, and another two had 10 and
15 per cent of such delegates so. (We assume that the overwhelming majority were elected, as delegates.) Nine periodic unions had between 97 and
100 per cent of such delegates from the rank-and-file.

The percentage of rank-and-file delegates is positively associated with
the closeness of elections, the correlations for top and next-to-top vacant-
post elections in the periodic group being $\cdot66$ and $\cdot39$ respectively ($N = 14$),
and for the corresponding periodic elections $\cdot28$ and $\cdot13$ respectively
($N = 15$). The correlation for top permanent-post vacancy elections is
negligible ($\cdot02$, $N = 13$).

We had hypothesised that a 'small to moderate' percentage of locally- or
regionally-controlled full-time officials as elected delegates is the optimum
condition for electoral opposition. In the periodic group this percentage
was not simply the opposite side to the coin of the percentage of rank-and-
file delegates, since the latter could also be substantially reduced by
national officials with *ex officio* status as voting delegates. The six periodic
unions with full-time local or regional officials as delegates had them in
these percentages: 30, 25, 15, 14, 10 and 3. The negative correlation in the
periodic group between the percentage of rank-and-file delegates and the
percentage of local or regional full-time officials as delegates is nevertheless
fairly high ($r = -\cdot75$, $N = 15$). It is $-\cdot99$ ($N = 13$) in the permanent-
post group. The percentage of such full-time delegates correlates $-\cdot56$
($N = 14$) and $-\cdot32$ ($N = 15$) respectively with the closeness of top vacant-
post and periodic elections. All other correlations with the closeness of
elections are negligible (under $\cdot04$). Thus, the percentage of subdivisionally-
controlled full-time officials as delegates is crudely similar, but inferior as
a predictor, to its superficial obverse: the percentage of rank-and-file
delegates.

If there is an optimum percentage of subdivisionally-controlled full-time
officials as delegates, one may speculate on the basis of our findings that it
is well under 20 per cent. As a practical matter, a firm prescription of rank-
and-file status for convention delegates may be the best formula for union
democracy. If lower-ranking full-time officials should indeed be given the
opportunity to politick with and gain reputations among rank-and-file
activists, including convention delegates, then perhaps some special format
at the convention or some other vehicle should be found.

THE FORMAL POWER OF THE CONVENTION

The convention was the supreme authority on questions of policy in the large majority of the British sample, but in five periodic and three permanent-post unions this authority was limited or absent, or the convention itself did not exist. The relationship of such authority to opposition was tested using a scale which provided for the convention's supreme authority, supreme authority on most questions (one permanent-post union), purely advisory powers (four periodic and one permanent-post), or absence (one periodic and one permanent-post). The directions of association in the periodic group are mixed, with the size of the positive correlations with the closeness of vacant-post elections ($\cdot33$ and $\cdot35$ respectively for top and next-to-top elections) outweighing the negative correlations with that of periodic elections ($-\cdot23$ and $-\cdot18$ respectively). The correlation with top permanent-post vacancy elections is $\cdot12$ (cf. Allen, 1954: 110).

As a set, the convention variables reported here and earlier, under convention frequency, were rather successful predictors of electoral competition. Some of the degrees of association are surprising, considering the fact that the elections in question were held by referendum.

CONCLUSIONS

Our organisational theory of union democracy was *strongly* supported in the sixteen British unions which elected their leading full-time officers periodically. This conclusion is based on an examination of the simple associations of forty-one predictor variables with the closeness of vacant-post and periodic elections to top and next-to-top offices. This overall finding was possible in spite of the very low, or moderately negative, correlations between closeness of vacant-post and periodic elections.

The theory received *no* general support, on the other hand, in the very heterogeneous group of fifteen British unions electing to top permanent posts. Seven of these unions either appointed rather than elected their second-ranking officers, or had none assigned to full-time national duties, so this conclusion is based solely on the closeness of elections to fill top vacancies.

The Unions Electing Periodically
The American variables.   Focusing for the moment on the twenty variables for which data were available for both the American unions and British periodic unions, it was found that eighteen of the twenty British correlations (90 per cent) with the closeness of top vacant-post elections were in the hypothesised directions (see Table 5.3). The corresponding figures for top periodic elections were seventeen of twenty (85 per cent). Those for

next-to-top vacant-post and periodic elections were lower: fourteen (70 per cent) and fifteen (75 per cent) of twenty respectively. (Only nine of twenty top permanent-post associations were in the predicted directions.)

A more wholistic view of the twenty variables' associations with the four measures of electoral opposition in the periodic group shows sixteen of the twenty with correlations predominantly as expected, e.g. three correlations of ·48, ·13 and ·09 in the predicted direction, and one of −·39 in the opposite direction. An even more wholistic approach shows twelve general areas of content, with from one to four variables in each area for the periodic group. Only two of the twelve, each represented by a single item, failed to correlate generally as expected: the time between regular conventions, and the formal direction of the top officer by the executive council. However, related but more sophisticated items covering these two areas, not available for the American analysis, were good predictors of electoral opposition.

The areas most highly associated with the closeness of elections to top posts in the periodic group were the appeals system, the composition of the executive council, the absence of a single logical successor, the number of elections of top officers, the number of levels of elected full-time officers, and the number of levels of hierarchical geographic organisation. The last was unsuccessful in the United States. The other areas associated as expected with electoral opposition in the periodic group, but less highly so, were the number of voting convention delegates (fewer being associated with more effective opposition), the electoral system, and the number of next-to-top officers. Of these, only the last was unsuccessful in the United States. Thus, there was, in the areas associated as expected with electoral competition, considerable overlap between the American unions and those British unions which elected periodically. The frequency of conventions may also be considered an area in common, *if* we may substitute, for Britain, the mean number of regular convention days in session per year during 1949–66. (See the conclusion to Chapter 5, pages 143–7.)

Additional British variables.   Of the twenty-one additional predictors tried in Britain, nineteen (90 per cent) correlated in the expected direction with the closeness of elections to fill top vacancies in the periodic group. The corresponding figures for next-to-top vacant-post elections were seventeen of twenty (85 per cent), for top periodic elections fifteen of twenty-one (71 per cent), and for next-to-top periodic elections fifteen of twenty (75 per cent). On the basis of the twenty-one sets of associations with the four measures of closeness of elections, twelve variables could be called fairly successful predictors, six might be described as from moderately to somewhat successful, and only three tended to disconfirm the hypotheses associated with them.

Eleven of the fairly successful predictors had at least one simple correlation of ·45 or more in the expected direction with a closeness of elections variable, and either no contrary correlations in its set or only one low contrary correlation. In terms of very broad content areas, the *most successful* predictors not available in the American analysis dealt with the status hierarchy, national power centres, civil liberties, and non-hierarchical structural relationships (the latter was entirely absent in the American study). The twelve fairly successful predictors follow (+ indicates an hypothesised direct relationship; − indicates an hypothesised inverse relationship):

— The percentage of the period 1949–66 with two top officers (+) (Hypothesis 1).
— The number of logical successors, under the constitution (categories ranked so that one such successor would be the least favourable alternative) (+) (H. 1).
— The number of elected, necessarily full-time national officers (+) (H. 1).
— The number of levels of elected full-time or permissibly full-time officers at and higher than major regions (+) (H. 3 and 2).
— The percentage of rank-and-file convention delegates, in practice (highly related to rules) (+) (H. 10).
— The mean number of regular convention days per year during 1949–66 (+) (H. 10).
— The power of the executive council to suspend or remove the top officer (+) (H. 10).
— An overall rating of the appeals process (+) (H. 10, and civil liberties).
— The number of branches per constituency for convention delegates (+) (H. 14).
— The number of members per constituency for convention delegates (+) (H. 14).
— The number of levels of non-geographic organisation outside a simple hierarchical structure (overlapping hierarchical geographic organisation) (+) (H. 21).
— The existence of geographic departures from simple hierarchical structure (e.g. optional or autonomous associations of branches) (+) (H. 21).

The following six predictors not available for the United States may be described as from moderately to somewhat successful predictors of the closeness of elections in the periodic group:

— The sum of the scores on ten appeals items (+) (H. 10, and civil liberties).

— Limitations on the top officer's voting rights in the executive council (+) (H. 10).
— The percentage of convention votes allotted by rule to national officers (−) (H. 10).
— The authority (and existence of) the convention (+) (H. 10).
— District rather than branch representation at the convention (+) (H. 14).
— The weighted average of the electoral system used in choosing the executive council (+) (H. 19).

The hypothesis must be tentatively rejected that electoral opposition is enhanced by a 'small-to-moderate' percentage of locally- or regionally-elected full-time officers among the elected convention delegates, if by moderate one means 25 to 30 per cent. However, the data were not suitable for testing this hypothesis on percentages under 20.

The percentage of branches with full-time officers was associated negatively rather than positively with electoral opposition, but we suspect that this is due in part to the common British prohibition on full-time officers serving as convention delegates and in other capacities where they may achieve a wider reputation. Periodic unions with greater percentages of full-time branch officers tended to have fewer levels of hierarchical geographic organisation, which was less favourable to opposition. It may be that full-time branch officers are a partial substitute for numerous full-time district officers, who, as in the Engineers, would be in a better position to compete for higher full-time posts.

There was no confirmation of our hypothesis that a supplementary part-time presidency alongside the general secretaryship might facilitate opposition by offering an alternative path to relatively high full-time office. However, this finding *cannot* be taken at face value because of the necessarily negative relationship between this variable and the number of top full-time officers (which, if two, would include a full-time president).

Finally, we explored the relationship between constitutionally-prescribed occupational–industrial representation, both at the convention and on the executive council, and the closeness of elections. Such representation presumably was usually a substitute for, rather than auxiliary to, geographic representation, and thus did not ordinarily provide departures from simple hierarchical structure. Such representation neither on the executive council nor at the convention was associated with closer elections in the periodic group, and its association with the closeness of elections to permanent top posts were moderately negative.

The Unions Electing Permanently

Chance may have been a factor in the lack of general support for the theory, since seven permanent-post unions had only one vacancy during 1949–67.

However, we attribute this lack of support primarily to: the heterogeneous nature of the permanent-post sub-sample, especially the inclusion of three general unions; the national appointment of some executive councillors and of second-ranking officers in some unions, which overshadowed and changed the significance of many other variables (especially those associated with organisational complexity); and the anomaly of the two railway unions, in which some fairly democratic features were associated with a strong general bias in favour of seniority for next-to-top officers.[20]

The large majority of correlations in the permanent-post group were quite low, and about as often as not in a direction opposite to that for the closeness of elections in the periodic group. The two most powerful predictors of the closeness of elections to fill top vacancies were both directly related to the question of succession: the absence of an apprenticeship title (assistant general secretary or vice-president) for a full-time officer, and the absence of a logical successor, all considered ($r = \cdot65$ for each). The latter is not a truly independent variable, and may be interpreted as showing that close elections tend to result when there is no single job title, held by a single individual, from which advancement to the top office takes place. The purely constitutional version of this scale, which had a substantial correlation with the closeness of top vacant-post elections in the periodic group, had a negligible correlation with the closeness of top permanent-post elections. The number of levels of nationally-appointed full-time officials, and the appointment rather than the election of next-to-top officers, were both negatively associated with the closeness of elections.

There is no direct evidence that election for life depresses opposition in elections to fill top vacancies, although it should be noted that permanence applies also to lower-level officials who may compete for the top post. Nevertheless, election for life takes away the practical possibility of removing the top officer prior to his retirement, and hence of a forceful way of demonstrating opposition to his policies.

Portrait of the Democratic Periodic Union: An Organisational Design
The composite portrait of the most democratic British periodic unions has features similar to the American, but there is much greater emphasis on organisational structure and much more severe limitations on the powers of the top and other full-time officers. The reader can compare these portraits with the models of oligarchy described in Chapter 2, and draw his own conclusions. With only some extrapolation beyond the reality of any particular union in Britain, the democratic union has a complex structure, with several levels of geographic organisation and many levels of elected full-time office, a few of which have the status of national officer. It is a large union, as it must be to sustain this structure. There are no appointed full-time officers whatsoever, and at each level of full-time office

short of the top there are a number of potential competitors for still higher office. At the pinnacle there is a division of power between two equal top officers with different functions. These top officers work under the direction of the executive council, which may suspend them and take steps to remove them from office. The executive council itself consists of full-time officers elected within geographic subdivisions of the union. The top officers have no vote on the executive council, even to break a tie. They also have no vote at the small annual conference, which meets for a fortnight, nor do any of the full-time officers. The annual conference and the final appeals court consist entirely of elected rank-and-filers (although arbitration boards with other compositions would be possible).

All full-time officers are elected by referendum with run-offs when necessary to achieve an absolute majority, but periodic elections are not held as frequently as in the United States. However, important vacancies are more frequent, largely because more than one officer exists at each rank, but also because of the retirement age. Elections to fill top vacancies are often close, but those against top incumbents are only occasionally so.

If the reader is reminded of the Engineers (see Chapter 9), this is appropriate; the only point of difference is that the Engineers lack as great restrictions on the powers of the president. Nonetheless, they remain a critical case for the theory, as do the Mineworkers.

NOTES TO CHAPTER 6

1 There were only two relatively pure craft unions, one among the periodic and one among the permanent-post group.
2 With pre-1949 data included, the correlation between periodic top and next-to-top elections rose to ·71 ($N = 17$), but that between top and next-to-top vacancies virtually disappeared, for both the periodic group and the sample as a whole. The number of next-to-top officers and their duties were not stabilised in some unions until after World War II. Two formerly periodic unions became permanent-post by 1949. The 1949–66 measures are more valid.
3 The findings were similar, but with generally lower correlations, for the frequency of regular *plus* special conventions. This mean interval between conventions was 4·2 months shorter.
4 The mean number of convention days per year was 3·8 for the permanent-post unions (the standard deviation was 3·1) and 3·5 for the periodic unions (the standard deviation was 2·3).
5 The Sheet Metal Workers, which according to Allen (1954: 170) used arbitration, was the missing case in this particular analysis.
6 The correlation between the six-point and nine-point scale was only ·20 among the periodic unions and ·63 among the permanent-post but it was ·85 in the United States. (In no more than a few British unions would the highest levels of appeal of officers and members have been different.)
7 The correlation between this scale and the six-point scale for *level* of appeal, also short of a referendum, was ·74 within the periodic group and ·34 within

the permanent-post. The correlations with appeal by a subordinate officer, including the possibility of a referendum, were $-\cdot03$ in each group.

8 Two almost uniformly bad items contributing towards the total score dealt with local jurisdiction in appeals cases. The greater culprit was: 'Was there a provision that a member may be expelled only by his own local union, or with its consent?' 'Yes', on a three-point scale, was scored as most favourable to democracy.

9 Each of the four periodic unions with two approximately equal top officers fell in a different group in Table 6.3.

10 We have not discussed larger general councils with the power to veto executive council decisions, but we doubt that they are much of an asset to democracy in themselves. The large executive councils in the permanent-post group have the full powers of governing bodies.

11 The Plasterers appear to have established such a post in 1948, only to abolish it in 1953 (see Newman, 1960: 120, 128–9).

12 The only instance was in the 1920s. The general secretary elected in 1966 went from the assistant general secretaryship to the executive council in order to achieve the top post.

13 The most favourable circumstance for opposition did not exist in the sample: the existence of *both* titles, assistant general secretary *and* vice-president, for full-time officers.

14 There was another anomaly involving this variable. It correlated $-\cdot17$ with the closeness of top periodic elections, while the *number* of next-to-top posts under the constitution correlated $\cdot30$, although the correlation between the two variables was $\cdot61$. The shrunken multiple correlation of these two variables together for predicting the closeness of top periodic elections was $\cdot48$ ($\cdot53$ before shrinkage).

15 We departed from a strict constitutional interpretation in the case of the Boilermakers, for reasons cited earlier.

16 Presumably the signed ballot papers were not scrutinised at the voting place, although there may have been instances where ballots were circulated and collected at work by individual branch officers.

17 This scale's correlations with the closeness of elections were $\cdot54$ and $\cdot21$ respectively ($N = 14$) for top and next-to-top vacant posts among the periodic group, and $\cdot34$ for top permanent-post vacancies. Those with that of periodic elections were negative but negligible ($-\cdot05$ and $-\cdot03$ respectively for top and next-to-top posts).

18 See Hall (1972: 109–71) for dimensions of complexity (vertical, horizontal and spatial) and for a review of research on size and complexity. There is little cited on membership organisations, which reflects the state of the field.

19 Six permanent-post unions, including the three general unions plus the Agricultural Workers, the Seamen, and the Bakers, had only one truly-elected official devoted full-time, constitutionally, to national duties. Three had only two such officials.

20 See note 5, pages 204–5, and page 194, regarding the moderate correlations of our organisational predictors with the extent of mixed leadership in the permanent-post group.

Chapter 7

Opposition, Factions and Political Culture

In this chapter we shall discuss factors apart from formal organisation which may have influenced the findings. In particular, we shall be concerned with some of the broader differences between the British and American labour movements, and to a lesser extent with historical and contextual factors within each country which may have influenced electoral competition.

FACTIONS

The finding of substantially closer British, as compared to American, elections to fill top and next-to-top vacancies was not paralleled with respect to contests against incumbents. It will be recalled that for top vacant-post elections there was a difference of 43·6 in the mean number of votes for the runner-up per 100 for the winner in favour of Britain, but a difference of only 5·9 where top periodic elections were concerned. Since by far most of the organisational variables we have discussed related as expected to both vacant-post and periodic elections within each country, we have to look further for an explanation. We speculate that the absence of openly-operating internal factions in British unions, to be described, accounts for our failure to find large differences in favour of Britain in the success of opposition in periodic elections, in spite of the otherwise much more favourable organisational climate. The logic is, simply, that effective opposition against an incumbent, and especially against an incumbent administration, requires effective internal oppositional organisation.

We shall use the term 'faction' for *an at least somewhat organised special-purpose political group within a larger organisation.* This definition seems to encompass its conventional meaning more or less. A local branch or other recognised stable unit of a larger organisation might very well support a faction, or engage in activities which a faction might undertake, without itself being a faction or a part of faction. Loosely speaking, any political activity of a controversial nature, or in support of some subgroup, could be called 'factional', but in the absence of an organised faction we would prefer to equate 'factional' with 'political'. A 'party' within an organisation would then be a stable faction, oriented towards political power, with an open appeal to a broad section of the membership.

In our increasingly organisational society, factionalism within membership organisations is an important part of the overall political process. This is most evident within political parties, where the outcomes of ideological struggles and contests for leadership often largely determine the choices available to an electorate. However, trade unions, professional associations and other membership organisations are often the arenas for political struggles which directly or indirectly affect the overall political process. American associations of anthropologists, historians and other professionals have recently been agitated by differences over the South-East Asian war, and by pressures from openly-organised factions of blacks, women and radicals.

Ostensibly apolitical union office-seekers in both countries periodically accuse incumbents of too soft a policy in the pursuit of wage demands, at times with a direct impact on government attempts to regulate wages. Indeed, it might be difficult to find in any moderately large membership organisation a struggle which does not have a rather obvious external political implication.

Political controversy within unions often reflects the influence of competing external organisations or forces, particularly those with structures penetrating or overlapping the structures of individual unions, e.g. the left–right division in the Labour Party. The fact of ideological penetration has been noted, and offered as an explanation for democracy in the Saskatchewan Wheat Pool, with the suggestion that, in general, a stable organisational democracy may be sustained by competition among external political forces (*a*) when 'the organization itself is non-partisan but provides only an opportunity, or a forum, within which contending positions may be heard', (*b*) when 'the issues themselves are not matters of life and death' to the organisation, and (*c*) particularly where 'a mechanism of structured conflict seems to be the only method' for determining the outcome of the ideological competition (Craig and Gross, 1970: 32). An important feature of such a forum is the right, supported by values and traditions, to further a policy through the available mechanisms. The major difficulty with this approach lies in the unspecified supportive organisational forms to be used in a society where, although democratic norms are assumed, these are ordinarily insufficient in themselves to provide the basis for a forum, even in the situation described.

Organisations usually try to control the spread of deviance. This may take the form of a *taboo on the formalisation of factions*. But permissiveness *vis-à-vis* factions does not *necessarily* lead to disruption, or even divisiveness (see Etzioni, 1961: 245). The organised expression of conflict may be necessary to *maintain the relationship* of the faction's members to the organisation (see Coser, 1964: 47). The alternative may be a break-away organisation, or expulsion of the members singly. British unions seem to have solved the latter problems while maintaining the taboo, at the expense of a more vital democracy.

British Factions

We agree basically with V. L. Allen's remark that 'There is never, in this country [Britain], a legitimate opposition admitted in a trade union' (1954: 234). B. C. Roberts has stated, along similar lines, that in Britain:

'The principle cherished in the trade unions is that of the "best man for the job," with candidates for office standing as active trade unionists and not as members of a group or party. The organization of a collective opposition has always been looked upon as an activity seriously endangering the sense of unity and brotherhood which is the bedrock of trade union organization. To this end many unions have rules which forbid canvassing, the circulation of correspondence between branches and committees, unless specifically authorized by the national executive council, and the attendance of members of one branch at the meetings of another' (1956: 243–4).

Many American trade union oligarchs have expressed and enforced such views (although most such interference is now illegal under the Landrum-Griffin Act), and caution has no doubt been the better part of valour where their rank-and-files have considered acting otherwise than in accordance with them. Nevertheless, factions have existed openly and in principle *legitimately*, a point of crucial importance, in many American unions, as we shall show.

British factions exist, but as internal organisations they are almost invariably only semi-organised, covertly organised, or at least relatively restrained in organisational techniques, although the situation is changing. For example, such techniques include:

1   Loose communications networks of like-minded, usually politicised, officers and activists, each participant establishing his own sub-network via the use of letters, the telephone and occasional personal contact. (May overlap with 3.)
2   Communications networks sometimes co-ordinated by members of outside political parties or groups, e.g. Communists, left-wing or Gaitskellite members of the Labour Party during 1959–60. (May overlap with 3.)

3 Shop stewards' movements, usually left-wing, often including members of various unions.
4 In a few instances, unpublicised but not entirely covert meetings of full-time officials, which may be held during annual or semi-annual meetings of full-time staff.

Communist and Anti-Communist Factions in British Unions
The political struggles in some unions have at times centred on specifically Communist and anti-Communist factions, with external organisations and publications playing some role in the outcome of elections. The Communists (Communist Party) have often been the best (or even the only) organised left-wing group in some unions, and have thus been in a position to take advantage of militant or left-wing sentiment to achieve elective office. Recently, however, Trotskyist groups like the International Socialists have been prominent. Presumably in response to this, organisations have been formed to operate within unions to counter what they claimed to be an organised attempt of the official international Communist movement to dominate the labour movement. In addition to these special anti-Communist groups, the official federation of national unions has at times intervened. This applies to the United States as well as Britain, but the struggle has been more prolonged in the latter (see Pelling, 1958). The mass media have, of course, often exaggerated the role of the Communist Party, particularly in unofficial strikes.

The persistence with which the official Communist Party has played a role in British intra-union politics can be understood only in the light of the organisational weakness of the non-Communist left, and of what may be characterised as the common British (but not American) view among not a small number of workers that the Party is still a part of the working class and socialist movement – i.e. still within an acceptable range of deviation.

Perhaps our statement that Communists are considered as a part of the working-class movement in Britain is an overstatement, but the fact is that anti-Communism as such is not socially acceptable among most groups of unionists. For example, the behaviour of a union member who publicly argues at a branch meeting that a candidate should not be elected to union office because he is a Communist would probably, we believe, be regarded as eccentric and socially unacceptable. At any rate, it 'just isn't done' in most local situations. This has not been the case in the United States, even before the 'cold war'. The greater British tolerance of dissent is no doubt a factor, but tolerance of vocal supporters of the Conservative Party is not particularly great in many unions, e.g. the Mineworkers.

As long ago as 1928, the Trades Union Congress attacked the influence of Communist organisations in the unions, and the 1929 Congress warned them of disruptive Communist activities. At that time the Party was trying to set up break-away organisations through the tactic of the 'Minority Movement', whose aim was to set up contacts in Britain for the 'Red International of Labour Unions' (RILU). This tactic failed and a consequent tactic of infiltration led the TUC in 1934 to counter the Communists, particularly in the trade councils (for fuller details see Martin, 1969). At that time the Communist Party was trying to secure affiliation to the Labour Party under the guise of the 'United Front' campaign. A similar 'United Front' policy was pursued from 1939 to 1941 for the purpose of 'stopping the war', and after 1941 for the purpose of 'winning the war'. There were also similar attempts in the immediate post-war period (see Trades Union Congress, 1948a and b). Two policy statements on the trade unions and Communism were published by the TUC in 1948, and there was considerable activity, via official union channels, during the 'cold war' years to challenge Communist influence within trade unions.

One anti-Communist counter-organisation, 'Common Cause', has been quite active in backing anti-Communist factional activity (see C. Jenkins, 1964; Fore, 1970: 5, 9). It was organised in England in 1951, although it had been founded in the United States in 1947. It was reported in May 1969 that 'Common Cause' was acting as the channel through which money from industrial sources was passed to the Industrial Research Information Services, an anti-Communist body organised by former trade unionists including Jack Tanner, former president of the Engineers. IRIS concentrates its activities on exposing Communists and left-wing militants in the union movement in its publication, *IRIS News*. It had been condemned by the TUC in 1960 as an organisation which appears mainly to be devoted to influencing union elections (see Foot, 1967). The organisation had been set up in 1956. *IRIS News* is still published and concentrates on 'exposing' to trade union members, candidates whom they believe to be Communists, Trotskyists or fellow travellers in coming union elections (see pp. 282-6).[1]

It would seem that the secrecy and deviousness in electioneering made necessary by the illegality and illegitimacy of open factions in Britain gives such Communist and anti-Communist organisations a special advantage: a good deal of secrecy is necessary simply to avoid disciplinary action and an invalidation of the results of the election. The effect of restrictive rules (and perhaps of such normative support as they may have) is illustrated by this credible news item by an 'Industrial Correspondent' for the *Sunday Times* (15 August 1965):

'Secret committees of anti-Communists all over the country are fighting a determined battle to ensure that the Amalgamated Engineering Union does not fall into Communist hands. The central point of the movement, which is believed to have the unofficial backing of the AEU's president, Sir William Carron, is in the Midlands . . .; committees have been established in other parts of the country. . . . A national organiser linking these committees is also believed to be operating from London. . . .

'The committees adopt the secrecy and discipline of the Communists themselves. They will not, for example, reveal their numbers or allow themselves to be quoted by name.

'Perhaps their most effective way of breaking the apathy of voters is to alert members whenever a Communist is standing. A typical method is being used at present by a Midland committee.

'A pamphlet has been printed which suggests, in none-too subtle a manner, that one of the candidates in a coming election is a Communist sympathiser, but the pamphlet is not sent to all union members. "It is given to a few trusted friends who then pass on the information verbally."

'The rules of the AEU expressly forbid the use of such pamphlets.'[2]

Prohibition of Campaign Literature

No union in the British sample has constitutional guarantees regarding the free circulation of campaign literature in union elections, and during 1949–66 only the Shop and Distributive Workers had, in practice, a wide and unrestricted circulation of such literature (B. C. Roberts, 1956: 245). A branch can circulate its literature through the machinery of the head office. Indeed, in 1967 there was a non-secret anti-Communist faction, the Progressive Labour Group, reportedly with a formal membership and a five-shilling annual subscription. Left-wing groups also operate rather freely, but it is not clear whether they have done so as openly as organised factions. There was a general prohibition on printed campaign literature apart from – possibly – material published by the union itself in thirteen of the sixteen periodic unions and eight of the fifteen permanent-post unions. In the remainder the rules were silent, but other formal bodies may have prohibited such electioneering. However, those unions with constitutional bans on general campaign literature were somewhat more likely to have rules requiring the circulation, by the union itself, of election addresses or, simply, biographies of candidates, the latter rated as a greater restriction than election addresses on a four-point scale (biserial $r = \cdot47$ in the periodic group, $\cdot21$ in the permanent-post).

Among the periodic unions, only two had no constitutional requirements for the circulation of some form of literature for top-post candidates, and in another two there was some doubt as to whether some such literature was mandatory. This was in contrast to eight permanent-post unions with no such requirements, and another one where this was in doubt. At the opposite end of a six-point scale, seven periodic but only two permanent-post unions required the distribution of candidates' election addresses, subject to either no or only mild restrictions as to content. Of the remaining periodic unions, one circulated biographies only and four circulated election addresses subject to severe restrictions. Each of the four remaining permanent-post unions required the circulation of biographies only. Where such literature was circulated by the unions, we believe that, in many cases, its volume was small and/or its method of distribution poor (in some unions only a very small number of copies going to each branch).

The six-point scale for the circulation of campaign literature by the union correlated moderately, in the expected direction, with all four measures of electoral opposition in the periodic unions,[3] but only negligibly so in the permanent-post unions. On the face of it, at least, some information on candidates is an aid to opposition. We expected a greater effect on periodic elections than on vacant-post elections because the incumbent would be so much better known', but this was not the case. The constitutional prohibition on unofficial campaign literature, on the other hand, was only weakly and inconsistently related to electoral opposition, probably because, in practice, there was little difference between opposition with and opposition without a constitutional ban.

Mixed Leadership

In spite of restrictions on free campaigning, fourteen of twenty-nine unions in the British sample had a mixed leadership throughout 1949–66, in the sense of having one or more recognised dissidents, or supporters of minority tendencies or factional groupings, either on the executive council or among other national officers of still higher rank. This was so in eight of the fourteen periodic unions for which we had information, and six of the fifteen permanent-post. In addition, two permanent-post unions had such mixed leadership for short periods. In the periodic group the percentage of the period 1949–66 with such mixed leadership correlated ·65 and ·55 respectively with the closeness of top and next-to-top vacant-post elections ($N = 13$), and ·32 and $-·13$ respectively for the corresponding periodic elections ($N = 14$). The correlation for top permanent-post elections was negative, $-·43$.[4] In this case, as in others cited previously, the negative finding is due partially to the two railway unions, which had the least-close top vacant-post elections but a mixed leadership throughout the period.[5]

Constitutional requirements for the union's circulation of campaign literature was associated with the presence of mixed leadership in both the periodic group ($r = ·49$, $N = 14$) and the permanent-post group ($r = ·23$, $N = 15$). We are sceptical that the circulation of such literature was effective enough, in itself, to produce this finding and the previously-cited association with close elections.

From other available data, it appears that there is a close relationship between the prevalence of a mixed leadership, and the continuity with which factional groupings operate *between* elections. This is true in both the permanent-post and the periodic groups. In the latter group, continuous factional activity is also moderately associated with the closeness of elections, except for top vacant-post elections. Our information on British factional organisation, we admit, leaves something to be desired, given the covert nature of British factionalism, but in our judgement factions operated in the periodic group, *between* elections, *continuously* in nine unions, sporadically in two more, and not at all (so far as we could determine) in five. The continuous operation of factions occurred in some unions outside the engineering industry: the Woodworkers, the Building Trades, the Plumbing Trades, the Fire Brigades, and – partially outside – the Sheet Metal Workers. The small Shipconstructors and the Patternmakers, which may be considered as in the engineering industry, did not seem to have any real factional activities between elections. The other periodic unions in which we could find very weak operations between elections were the Boilermakers, the Boot and Shoe Operatives, and the Operative Printers.

In the permanent-post group we could find continuous operation of factions between elections in only the Shop Workers, the Tailors, and the Painters. We considered the operation of factions between 1949 and 1966 to be sporadic in the Transport and General Workers, the Mineworkers, the Railwaymen, the Health Service Employees, and the Seamen.

These conclusions on factions suggest themselves:

1   It would appear that periodic elections are a stimulus to the creation and continuous operation of factions.
2   Even in Britain, periodic elections do not necessarily lead to the organisation of factions or, where they exist, to their continuous operation.
3   The continuous operation of factions in periodic unions is *not* necessarily associated with close elections (e.g. the Woodworkers), nor even with contested periodic elections for the top post (e.g. the Fire Brigades, the Plumbing Trades, and the Sheet Metal Workers). It is negatively associated with the closeness of top permanent-post vacancy elections ($r = -·52$, $N = 14$).
4   There is no simple relationship between the continuous activity of factions and the type of industries in which unions operate, although the four largest engineering unions did have such activity (see p. 282).
5   The more continuous operation of factions is strongly associated with the existence of a national union leadership of mixed political complexion (in both the periodic and permanent-post groups), but we believe that the mixed leadership is more a cause than an effect. Since in the permanent-post group neither a mixed leadership, nor a more continuous operation of factions, is positively associated with close

elections (in fact, the opposite is the case), it does not appear that mixed leaderships are due to electoral successes of factions.

On the whole then, there is no evidence that factions offer an alternative explanation for electoral opposition in Britain, especially where top vacancies are concerned. Continuously-operating factions seem to be a necessary, *but not a sufficient, condition for closer periodic elections.* Factions themselves are probably stimulated by a favourable organisational climate (the correlation of their continuity of operation with constitutional requirements for the union's circulation of campaign literature is ·66 in the periodic group), and by the conditions in the industries within which the unions function (most evidently, in the engineering and building trades). Many of these unions have much in common organisationally, for historical reasons, so that the direct effects of external context cannot easily be separated from the effects of formal organisation. More research on British factions as such should be done, but the covertness and illegitimacy of their existence (with the possible exception of the Shop Workers) makes large-sample comparative research difficult and less worthwhile (cf. Martin, 1968).

American Factions
The situation in the United States has long varied greatly from union to union (see Muste, 1928). There is the well-known, but exceptional, formal two-party system (unrelated to external political parties) of the Typographers (see Lipset *et al.*, 1956). Even in American unions, however, factionalism has often had a disreputable connotation. Militants are exhorted to 'Fight the Chamber of Commerce, not the union!' Many union constitutions have barred political subversives from membership. But in numerous instances, internal factions have operated flagrantly as national 'caucuses', 'clubs', 'committees', etc., with formal names, officers, flyers issued in the name of the faction, and sometimes periodicals. In addition, large locals in some unions have had similar organisation at times when there was little factional organisation nationally. 'Outside' pressure-group alliances (see Barbash, 1967: 132), e.g. the Association of Catholic Trade Unionists and the Negro-American Labor Council, have also played a role, although the former organisation was more active when the Communists were stronger in the unions.

In the million-member United Auto Workers, organised opposition had re-asserted itself by 1959 in the form of a body called the National Committee for Democratic Action in the UAW (NCFDA). It started from a demand for a referendum vote on dues increases, and a steering committee and 'post-convention' caucus was formed (see Steiber, 1962: 149; cf. also Ulman, 1962: 47–8). With local caucuses, and formal membership cards, it set out to run candidates for union posts. Some ran on a 'leftist' ticket; others merely wanted more local-union control of UAW policies (Steiber, 1962: 152).

According to the *New York Times* (1 October 1968), 'a black caucus has formed within the United Automobile Workers and is demanding full equity for Negroes within the big union. The group is called the National Ad Hoc Committee for Concerned Negro UAW Members and is headed by Robert Battle, 3rd. Mr. Battle is a vice-president of Local 600, the union's largest, at the Ford Motor Company's Rouge works in Dearborn, Mich.' The leadership of the UAW has devised ingenious ways to diffuse such factional tendencies. At conventions, a period of time is set aside on one day for rank-and-file demonstrations. So, rank-and-filers drive in from miles around with their signs and demonstrate before the delegates. In the past these 'demos' have been long ones. At the 1967 convention in Detroit, for example, there was such activity for about an hour inside the convention hall. It is said that this helps alleviate the gap between the rank-and-file and the delegates, many of whom are local officials.

Other recent American examples of openly-organised factions are abundant in the pages of publications like *Union Democracy in Action*[6] – a forum for the discussion of opposition against political 'machines' in the labour movement, started in 1960. These factions include: the 'Inter-Local Council of Progressive Painters' and the 'United Committee for Democracy' (both in the Painters), the 'Better Union Committee' (in the United Paperworkers), the 'Rank and File Movement for Democratic Action' (in the Pulp, Sulphite and Paper Mill), the 'Committee for NMU Democracy' (in the National Maritime), and many more.

Slates of candidates in one union, the International Ladies' Garment Workers' Union (ILGWU), may be actually registered under the constitutional provision that 'any group of candidates for any office or any elective position . . . who shall desire to appear upon the ballot under a group name or designation shall file a request in writing with the Executive Board of the Local Union at least ten days before the date set for . . . the election' (A. H. Cook, 1963: 21, n. 31). These groups are, however, permitted as open organisations during this period only; the net effect, in the American context, is to limit rather than to encourage factions.

One of the problems in generalising about the conditions which promote open factions in the United States is that such factions have sometimes existed under repressive regimes, in reaction against them. Oppositionists in some unions have been blacklisted for employment, expelled from the union, slugged, even murdered – as in the Painters in 1965 and the Miners in 1970 – while usually remaining 'invisible men' (see Benson, 1972). The poorly-enforced Landrum-Griffin Act 1959 provides for the rights to meet and assemble freely with other union members, to express any views, and to support candidates without being subject to reprisals. The union is supposed to comply with the reasonable requests of candidates to distribute campaign literature at the candidate's expense, by mail or otherwise, in a non-discriminatory way, and to refrain from discrimination in granting lists of members. General bans on factions would appear to be illegal. There are also provisions on the conduct of elections, on trusteeships, and on reports of financial transactions. However, factions have sometimes survived for long periods under repressive conditions, particularly where they have won a local base. It should be clear that the persistence of factions, even open ones, is not as good an indicator of democracy as the effectiveness of opposition in elections or policy making (cf. Martin, 1968).

POLITICAL CULTURE

Any attempt to explain British–American differences in union factionalism on the basis of political culture is hazardous, although it may be intriguing. First of all, 'The usefulness of an exposition based on political culture is circumscribed . . to the extent that it is not an independent determining variable, that is, to the extent that values and ideas that are seen as determining are in fact created and maintained by the very structures they are supposed to determine' (Panitch, 1971: 186). For example, the more favourable opportunities for electoral opposition provided by the formal organisation of British unions may ultimately make opposition more acceptable; also, without its rules against electioneering, in the Engineers such restrictions might not last through one important election. Second, there is a tendency for explanations to be circular also because there is often no direct way to judge the ideational aspects of political culture: these may be inferred from expedient, conventional organisational practices and personal behaviour.

When the concept of culture is applied (perhaps implicitly) to life within a large organisation, too much may be assumed concerning the capacity of the organisation to envelope the individual in its unique system without administratively-controlled sanctions and the structuring of opportunity to achieve individual goals. Even proponents of the idea of organisational culture have recognised that it is dependent less upon personality development and more upon the 'tribulations and rewards of adult behavioural requirements'. Concerning the prevalence of internalised organisational norms, it has been stated, 'It is not necessary . . . to find a miniature reflection of the ideology of the system in the individual motivational patterns of most members in order to have an effective set of group values' (Katz and Kahn, 1966: 56–7; see also 65–6).

Mann (1970: 435) has argued along similar lines, after a survey of the evidence concerning the political and economic attitudes of the British and

American working classes: 'Their compliance might be more convincingly explained by their pragmatic acceptance of specific roles than by any positive normative commitment to society.' He has also argued that 'working-class *individuals* [our emphasis] . . . exhibit less internal *consistency* in their values than middle class people', and that 'the working class is more likely to support deviant values if those values relate either to concrete everyday life or to vague populist concepts than if they relate to an abstract political philosophy'. Furthermore, most general norms, values and beliefs 'can be used to legitimate any social structure, existing or not' (pp. 432, 424).

The working class, and even more so the labour movement, is a sub-culture, with strong contra-cultural elements (see Yinger, 1960: 628ff.), meaning that its norms have a functional value for the individual in reducing a sense of strain and frustration induced by the cross-pressures of conflicting demands. Britain is an elitist and inegalitarian society, yet the Labour Party's norms are egalitarian and predominantly anti-deferential (see Rose, 1964: 56–7). The norms of the country have been characterised as deferential (see Almond and Verba, 1963: 173, 181). In the United States, the group identity and solidarity of the working class appear to be weaker, and stresses on workers probably manifest themselves in more individualistic ways.

Apart from subcultures, every society has different patterns of authority in different spheres – e.g. the economic, the political, the arts – and often various patterns within such spheres. '[T]here is no single set of values, interests, and institutions that completely commands allegiance within the economic, the social or the political systems' (Rose, 1964: 106). Thus, among union members it is dangerous to assume attitudes and values with respect to trade union government on the basis of the members' apparent attitudes towards the national government and its leadership. One is on much safer ground when there is evidence of similarity between the membership and society at large.

Indeed, there may be important differences from union to union with respect to the role of union leaders, factions and other aspects of democracy. Thus, an unavoidable problem in the armchair approach to political culture is that one may choose at will among national, subcultural and organisational norms when these are in conflict with each other. We ourselves prefer to emphasise what we believe to be organisational norms, i.e. those of trade union activists, and secondarily the apparent implicit assumptions in written rules and formal organisation which may be accepted by such activists. In British unions such norms appear to be:

(1) *Any union member has the right to be considered for any union office, on his own merits, without too many obstacles being put in his way.* In some unions, knowledge of the industry and union must be demonstrated in a

formal test before candidacy is permitted, but these seem to be objective and, where used, have not resulted in a dearth of candidates, e.g. in the Railwaymen. In four of the British sample it is exceptionally easy to be nominated for the top office: in the Locomotive Engineers the prospective candidate simply completes an application form; in the Engineers and the Printing, Bookbinding and Paperworkers a single member may nominate; and in the Operative Printers ten members may nominate a candidate for the top post.

There is a curious parallel in the nomination of candidates in Parliamentary elections: the assents of ten electors plus the candidate are all that is required (see British Information Services, 1958), plus a deposit. Nevertheless, we do not want to make too much of this. In the British sample, in twenty-five of thirty-one unions candidates were nominated for the top post by single branches *or* small numbers of members, in four by groups of locals fewer in number than the median number in a major region, and in two (both permanent-post unions) by major regions or the equivalent. The Vehicle Builders, included above, nominated by branch with the subsequent approval of a national selection committee. In the Railwaymen and probably in other unions also, candidates had to pass competency tests for higher but not the highest (top) office. We do not have similar information for the American unions, but believe ease of nomination to be less the case.

Any casual reader of the journal of many a British union could not escape the formal notices of forthcoming elections, the long lists of candidates to numerous offices, and in many cases the branch-by-branch listings of the votes for each candidate, often in a second as well as a first ballot.[7]

(2) *Any union member, including a candidate for office, may belong to any outside political party or outside union reform movement, provided it is a working-class group.* This norm is, in fact, violated by a number of unions, originally under pressure from the Trades Union Congress during 1949–50.

(3) *Organised internal factions are unnecessary, unfair and probably conspiratorial.* While we have argued that such norms as exist would probably be insufficient to prevent free campaigning, the common rules on these matters probably have some support. There may also be some carry-over of norms from Parliamentary elections, norms based on the strict limitations on campaign expenses together with the provision of one free mailing and a short campaign period. These may represent, or project, the fear that unrestrained political aggression could be unfair to the weak or the more scrupulous.

(4) *There is no harm done if a member tries for high office but gets comparatively few votes.* It has been alleged that, while Americans support 'underdogs' but reject the defeated, the British are peculiar in honouring the defeated. In any case, British aspirants for union office may eventually

build a national reputation in this way, and so get elected. But one should not run for too many different kinds of specialised offices, since one cannot be qualified for everything. These norms plus the ease of nomination encourage minor candidacies, and help explain the fact that the mean number of candidates for vacant top posts in Britain during 1949–66 was *much* greater than in the United States.

Permanent Posts and the View of the Job
It is a reasonable conjecture that the prevalence of permanent tenure for British union officials affects the general social climate in which periodic elections are conducted in those unions which hold them. This social climate may be partly responsible for the uncontested periodic elections for the top post in seven unions. Indeed, the Painters shifted from periodic elections to permanent posts in 1948.

Lipset (1962b) has suggested that permanent posts, as in British and Swedish unions, are more likely in societies in which deferential values, e.g. a strong respect for superiors, are more prevalent. There is no doubt that the idea of permanence would be repugnant to most American activists and even most union members. However, many professional associations in the United States have had executive secretaries, appointed for indefinite terms, and in such cases there have been no expressions of shock and no general outcries of oligarchy. We suggest that the hypothesised effect of permanence on periodic elections derives less from deference than from its implication for a view of the job of union official, including the top officer.

First of all, there is some misunderstanding of what 'permanence' means, constitutionally. The 1965 Rules of the Railwaymen provided that the executive council 'shall suspend, prosecute, and may dismiss the General Secretary if found guilty of fraud. It shall also suspend the General and Assistant General Secretaries for absence from, or gross neglect of duty, and report [this] to the Annual General Meeting' (p. 16). In addition, the very top officer 'shall remain in office during the will and pleasure of a majority of the members, who shall, through the Annual or Special General Meetings, have power to dismiss or call on him to resign' (p. 21). With very few exceptions, British executive councils can suspend the top officer and dismiss him subject to appeal (B. C. Roberts, 1956: 275). The phrase 'will and pleasure of the members' is normal in British union constitutions, with reference to the top official's continuance in office, and in the large majority of British unions discontinuance is by vote of the convention (Allen, 1954: 215, 228).

The Railwaymen, in fact, dismissed their general secretary in 1874 and 1897, and in 1931 the general secretary resigned on request of the executive council after a dispute about his entering the government. The Foundry Workers dismissed their general secretary in 1937, the Painters in 1910, the

Plumbers in 1909, the Electrical Trades in 1901 and 1907 – to cite instances occurring in our sample between 1900 and approximately 1953 (see Allen, 1954: 226–45, 271–93).[8] Most of these dismissals were for defalcation or embezzlement, and it may be that their decline after 1910 was due to better administrative and accounting practices and more 'professional' officers.

In all, ten of the twenty-seven unions in our sample (or their predecessors) surveyed by Allen either dismissed, defeated or forced the resignation of general secretaries, on eighteen different occasions between 1848 and 1937 (surveyed until 1953, as stated above).[9] On only two of these occasions were top officers removed, in the Engineers and the Woodworkers, in the course of standing for re-election. In the periodic unions (seventeen of the twenty-seven), fourteen top-officer removals occurred.

The significance of the 'permanence' of officials is modified not only by the terms under which permanent officials hold office, but also by the conditions under which they supposedly work: 'There is no exception in British trade unions to the ruling that the general secretary must work under the control of his executive council' (Allen, 1954: 242). To the extent to which this is true, and it is true to some extent as compared with the situation in American unions, there is less reason to remove the top officer.

A failure to oppose the general secretary in periodic elections may also derive in part from a view of him as a salaried employee and servant of the union, with a status equivalent to that of a civil servant. In referring to the view of Vic (now Lord) Feather, the then general secretary of the TUC, on Britain's entry into the European Economic Community, a view opposed to that of the TUC General Council, *The Times* of 7 July 1971 wrote: 'Of course as general secretary, Feather is the unions' top "civil servant" and supposed not to have a public view.' This would never be said of the president of the American labour congress.

One does not remove such an employee except for technical incompetence or financial dishonesty. The following was no doubt the original view of the job:

'. . . In most constitutions . . . the duties of general secretaries are explained in detail. This practice dates from the days when it was necessary to give elementary guidance to general secretaries . . . General Secretaries are reminded that they must correspond with their branches, countersign all cheques . . ., arrange an audit of the union books, prepare monthly, quarterly or yearly reports, preserve all union documents committed to their charge, provide branch secretaries with stationery, convene executive-council meetings and so on' (Allen, 1954: 241; c.f. S. and B. Webb, 1901).

While secretaries may not currently do these things personally, they are still responsible for them. General secretaries were also required to keep regular office hours in a number of unions, mainly craft or ex-craft, including the Engineers, the Boilermakers, and the Foundry Workers (245).

One curious bit of evidence for the view of full-time officials as civil servants is the 'no canvassing' rule in elections in some unions. This means not only no printed literature, but also no open attempt to influence voters. It parallels the quite common rules governing the appointment of local government officials and teachers. The perception of the union official's job seems to be related to restrictions on factional activities. Many years ago when Sam Watson first became an Area official in the Durham Mineworkers, he jocularly said that he had won because some of his friends had done more and better 'canvassing' in local pubs and working-men's clubs than his opponents had. This occasioned an investigation, during which he was asked whether he had, in fact, sent three friends as canvassers. He replied that this was untrue: that the number was five. Somehow he survived – the matter was dropped. The inherent contradiction between the values of non-partisanship and practical politics seems never to have been resolved, and to have remained to plague the conscience.[10]

Side-Effects of Labour Party Affiliation
It could be argued that the affiliation of the unions to the Labour Party in Britain has stimulated opposition not only by injecting political issues into union life, but also by increasing the turnover of full-time officers and by occasionally offering an indirect path to union office[11] via Labour Party candidacy or office. However, the opposite point could also be argued: that the opportunity to achieve office through the Labour Party (or to achieve posts in worker education) has defused opposition by removing dissidents from the unions.[12] Indeed, the anticipation of the achievement of such posts may have reduced the bitterness of some internal oppositionists or tempered their style, perhaps making them more acceptable in the context of a general bias against explicit factions. Thus, on the whole, the limited opportunities for positions elsewhere, insofar as these can be separated from the general politicising effects of Labour Party affiliation, have probably not greatly influenced the effectiveness of internal opposition, but they may have had a modest effect on its style and the particular nature of its legitimacy.

The top officers of the following unions in our sample are known to have resigned to accept government-related posts during the Labour Government of 1945–50: the Mineworkers (1947), the Railwaymen (1947), and the Locomotive Engineers (1947), all permanent-post unions; the Electrical Trades (1947), and the Plumbers (1949), both periodic unions (see Allen, 1954: 271–93). It is doubtful that such resignations had any considerable effect on the general level of competition for top office in Britain during 1949–66, partly because of their dates, but also because some of these leaders were probably due to have retired shortly (e.g. the Plumbers' general secretary had been in office for twenty-one years).

The absence of open factions in British unions and the common restraints on electioneering are probably factors in depressing the level of electoral opposition to incumbent top officers. The prevalence of permanent posts in British unions may create a social climate unfavourable to such opposition in the periodic unions, but this is difficult to separate from the superficially apolitical nature of the top post in both permanent-post and periodic unions. It is unwarranted at this time to explain either permanence or restrictions on factionalism on the basis of a more deferential national political culture. Such greater confidence as British union members *may* have in the fairness and honesty of their leaders may be deserved in certain respects – at any rate, their leaders' powers are more limited and less crudely oppressive. It does appear that certain specific aspects of trade union political culture have parallels in, and may be supported by, British norms and attitudes concerning electioneering.

Trade union norms concerning fairness in electioneering and the acceptability of defeat may be supported by similar national cultural norms. The ideologists of the militant and left wing of British unionism have raised as an issue the permanency of full-time posts, but not, to our knowledge, the restraints on the organisation of factions. We doubt that it has occurred to them to do so.

NOTES TO CHAPTER 7

1 See B. C. Roberts (1956: 259–60) on the activities of trade union Advisory Councils of the Conservative Party in the constituencies, and on Catholic trade union committees. Such organisations continue to exist.

2 See Chapter 8 on the Mineworkers and Chapter 9 on the Engineers for related examples of campaigning in the face of restrictions.

3 In the periodic group, the correlations were ·33 and ·38 respectively with the closeness of top and next-to-top vacant-post elections, and ·23 and ·38 respectively for the corresponding periodic elections.

4 The measure's correlations with union size were ·29 in the periodic group and ·23 in the permanent-post group. Another, more global, measure of the extent of mixed leadership at the national level, a seven-point rating scale, correlated ·30 and ·37 respectively with the closeness of top and next-to-top vacant-post elections ($N = 14$), and ·39 and ·01 respectively for the corresponding periodic elections ($N = 15$). The correlation for top permanent-post elections was − ·44. The rating scale's correlations with the percentage of the period 1949–66 with mixed leadership were ·71 in the periodic group ($N = 14$) and ·92 ($N = 15$) in the permanent-post group.

5 In the permanent-post but not the periodic group, a mixed leadership was associated with some of the more important organisational features which we have hypothesised as being favourable to union democracy. The correlation of mixed leadership was ·47 with the number of elected, full-time national

officers, ·54 with the number of levels of such officers, and ·33 with the number of top officers. Other correlations were ·34 with the number of top vacancies, and ·45 with the electoral system for top office.

6 It ceased publication under this name in 1972, with the formation of the Association for Union Democracy (Room 805, 23 East 16th Street, New York, N.Y.10003).

7 For example, the February 1972 *Monthly Report* of the Boilermakers (their journal) devotes nine pages to the branch-by-branch first-ballot votes in the elections within eight subdivisions to choose eight delegates to the Trades Union Congress, with a median of eight candidates, and ten pages to similar results in the elections to choose delegates to the Labour Party Conference and the Scottish and Irish Trades Union Congress.

8 The 20,000-member Constructional Engineering, not in our sample, dismissed its secretary in 1939 (see Allen, 1954: 289).

9 Some unions did not exist in 1848. Only two of ten permanent-post unions were involved, but as a group the permanent-post unions were formed later.

10 The illustration is based on interviews with Sam Watson and a staff worker in the Durham area in 1961.·

11 W. F. Cooke has noted that 'the present General Secretary of the Boot and Shoe Operatives was elected to General Officer (logical successor to either of the two top posts . . .) as a rank-and-file member holding the office of union-sponsored Parliamentary candidate, known in NUBSO as "Parliamentary Agent"' (in correspondence with the senior author).

12 Cooke also has noted that Eric Heffer, an unsuccessful left-wing candidate for general secretary in the Woodworkers, was elected Labour MP for a Liverpool constituency in the 1960s, and later became a junior minister in the 1974 Labour Government.

Part Three

CASE-STUDIES IN OPPOSITION

Chapter 8

Case-Study 1: Sustained Electoral Opposition in the British Mineworkers' Union

The British Mineworkers' union combines perhaps the highest degree of regional administrative autonomy in Britain – a carry-over from a previously federal form – with national decision-making on industrial and political policy. The decision-making processes have entailed a high level of electoral opposition over a prolonged period of time, and have resulted in important posts being shared among different political tendencies, a pattern which has persisted into the 1970s. We will show how the distribution and regulation of power in the Mineworkers have resulted in another important exception to the iron law of oligarchy. The explanation will primarily be in terms of *formal* organisational factors rather than a by-passing of the official structure. It will focus on the last two *presidential* elections particularly, in 1960 and 1971, as well as the two *general secretary-ship* elections of 1959 and 1968.

THE MINEWORKERS IN BRIEF

The Miners' Federation of Great Britain (MFGB) was formed in 1889, after a long history of regional unionism in mining and the formation of a less inclusive and unsuccessful national union in 1863 (Arnot, 1949: 34–87). In 1945, in preparation for an extension of national collective bargaining, and with the affiliation of additional regional associations of craftsmen as well as the Colliery Officials and Staffs Association, the name was changed to the National Union of Mineworkers (NUM) (Arnot, 1961: 404–30). The overwhelming majority of the members came from the already affiliated non-craft regional unions, called Areas. The significance of the change was in the now mandatory adherence of the sections to national collective-bargaining agreements. There seem to have been no important changes in 1945 relevant to the election of top officers, apart from the re-institution of the full-time status of the president alongside that of the general secretary (to be discussed shortly).

The history of British coal mining was marked by destructive competition between companies and bitter industrial disputes, as in mining everywhere, until the nationalisation of the industry in 1947. Since that time a national negotiating machinery and less intransigent management have resulted in an improvement in working conditions and local industrial relations, although unofficial strikes have remained numerous (Jencks, 1966; Silver, 1973).[1] Nationalisation and the change to national-union status have had no apparent effect on the closeness of competition for the union's top posts. The union and its members have, of course, had no shortage of serious problems.

In its direct negotiations with the Coal Board the NUM may raise any question at any time, as is usually the case in British industrial relations. Unresolved disputes originating in the Areas *may* be referred to the national levels of the NUM and Board, and eventually to arbitration. Some negotiations take place in concert with other unions in coal mining, where the NUM does not have exclusive jurisdiction over certain classes of employees (to be mentioned shortly). Arbitration is by a three-person neutral board, appointed by the Master of the Rolls after consultation with the NUM and the Coal Board. It was used in 1971 on the holidays question, but was not employed in the 1973–4 major disputes over wages. (See Meyers, 1961: 74–80 for a description of the formal machinery for conciliation and arbitration.) However, the divisions of the Coal Board and the union's Areas have retained very considerable autonomy, even in matters affecting wages, and the arbitration on Area or national matters that has taken place has had no major effect on industrial relations.

In 1960, at the beginning of the decade or so we intend to discuss in detail, the NUM was the fourth-largest union in Britain, having 639,000 of the 8,128,000 members of the unions affiliated to the Trades Union Congress. Its peak size was 945,000 in 1920, and the minimum between 1908 and 1960 was 497,000 in 1933 (Arnot, 1949: 393; 1953: 545; and 1961: 434). The membership has been declining due to pit closures and mechanisation: it was approximately 450,000 paid-up members in 1967, and 259,000 in July 1973.

The Mineworkers is an industrial union, in the sense that it includes the overwhelming majority of manual workers (both surface and underground) in a single industry (coal mining and the production of coke), and is limited to this industry. The white collar workers in the Colliery Officials and Staffs Association were affiliated after the formation of the NUM. Their organisation, with 31,000 voting members in 1960, remains in competition with the successor to the Clerical and Administrative Workers' Union (now APEX), with an estimated membership of less than 10,000 in the industry. The British Association of Colliery Management, and the National Association of Colliery Overmen, Deputies and Shotfirers (37,000 members), remain outside the NUM, although many shotfirers are in it. Thus, over 90 per cent of the employees of the National Coal Board are members of the NUM, as well as an estimated 3,000 to 4,000 of those employed in licensed (private) mines. The Coal Board has agreed to a dues check-off, and in a few regions to a union shop (i.e. compulsory union membership after employment), at least for underground workers. However, for most manual workers in coal mining there is a virtual but unofficial union shop (Meyers, 1961: 10–12).

While the overwhelming majority of the 627,000 voting members in 1960 (at the time of the first of the two presidential elections we shall later examine in detail) were in fourteen geographic Areas such as Yorkshire, Durham and Scotland, there were also 86,000 in six industrial or occupational 'Areas': the Cokemen; the already mentioned white collar COSA; two artificial groupings of certain local craftsmen's associations for purposes of representation at the national level; and two groups of workers who, by special agreement, maintained a dual affiliation, with both the NUM and one of two other national unions (see Table 8.1).

Several of the Areas were themselves federations almost until the date of formation of the National Union in 1945, and in the case of the Midland Miners' Federation two constituent organisations themselves retained the title of federation (Arnot, 1961: 414–16). While the relative isolation of the mine-workers' communities might with justification be invoked as an explanation for the slow process of accretion and amalgamation, other important British national unions were also formed 'from below' in local areas during the nineteenth and early twentieth centuries.[2]

The well-known solidarity of the miners seems to be based on: their opportunity for informal contact at work, in Coal Board-supported recreation centres since nationalisation, and in the mining communities generally; their relative geographic isolation; the dangerous nature of their work; a knowledge of the union's history of struggles; and their psychology as a very special elite, partially in reaction against their formerly very low status (in turn related to the dirty nature of the work and the widespread absence, until nationalisation, of pit-head baths). In addition, there is the belief among many or most miners that their union is among the most democratic in Britain. In the 1960s, we were told that many Durham miners were living outside the mining communities, commuting to work by automobile, and that some of the branches participating in the annual Durham miners' gala had had to hire bands for the traditional parade, since they no longer had their own. Since that time, pit closures and transfers to other mines must have had their effect in disrupting community life, which the energy crisis will hardly reverse!

This general description of the Mineworkers does not distinguish it radically from most other unions with respect to features which might

TABLE 8.1   *The membership of Areas and percentages voting in the May 1960 NUM presidential election*

Area	Eligible members[a]	% Total	% Voting	% Ballots invalid
Geographic				
Yorkshire	111,846	17·83	60·19	2·61
South Wales	84,852	13·53	66·68	2·18
Durham	78,012	12·44	65·21	3·40
Scotland*	62,956	10·04	78·19	3·73
Nottingham*	47,022	7·50	55·47	4·85
Midlands*	37,445	5·97	73·74	3·80
Lancashire*	32,725	5·22	64·99	3·12
Derbyshire*	32,017	5·10	66·56	5·98
Northumberland*	28,669	4·57	88·10	5·48
Cokemen[b]	6,548	1·04	55·04	0·78
Leicester	5,847	0·93	61·89	6·36
North Wales	5,765	0·92	68·03	8·87
Kent	5,451	0·87	74·81	2·92
South Derbyshire	5,070	0·81	65·56	5·14
Cumberland	3,766	0·60	74·61	3·62
Combined geographic	547,991	87·36	66·95	3·60
White collar and craft (except 'other')				
Colliery Officials' and Staffs' Association*	31,168	4·97	82·50	0·32
Group No. 1 (Craftsmen[c])	19,978	3·18	82·95	0·39
Group No. 2 (Craftsmen[c])	14,889	2·37	66·79	0·68
Combined white collar and craft	66,035	10·53	79·10	0·41
Other (dual union affiliates)				
Power Group No. 1 (Transport and General Workers' Union)	9,640	1·54	53·55	0·41
Power Group No. 2 (National Union of General and Municipal Workers)	3,632	0·58	47·78	1·84
Combined other	13,272	2·12	52·00	0·77
ENTIRE UNION	627,298	100·00	67·91	3·16

*The Area had its own candidate.
[a] As of June 1960.
[b] The National Union of Cokemen and By-Product Workers has been placed under geographic Areas, rather than elsewhere, because its membership includes unskilled as well as skilled workers, on an industrial basis.
[c] Each of the two craftsmen's Groups is composed of several relatively independent associations limited to certain geographic Areas. The Groups are artificial entities for the purposes of voting and representation on the national executive committee. Jurisdiction has been complicated and confused, and there have been break-aways. In 1967 attempts were being made to negotiate a return.

foster electoral competition – with the exception of the occupational community. We pass now to a summary of the major formal features of organisation which tend to promote close elections to national office.

Regional and Local Substructures
Two general structural principles flow directly from the general notion of equality. First: *Elections tend to be more closely contested where the major formal regional units are less unequal in their available voting strengths;* and second: *A greater number of fairly large regional units is conducive to close elections.* Perhaps the greatest departure from the countervailing-powers model in the Mineworkers lies in the distribution of the twenty Area memberships over a wide range of size. Focusing again on 1960, the four largest Areas, with from 112,000 to 63,000 members, had a combined membership of 54 per cent of the total. The six Areas which followed had from 47,000 to 29,000 members and constituted 33 per cent of the total, while the remaining ten, with from 20,000 to 3,600, constituted only 13 per cent. The power of the smaller Areas is somewhat enhanced by the voting system, which is discussed below, and in 1960 the general secretary of COSA, the white collar 'Area' with 31,000 voting members, won the presidency. This will be discussed in detail later.

The power of the Areas as against that of the national officials is manifest in more than simply internal administrative autonomy. The Areas are the sole source of nominations for all national posts, and the national officers themselves have no powers to appoint union officials, national or otherwise. The Areas are also directly represented on the national executive committee and at the annual conference (i.e. convention).

The industrial unionism of the Mineworkers and the nature of its industry determine the concentration of the membership into large single-shop local unions. Opposition is more likely to arise in larger locals, particularly when their membership is not unduly dispersed. In the Durham Area in 1958, roughly 60 per cent of the membership was concentrated into thirty-four branches (local unions), each of which had 900 or more members. (Sixteen had 1,500 or more.) While it is also true that there was a total of 130 branches, forty-nine with fewer than 300 members, the absolute number of large branches seems more significant for branch-based competition in elections for Area or national offices.[3]

The Status Hierarchy
The two major principles which apply are, first: *A hierarchical structure which provides two or more offices of the same rank at each level, including the top, is favourable to the production of close electoral contests.* This principle is less relevant where the path upward may be through appointment as well as election, so that: *A higher proportion of elected full-time*

officials tends to produce closer elections. In the NUM there are two approximately equal top officers, a president and a general secretary, and *no other* full-time national officers (the nature of the vice-presidency will be discussed later). Thus, at the next-to-top level we find the formally equal top officials of the twenty Areas, the larger of which in turn have Area presidents and general secretaries, and then in some cases, below these, undifferentiated full-time Area officials. It is true, of course, that the top officials in the larger Areas would ordinarily poll more votes in national elections.

The salary differentials are moderate, by American standards, between adjacent ranks and even between the top officials and the membership, but this is the usual case in British unions. *All* national and Area full-time officials in the NUM (and probably also full-time branch officials where these exist) are elected (by ballot of members) – none is appointed. Finally, as in most British unions, full-time posts are 'permanent' – i.e. not subject to periodic elections.

The National Power Centres

Power may be distributed within or between national power centres. It has already been implied that, as the president and general secretary share power, they may be divided against each other. The principle here is that: *The greater the independent power exercised by national committees and conferences, the less the probability of the domination of an organisation by a single tendency, and the closer the elections.* The Mineworkers' annual national conference consists of Area delegations which are mandated on most of the important questions at prior Area conferences and, hence, not easily subject to manipulation. Only seldom are important matters allowed to arise unexpectedly. The national executive committee also consists of representatives from the Areas, who include ordinarily a top Area official and are relatively independent of the national officials for support or favours.

The Voting System

The major principle here is that: *Any method of casting or counting votes which permits a combination of the supporters of oppositionists or minor candidates, or of their votes, tends to lead to closer elections than the plurality system.* The Mineworkers uses the alternative vote, a form of preferential balloting. Voters mark their preferences 1, 2, 3, etc., and the candidates with the least first preferences are eliminated, in turn, until one candidate has an absolute majority of the remaining active ballots. (There are nontransferable votes when voters who support minor candidates fail to rank all the candidates.) The fact that voting takes place through referenda, rather than at national conferences, tends to diminish somewhat the tendency towards domination by the coalition of Areas which has the largest combined membership. Full-time Area officials, as well as national, are elected under similar voting systems. In national and some Area elections, balloting takes place at the mines (or at least in the geographic Areas), with the count being conducted by an impartial outside agency.

We turn now to an examination of the results of elections, with a focus on competition, power sharing and democracy.

FULL-TIME TOP OFFICERS SINCE 1918

The first referenda for secretary and president took place simultaneously in 1918, on the retirement of the secretary who had been in this full-time office since the founding of the Miners' Federation, and on the establishment of the presidency as a full-time rather than part-time position. The full-time presidency was discontinued in 1922 on the retirement of the first such office-holder, but was re-established in 1945 under the NUM. The findings will be presented for all referenda to full-time top office since the founding of the Federation. Since these elections were to permanent positions, the posts at elections were vacant except when the incumbent part-time presidents ran in 1918 and 1945 (and were re-elected). Excluding these, there was a total of ten vacancies, seven of them since 1946.

Shared Political Power
The full-time presidency and general secretaryship of the Mineworkers have generally been regarded as having approximately equal status and power. The holder of neither position would run for the other. Both Allen (1954: 207–8) and Roberts (1956: 262) point out the importance of 'personality' as the determinant of which leader may become dominant in such cases, although Roberts states that the president of the NUM is probably the senior officer. Allen cautions against assuming that greater administrative control is associated with greater prominence, in unions with full-time secretaries and presidents. The president presides at meetings of the conference and national executive committee, performs duties 'entrusted to him' by the latter, and sees 'that the business of the Union is conducted in a proper manner and according to the Rules, and that in the conduct of affairs of the Union the Rules are duly and properly carried out' (NUM *Rules*, 1947: Section 15). The general secretary also acts as treasurer and conducts the correspondence 'for and on behalf of the Union and the National Executive Committee and keeps records of their proceedings' (Section 17).

A communication from a member or branch to the national office would be expected to be addressed to the general secretary. Both top officers are *ex officio* members of the national executive committee, normally without

vote but with the president voting to break a tie. Between national conferences the executive committee 'shall administer the business and affairs
of the Union' (Section 8). The powers of the conference and national
executive committee are specifically referred to in the *Rules* under a section
entitled 'Government', while those of the top officers are not, so that it is
clear where constitutional power lies. By and large the reality conforms to
the rules.

Since 1946 the presidents seem to have had the edge in power over the
secretaries, but they along with the majority of the national executive have
been orthodox Labour Party supporters, while three secretaries have been
either officially members of the Communist Party or (currently) left-
Labour ex-Communist.[4] Thus, the sharing of power between the two top
officers has to some extent involved a sharing of political influence outside
the union as well.

Previous Defeats for Top Office

The existence of two top officers, of course, tends to increase the number
of succession crises, the chances of any particular Area official winning
such a post, and ultimately the legitimacy of opposition. In many British
unions it is acceptable to use the electoral machinery to become known,
and thus internal communications and knowledge of the candidates are
fostered by a greater number of top vacancies.

The rate of turnover in office is increased by the mandatory retirement
at sixty-five (at least since 1945 – retirement at seventy was apparently made
mandatory at the 1933 annual conference) and the late average age (forty-
seven) at which full-time office is obtained in the Areas (although the current national secretary achieved that post at forty-three). Those who have
reached sixty are not permitted to be candidates for full-time offices, which
also probably increases Area officials' motivation to try for such national
openings as arise while they remain eligible. All these factors, plus the
nature of the electoral system, promote a larger number of candidacies and
victories for candidates who have been defeated previously. Such victories
are, of course, of far greater significance as a sign of the winners' having
fought their way into office, than they are of their having been advanced,
without much opposition, by a ruling group.

The results of all referenda for top offices are shown in Table 8.2.[5] Five
winners were previously defeated, in four instances as the runner-up, in the
nine genuine vacancies for which this was possible. (The two *initial* referenda
and the 1945 presidential election are excluded.)

Numbers of Candidates

There have been *no uncontested elections* under the referendum system, and
in eight of the twelve elections since 1918 there were three or more candi-

dates. The median number of candidates was 4·0 for the twelve elections, and 4·5 for the ten genuine vacancies (see Table 8.2).

Since elections are by transferable votes, there is less reason to expect easier victories for the leading candidate when there are more competitors, than there would tend to be under a plurality system. There is a weak tendency for a greater number of candidates to be associated with closer elections, but this may be coincidental. The leading candidate has an

TABLE 8.2 *Referenda by preferential ballot (transferable votes) for full-time permanent general secretaries and presidents of the British Mineworkers' union, 1918–74[a]*

Year	Post	No. of candidates	Final votes for runner-up per 100 for winner	First preference votes for runner-up per 100 for winner	Winner's defeat in previous referenda	Comments
1918[b]	Secretary	8	62·1	59·8	(not possible)	1st referendum in 1918.
1918[b]	President	2	31·3	(1 count)	(not possible)	1st referendum in 1918. Winner was part-time president since 1912.[c]
1924	Secretary	9	92·9	71·7		
1932	Secretary	4	67·5	59·3	4th, 1924	
1945	President	4	51·4	57·1		Winner was part-time president since 1939.
1946	Secretary	3	73·7	(1 count)		
1954	President	2	46·6	(1 count)	2nd, 1946	
1959	Secretary	5	79·0	71·7		
1960 (Jan.)	President	5	62·4	61·3	2nd, 1945	Winner died before taking office.
1960 (May)	President	7	95·0	124·8	2nd, 1959	Winner was 2nd in first preferences.
1968	Secretary	2	91·2	(1 count)		
1971	President	2	78·9	(1 count)	2nd, 1968	

[a] The only previous vacancy was filled at the founding conference, in 1889.
[b] The 1918 elections were simultaneous, with voting taking place from one to three days after the Armistice.
[c] The presidency became part-time again in 1922, after this winner left office, and remained so until 1945.

advantage even under a transferable vote system, since many voters fail to list preferences among some or all of the minor candidates. Some minor candidates may not be known to the voters.[6]

Posts Held Previously

The consistent advancement of assistant top officers to vacant top posts in unions has been taken as implying oligarchic control. In the NUM, where the leading candidates in the referenda have ordinarily been the presidents or secretaries of their Area governments, the only possible higher offices short of the two top national posts have been the part-time vice-presidency and, during certain periods, the part-time presidency. Both posts were filled annually or, after 1945 for the vice-presidency, biennially at the national conference, almost invariably by Area secretaries or presidents who continued in their full-time Area posts. It might be thought that such Area leaders, in serving as part-time national officials, would have an advantage over others through their becoming better known and appearing to be the logical successors to the top officers.[7]

The winners of eight of the ten vacant-post referenda had never held such part-time national posts, and the other two had been defeated in national referenda *before* achieving the vice-presidency some years later, and then finally a top office. Arthur Horner, the Communist secretary elected in 1946, never achieved part-time national office in spite of his having tried to displace incumbent vice-presidents on three occasions and an incumbent part-time president on one.

It may be that the vice-president carries little weight in the NUM. The rules assign him no regular powers or duties, although he sometimes substitutes for the president and may decide disagreements between the president and secretary. Or it may be that vice-presidents have been intentionally chosen (under the NUM) so as to be over-age for eventual candidacy for the top posts. For example, F. Collindridge was elected vice-president in 1961, three years before his mandatory retirement (see Moffat, 1965: 290). This would, of course, enhance the chances of other Area officials for eventually achieving a top office. Perhaps the vice-presidency has come to be regarded as a semi-honorary post for senior officials and a consolation prize for large Areas holding neither of the two top offices.[8]

The Closeness of Elections
A persistent absence of opposition, or of effective opposition, in elections to top posts is not compatible with representative democracy in a large organisation, as we have already argued. On the other hand, persistently close elections are *inconsistent* with oligarchic control, unless one assumes that close elections can readily be kept under full control through the falsification of results.

Top vacancies in the Mineworkers.   The number of votes for the runner-up per 100 for the winner, in all referenda for top office since the foundation of the union, are shown in Table 8.2. The median for the ten genuine vacant-post elections since 1918 is 76·3 per cent, and the mean is 74·9 per cent. In only one did the runner-up receive fewer than 62·1 votes per 100 for the winner.

There appears to have been no long-term decline in the closeness of these vacant-post referenda. This in itself is a finding of some importance, in view of Lipset's suggestion that competition may be expected to fade with the passage of time if there is not some special sustaining mechanism, e.g. an established party system.

Final as compared to initial counts.   When there are three or more candidates and none has a majority of the votes, a reversal of the standing of the leading candidates is possible under a system of transferable votes. When the initially-leading candidate loses, an element of drama enters the situation, even if only retrospectively. The candidate leading initially and his supporters can more easily rationalise their defeat, and perhaps rebound more readily for another try later. When there is no actual reversal but the final count is closer than the first, this seems to emphasise the potential in the voting system for a combination of oppositionists, which might perhaps be more effectively welded in the future.

In the Mineworkers there was only one reversal, in the second 1960 presidential election. However, the logic of the preferential voting system was also sustained, in the form of closer final counts, in five of the six remaining referenda in which a majority was not obtained on the first count (see Tables 8.2 and 8.3).

More-than-Nominal Minor Candidates

While one cannot say categorically that a greater number of more-than-nominal minor candidates is a sign of more effective opposition, it *is* a sign of the breadth of the competitive struggle. At any rate, the findings in this respect shed light on the political process in the Mineworkers, in that they rule out the two-party system as a reasonable possibility. For example, the *third-place* candidate for the secretaryship in 1959 received 117,497 votes, as compared to 139,891 for the runner-up, according to the last count on which the leading three candidates appeared. Thus, the third-place candidate received 84·0 votes per 100 for the second-place. For the seven vacant-post referenda in which there were three or more candidates, the median such figure was 73·5 per cent.[9]

To indicate the breadth of the competitive struggle in another way: the candidates leading on the first count in the three elections in 1959 and 1960 received respectively only 36, 41 and 28 per cent of the first preferences. When one considers that each candidate must be nominated by an Area, and ordinarily by one of the ten largest, the very fact of a median of 4·5 candidates for genuine vacant posts since 1918 casts doubt upon the existence of a meaningful party system. Nevertheless, important differences in the political views and backgrounds of the candidates have usually existed.

TABLE 8.3 *The May 1960 presidential election: first preferences and the deciding count*

Candidate, Area and Area office	Additional nominating areas	% of national members	% of national valid ballots	Candidate's % of first preferences	% of national vote: deciding count	Candidate's politics
Moffat, Scotland, vice-president	Yorkshire S. Wales Kent Cumberland	42·86	42·41	28·16 (116,174)	48·71 (187,873)	Member of Communist Party
Ford, COSA, secretary	Durham Gp No. 1 N. Wales S. Derbyshire Power Gp No. 2	22·90	24·17	22·56 (93,084)	51·29 (197,854)	Labour
Ellis, Nottingham, agent	—	7·50	6·02	14·88 (61,389)		Member of Communist Party
Southall, Midlands, secretary	Leicester	6·90	7·26	8·18 (33,752)		Labour
Hammond, Lancashire, agent	—	5·22	4·99	6·99 (28,853)		Ex-Communist Party[a]
Wynn, Derbyshire, secretary	—	5·10	4·86	7·77 (32,040)		Ex-Communist Party[a]
Holliday, Northumberland, president	—	4·57	5·79	11·46 (47,264)		
TOTALS		95·05	95·49	100·00 (412,556)	100·00 (385,727)	

[a] Politically left of orthodox Labour.

Participation in Elections

We believe that, within very broad limits, there is little relationship between the percentage of the membership voting in union elections and the effectiveness of electoral opposition. Nevertheless, formal democracy presumes some reasonable degree of participation, and, other things being equal, a greater participation on a reasonably-informed basis is apt to yield a result more representative of opinion among the members of an electorate.

In the Mineworkers the percentage voting has always been high, ordinarily well over 60 per cent since 1945. In 1971 it was over 70 per cent.[10] In the May 1960 election the membership in the higher-status white collar and craft Areas participated somewhat, but not dramatically, more than those in the predominately lower-status geographic Areas, 79·1 as compared to 67·0 per cent (see Table 8.1). This *may* be due to the mechanics of conducting elections in the white collar and craft Areas, which present different problems in the casting of ballots.

A CLOSER LOOK AT THE NATIONAL REFERENDA

One requirement for a formal representative democracy is an electorate separate and apart from the chief competitors for office. This leads us to two related questions: To what extent and how do Area officials control the votes of their memberships in national referenda? And to what extent are the Area governments internally oligarchic? An attempt will be made to answer these questions, first by taking a closer look at the national elections, and then by examining the competition for Area offices.

'Favourite Sons' and Other Candidates

The two major ingredients for victory in a national referendum have been a national reputation and a sufficient number of Area nominations. It has been common in the Mineworkers for Areas to nominate – in effect, to endorse – candidates from other Areas when they were not running their own. Joint nominations have at times been arranged by agreements among the leaders, sometimes on the basis of an obvious similarity of political views. The South Wales and Scotland Mineworkers, under Communist leadership and with memberships probably more left-wing than that in most Areas, backed each other's candidates and jointly backed Yorkshire's in the three elections during 1959–60. The small Communist-led Kent Area also made identical nominations in all three elections. There have also been more covert coalitions, to some extent cutting across political lines. These will be discussed later.

The information on the ballot papers, and on the nationally-prepared wall posters announcing the election, has undoubtedly been a factor in the membership's following the recommendations of their Area governments.

The Area of origin *and* other nominating Areas have been shown on the ballot paper, at least in the three 1959–60 elections. Thus, most voters could discover the recommendation of their own Area by a glance at their ballot papers, and the identity of the leading candidates (usually two) as well, although the latter identification would play a greater role in the listing of their second and later preferences.

In the 1959–60 elections, the total numbers of Areas nominating were respectively twelve, thirteen and seventeen. In the May 1960 election, 95 per cent of all eligible voters and the same percentage of the 413,000 actually voting belonged to Areas which had nominated candidates. Two-thirds of the national membership belonged to the Areas nominating the two leading candidates, who had five or six nominations (see Table 8.3). There was a proportionately greater support for minor candidates, due to their source of strength coming primarily from within their own Areas, and to the lack of unity within the Labour and Communist forces.

Let us examine the degree of support for 'favourite sons' and other nominees (see Table 8.4). There was a total of only ten persons involved in the seventeen candidacies in the three elections. Two candidates (Wynn and Southall) ran in all three elections, three ran twice (Hammond, Holliday and Ford, the latter being elected), and five ran only once (Allan, Ellis, Moffat, Machen and Paynter, the latter two being elected). Ignoring this overlap, the median percentage of the first preferences for the seventeen favourite son candidacies within their own Areas was 66·5 per cent, while the corresponding median for the twenty-five nominations of outside candidates was 49·2 per cent. The highest median percentage of first preferences for favourite sons in any one election was 74·3 per cent in January 1959, while the lowest was 54·6 per cent in May 1960. The corresponding figures for outside nominees were 55·7 and 38·3 per cent respectively. On the whole, there were *no* important differences between the larger and smaller Areas in the degree to which they backed their favourite sons or other nominees.[11]

Thus, on the average, about *one-third* of the memberships in Areas with favourite sons *failed* to give them their first preferences in the three 1959–60 elections (again ignoring the overlap), and about *one-half failed* to support outside nominees. However, the non-conformist votes were generally distributed widely, although not evenly, among the remaining candidates. For example, in the May 1960 election the smallest absolute and relative lead of any favourite son in his own Area was that for Hammond, of Lancashire, with 53·0 per cent of the first preferences as against 20·4 per cent for his leading opponent. The median relative lead of favourite sons in their own Areas was better than 4·5 to one, in this election. Thus, the 'opposition' within the Areas was considerable, but divided or lacking in organisation. The ultimate national effect of such 'opposition' can be interpreted only in the light of the transfers of the votes, which will be considered shortly.

TABLE 8.4 *Percentage of the initial count for nominees and leading candi-dates within the twenty Areas of the NUM in three national referenda for top post, 1959–60*[a]

	Areas with:		
% *Initial Count*	*Favourite Sons* (n = 17)	*Nominees —from outside* (n = 25)	*No Nominees* (n = 18)
90–99	—	—	—
80–89	4	—	—
70–79	4	—	—
60–69	4	4	3
50–59	5	8	4
40–49	—	4	7
30–39	—	8	3
20–29	—	1[b]	1
10–19	—	—	—
0–9	—	—	—
Median	66·5%	49·2%	48·7%
Median January 1959	74·3% (n = 5)	46·2% (n = 7)	46·1% (n = 8)
Median January 1960	82·7% (n = 5)	55·7% (n = 8)	50·3% (n = 7)
Median May 1960	54·6% (n = 7)	38·3% (n = 10)	45·2% (n = 3)

[a] The numbers of candidates were five, five and seven respectively.
[b] In this instance only (Group No. 1, in January 1960), a nominee of an Area received fewer first preferences in the Area than another candidate.

The Meaning of Nominations and First Preference Votes

It appears incongruous that the Areas *without nominees* gave about as much support to their leading candidates as those Areas with *outside nominees* (see Table 8.4). It may be that in some cases there were endorsements sub-sequent to the closing of nominations. However, the following partial explanation emerges from an examination of the voting figures: (*a*) there appear to have been distinct *pre-nomination preferences* among the voters, or at least the active rank-and-file, based on a differential knowledge of the candidates (this, in turn, being based partially on the propinquity or over-lapping of Areas) and perhaps on politics; and (*b*) where Area nominations were counter to these preferences, the nominations took precedence but with a substantially-decreased effect. Thus, there are definite limits to how much influence Area officials can exert on the votes of their members.

The voting of Durham in the three 1959–60 elections is an example of both points. Durham was led by its orthodox Labour general secretary, Sam Watson, who was often regarded as dominating his Area by virtue of outstanding competence and his 'strong' personality. Watson had for years been on the national executive of the Labour Party. Durham did *not* nominate in the first two elections, and 51·6 and 55·6 per cent respectively of its first preferences went to the candidates from the neighbouring Northumberland Area. In the second election the Northumberland candidate was Allan, an ex-Communist who was probably more left than the Communist-supported Machen, who won the election.[12] Machen was centre-left within the Labour movement. He opposed Gaitskell, the leader of the Labour Party, but also actively opposed the Communists on many issues within Yorkshire. Allan had left the Communist Party at about the time of the 1956 Hungarian revolution, but apparently had never publicly attacked the Party and was still regarded as a left-winger. Largely as a result of support within Durham, which was the third-largest Area, Allan rather than Southall, the leading orthodox Labour candidate, became the national runner-up in the January 1960 election, with 62·4 votes per 100 for Machen.

In the third 1959–60 election, Durham nominated Ford for the presidency against (among others) Holliday of Northumberland, who had received over half of Durham's first preferences in the first election, in opposition to Ford among others. The nomination resulted in Ford leading the field within Durham, gaining, however, only 34·7 per cent of the votes. Holliday remained relatively strong, polling 13,169 votes to Ford's 17,060. In the first election the vote had been 28,184 for Holliday and 12,437 for Ford. Thus, there is strong evidence within Durham for a 'natural' preference for candidates from the adjacent northern Area over other candidates in the field. Other but less striking examples could be cited of the ineffectiveness of outside nominations.

Finally, it must not be assumed that a nomination always reflects the wishes of the top officials within an Area. The full-time officials in most large Areas are not politically homogeneous, and the nominations are the result of a formally democratic process and are often difficult to control. Nominations are usually made: by Area councils, consisting of rank-and-file delegates from each local union (e.g. in Derbyshire); by rank-and-file Area executive committees, usually elected on a ward basis (e.g. in South Wales and Durham); or by a direct vote of branches (e.g. in Yorkshire).

When a top Area official is not available for candidacy, a *minor* official of a *different political hue* may receive enthusiastic support. Thus, Ellis, an agent in Nottinghamshire and an official Communist, received his Area's nomination in the May 1960 presidential election, presumably over the objection of the quite right-wing Labour senior official. The desire for Area representation nationally is strong, and most active members do not take political differences as seriously as one might think.

Yorkshire provides an example of an uncontrolled *outside* nomination. Machen, president of the Yorkshire Area, won the national presidency in

January 1960 but died before taking office. Collindridge, the right-wing secretary, could probably have been nominated if he had not been over-age. His co-officers were comparatively new and did not wish to run. Moffat's name was submitted and apparently there were no other prominent contenders. In the national election: Moffat, the leading Communist candidate, received 21,225 votes within Yorkshire (32·4 per cent); Ellis, the other Communist candidate, 11,794; and Ford, who won the election, 11,520. One may wonder whether the orthodox Labour Yorkshire officials could have put Ford (whose politics were the same as theirs) over as a nominee, after Yorkshire had nominated the Communist Paynter in 1959. We shall soon see the political logic behind the latter nomination.

A Dearth of National Figures

The lack of unity among the orthodox Labour forces, and perhaps among the Communist forces in the May 1960 election, may have been due to a shortage of potential candidates of truly national reputation and sufficient stature. This may also partially explain the wide dispersion of votes among the 'oppositional' candidates in the Areas.

By May 1960, the best-known individuals in the four largest Areas were either over-age or – in the case of South Wales – not in the running because the Area had already contributed one of the two top national officials (the general secretary). Of the ten individuals involved as candidates in the 1959–60 elections, according to an evaluation by one of the minor candidates, four were 'well known generally', five were 'well known to active members in the branches', and one was 'known somewhat to active members'.[13] Three of the four best known were elected. Not all of these four were popular or well known in their own right. For example, Ford, who lost the first election but won the last, was widely objected to because he had been a clerk but never a miner; and the name of Moffat, the Communist runner-up in the last election, was known primarily through the reputation of his more prominent brother, who was then president of the Scottish Area.

The absence of a secondary leadership at the national headquarters, and of a national union newspaper or member-oriented journal, accounted largely for this dearth of national figures. These considerations lead us to doubt that as many as four of the candidates could have been known to most voters *before* the opening of nominations for the 1959–60 elections. However, the situation is undoubtedly similar in those many unions which differ in these respects but nevertheless have poor internal communications.

Votes in the Branches for 'Opposition' Candidates

In spite of the often moderate-to-large support for candidates other than the nominees of the respective Areas, the 'oppositional' votes tended to be spread widely among the branches, with comparatively few branches apparently being effectively controlled by the supporters of particular opposition candidates. Thus, Machen obtained 82·7 per cent of the first preferences in his own Area, with an absolute majority in *each* of the 107 branches. When Yorkshire nominated the Scottish Communist, Moffat, who received only 32·4 per cent of Yorkshire's first preferences, he gained an absolute majority in only eight of 105 branches,[14] but nevertheless had a plurality in seventy-six branches. Ford, the leading opposition candidate in this election both in Yorkshire and nationally, had a plurality in seventeen Yorkshire branches, but gained an absolute majority in only three. The large number of candidates, differences of opinion within the Area itself, and poor communications outside the Area probably contributed to this relative absence of strong local concentrations of oppositionists. In these circumstances, a further polarisation into political camps could take place *only* by means of the electoral system.

The Significance of the Vote Transfers
The transferable vote system permits the defeat of an initially-leading candidate, as occurred in May 1960 (see Table 8.3), and – as shown previously – ordinarily narrows the gap between the leading candidates. Since absolute majorities on the first count have not occurred in the seven referenda to top office with four or more candidates, the transfers have usually determined the elections. While, in these circumstances, competing right-wingers or competing left-wingers might agree to recommend an exchange of their followers' second or later preferences, this does not seem to have occurred on any scale, at least during 1960. In practice, the voters appear to have been extremely intractable and politically illogical. Political gamesmanship could probably not have been relied upon to manipulate the transfers, or perhaps even to determine their direction.

The prime example of political inconsistency involved the transfer of Ellis's votes in the May 1960 presidential election. This election was rare, and perhaps unprecedented, in that two official Communists were candidates, although only one was backed by the Party nationally. On the fifth count only three candidates remained, with these votes: Moffat (Communist), 160,238; Ford (orthodox Labour), 135,635; and Ellis (Communist), 102,371. Ellis's votes were then transferred, 62,219 going to Ford and only 27,635 to Moffat (12,517 were non-transferable – these voters had not listed subsequent preferences). Thus, Ford won the election by 197,854 votes to 187,873. Many of Ellis's votes had come from his own Area, on the basis of his local reputation rather than his politics. (The top leadership in his Area was orthodox Labour, as mentioned earlier.)

In this same election, the predominant trend was *politically* illogical in four of the five transfers, and in one of these four the major Communist candidate benefited (in the transfer of Southall's votes). It may be a coincidence, but the plurality of each illogical transfer went to an adjacent position on the ballot paper (on which the names were placed alphabetically, as is customary). Some of the Ellis-to-Ford transfers may be explained on this basis, although probably not a decisive number. There is also the matter of Ellis's first position on the ballot paper: the savants in the Mineworkers generally accord the first position an advantage of from 5 to 15 per cent. Some also grant an advantage, but a lesser one, to the last position on a long ballot paper. Thus, the irrelevancy of alphabetical placement no doubt puts some votes beyond potential oligarchic control, although in the NUM this seems hardly necessary for democracy.

COALITIONS IN NATIONAL ELECTIONS

There is reason to believe that the potential for bloc making and division of the spoils, inherent in the countervailing-powers model presented earlier, manifested itself first in the 1945–6 elections for the national presidency and secretaryship, and then again in the first two elections during 1959–60. These pairs of vacancies were both expected and proximal, and hence particularly well suited for horse-trading. However, it appears that such arrangements were covert, not fully inclusive of the largest Areas and not entirely unprincipled politically. Such arrangements would have been considered improper, as would any sign of open factional organisation. In this respect the union was similar to most other British unions. When asked in 1961 whether such coalitions among Area officials might be inevitable, in view of the regular contact of such officials on the national executive committee, one Area official answered that they might be inevitable but that there would be 'hell to pay' if they were known.

A number of persons in and close to the union believed that these blocs existed. One Area secretary claimed a knowledge of a pact for mutual non-opposition in 1945–6, based on an advance conversation with one of the winners. The supporting evidence is that the home Areas of both the newly-elected president (Will Lawther, from Durham) and the vice-president (from Northumberland) refrained from opposition to the Communist Arthur Horner of South Wales, in 1946. At this time Lawther was regarded as fairly left-wing and friendly towards Russia. The memberships of Durham and Northumberland were about 105,000 and 28,000 respectively – almost enough for an endorsement which would have swung the election to the leading non-Communist candidate. Horner won by 59,500 votes. An explicit endorsement of the leading non-Communist would have influenced votes in other Areas as well. Scotland, which is also supposed to have been a party to the pact, nominated both Lawther and Horner.[15]

In the 1959–60 elections the three Communist-led Areas (South Wales,

Scotland and Kent) and Yorkshire, Machen's Area, had a mutual exchange of nominations in the first two. Machen was farther from the Communists politically than three of the other candidates in his election, but was better known (he had participated in the 1926 general strike) and from a larger Area. And, from Machen's point of view, the discipline of the Communists could be relied upon to deliver the nomination in the three Communist-led Areas. Thus, three of the four largest Areas were in league with each other, and the fourth, Durham, made no nominations.[16]

The 1945–6 apparent agreement is more understandable in the light of the situation during and shortly after World War II, when the political mood of the day, in the British labour movement, was not antagonistic to either Russia or the British Communist Party (see Moffat, 1965: 89).

This, of course, did not apply to the 'cold-war' days of 1959–60, but there was the additional factor of the industrial tameness of the Communists in the Mineworkers, largely under Horner's leadership. A review of Horner's autobiography, *Incorrigible Rebel*, remarked that:

'. . . he never led his men into a major strike either in South Wales or during his later period as secretary of the N.U.M., and he was soon boasting of his moderation. "Let the 'rights' sneer . . . let the 'lefts' . . . jeer," he wrote in 1937, apparently regarding fully paid-up membership of the Communist Party as entirely compatible with a "centre" industrial position; and he issued stern instructions that agreements with the employers were to be fully honoured and unofficial strikes relentlessly stamped upon. After nationalisation he entered into the friendliest relations with members of the National Coal Board . . .

'. . . A Communist secretary of the N.U.M. who promoted no major strikes during the period of maximum British coal shortage and who failed to get his union to vote against German rearmament was about as much practical use to Moscow as Senator Kennedy in the White House is likely to be to the Pope. But practical influence aside, Mr. Horner's office had the same sort of prestige value . . . The Communists were therefore glad to keep him, and even to give him unusual latitude' (R. Jenkins, 1960).

Horner, of course, publicly endorsed Paynter, the Communist candidate in 1959, who was also from South Wales. The Scottish Communists in the NUM appear to have been less acceptable and popular than those from South Wales, perhaps enough to have turned the balance in Moffat's defeat by 10,000 votes in May 1960. The vicissitudes of the path to top office through the referendum are also illustrated by this press comment: 'The most serious setback for Mr. Moffat is likely to be caused by the Summit failure. It has been estimated that Mr. Kruschev's performance will lose him up to 30,000 votes' (*Birmingham Post*, 23 May 1960).

ELECTIONS AT NATIONAL CONFERENCES

While the conference has been exceptional in its freedom from control by the top officials, its elections for the part-time presidency were seldom closely contested. Of the six such vacancies between 1912 and the change to the full-time presidency (and the referendum) in 1945, three involved uncontested elections, two involved better than three-to-one victories, and only the last (in 1939) approximated the median closeness of referendum elections.

Incumbents ran for the part-time presidency in fifteen elections by conference between 1922 and 1943, but were opposed in no more than four. The incumbent was overwhelmingly defeated in 1930, but in very special circumstances: he stood behind the industrial policy of his Area (which he was virtually required to do), in disagreement with the remainder of the Miners' Federation (Arnot, 1961: 35). Apart from this there was only one election in which the incumbent president did not win overwhelmingly: the 1940 election, when the runner-up percentage was 86. Thus far, elections at conference do not appear to generate as much opposition as national referenda.

An examination of the part-time presidents' path up the status ladder shows that, in *each* case, they had been elected to the vice-presidency no more than five years before becoming president – and within two years in three instances. It might be argued that the delegates (or those instructing them) had suitability for the presidency in mind when electing vice-presidents. While we would not accept this as a justification for the low level of presidential competition, let us nevertheless turn to the elections for vice-presidency vacancies.

There was, indeed, closer competition at the vice-presidential level. Only one of the fourteen vacancies for the vice-presidency between 1909 and 1961 was uncontested, and the median number of candidates was 3·5. There were as many candidates in the more recent elections as in the earlier. Four vice-presidential winners were previously defeated at conference for the vacant part-time vice-presidency or presidency, and another two were previously defeated in referenda for the general secretaryship. Apparently, then, at least six of the fourteen vice-presidents fought their way into this office or, at least, were not hand-picked by a monopolistic administration. However, no incumbent vice-presidents were defeated.

The electoral system used at conference varied from period to period. Although this was a matter of practice rather than rule, the consistency of each practice allowed us to place all but one election in periods within which the electoral system was presumably known in advance. The absence of a trend in the closeness of the referenda elections between 1918 and 1971 seems to warrant a comparison of the 1909–61 conference electoral systems at different periods.

The six vice-presidential vacancy elections filled at a conference requiring an *absolute majority* of conference votes had a median of sixty-seven votes for the runner-up per 100 for the winner, which was reasonably close to that for the referenda (one was a precise tie and required a further ballot). The seven vacancies requiring a *plurality* had a median runner-up percentage of only 33. Absolute majorities were required either through successive run-off elections (four between 1909 and 1917 and one in 1961, the latter being excluded because its system was inconsistent with that of adjacent elections), or through transferable votes (in 1934 and 1939). Five were filled under the plurality system between 1922 and 1932, and two in 1951 and 1955. Conceivably, the electoral system might be altered to favour a particular candidate.

Thus, it appears that, as expected, the requirement of an absolute majority tends to produce closer elections. If one is willing to assume that elections to lower national posts tend generally to be closer than those to higher, other things being equal, then the failure of the vice-presidential elections to surpass the closeness of those to top office indicates that the referendum is more effective for opposition than the conference, even a conference far more powerful than the conventions of most large American unions.

THE STATUS HIERARCHY AND COMPETITION IN THE AREAS

The situation in some larger Areas mirrors that in the national union. There are full-time permanent presidents and secretaries of equal status, and beneath them a number of full-time permanent 'agents' who are elected by referendum (again by transferable votes) in districts within the Areas. Such Areas include South Wales, the Midlands and Scotland. It is common for the agents (who serve the pits in their districts) to run against each other when top Area posts become vacant.

In some cases agents are elected on an Area-wide basis, and in other cases treasurers and other differentiated officials rather than agents are elected (e.g. in Northumberland). Very small Areas may have only one full-time official. Durham elects only agents, but these are then assigned, by seniority, through custom and practice to the various offices.[17] All full-time Area officials are elected by referendum, under the same voting system as for the national president and secretary. Prior to 1945, some Areas used elimination balloting (two or more run-off elections) rather than the single transferable vote, to achieve absolute majorities. Some Areas still provide for, and in practice require, preliminary branch votes (each branch casting its assigned votes *en bloc*) to reduce the number of candidacies to a reasonable figure. Durham, which is unusual, submitted eighty-three nominations for agent to a preliminary branch vote in 1953. In 1945 the number was 147.

Each branch must vote for as many candidates as will appear on the final referendum ballot – at one time eight, currently four.

The most logical contenders for the lowest level of full-time Area vacancies are in some cases the rank-and-file executive councillors, especially where both types of officers are elected on the same ward basis. However, in other Areas the part-time vice-presidents or presidents have been in a position to compete in Area-wide elections for the lowest full-time post.

The following excerpt from an election address, for the post of Area official in Derbyshire, provides an indication of the line of progression and extent of experience – the latter is somewhat beyond the average in this case, but not unusual:

'36 years membership of the Union [age 50];
17 years delegate to Area Council [conference];
13 years Area Executive Member;
Two years Area Vice-President [part-time office];
Five years Area President [part-time office];
20 years active member of the Labour Party;
12 years Labour Party Member Heanor Urban District Council' (*Derbyshire Miner*, January 1959: 3).

There are frequently two different orientations to advancement in the union: one towards local and the other (perhaps passing briefly through a local phase) towards wider horizons. The division of function and perspective resulting from this separation, which is largely required by the heavy burden of servicing a large branch, may be the basis for different opinions on whom to support in union elections.[18]

Elections in South Wales

The closeness of referendum elections to full-time Area posts is generally comparable to, but a little closer than, that to the top national posts. The seven elections to fill vacancies in the South Wales presidency and secretary-ship during 1940–66 had a median runner-up percentage of 76, which is roughly typical of such Area elections in the Mineworkers.

The South Wales rank-and-file executive councillors were elected for two-year terms within five wards. During 1949–59, each ward chose either two or three councillors simultaneously, in transferable vote referendum elections superficially resembling proportional representation (the Hare system) but requiring for each winner an absolute majority of the votes. In practice, this system is more favourable for an 'oppositional' candidate than for the weakest candidate of the leading tendency (although, in principle, winner-take-all elections are possible with a factionalised and disciplined electorate). Of the thirty regular separate ward elections held during 1949–59, ten resulted in the defeat of an incumbent.[19] The mean closeness of thirty-four separate elections (including four by-elections) was eighty-three votes for the runner-up per 100 for the lowest winner.[20]

The executive councillors are the logical competitors for the full-time agent posts, since they are elected from within the same wards. In the fifteen South Wales elections of agents during 1939–55, seven runners-up had eighty-five or more votes per 100 for the winner. The median runner-up percentage was 75.

The separate wards seem even more divided internally in elections to the Area top posts, than the Areas are in national elections. This is so in spite of the fact that three wards represent natural and historical subdivisions within South Wales. (The other two include two such subdivisions each.) In the 1958 election of a general secretary, none of the six candidates received a majority of first preferences in any ward. The Communists were strongest in Swansea, but even the Swansea Communist candidate (who won the secretaryship) did not quite receive a majority in the Swansea ward. Furthermore, the votes in opposition to the leading candidate within each ward were not as divided as in the national referenda.

Elections in Other Areas
The elections to full-time posts in other Areas are also close, although our data are not complete. For example:

> *The Midlands.* A median runner-up percentage of 83 in five top-post elections, 1948–66.
> *Kent.* A median runner-up percentage of 77 in two top-post elections, 1950 and 1960.
> *Yorkshire.* A median runner-up percentage of 61 in two top-post elections, 1952 and 1954; a median of 93 per cent in three elections for vice-president, financial secretary and compensation agent, 1952–9; and a median of 73 per cent in seven elections for agent, 1953–60.
> *Durham.* A median runner-up percentage of 76 in five Area-wide elections for agent, 1945–58.
> *Nottingham.* A median runner-up percentage of 80 in four Area-wide elections for 'Area official', 1951–7.

THE NATIONAL AND AREA CONFERENCES

The formal organisation of national conferences not only reflects, but also has contributed greatly to, the independence of the Areas from the national officials and each other. Thus it warrants consideration in itself.

In 1960 the four-day national conference was attended by only 135 voting delegates from the Areas. In addition, attending as non-voting *ex officio* delegates, there were the twenty-eight members of the national executive committee and the two national officials (the presidency was vacant). The NUM is one of the few British unions which completes its conference business.

Resolutions proposed by the national executive committee or Areas – with no more than three resolutions and two amendments permitted per Area – 'shall be in the hands of the Secretary not later than fourteen weeks prior to the date of the Annual Conference in order that they may be sent to the Areas at least twelve weeks prior to the Annual Conference' (NUM *Rules*, 1962: Section 23).[21] Amendments to resolutions must arrive at the Areas at least six weeks in advance. Usually no more than forty resolutions appear on the agenda, and some of these are subsequently withdrawn.

While the business committee for the conference may ask an Area to withdraw its resolution in favour of a suggested composite, Area conferences have been known to take formal votes as to whether the composite resolution should be accepted in place of the resolution originally submitted.[22] Emergency resolutions may be submitted to the national conference only with the consent of at least 75 per cent of the delegates present, and in 1960 only one such resolution was presented – by the national executive committee.[23]

One can appreciate the decision making at the conference only in the light of what happens in the Areas. Some Areas (probably all the large ones) hold conferences preceding the national conference itself. Branches have the opportunity to initiate resolutions for consideration first by the Area conference, the supreme authority within the Area, and then, if approved, by the national conference. The Area conferences (sometimes called councils) consist of delegates from the branches and meet regularly throughout the year. One such meeting is considered as the Area's annual conference, and is usually held at a time when decisions can be made on matters to come before the national conference.

Area delegations to the NUM national conference usually arrive instructed on nominations for the vice-presidency and other NUM offices, and, possibly, on NUM representatives to the Labour Party and Trades Union Congress. Derbyshire has actually conducted votes in the branches on all these questions.[24] In Durham, all resolutions passed at the Area conference (and apparently at the council) go back to the branches for votes of approval, together with brief summaries of the arguments presented for and against. The Areas follow through by casting the traditional block votes at the national conference. While the four largest Areas could dominate the national conference, they are usually divided politically.

On some matters the Areas leave the voting on resolutions in the hands of the delegations, which are expected to vote in accordance with the views expressed at the recent and previous Area meetings. In much of the British labour movement it seems to be assumed that a policy resolution stands as binding until altered by a subsequent conference, barring, of course, radically-changed circumstances.

The delegations need room for manoeuvre on the more tricky political questions: 'More than in most unions the drafting of a motion and the way in which it is advocated make all the difference between success and failure. Militant Areas like Scotland often try to word resolutions so innocently that they will command wide, and unsuspecting, support in the coalfields' (M. Harrison, 1960: 142). On the whole, however, the orthodox Labour majority has been more than their match.

While most questions at regular national conferences are thus settled in advance, the average delegate is probably unable to predict the vote on many questions. The debate proceeds (from observation and the minutes) in full seriousness, in an atmosphere of importance and occasional drama, with a mutual respect being reputedly even more characteristic of the Mine-workers than of other British groups. It would seem to be a good show-place for potential national officers.

Given the cohesiveness of the Mineworkers and the opportunity for communication which the relatively small conference affords, a sense of solidarity seems to be achieved, in spite of the prior decentralised decision making, which in the conventions of most large American unions is achieved only through manipulated fanfare and showmanship.

The creativity and overall quality of decision making are another matter. These can hardly be discussed apart from the union's possibilities for political and industrial action, nor, in recent years, outside the contexts of nationalisation and financial crisis for the industry. Most resolutions which involve economic demands require implementation by the national executive committee. Many which are believed by the leadership to be impracticable are 'remitted' to the national executive, since – as an official remarked to us – the members 'would never understand' the defeat of these proposals. Thus, the willingness to use the power of the union in disputes is usually involved, and this depends partly upon the political nature of the leadership.

On the whole, the policies of the orthodox Labour majority have generally prevailed. Major improvements in the working conditions of the mineworkers were begun in 1947 under the Labour Government, after nationalisation and during a coal shortage, and then a uniform national wages agreement for day-wage workers was negotiated and went into effect in 1955 (Jencks, 1966: 98–103). Since that time the main problems of the union have been to protect the mine-workers' interests in the face of the increasing mechanisation of coal cutting, pit closures and, more recently, the decline in their wages relative to other workers'. It would be difficult to say that the national conference as such has done more than provide pressure in the directions taken by the union. While facile judgements on the quality of the conferences' industrial decisions are not in order, the conference itself appears to have provided the basis for an overall legiti-mated national policy, formulated after considerable democratic involve-ment at lower levels. Superficially the entire process appears unwieldy, but the relatively small annual conferences, plus at least annual special con-ferences since 1949, have permitted the union to avoid a backlog of problems.

Some of the much-discussed disadvantages of mandating delegates (Allen, 1954: 131–3, 265–6, 309) do not apply to NUM national conferences. First of all, the objection that delegates should make decisions only after mutual confrontation and adequate discussion may be answered by refer-ence to the well-run Area conferences (that are, in turn, preceded by branch discussions), some of which meet both before and after other Areas have communicated their proposals. Second, mandating usually occurs in the NUM on broad questions of policy, and it is precisely here that members should expect the outcomes of conferences to conform to their views. Third, the gradually-changing structure of the coal-mining industry has allowed time for a slow development of ideas and their implementation. Finally, the union's conferences are frequent enough to permit a reversal of most policy decisions.

Some of the advantages of the decentralised preliminary decision making include (*a*) a clear check on the manipulation of the national conference by the national officials or even a strong minority of delegates, and (*b*) a respect for the decision-making process itself, reinforcing the cohesiveness of the union and contributing towards 'a political system allowing the peaceful "play" of power, the adherence of the "outs" to decisions made by the "ins", and the recognition by the "ins" of the rights of the "outs" – [without which] there can be no democracy' (Lipset, 1960a: 21).

Nevertheless, the NUM's conference cannot be recommended as a general political model: the block vote of its four disproportionately large regions *could* systematically dominate the conference and be disastrous for demo-cracy. It has worked as well as it has in the NUM partly because the top officers are elected elsewhere, and partly because of an accident of history: the domination of two of the four largest Areas – South Wales and Scot-land – by politically dissident (in this case, left-wing) forces. It is true that the political and administrative autonomy granted to the Areas has facilitated this political division (as has the geographic isolation of some of the coalfields), so that other democratic features of the Mineworkers must take much credit for the success of its conference in practice. But the block vote of such large subdivisions is indefensible, whether this is required by rules, based simply on tradition as in the Mineworkers, or based on the discipline of the dominant regional faction under a winner-take-all system for electing delegates. Yorkshire, until the early 1960s, was entitled to the maximum allowable delegation of twenty. Surely some system of proportional representation within 112,000-member Yorkshire would have been more democratic, with the delegates voting accordingly at conference, or, failing that, representation based on the several natural political subdivisions within Yorkshire itself.[25] However, as we shall see later, a direct ballot of members or branches is also available in the NUM for settling major policy-making questions.

THE NATIONAL EXECUTIVE COMMITTEE

One should not expect national conferences in organisations of several hundred thousand or more members to achieve co-ordination of policy and effort without leadership from smaller groups. In the Mineworkers the national executive committee has served this function, under the leadership – at times – of the top officer representing their majority view, and through the medium of a loose factional organisation among the important full-time officials.

Composition

The national executive committee consisted in 1960 of twenty-eight representatives from the Areas, plus the national president, vice-president and secretary as *ex officio* members. All but the representatives of the two Power Groups were elected in the Areas by branch vote (block votes of the individual branches) for two-year terms. Until perhaps the late 1950s, some Areas were permitted to use their own methods of election. While it has been theoretically possible for working mine-workers to dominate the committee, the Areas have usually included a chief officer – president or secretary – in their delegations or, failing that, another full-time Area officer. In 1958 there were five at least nominally-working mine-workers on the committee, which is perhaps high when one considers that most Areas had only one representative. The basis for representation was one delegate for fewer than 40,000 members, two for from 40,000 to 72,500, and three for 72,500 or more. Some recent problems of representation are discussed later.

Constitutional Power

The executive committee has considerable constitutional power. It holds Area officials and executive committees responsible to it for membership and financial records, negotiations at district or colliery level, and monthly reports of 'work done and proceedings taken' (Section 34). No Area has the power to complete an Area or district agreement 'without the previous approval of or under power delegated to them by the National Executive

Committee' which may 'withhold its approval . . . with a view to any out-standing points of difference being reconsidered or otherwise' (Section 36). Any Area or branch disputes 'likely or possible to lead to stoppage of work . . . must be immediately reported . . . to the National Executive Committee . . . and in no case shall a cessation of work take place . . . without the previous sanction' of the national executive committee or a committee to which it has delegated power, and strike pay shall not be available without this sanction (Section 41).

The Exercise of Leadership
One may well ask how and to what extent the pseudo-federal structure of the NUM has been able to provide the basis for an effective national leader-ship. It has been remarked that the inclusion of the chief Area officers on the national executive committee 'of course, increases the strength of the federal tendencies within the union. Each of these officers is reluctant to interfere with his peers lest he suffer in his turn' (Clegg *et al.*, 1961: 12). More specifically, an American observer commented: 'One feels that the NUM executive has not as yet been transformed wholly from an aggregation of powerful Area leaders into an effective unified national leadership' (Meyers, 1961: 77).

It is difficult to evaluate this criticism, but one official expressed the view to us in 1967 that it applied only during the incumbency of the second of the three NUM presidents (which ended in 1960, approximately the time the criticism was written). The point is that the chief executive plays a special and crucial role, as has been well stated elsewhere:

'Normally, we think of this organization-directing function [discovering opportunities in the environment and winning environmental support] as the responsibility of a board of trustees or directors or of a commission or a legislative body, such as a city council. But we know that often the chief executive is the key member of such a group and that when the board or council does effectively discharge organization-directing responsibilities, this fact frequently reflects the chief executive's capacity to energize his board or council . . . this also enables him to link the directing function to . . . the "organization-managing" function' (Thompson, 1966: 113).

In a few British unions it appears that the chief executives or their assistants spend considerable time before executive council meetings, often on the telephone, promoting their views on questions to be considered. *Perhaps* the structure of the Mineworkers makes such integrative leadership especially necessary, but there is no strong evidence that this is the case.

The following somewhat paraphrased remarks of a knowledgeable in-formant during an interview suggest the importance of personal leadership, even in the highly-structured situation of the NUM, and some of the factors which may make acceptable or effective leaders unavailable:

'Will Lawther [the first NUM president] was the acknowledged leader – where the noise came from. He was a brilliant orator, and dominated the annual conference. His style was flamboyant and free-wheeling [and, according to another informant, he was not averse to occasional trickery to get his way]. Lawther became very important nationally, in the union. He also became important in the Labour movement, based on his personal relationships in politics and in trade unions. This was very manifest. There was a slight recession in his importance later . . . The non-Communists couldn't get anyone satisfactory to them to run, on Lawther's retirement. A matter of money and "perks" [privileges and benefits, as Area officials]. They just kept asking for nominations. The big men, personality-wise, were outside of this office [not really interested or available].'

There were various points of view within the NUM in the early 1960s concerning its degree of centralisation. One Area official remarked that the 'federalism' of the union was more psychological than actual, while a national officer remarked that the union was well along the way to becoming a centralised national union. This point of view seemed to be more prevalent among officials who considered themselves to be in the minority, politically. (On the other hand, many members still spoke of their Areas as 'autonomous'.) A related but more complex view was presented in an interview in 1961 by an Area secretary and member of the national executive committee, in answer to the question: 'What feature of the union would you most like to change?':

'We need a complete reorganisation of the head office, its duties, and its relationship to the national executive committee. There are two people there [the president and general secretary], relatively detached from the rest of the union, and I am in my office here. The reason that there are not more meetings of committees is that they [the national officers] are overworked. They should devolve the work more, and use others to head the committees. [Could they appoint anyone to head a committee?] Yes, they could. In fact, Jones [the previous president] agreed, and Paynter [then general secretary] really agrees, but no one does anything.[26] We are a relatively new union [since reorganisation as the NUM], but too involved to sit down and evaluate: "Does the apparatus really work?" We are very conservative on organisational matters.'

Criticism of this type is not only familiar, but also classic. It does raise the question as to whether a weakness in the directing of the NUM, *if* greater than typical for a British union, may be due less to its pseudo-federal form directly than to starving the head office of the officers and staff necessary for it to function within its assigned sphere as a national office. However, the national office does have less to administer because of the decentralisation.

The 1965 conference passed a resolution to strengthen (or establish) national departments for industrial relations, safety, social insurance, research and a national magazine. The speaker for the resolution stated:

'The specialist departments in the areas are often stronger and more effective than those at headquarters . . . We know and fully recognise that to the extent that you improve, strengthen and make dominant a central authority, you will perhaps be taking away from the various Areas some of the authority that they now enjoy, but in this era some of that authority will disappear anyway. It is much better that it is surrendered in a planned and methodical way' (NUM, *Report of Annual Conference*, 1965: 99–100).

The recent financial situation of the union has probably hampered implementation. One may doubt that such centralisation of services would seriously reduce opposition for office, except where possible misuse of the magazine is concerned.

The national executive committee is allowed considerable discretion in handling negotiations with the National Coal Board, as is indicated in this analysis of the situation a little more than a year before the national strike in 1972:

'. . . for the first time since the war, the annual conference last summer passed a resolution coupling a claim [for a £20 minimum] with a call for strike action if it was not met in full. When the claim was duly not met, they [the militants] argue, it was open to the executive to recall the national conference, which could at least have fired a warning shot at the National Coal Board. It could also have called for a "proxy" vote [i.e. coalfield by coalfield] instead of a full-scale, referendum-style ballot. And it could have called for selective area strikes, rather than a national effort, without any ballot at all.

'The leadership chose to avoid all courses that were likely to bring them into conflict with the Coal Board. They went instead for a quick ballot [of members] on a national strike and it predictably turned out against such action [a two-thirds majority was required, but only 55·5 per cent approved]. They have arranged a ballot on the NCB's 12 per cent offer for this week, and it is predictable that this, too, will be in favour of acceptance [it was]. The NUM executive should not, however, be surprised that their tactics have led to a good deal of disillusion among rank and file miners' (Eric Jacobs, *Sunday Times*, 15 November 1970).

*   *   *

A letter to the *Scottish Miner* of December 1970 cited these arguments, and demanded the printing of the minutes of the executive committee in the union press so that the rank-and-file could see who voted how in two close votes on these matters.

In such circumstances, it was inevitable that the composition of the executive committee should be questioned, sooner or later. The retention of Area representation in a federal or pseudo-federal structure can lead to great imbalances in a committee of reasonable size, when the subdivisions are numerous and grossly unequal in membership. By 1973, some Areas had minuscule memberships, and it was claimed that groups with a total membership of no more than 10,000 had disproportionate power. Indeed, one source claimed they had ten votes on the executive – votes 'which were used on almost every occasion to stifle progressive policies' and 'to out-vote the other members who represented the majority in the union' (*Scottish Miner*, May 1973).[27] The 'headquarters' view' was that this was 'nonsense'. A resolution was on the books for the 1974 conference, but no change had taken place to correct the possible imbalance in recent years.

Discipline
Decentralisation in the NUM extends to the complete and constitutionally-guaranteed control by the branches and Areas of all funds (including sickness and retirement) retained by them. The national office is dependent upon being sent a modest portion of the dues collected locally.[28] The national executive committee retains only the right to approve small strike benefits (which were never granted until 1972) and payments from a political fund in support of Area-endorsed candidates for government office.[29] The American concept and practice of 'trusteeship', in which the national office (often the president) appoints local administrators to take over the duties of supposedly derelict local representatives, is unknown in the NUM and apparently in British unions generally.[30] To what extent then, and how, does the national office obtain compliance with its decisions?

First of all, the really important industrial decisions – those involving national agreements negotiated between the national executive committee and the Coal Board – are legitimated by special conferences, national ballots or both, as described above. Left-wing and militant officials in some Areas often loudly oppose acceptance, and sometimes receive sizeable votes, but only once since the formation of the NUM has a major Area failed to abide by a decision: Scotland supported a strike briefly in 1970, during the negotiations described above. In the last analysis, Area officials could probably be constitutionally removed by the national executive committee for breaches of discipline, unless their Areas seceded from the NUM. Thus far the latter has happened only with certain regional groups of craftsmen, some of which may have returned.

In general, the national office rules with a light hand. On lesser matters an Area council may refuse to comply with instructions from the general secretary, and then again with further instructions from the national executive committee, but we have been told at head office that they 'invariably' fall into line eventually (the craftsmen excepted), without explicit threat of disciplinary action. As the head office sees it, they point out painstakingly, systematically and unobtrusively what the rules and national decisions have meant over the years. They ordinarily have in their favour the solidarity of the miners, which is extended to the national union.

BEYOND LEGITIMACY

There have been three major cases in the NUM, all centring on Yorkshire, where local industrial struggles, reached almost Area-wide proportions outside and beyond the control of the established union machinery, or even spread to other Areas (to South Wales, in 1969). In addition, there have been infrequent accusations of irregularities in elections. It is instructive to see how such breakdowns in legitimacy have been resolved.

The 1961 Strike in Yorkshire
Unofficial strikes in British coal-mining have usually centred on immediate situations at the workplace, and have most often involved piece-work rates under highly variable conditions of work. While strikes tended to occur more often than in other industries, they have also been shorter, involved fewer workers and resulted in fewer days lost annually per worker (Jencks, 1966: 109). Officials in even Communist-led Areas have generally neither promoted nor condoned unofficial strikes, but officials in most Areas have accepted them as a fact of life.

The 1961 Yorkshire Area strike lasted over two weeks and involved, at its peak, about half of the Area's 120,000 workers, on the basis of general demands for a 10 per cent increase in piece-work rates and a guaranteed wage per shift. The Labour Party was divided at that time over the issue of unilateral nuclear disarmament, and the Yorkshire officials accused Communist and other left-wingers of attempting to take over the Area politically and then swing the entire NUM into the anti-Gaitskell camp.

The outcome is illuminating. The strike was lost and one man was expelled from the union about five months later (without losing his job, in spite of the closed shop), only to be reinstated in two weeks by a vote of delegates from the 104 pits, taken at an Area council meeting. Of three men severely censured at the time of the expulsion, one – a Communist, Jock Kane – was elected as a full-time official in 1963, while another was runner-up in this same election. The national executive committee took no concrete disciplinary action.[31]

Disputed Decisions and Election Results

We found only one accusation of large-scale ballot rigging after 1945, in one of the small group of larger Areas which did not have (at that time, at least) their ballots counted by the Electoral Reform Society. The election, in the Lancashire Area, was re-run, and the same candidate won although with a lesser, but still considerable, majority: by approximately 3,000 votes as compared to 5,000 initially, out of approximately 18,000 total in the second election (see *The Times*, 18 and 31 October 1960, 15 and 16 January 1961; *News Chronicle*, 17 October 1960; *Daily Worker*, 18 October 1960; *Daily Herald*, 24 October 1960). The tally sheets of the Electoral Reform Society for the 1959–60 elections for the national secretary and president show 964 ballot papers disallowed for 'similar handwriting' and 468,667 valid ballots (plus ballots invalid for other reasons) in the first election, and 1,798 and 412,556 respectively in the third. (The tally sheets for the second election made no reference to similar handwriting or any other specific cause for invalid ballots.) In the first election, fourteen branches were involved in such disallowances (in three large and two small Areas), with the four branches contributing the greatest numbers of similar hand-writings having from 108 to 152 such ballots each. In the third election, 1,466 similar handwritings came from twenty-seven branches in three Areas (with a total of four large and four small Areas involved). A total of 1,230 branches was shown individually on the tally sheets for the third election, but in addition there were grouped data for South Wales, Cumberland, Power Group No. 2, and the Derbyshire and Nottinghamshire Winding Enginemen's Association. It may be inferred from the Areas involved, and from the candidates most favoured by the particular branches, that irregularities were perpetrated especially by local zealots in support of their favourite sons or politically-favoured nominees. However, certain Areas with such nominees were involved hardly or not at all. The counts by the Society have never, to our knowledge, been challenged by any union.

In other instances there have been disputes over irregularities in particular branches or over technicalities (see *The Manchester Guardian*, 31 January 1961; *The Times*, 26 September 1961). The cases where a full-time Area or national official has been forced to resign, or has been removed, once over the initial hurdles, have been extremely rare, and with one possible exception since 1945 have not involved political differences. (One left-wing Area official among others predominantly more right-wing in his Area told us that the others would protect him against potential threats to his job.) In general, the union has not appeared to be reluctant to re-run elections (although the outcomes have almost invariably been the same), but neither have the members appeared to be reluctant to use the courts where necessary. The surprising aspect of this is that both left- and right-wingers, in the Mineworkers as in other British unions, accept the right of members to appeal to the courts in defence of their rights, as laid down in their union's own rules. Where elections in the NUM are concerned, the courts have not been as effective as the desire of the union's representatives to avoid the basis for any serious charges or to support democratic values.

COMMUNICATIONS

One common cause of oligarchic control in national unions, exclusive control over the formal means of communication, is lacking in the NUM nationally and even within most of its Areas. The national union's monthly *Information Bulletin*, published at least during most of the 1950s and 1960s, was slanted towards the union's officials and staff and perhaps at least equally, one suspects, towards interested people in the Coal Board and in politics. It lacked news-stories and articles directed towards even the most active members, and would not qualify as a union journal. The current newspaper, *The Miner*, was established only in recent years. Only the NUM and the Boot and Shoe Operatives did not have journals in 1952, among the eighteen largest unions affiliated to the Trades Union Congress (B. C. Roberts, 1957: 323–4).[32]

The union circulates minutes of the national executive committee meetings to Area and chief branch officers, probably one or two copies per branch. Since the executive committee must first accept the minutes of its preceding meeting, there is usually a lag of about two months between a meeting and the arrival of its minutes at the branches. With appendixes these minutes can run to sixty pages. They contain valuable information, particularly in reports of negotiations with the Coal Board, but, as one Area official remarked, it would take 'the studious type' to read them regularly. (The minutes have not normally reported how individual representatives voted.)

Of the nine large geographic Areas in the NUM (see Table 8.1), only South Wales, Scotland and Derbyshire (all left-of-centre) had journals or newspapers in late 1960 (Derbyshire's was started in 1957). The Colliery Officials and Staffs Association, a right-wing Area, may also have had a publication then, since we discovered one some years later. Apart from these there could not have been much else of significance, and it is doubtful that these publications had much circulation outside their own Areas. Furthermore, seven Area secretaries with whom we were in correspondence believed that there were no branch journals or newsletters in their Areas, and three made no mention of them.[33] Thus, few official publications existed which could have influenced either the general opinions of the mineworkers or their votes in union elections.

The situation has been similar with respect to campaign literature in the NUM's national elections: the union has never printed election addresses (although a subcommittee of the executive committee proposed this in 1945), and flyers by branches, Areas or the candidates themselves have been considered illegal. A Scottish branch which was charged with issuing a flyer in support of a presidential candidate in 1954 apologised 'unreservedly' for this in a letter to the national executive committee (Proceedings of the National Executive Committee, 1954: 215–16). The apology was simply 'received'; the election was not close. Derbyshire printed election addresses of candidates for its full-time posts in 1959, and displayed them prominently in its newspaper, but it claimed to be unique in this respect.

One of the minor left-wing candidates in the May 1960 presidential election, when asked in July 1961 what would be an ideal system for running such an election, gave this somewhat bitter though perhaps only half-serious reply: 'I would take each candidate, and put him in a room by himself, and give him an hour to write his election address, with no opportunity to have anyone else write it for him. Then I'd have these addresses distributed to the membership.' He argued further that the absence of election addresses was generally to the benefit of the right wing in the union.

Much of the communications void is filled, when important votes are scheduled, by the nation's daily and weekly press, and often radio and television. The NUM is one of the least secretive of British unions, and the communications media seem to grant it attention even beyond the union's place in the economy. Basic biographies of candidates, such as some organisations might circulate along with ballot papers, are common and sometimes lengthy. It is often possible to tell left-wing from right-wing candidates, with the two leading candidates indicated. Descriptions of the NUM's voting system appeared frequently during the three national union elections in 1959 and 1960, often with editorial praise and suggestions that other unions should follow suit. (The Electrical Trades Union, under Communist leadership, was then under scrutiny regarding possible fraud in its elections for national officers.) The praise for the voting system did not cease after a Communist was elected in the first election, in 1959.

Publicity for a militant or other position taken by an Area before a national conference, or before the completion of a national referendum, may influence members in other Areas or exert pressure on the national executive committee. Of course, it can also build up an Area's leadership in the eyes of its own members. For example, one national newspaper reported, prior to the 1961 national conference, that the South Wales Area had 'passed a resolution instructing the union [national] executive to press the National Coal Board for a substantial increase in wages. The resolution ended: "If it fails to obtain a satisfactory conclusion, the union will consider using its industrial power until the wage increase is granted"' (*The Manchester Guardian*, 13 March 1961).

The Areas have not always been broad-minded when individual members have utilised the press. A branch secretary in Leicestershire was 'suspended from membership of the union for two years because . . . he wrote to *The Manchester Guardian* . . . [claiming] that the agenda for the union's annual conference was not seen or discussed by local branches . . . He described the situation as "totalitarian"' (*The Observer*, 4 December 1960). He appealed the suspension to the national executive committee, which we presume overturned it. In another case in early 1974, Frank Smith, the Leicestershire Area secretary and a member of the NUM executive council, was called to task during the then ongoing dispute (and, indeed, precipitated a one-day strike) because he had allowed his own unmilitant line to be used by the media. For this he issued an apology (*The Times*, 8 January 1974).

There are, of course, dangers in having to rely primarily on external sources. In one national election with several candidates a newspaper erred in focusing attention on a supposedly-leading but actually minor orthodox Labour candidate, to the possible disadvantage of this cause. And the Communist secretary of the NUM complained to us that the press became really interested in only those elections where there were Communist candidates, who were then given less than fair treatment (but in our view, more than their share of publicity, which often helps). On the whole, however, the press seems to have played a useful role in partially filling a vacuum, at least since 1959. This applies equally to the engineers' union, to be discussed in Chapter 9.

Nevertheless, the absence of adequate official channels has encouraged candidates or their supporters to use subterfuge to influence some members in other Areas, or to stimulate the vote in their own. The first case we are aware of occurred in the huge Yorkshire Area. The *Yorkshire Miner*, the first official newspaper in 101 years of the Area's history, was launched in May 1959 by decision of the Area council, and published its second issue in January 1960, shortly before the voting took place which elected Machen to be president. Machen himself contributed, or was the subject of, about one-third of each issue (ten and eight pages total, respectively). The newspaper went out of existence after the election. Also published in the latter part of 1959 was a 130-page report of a delegation to China, with Machen recognisable in over 35 of the 105 photographs (see Yorkshire Area, NUM, 1959). These publications made no mention of the coming election.

THE 1968 NATIONAL ELECTION

The most recent elections for national secretary and president show the development of a more organised and less restrained factionalism cutting across Area boundaries. The 1968 election of Lawrence Daly also shows a more than superficial relationship between the programme of the winner and the industrial policy of the union, pursued in the 1972 national strike and continued in the protracted dispute of 1973–4 against the government incomes policy. Lastly, the 1968 election shows how a rank-and-filer fought his way from this status to one of the two top offices in just a few years. All these events are, of course, interconnected.

Daly's initial steps towards the top were taken in Scotland, in opposition to the Communist Party. The general Scottish background is therefore important. In 1929 there was a split in the Scottish section of the Miners' Federation of Great Britain, and the United Mineworkers of Scotland was formed under left-wing, largely Communist leadership. It did not have the recognition of the Federation, of course, and finally dissolved itself in 1936, advising its members to join the recognised union. However, Communists in other Areas did not take similar action, and the account of the principal chronicler of the mine-workers' unions attributes this development to the unwillingness of right-wing officials to relinquish power after a landslide defeat in the union's elections (Arnot, 1955: 185–96, 213–22).

We have been told that the Communist Party in Scotland gained greatly, both in experience and in the development of a core of disciplined members, from leading its members out of, and then back into, the Miners' Federation. The Scottish and South Wales Areas are probably the only ones in which the Communist Party as such has considerable strength, and in the Scottish Area it has so much that, it has been stated, if Communist memberships in British unions generally were comparable, the Party would constitute a mass movement.

The strength of the Scottish Communists no doubt reflects a greater support for left-wing politics in sections of Scotland than elsewhere in Great Britain. At any rate, the only long-term Communist MP, from 1935 to 1951, represented a Scottish constituency. It is significant that Daly made some political progress within this same constituency, as will be shown.

Prior to Daly's first achievement of full-time Area office, both of the Scottish Area's top posts were held by Communists. Since 1960 at least, pro-Eastern bloc political views have set the general tone for the *Scottish Miner*. Signed articles on international affairs have usually been critical of American policy, but either silent on Russia's role or accepting of its peace proposals. There is the usual quota of reports of visits made by Scottish mine-workers to Eastern bloc countries at the invitation of their miners' or other unions, usually with favourable comments or implications.[34] One interesting aspect of the numerous official foreign visits in the NUM is that these are shared, on a rotation basis, among the members of the appropriate committee – usually the national or an Area executive committee. At the Area level it is common practice to send one full-time official along with the rank-and-file executive committee members. Thus, there is an incentive for all to accept the invitations of even the government-dominated unions of the Communist countries, which account for most of the invitations received. It must be admitted that, in Britain, these are not sure signs of Communist domination; it is a matter here of degree. But deviations from the Party line have occurred. For example, Frank Allaun, MP, a frequent contributor, has praised the Yugoslav trade unions and government as being 'independent both of American and Russian governments' (*Scottish Miner*, February 1963: 5). For whatever reason, the Scottish Area Communist leaders, who certainly included some hard-liners (note Moffat, 1965), seem to have displayed a non-totalitarian public face. Such was the climate for Daly's rise.

Daly's political background has been described by *Tribune* (1 January 1965: 4):

'Daly was an active Communist until 1956, when he broke with the British party because of its automatic endorsement of Soviet policies. Instead of swinging wildly Right, he became closely associated with the New Reasoner Group and the *New Left Review* and, in 1957, formed the Fife Socialist League, advocating positive neutralism and unilateralism for Britain, and the extension of public ownership with democratic control. He regards E. P. Thompson's "Essay on Socialist Humanism" (*New Reasoner* No. 1) as his "Socialist Bible."

'Standing on behalf of the Fife Socialist League, he became a Fife County Councillor in 1958, with a sweeping victory over Labour and Communist opponents. Even in the 1959 General Election, he secured 5,000 votes in West Fife, pushing the Communist candidate down to below 4,000 in the seat that Willie Gallagher [Communist M.P.] held until 1951.

'On the county council he harassed the Labour machine, which he thought bureaucratic and over-orthodox, while he himself was harassed at every turn, inside and outside his union, by the Communists.

'Earlier this year [1964], the Fife Socialist League dissolved and Daly joined the Labour Party, as other members were advised to do . . .

'This does not mean that Daly has compromised his *New Left* views . . .'

Daly's early union career included his membership of the Scottish Area Youth Committee, the posts of branch secretary (in 1946) and chairman and, in 1957, of pit delegate to the Area council. Some time later he was elected to the Area's rank-and-file executive council.

He achieved his first full-time post, as mine-workers' agent in Fife, Clackmannan and Stirlingshire, in 1964 at the age of thirty-nine, beating a Communist-backed opponent by better than two to one. In this election he had the support of the newly-formed anti-Communist Scottish Labour Miners' Association, and of the virulently anti-Communist *IRIS News*, which concentrates on union elections. This was an unusual development for both the NUM and the British union movement, because such an association, consisting only of mine-workers, would have to be an admittedly intra-union faction. *IRIS News* quoted Sid Ford, the national union president, as saying, 'I will not lose any sleep over its formation,' in the context of an anti-Communist speech, and added, 'Scottish Labour Miners have interpreted the comment as an official blessing of the Association' (January 1964: 1, 8).

It was at about this time, but probably after this election, that the Fife Socialist League was dissolved. One may surmise that Daly's participation in local politics did no harm to his progress within the union to that point. This avenue for the building of local reputations is not unusual for British unionists who achieve full-time office, but it is normally done through the Labour Party.

From this point on, Daly's rise in the union was surprisingly rapid. He was elected general secretary of the Scottish Area one year later, in early 1965, to become the first non-Communist to hold that office in almost twenty years. According to *Tribune*, 'Alex Moffat, the Communist president of the Scottish NUM, holds the press largely responsible for the defeat of his party's nominee' (1 January 1965), who was defeated by approximately 20,000 votes to 12,000 in a 79 per cent poll. Only thirteen branches had backed Daly officially, as against forty-one backing the Communist.

Just a few months later Daly was declared the loser to two Communists in a branch vote for two Scottish posts on the national executive committee. Daly claimed that the result was based on irregularities in the conduct of the election, as two of the branches that submitted votes had never held meetings. This allegation was forwarded to the national office. Alex Moffat, the Scottish president, reportedly stated at first that the letters of complaint were fraudulent and part of a campaign which was a 'gross interference with the work of the trade unions' (*IRIS News*, May 1965: 1). However, a short time later the Scottish executive committee backed Moffat's initiative as president (at least technically) in disallowing the disputed votes, and declared Daly one of the two winners, by a very close margin, along with Moffat himself. Moffat finally argued that the mistakes were honest ones, committed by branch committees 'acting on branch decisions', and that a similar unconstitutional vote had occurred in another branch in 1961 to the disadvantage of the Communist candidate for the Area vice-presidency. Finally he said, 'People who scandalise the good name of this Union by running to the press instead of using the Union machinery to deal with complaints, haven't got the interest of the miners at heart' (*Scottish Miner*, May 1965: 1). Daly's post on the national executive committee was no doubt useful, perhaps even critical, in the 1968 national election, which he won by just 10,000 votes.

Perhaps the major factional innovation in Daly's campaign for the national secretaryship in 1968 was the publication of his pamphlet, *The Miners and the Nation*, by the Scottish Area. This programmatic statement called for the public ownership of all fuel industries by a single national energy authority responsible to the government (*Scottish Miner*, September 1968). The NUM's 1961 conference, in fact, urged the Labour Party and the Trades Union Congress to campaign for the public ownership of all basic fuel industries (*Tribune*, 14 July 1961). Daly's pamphlet also advocated guerrilla strikes both against the Coal Board's policy of pit closures and in favour of his fuel policy, which called for underwriting the coal industry at its current level. We don't know how widely Daly's pamphlet was circulated outside Scotland, but it was reviewed in the *Scottish Miner* (September 1968: 5) by officials of the Kent and South Wales Areas. The latter stated that it 'should be "A Must" to be read by all miners in the British Coalfield'.

Daly's only opponent in the 1968 election was Joe Gormley, of Lancashire, who was the secretary of the newly-named North-Western Area of the NUM and a member of the Labour Party's national executive. Gormley argued, in an open letter to Daly which was quoted at length in the press, that Daly's strategy 'means taking industrial action at the most productive collieries. I know of no more certain way of hastening the demise of this industry than to cripple the strongest units first . . . Threaten a stoppage and the busiest people in the country will be the sales representatives of oil, electricity and gas.' Concerning the pamphlet itself, Gormley found it 'presumptuous of any area to circulate a booklet on the pretence that it should form the basis of discussion when discussions have been proceeding within the union for more than a decade and when policy has been formulated and approved by conference' (*Daily Telegraph*, 1 November 1968). He was saying, by implication, that the publication of Daly's pamphlet was an unfair campaign tactic.

Daly received the support of the Communist Party in the secretary's election, in spite of his having received anti-Communist support in his rise to the Scottish secretaryship, but according to *IRIS News* (October 1968: 5) this was only after many Communists bitterly opposed to this decision had fallen into line.[35] He also received the aid of the non-Communist leftist *Voice of the Unions* and its various loosely-associated supporters, this apparently being the first such organised effort at campaigning in the NUM on a national or near-national scale. Shortly before the election *IRIS News* (November 1968: 5) said that there was little sign of any organised support for Gormley, while the 'Communist Machine' was 'highly geared for this particular election and they are leaving nothing to chance particularly in the Yorkshire and Midlands coalfields.'

The Areas originally supporting Daly were Scotland, South Wales,

Derbyshire and Kent, and those supporting Gormley were the North-West (which included Lancashire), Durham, Cumberland and South Derbyshire. *The Times* (5 September 1968) reported: 'The result may depend on the choice of a nomination by the big Yorkshire Area . . . Both Mr. Daly and Mr. Gormley will be among the half-dozen names they consider.' The *Scottish Miner* (September 1968: 1) reported: 'It was the first time a Scottish Area nominee had been chosen unanimously [in Scotland] for a national position.'

Gormley lost the election, no doubt largely because of the disillusionment of the mine-workers with the Labour Government's policies towards the trade unions and coal industry. In fact, the Government White Paper on the coal industry led some NUM leaders to threaten a disaffiliation from the Labour Party and the putting forward of the Mineworkers' candidates in appropriate constituencies. Gormley himself led this short-lived move, which was in character in the light of his impetuous manner and 'his sudden and not always consistent enthusiasms' (*The Times*, 11 June 1971), but it has been suggested that it was designed to outflank the left and to avoid his being stuck in the position of being identified with unpopular government measures. In 1967, the leading right-wing candidate for the presidency of the Engineers, John Boyd, had made a similarly rebellious move, also unsuccessfully.

THE 1971 NATIONAL ELECTION

Gormley's only competitor in the 1971 presidential election was Michael McGahey, who was on the executive committee of the British Communist Party. McGahey had won the presidency of the Scottish Area less than a year before by 13,149 votes to 8,499, evidently in a bitter campaign since shortly after the election he inveighed against 'certain elements, who are prepared to enter a smear campaign' (*Scottish Miner*, January 1968: 1) based on his politics. McGahey, who was to rise to national prominence in 1973–4, appears to have been a less than ideal candidate for the left, because Daly had been the first Scottish candidate to achieve a top post in the NUM, and the capture of the second top post by the same Area would have been unprecedented.

This time Gormley was not to be caught napping, as is evident from this news item which appeared about three weeks before the voting:

'Mr. Joe Gormley . . . yesterday defended the decision of his Area executive to vote £8,000 for his campaign in the NUM presidency election. He has been accused by his Communist rival . . . of "unscrupulous tactics" in the campaign.

'Mr. Gormley told the union's North-Western Area conference at

Blackpool: "It will be money well spent if a man who understands the problems of the North-West is elected"' (*Daily Telegraph*, 7 May 1971).

The authorisation of these funds caused the resignation of an elected trustee of the North-Western Area, reported shortly after the voting had started and probably 'too late to do much harm to Gormley's chances'. 'A great deal of the money goes in expenses paid to canvassers whipping up support for their man in other coalfields. Gormley has politely pointed out that election campaigners are on union business and therefore are due to be paid for loss of earnings' (*The Times*, 28 May 1971).

Gormley won the election by 117,663 votes to 92,883. Given the fact that there were only two candidates in the 1968 election, we strongly suspect that, if Gormley had won this previous election, Daly would have won against any available candidate in 1971. McGahey was elected vice-president at the 1973 conference by 155 votes to 126.

We have been told that Daly visited Yorkshire as part of his 1968 campaign, but only under the pretext of having been invited to deal with the problems of the many displaced Scottish mine-workers who had been transferred to this Area. In contrast, Gormley's canvassers represented a radical break with the tradition of non-interference in the affairs of other Areas – an even greater break with past practice than Daly's circumventing the supposed prohibition on campaign flyers by his Area's publication of his pamphlet.

The trend towards open internal American-style factions (see Chapter 7) has gone even further. The Yorkshire Association of Labour Miners, formed in 1972 to prevent the takeover of the Yorkshire coalfield by left-wingers, is open to any NUM member who has 'no connection with proscribed organizations' (*IRIS News*, September 1972: 9). The chairman of the new association granted an interview to the press, and an editorial welcomed the formation of the association. Surely, left-wingers could respond in kind if they wished to.

TOWARDS LEGITIMATE FACTIONS?

There is a great difference between a break with past practice and the establishment of a new legitimacy. The NUM has not had a chance to resolve these contradictions to its established order, and it seems doubtful that Areas of grossly unequal size will be granted *carte blanche* for the financing of election campaigns. And so far as we are aware, election addresses are *still* proscribed where national office is concerned. Either (*a*) the NUM will have to move towards a greater and more explicit permissiveness in electioneering and internal political life, probably with some consideration to fairness and perhaps with the provision of informational facilities, or (*b*) in reaction against the most indefensible campaign practices, there will be an attempt to tighten up generally and a return to the more usual limitations on civil rights in British trade unions, which exist under the guise of equal opportunity for all. Such an attempt would probably fail in the NUM, as it has in the past.

May a further politicisation in the NUM lead to the formation of a two-party system? The fact that there were only two candidates in both the 1968 and 1971 national elections may have been the result of bloc making in advance – we are not informed on this. However, such a coalition would not represent a party, at least on the left. First, it is too heterogeneous and takes its internal political differences too seriously; there is no love lost between the Communists and many of the non-Communists on the left, and many of the latter support particular left-wing sects. Second, the political situations within the Areas are too different for the regional political line-ups to be equivalent; for example, the leading opponents of the Communists in Scotland and South Wales are unlikely to be orthodox Labour. Third, the diffuse competition in the Areas, at all levels, is not likely to be channelled exclusively into party lines, and certainly not into two parties. Finally, the electoral system is such as to permit at least a three-way race with little if any loss in votes to the opposition (or the leading runner-up). *A two-party system is therefore unlikely, and is unnecessary for close elections, as we have shown.* Also, it would place too many constraints on the political process for it to be optimal for democracy. The continued development of more open and organised factions *might* lead to what some would choose to call a multi-party system, but this would be a far cry from its supposed governmental model, unless there were a great politicisation of the British working class – and an electoral system in the union which could reward political tendencies according to their degree of support – i.e. proportional representation.[36]

UNION POLITICS AND THE 1972 NATIONAL STRIKE

The historic seven-week national strike of the Mineworkers in 1972 resulted in an overwhelming victory for the union. It was the first official strike since the major defeat in the 1926 'general strike' (or lock-out), and there is no doubt that this experience had much to do with the long-term reluctance of the majority of the national executive committee to consider official strikes seriously. However, we have the impression that, for some of those in the upper ranks of the union's officialdom after nationalisation, official strikes were simply unthinkable and beyond questions of pragmatic judgement. The National Union of Railwaymen, which came to the aid of the Miners' Federation in 1926 and also sustained a serious defeat, was not similarly affected.

We are interested here only in the highlights of the decision-making process, and what these show about the strengths and weaknesses of the Mineworkers' democracy. The decision to strike in 1972 was certainly the
culmination to well over a decade of discussion and agitation by the more
militant Areas for national 'industrial action', with formal decisions taken
at Area and national conferences, in the national executive committee and
in membership ballots playing important roles. Daly's platform on industrial action in his 1968 campaign was also directly relevant, as was his
behaviour after the election (to be touched on below).

However, the 1972 strike was also the result of the wildcat strikes in
Yorkshire described earlier, and of the more comprehensive wildcats in
1969 and 1970. The national membership was divided and never overwhelmingly in favour of a strike, which was part of the problem. But the
majority of workers in any industry are rarely in favour of a major strike
until such is advocated by their recognised leaders. Ultimately, one must
face the questions of whether the leadership could and should have avoided
the massive wildcats prior to the strike by taking the leadership earlier, and,
if so, of to what extent the leadership failure was due to the NUM's political
system.

The background to the 1972 strike (and subsequent industrial relations
developments in 1973–4) can be found in changes in the mining industry
(and for the latter the onset of the 'world energy crisis'). In 1947 there were
over 700,000 mine-workers producing 197 million tons of coal (including
10 million tons from open-cast workings); twenty-five years later, 286,000
mine-workers were producing 133 million tons of coal. The number of
collieries in 1947 was 958; by 1971 this had been reduced to 292.

The drop in employment was due to increased competition from fuel oil,
particularly after the peak output year of 1957, to an increase in the world
production of coal and nuclear power, and to the extensive mechanisation
of British coal mining. The output per man shift, which was 21·5 tons in
1947, reached 44·2 tons in 1971 (according to NCB figures for 1971). The
ratio of these outputs per man year was 262 to 463. Over this period the
mine-workers' earnings declined both relatively and absolutely. The 1971
conference, under pressure from militants, demanded increases in the
minimum wage rates that would have cost £120 million per year. The bulk
of these increases were finally won.

The wildcat strike in October 1969 preceded the decision of the national
executive council to recommend acceptance of the Coal Board's proposal.
At its peak the strike affected 130,000 mine-workers in 140 of the Coal
Board's 306 pits, with 70,000 strikers in Yorkshire and 10,000 or more in
each of the South Wales, Scottish, Derbyshire and Nottinghamshire Areas.
The leaders of the Yorkshire strikers called for the resignation of the two
top national officers (including Daly), and led a lobby of 150 mine-workers

to the meeting of the national executive committee. During the strike the South Wales Area announced that a large majority of its branches favoured a national strike, and the Coal Board made what *The Times* described as an offer of a 'substantial' increase in wages (20 October 1969; see also 21 and 22 October). The executive council voted to accept this offer, over the opposition of the strikers (pay was not the only issue), and subsequently a national delegate conference and a ballot of members confirmed this decision.

Shortly afterwards a manifesto by a group of mine-workers appeared in the *Voice of the Unions* (Christmas 1969), taunting Daly (whom the *Voice* had supported for office) and offering a programme for action:

'Well, Lawrence, what happened? Are you a prisoner of the Executive? Have you given up so soon? Don't they play the game according to the rules? Well, you know where the basis of your power lies. It's in us, the members who elected you to high office. It's not too late to stand up and defy the National Executive, to call for a ballot for strike action behind the 40-hour week . . . – not a ballot for or against the 27/6; that's an N.E.C. trick, since of course everyone wants the 27/6 for the day-wage men; but a straight vote for a strike on the 40-hour week.

'Let the N.E.C. do what it will then; we shall support you. If you don't support the very actions you encouraged, then you've said it, "we become ineffective and discredited as a Union." Over 100,000 men on unofficial strike understand what you meant. Did you?'

The manifesto's programme for democracy in the union included:

'(11) Periodic election of all full-time officials at all levels;
'(12) A National Executive of lay members elected by areas from working miners;
'(13) Rationalisation of areas to come in line with [Coal] Board areas, with assignment of greater funds to the centre where these can be more economically centralised.'[37]

The programme advocated for the industry included union control of pit management, and union power to veto major appointments to both the Area and national levels of the Coal Board. To discuss and develop a programme further, branch action committees were advocated as well as joint action committees with other branches.

The 1970 wildcat activity, which also involved over 100,000 strikers, was exceptional in that it had the official backing, for a time, of at least one Area. The politics of the situation are conveyed by these selections from a letter by a Scottish mine-worker (Michael Fitzpatrick, *Scottish Miner*, January 1971: 6):

'Along with hundreds of others I attended a mass rally and demonstration in the Usher Hall.

'I recall with amusement – and sorrow – some of the verbal barbs let loose from Lawrence Daly's armoury.

'"Let there be no compromise, we are asking for and shall accept no less than five pounds."

'"I shall be in the forefront of the strike when it comes, official or unofficial."

'The rejection of the compromise came shortly afterwards; not by Lawrence Daly and his compatriots, but by the South Wales, Scottish and Yorkshire divisions.

'At a delegate conference in Edinburgh the Scottish executive were given a mandate to strike, with the exception of some four Ayrshire pits.

'The struggle was on with a vengeance, and soon the effects were beginning to tell. . . .

'Here I come to the saddest part of the story.

'Like a bolt from the blue came an invitation to a recall conference by the Scottish Executive, where our delegates, among others, were exhorted by the executive to return to work.

'May I pose the following questions.

'WHERE? WHEN? WHY? were these decisions taken.

'Mr. McGahey, in his television confrontations, backed the strike all the way, yet capitulated when it had reached its full momentum. I aver that it was a complete betrayal of our South Wales comrades, and they were left to play an abortive rearguard action.

'How can we deprecate the actions of such as Lawrence Daly when our own leaders in Scotland have displayed such temerity?

'I write this with the complete backing of the officials and members of our branch . . .'

The apparent ambivalence of the full-time left-wing leaders of the unofficial strike may have been based on a fear of removal from office for outright defiance of not only the national executive council, but also (technically) the membership. A motion for a national strike had been defeated some months before under the two-thirds rule, only 55·5 per cent being in favour of striking. At any rate, it could be argued that a wildcat which had little chance of becoming official in short order was unlikely to result in a comprehensive national agreement with the Coal Board. At the July 1971 conference the constitution was amended (not unanimously) to require only a 55 per cent majority for a national strike, and a ballot conducted in late November 1971 showed 58·8 per cent in favour of a strike, with 85 per cent of the members voting. Shortly before the count was announced, *The Times* (29 November 1971) reported that the left-wing leaders had been striving to prevent further wildcats in the hope of achieving an all-out national strike.

The strike began in early January 1972 and continued for more than a month. The rank-and-file refused to allow safety work to be done at the majority of mines, contrary to the policy of the national union, and spontaneously organised the picketing of coal reserves at electric power stations and other key points, although much time was lost before this began. The threat of a national power crisis hastened the successful end of the strike. It would appear that this mass participation was informal and unstructured, or at any rate not officially inspired, and that there was again a gap between the formal leadership and rank-and-file (as there often is in such mobilisations, especially when the leadership has been somewhat reluctant – in this case, possibly through fear of prosecution under the relatively new and untried Industrial Relations Act 1971).

Where union democracy is concerned, what can one make of the extremely tardy use of the strike weapon, and the apparent lack of responsiveness of the union to the continuing unrest in Yorkshire and elsewhere? Before attempting this evaluation, let us note that union democracy is unlikely to resolve all problems of industrial relations, that unofficial strikes are often an adjunct to democracy, which is always imperfect, and that probably the least democratic unions are the harshest in their treatment of wildcatters.

There are also some more directly pertinent mitigating factors for the behaviour of the union and its leadership. First, the two-thirds requirement for a national strike ballot, which existed for historical reasons, undoubtedly delayed the strike decision. Second, there were important differences in pay and problems from Area to Area, and the potential support for a strike was bound to differ accordingly. For example, a crucial national agreement made in 1966 to equalise the earnings of face-workers delayed a considerable portion of the raise (£2·77½ per week) until the end of 1971 for face-workers in South Wales, Scotland and some other Areas, although there is no simple relationship between profitability and strike-proneness (see Eric Jacobs, *Sunday Times*, 6 February 1970). Third, perhaps some of the unofficial strikes, even though unwanted, were utilised for reaching better regional or national agreements. Finally, disagreements over particular strikes at least are legitimate, and one cannot expect leaders who oppose a strike to advocate one.

The latter point does, however, relate to the one obvious flaw in the formal government of the NUM: the permanence of full-time officials at all levels. The unofficial strikes of the Yorkshire mine-workers were usually condemned by their top Area officials, but there was no practical opportunity to campaign for an alternative leadership.[38] There is every reason to believe that the full-time officials in politically-divided Yorkshire would have had to fight for re-election. Perhaps a greater latitude for official Area strikes was also necessary for democracy, although sometimes even the Area itself was too large a unit for decision making. The Coal Board allowed considerable autonomy to its divisions in negotiations with the union. However, it would be hard to argue for the formalisation of Area autonomy with respect to the right to strike in a once declining nationalised industry in which the Areas would to some extent be competing against each other. Periodic elections are no cure-all, as we shall see, and are anathema to the technocratic mind, but together with other democratic features of organisation they may make a difference. The NUM is an excellent candidate for such a possibility.

CONCLUSIONS

The Mineworkers has sustained moderately close elections in filling vacancies in its top national and Area posts since 1918. There are no signs of any tendency for the competition to fade. The leading competitors for the top posts have usually been top full-time Area officials, and there have usually been three or more such candidates in any one election. The two top posts have been shared by relatively left-wing and right-wing political tendencies, at least since 1946, and the leading runner-up in a top-post election has had an excellent chance to win the next such election. At the lower levels of full-time office, in the Areas, the competition has been more diffuse and elections somewhat closer. It is clear that no one faction has had a monopoly of political power nationally, and that the two full-time national officials have lacked the staffs, financial resources and political power to dominate the union.

In generalising, it is reasonable to attribute the effectiveness of opposition in the Mineworkers to the four kinds of inequality-reducing factors suggested in our formal theory of union democracy: the status hierarchy, the regional and local substructures, the limited powers of the top officers and the existence of other power centres, and the voting system.

While the union generally approximates the countervailing-powers model in which the powerful officials of large independent and relatively equal substructures compete against each other, there are a number of departures apart from the obvious one of the regions covering a range of sizes. First, the larger Areas have taken distinctively different sides in the right–left split in the union. Second, the number of available and highly acceptable candidates for a top post has sometimes been quite limited, due to the lack of truly national reputations, ineligibility due to age, and political unacceptability in a particular national election (e.g. being from the same

Area or of the same political persuasion as the national officer already holding a post). The political differences have made the competition for posts more meaningful, and the unavailability of equally acceptable candidates has been haphazard and therefore not susceptible to the control of any political tendency or bloc. However, both these considerations have detracted somewhat from the equality of the candidates and the closeness of elections.

The permanence of full-time posts and the illegitimacy of open factions, so prevalent in British trade unions, has been discussed earlier in a broader context. However, it appears that the elective nature of the permanent full-time posts, and the security against reprisals from higher-ups accorded to their occupants, have reduced or nullified the counter-competitive effects of permanence. However, we may speculate that permanence has shielded some national officers from membership pressures for more militant action, and thus has detracted from democracy in the area of policy making. The NUM has recently been moving towards a more intense competition between openly-operating internal factions – an unresolved situation which bears watching.

The average level of competition for important posts in the Mineworkers has remained remarkably stable over a protracted period of time. Depressions, wars, expansions and contractions of the industry, and changes in the country's political situation have had no simple and direct effect on the national elections, except to add grist to the mill of union politics. From our perspective, the union may be conceived of as a competitive system, relatively independent of its particular situation in its production of close elections.

The Mineworkers' combination of decentralised administration, national decision making and democracy should continue to be viable for some time, even in the face of further changes, so long as its basic formal organisation is left intact. Its rarity elsewhere may be explainable in terms of sociological or historical trends which have little inherent relationship to organisational effectiveness. We will return to the Mineworkers in Chapter 9, in a comparison with the Engineers.

NOTES TO CHAPTER 8

1 Goldthorpe (1960: 4) has pointed out that conflicts between workers and supervisors over wage rates have been particularly prevalent in coal mining, where 'the physical conditions under which men work are likely to change from day to day, even from hour to hour'. The required adjustments in wages 'depend upon on-the-spot judgments by deputies which must in some degree at least be of an arbitrary kind and which seem almost invariably to involve a good deal of negotiation and bargaining with the workmen concerned'. This applied particularly to those on piece-work, about 40 per cent of the total.

The situation has probably changed somewhat with further mechanisation and an agreement in 1966 to standardise wage rates at the coal face. Until fairly recently, at least, the piece-workers at the face (where the coal is cut) were the centre of most local industrial disputes, and former face-workers held the large majority of full-time posts in the union. The solidarity of the miners has nevertheless been high, partly because a considerable percentage of non-face-workers have been older workers formerly at the face.

2 Lipset *et al.* (1956: 395–6, 414) suggest that formation as a federation (or from below) favours the emergence of internal opposition.

3 The figures are based on data provided by the union to the Electoral Reform Society for the conduct of the 1959 election of the national general secretary. Two branches with no stated membership are not included. Probably their voting membership had dropped to zero.

4 The consistency with which this has occurred leads one to suspect that many miners would prefer to keep a balance of power at the national level. Such a motivation has been attributed to convention delegates in the early days of the American United Auto Workers (see Howe and Widdick, 1949: 81–2).

5 Most of the Mineworkers' election results reported here are from printed minutes and proceedings of the union and its Areas. We have also utilised data sheets and correspondence at the NUM and Area headquarters and at the Electoral Reform Society, the works of Arnot (1949, 1953 and 1961), Area periodicals, and the daily press.

6 The five genuine vacant-post elections with five or more candidates each had a mean runner-up percentage of 78·3, while the four with three or fewer candidates each had a mean of 72·6 per cent. The three such elections with seven, eight and nine candidates respectively had a mean of 83·4 per cent, as compared to 72·2 per cent for the three with two candidates each. The very fact that there were as many as seven candidates may indicate that none was truly outstanding, in the eyes of the membership.

7 Allen (1954: 202–7, 271–93) shows that, in Britain as a whole, 'in sixty-eight known cases of assistant general secretaries contesting elections to fill vacancies for the position of general secretary . . . on only six occasions did they prove to be unsuccessful' (202). Ordinary members regard the assistant position as a stepping-stone.

8 Collindridge was secretary of the Yorkshire Mineworkers, the largest Area. R. Page Arnot remarked (personal interview, 21 June 1968) that it was 'almost unthinkable' that Yorkshire should not have at least one of the three national offices. It was as though the union were still a federation, in this respect. Arnot added that a number of early coincidences helped to determine the pattern of succession and the relationship between the vice-presidency and Areas. In particular, Smillie, who achieved the vice-presidency in 1909 (and was president from 1912 to 1921), was kept out of that office for many years because he was a socialist, although he 'deserved' higher office. (Also see Arnot, 1949: 322–3.) The situation has been changing.

9 The remaining percentages for vacant-post elections with three or more candidates were: 1918, 93·6; 1924, 73·5; 1932, 48·1; 1946, 16·3; January 1960, 67·0; and May 1960, 75·5.

10 H. W. Wynn, secretary of the Derbyshire Mineworkers, claimed that in his Area 67 per cent voting represented nearly 85 per cent of those actually available, considering absenteeism, injuries and hours of work.

11 The Areas giving the most support for favourite sons were Northumberland

(89·9 per cent for Allan), COSA (88·6 and 87·8 per cent for Ford) and Yorkshire (82·7 per cent for Machen).

12 The role of Durham is discussed again below under coalitions in national elections. It appears that Watson did not prefer the Northumberland candidates.

13 The evaluation is by H. W. Wynn, interviewed in 1961. These judgements were consistent with the results of other, less structured interviews.

14 One branch with fewer than thirty valid ballots has been neglected.

15 South Wales, Horner's Area, nominated its own non-Communist (and apparently orthodox Labour) W. H. Crews against Lawther, but the Communists did not hold both leading posts in South Wales at that time. Moreover, a credible source has informed us that few in South Wales took Crews' candidacy seriously.

16 According to Abe Moffat (1965: 286–7), the brother of the candidate in the May 1960 election: 'Whilst Sam Watson [the leading Durham official] was always a rabid anti-Communist in public, he nevertheless recognized . . . that it was wise to have at least one of them holding an official position. This was openly revealed when . . . even at an Executive dinner in London he could declare that Bill Paynter would be the next General Secretary.' However, a highly credible source has written to us that he was told by a participant, on the day following the dinner, that Watson merely said he was resigned to Paynter becoming secretary – he could see no way of stopping it.

17 The weakness of custom and practice without formalisation in rules is illustrated by the case of Sam Watson, who in his own account 'refused' to step down from the post of Area secretary to the more senior, but less demanding and less important, post of president. Presumably he had the assent of Durham's Area council. In Nottingham only full-time 'officials' are elected, and the Area conference selects the permanent president and secretary from among these.

18 Branches are permitted to have full-time secretaries. In South Wales these are barred from competing for the Area executive council, as they are not rank-and-filers.

19 Two of the five wards, Monmouthshire and Merthyr-and-Rhymney, had four defeats each (i.e. in two-thirds of their regular elections). This was due in part – in the case of Merthyr-and-Rhymney – to the demography of the ward (the pits are strung out in separate and apparently competing valleys).

20 In this computation we have not employed the formula, to be used later, which allows the runner-up percentages for defeats to exceed 100.

21 The 1947 *Rules* specified eight and six weeks respectively, rather than fourteen and twelve.

22 Minutes of the Derbyshire Area Council, 18 June 1955.

23 NUM, *Report of the Annual Conference*, 1960: 134. It is possible that other resolutions were presented in private session. If so, they were probably on problems of internal organisation.

24 In its branch vote in 1955 on the NUM's nomination for the treasurership of the Labour Party, Hugh Gaitskell won over the relatively left-wing Aneurin Bevan by 330 votes to 307 (Minutes of the Derbyshire Area Council, 18 June 1955).

25 The size of recent conferences has declined with the declining membership. Each Area was entitled to two delegates for its first 10,000 members, plus one for each additional 5,000, to a maximum of twenty. The basis of representation has not been changed.

26 The current president had been in office less than a year at the time of the interview.
27 By early 1973, the membership requirements for the maximum number of representatives (three) from an Area had already been reduced and a consolidation of Areas had taken place. As early as the late 1950s, South Derbyshire and Leicester were taking turns in electing an executive committee representative, as were Kent and Somerset.
28 See Roberts (1956: 364) and the NUM *Rules*.
29 All twenty-eight names of prospective Parliamentary candidates submitted by nine Areas for sponsorship in 1966 were approved by the national executive committee, after approval by the Labour Party, and the overwhelming majority were subsequently elected (Minutes of the National Executive Committee, 10 March and 14 April 1966).
30 In 1965 the United Mine Workers of America had seventeen districts and one local which had been under trusteeship since 1959 or earlier, of a total of twenty-one trusteeships in existence for that entire period among all American unions (see United States Department of Labor, *Summary of Operations, Labor-Management Reporting and Disclosure Act, 1965*, Washington D.C.).
31 *The Times*, 20 and 28 February, 1, 2 and 4 March, 15 and 17 August 1961; *The Manchester Guardian*, 8 and 10 March, 21 August 1961; Socialist Labour League, *Newsletter*, 4 and 18 March 1961; *Daily Herald*, 1 March 1961; *Daily Express*, 2 March 1961; *Daily Telegraph*, 4 March 1961; *Daily Worker*, 29 May 1961. A similar strike in 1955, in which J. Kane also participated, was apparently more successful. W. F. Cooke's notes indicate that Kane took a job with the Coal Board on nationalisation, and later resigned to return to the pit. Some efforts were made to expand the 1961 strike into Lancashire. The differences in the number of unofficial strikes from Area to Area (see Jencks, 1966) are difficult to explain (see Hughes, 1960–1 for one approach), but their greater contagiousness within Yorkshire seems related to its 'panel' system, under which representatives of adjacent mines meet regularly. In 1961 the Yorkshire leadership had tried unsuccessfully to limit what could be discussed at panel meetings (see also Ronald Kershaw, *The Times*, 27 October 1969). A working mine-worker told us that he attributed the strike-proneness of Yorkshire largely to the presence of many mine-workers who had been displaced from other Areas in earlier decades, but had never become fully reconciled to this nor been fully accepted in their new locations. Finally, the Yorkshire pits are among the largest (the average pit had 1,640 miners in 1969; *The Economist*, 25 October 1969: 66).
32 During 1926–31 the Mineworkers had a semi-official and then an official journal, which apparently could not be kept up for financial reasons.
33 The correspondence with the Area secretaries was made in late 1960. No information was available from the Cokemen, nor from four very small Areas.
34 Robert Whiteside (of the Youth Committee), 'East Germany's Young Workers Defend "The Wall"', *Scottish Miner*, November 1962: 3.
35 In 1969, the British Communist Party joined the Italian and the Australian (and two minor Parties) in declining to endorse the declaration of an international Communist conference in Moscow, although the declaration was called a 'valuable basis' for discussion (*The Times*, 30 June 1969: 8). The British reservations concerned 'the mutual responsibilities of communist parties and by implication, the rights and wrongs of the intervention in Czechoslovakia'. In 1971, Lawrence Daly wrote in the Communist Party

newspaper, the *Morning Star*, challenging the Party to clarify its stand on Czechoslovakia (see *IRIS News*, September 1971: 1). It seems significant that Daly's criticism should be published.

36 Proportional representation in the election of the executive council of the British National Union of Teachers, for example, has not led to the development of a party system. The election of two or more representatives from each region is similar to the system used for the Irish Parliament.

37 In 1967 the number of divisions of the Coal Board was reduced from forty to seventeen, with further cuts planned by 1975 (*The Times*, 2 July 1969: 20). In the early 1960s there were nine divisions. Thus, the boundaries of the divisions did not always coincide with those of the NUM's Areas. With a flexible union leadership, some solutions might be found short of a break-up of the historical Areas, which have been so intimately related to the Mineworkers' democracy.

38 However, the right-wing secretary of Yorkshire was also elected vice-president of the NUM in 1961, a few months after the wildcat, undoubtedly with the support of his Area. Top Area officers are usually included in their Area's elected delegations to the national executive council, which is also elected periodically. It would be unusual to deny them this prerogative.

Chapter 9

Case–Study 2: Sustained Electoral Opposition in the British Engineering Union

This chapter will show that the million-plus-member Amalgamated Union of Engineering and Foundry Workers (AUEW), formerly known as the AEU, also meets most of the criteria for non-oligarchy and for a moderately stringent conception of valid opposition. It thus constitutes a critical case, as did the Mineworkers. The democratic national union is like the mentally healthy person in that the recognition of either is difficult: the criteria for illness are more fully developed than the criteria for health. We will therefore describe the Engineers' political system and show the character of opposition within it, while making liberal use of those specific measures of the success of opposition already utilised in our study of the Mineworkers. This study will cover the same period and include the election of the present president, Hugh Scanlon. The Engineers have had close competition in the filling of top and other vacancies for over fifty years – indeed, if one includes the union's predecessor which had many similar features, for over 120.

THE UNION IN BRIEF

The Amalgamated Society of Engineers, established in 1851 as a union of several crafts in the engineering (machine-tool) industry, was the first successful attempt in Britain at forming a national union. It became the Amalgamated Engineering Union in 1921 as a result of a further amalgamation which it dominated. In 1926 the union was opened to all males in the industry regardless of job or skill, and women were admitted in 1943. Skilled workers have made up only about one-third of the membership since 1960 or earlier, but they have continued to dominate the full-time officer force and the various committees (Clegg *et al.*, 1961: 17). The basic structure and procedures of the Engineers have been the same since 1921.

On 1 July 1967 the Amalgamated Engineering Union joined forces with the Amalgamated Union of Foundry Workers, a very old union with many organisational similarities to the AEU. Although fusion took place, under the name of the Amalgamated Engineering and Foundry Workers' Union (known as AEF), the two organisations kept their separate rules. The Engineering Section also retained its identity, and separate rules, after a further amalgamation on 26 April 1970 with two small unions: the Constructional Engineering Union and the Draughtsmen's and Allied Technicians' Association (see *Tribune*, 14 April 1972: 4). The product of this amalgamation was the current AUEW, which began with 1,297,000 members. It was only in 1972 that working discussions started in order to bring about a single set of rules for the AUEW. By the winter of 1973–4, the membership had risen to 1,324,000 and was moving up to 1,400,000, according to union sources.

It is amazing that the Engineers apparently escaped sociological analysis until recently; they *were*, after all, an important union in 1911, when Robert Michels published his classic study of oligarchy in labour and socialist organisations. They had 44,000 members in 1857; 88,000 in 1900; 460,000 after a rapid growth during World War I; 192,000 in the depression year of 1933; followed by a recovery to 413,000 at the tail end of the depression. The World War II peak of 912,000 members only fell to 808,000 in 1947. There was fairly steady growth in membership from 1950 to 1960, when it reached 1,054,000, and then further growth in 1964 and 1965 to 1,113,000 (Amalgamated Engineering Union, 1965: 9).

The membership of the Engineers at the end of 1960 included 947,000 in Great Britain, 26,000 in the Irish Republic and Northern Ireland, and 82,000 overseas (mostly in Australia). Only 77,000 female members were included in the above, in the British Isles.[1] The overseas members belonged to essentially autonomous unions, but could (and did) vote in the Engineers' elections for president and secretary until 1967. (Future references to the Engineers will ignore the overseas sections except insofar as the votes of their members contributed to these national elections.) The members in the Irish Republic and Northern Ireland were fully integrated into the life of the union; for example, all Ireland was combined with Liverpool, Blackpool and many other districts for the election of one of the seven members of the executive council.

The Engineers are important in Britain not only because they are the second-largest union, but also because they form 'the keystone in the Confederation of Shipbuilding and Engineering Unions [CSEU], whose procedural agreement with the Engineering Employers' Federation [EEF] covers some 3·5 million workers in about thirty unions – the largest collective bargaining agreement in the British industrial relations system' (Richter, 1973: 29). The Engineers have had a considerable number of members outside the machine-tool industry proper – e.g. in automobile and aircraft production, maintenance and repair, and in the maintenance and repair of buses and railway equipment – and enough members to warrant the union's involvement in negotiations for pay and conditions in the iron and steel, chemical, paper-making, plastics and textiles industries (see Amalgamated Engineering Union, 1965: 86). In 1965 there were twenty-nine such industries or sections of industries, with textiles accounting for four of these, railways for three, chemicals for two, and various non-industrial local or government authorities or services for three. In other words, there was bargaining in twenty-one rather different kinds of industries. The Engineers have not had exclusive bargaining jurisdiction at the places of employment where most of their members have been found.

The Basic Structure
The union had 2,300 branches in 1960, most of them multi-shop, grouped into 263 districts which, as we shall see, had considerable autonomy in many matters. The mean branch size was 420 members and the mean district size was 3,700, with a mean of 8·7 branches per district. However, the mean district sizes are somewhat misleading, since there were approximately eighty small single-branch districts, located disproportionately in Scotland and Ireland (correspondence with G. S. Aitken, Research Officer) and, we assume therefore, in other more isolated locations. These single-branch districts were certainly much smaller in membership.

The branches were based primarily on localities rather than places of work, due largely to the Engineers' lack of exclusive jurisdiction at the workplace, but also to the union's (or the leadership's) explicit preference for the geographic basis and for relatively small branch sizes. There were only about sixty branches with as many as 800 members, as late as 1967. (The *Quarterly Report* of July 1958 showed approximately ninety.) If a branch's membership grew bigger than 500, consideration was given to the opening of another branch or, increasingly, to the collection of dues by shop stewards rather than branch officers (interview with G. S. Aitken). The dues check-off was rare. Although one might think that a small-to-moderate branch size would encourage conformity and deter the expression of political differences, the Engineers' regularly-published reports show considerable internal division with preferences for different candidates at all supra-branch levels of office, even within most fairly small branches.

The number of geographic subdivisions above the district are constitutionally prescribed, and have remained constant since 1921. There are twenty-six divisions and seven executive council regions. The officers of the divisions have the function of organising non-union workers, 'But probably their main function today is that of negotiating with the Employers' Associations at Works and Local Conferences. This they do on request from the respective Districts and theirs is the responsibility of carrying out the various stages of the Procedure Agreement in the Engineering Industry up to – but not including – national level' (Amalgamated Engineering Union, 1965: 11). Each of the twenty-six divisional committees elects two of its lay members to the Engineers' annual conference, known as the national committee, which is the highest legislative authority in the union.

Finally, at the national level, there are the seven-member full-time executive council, other national officers to be described, and an eleven-member rank-and-file final appeals court, each member representing a region which exists for this purpose only.

THE ENGINEERS COMPARED TO THE MINEWORKERS

Before describing the Engineers' organisation in greater detail we will compare it with that of the Mineworkers. The two unions have much in common, particularly at a level of abstraction which focuses on the equality of status of potential competitors for office, the equality of votes in the regions or substructures supporting such competitors, the existence of independent national power centres, and the voting system. This is why we have selected them as *critical cases*, for greater study in depth. There are, of course, differences of some importance as well.

Similarities
These are the specific similarities:

1   All full-time officials are elected. None is appointed.
2   The vast majority of full-time officials are elected within and are responsible to substructures, entirely regional ones in the Engineers and primarily so in the Mineworkers.
3   Each union has two top officers of approximately equal status.
4   There are at least two full-time officers of exactly the same rank in a position to compete for each full-time office, except the very lowest.
5   Full-time officers must retire at the age of sixty-five.
6   There is a high degree of regional autonomy, in spite of the fact that quite a bit of national bargaining takes place in both unions.
7   The annual national conferences of both unions are relatively small (although much smaller in the Engineers) and cannot be easily manipulated. For example, resolutions submitted by the regions cannot be removed from the agenda or altered without their consent.
8   All full-time officials are elected in a multi-stage process which permits a combination of weaker against stronger tendencies.
9   Referenda are held for all full-time posts.
10 The casting and counting of ballots in national elections are fairly well supervised.
11 The mass media give excellent coverage to important elections within these unions, and to their factional situation generally (although

industrial relations in the engineering industries receive even more coverage).

12 Many of the active rank-and-filers are politically interested and some are ideologically committed, although perhaps not more so than in some other British unions.

13 Internal factions have been somewhat illegitimate and therefore somewhat covert, and there have been restrictions on free campaigning (although with the passage of time these have been increasingly circumvented in both unions).

Differences

In spite of a comparable closeness of elections to fill top vacancies, the two unions differ in many respects – some of them surprising. The differences are summarised in Table 9.1.

The Engineers depart significantly from the Mineworkers' approximation to the countervailing-powers model of effective opposition, and are a step in the direction of the random model (see Chapter 3). It will be recalled that under the countervailing-powers model the contending forces are few, equal, powerful and secure, and there is a likelihood of bloc making among them (which is ameliorated by free campaigning among the electorate). These are the major departures:

Large number of districts. With effective functional autonomy at the level of 263 districts, a division of the electoral spoils by prior agreement is very unlikely.

Large, arbitrary areas for the election of executive councillors. Although the seven full-time executive councillors are very powerful figures, they are in no position to make blocs to deliver the votes of their areas in union-wide elections, including those for top office. The councillors are elected from large, somewhat arbitrary areas with few functions as such. The union's twenty-six divisions also have few functions. Neither the areas nor the divisions within them have an internal structure capable of effectively co-ordinating (or controlling) the large number of relatively autonomous districts. For these reasons a diffuse anarchic competition for office may result, which can be resolved only through the electoral process itself. This is particularly the case with a large number of candidates, a common situation because nomination for any office may be made by a *single member*, without a seconder being required (Rule 2.5).[2] In the Engineers monopolistic tendencies are also rather weak since the top officials lack the power to suppress opposition even at the national level, and because the union is a suitable arena for personal and political competition for other structural reasons as well, to be explained.

TABLE 9.1   *Summary of differences between the Engineers and the Mineworkers*

The Engineers	The Mineworkers
1 Periodic elections for all full-time officials.	All full-time officials are permanent.
2 Low percentage voting (as low as 8%) at meeting halls (until recent change to postal ballot).	High percentage voting (usually over 65%) at place of work.
3 Seldom has exclusive bargaining rights at workplace.	Approaches exclusive bargaining rights.
4 Many employers.	One major employer (National Coal Board).
5 Membership usually voluntary (members may choose other unions).	Virtually a closed shop, except for minor occupations.
6 Little occupational community.	Occupational community based on residence, recreational facilities and relationships at work.
7 Basic structure developed after its formation.	Basic structure existed at time of formation (federation).
8 Ambiguous position for shop stewards in union structure (due to absence of exclusive bargaining).	Fairly clear place for workplace representatives in union structure.
9 Annual conference with only rank-and-file voting delegates.	Annual conference with full-time officials as voting delegates (strong minority, in practice).
10 Small (7-member) full-time executive council.	Moderately large (approximately 28-member) executive council, overwhelmingly full-time officials in practice.
11 Independent rank-and-file appeals court.	No independent appeals court.
12 Three levels of nationally-elected full-time officers.	Single level of nationally-elected full-time officers.
13 263 important functional sub-divisions (districts) in 1960.	20 important functional sub-divisions (regions and occupational groups).

However, the union does *not* approach the random model of electoral competition either; the anarchy of the electoral process is far from complete, even on the first ballot. The first-ballot votes within most branches, when vacancies exist for national offices, show a division of opinion which rules out both the narrowest parochialism or partisanship (manifest in unanimity), and a random marking of the ballots.

One may conceive of two kinds of 'randomness' in the marking of ballot papers. One is based on the individual voter's 'preferences', which are influenced by superficial and haphazard pieces of information (with some greater likelihood of local or regional candidates being known). This would still be an unbiased system, even with such a bias in favour of local candidates, if the membership were widely and equally dispersed and if the same were true for the branches and districts. The other kind of 'randomness' is based on the equally-limited information available to local leaders; the branch members follow their recommendations since there is nothing better to go on. This is very common in the trade union movement, and often results in near-unanimous votes within the particular branches. With poor communications between local leaders and many voters, both kinds of 'randomness' can operate simultaneously.

Given the possibility of these two kinds of 'randomness', one resulting in no clear preferences among a wide field of candidates and the other in virtual unanimity, it is difficult to interpret the fact that 40 per cent of the Engineers' branches failed to give a majority to any one of the eleven candidates in the closely-contested 1967 election to fill a presidential vacancy. The votes for the non-leading candidates in each branch were usually spread over several candidates, as in the Mineworkers. However, it is reasonable to consider that much of the minority voting within the branches on the first ballot was due to disagreement or opposition, since: (*a*) the union circulates uncensored election addresses (although some of these say little or use Aesopian language); (*b*) the mass media, and the literature of external political organisations, pay attention to the campaign; (*c*) those voting are primarily active members and should be better informed (only 11 per cent voted); and (*d*) four of the seven executive councillors were presidential candidates, and therefore most voters were in the position of having to vote for or against an important 'favourite son'. Other regions or divisions must have been similarly represented, but by lower-ranking officials. There remains, in addition, the matter of the run-off election between the two leading candidates. In the 1967 presidential run-off, about one-half of the English branches gave one-quarter or more of their votes to the less favoured candidate in the particular branch. With a clear-cut choice between an orthodox Labour and a left-wing Labour candidate quite similar to that between Gormley and Daly in the Mineworkers in 1968, it may be assumed that the intra-branch minorities represented 'opposition' rather than a random familiarity with the candidates or their supporters.

A more clear-cut example of informed partisanship in the 1967 presidential run-off is shown by the vote in Scotland, where 84 per cent of the branches submitting votes showed a majority for one of the eleven candidates on the first ballot. Boyd (orthodox Labour), one of the two leading candidates, was from Scotland and had sat in the executive council for fourteen years. A further breakdown of the first-ballot votes in Scotland shows 63 per cent of the branches with a majority for Boyd, 21 per cent with a majority for Scanlon, his chief rival nationally, only 17 per cent with no majority for any one candidate,[3] and just one branch out of 245 with a majority for a minor candidate. In the run-off election, 26 per cent of the Scottish branches gave a majority to the left-wing non-Scottish candidate (who won the election nationally). Certainly the Scottish vote was polarised, and while more so than is typical in the Engineers it shows that much of the vote is indeed far from random.[4]

The absence of a subnational constituency for some second-ranking officials. The Engineers also depart from the countervailing-powers model in that their two assistant general secretaries, the most logical competitors for the post of general secretary, are elected by referendum by the entire general membership. They control no blocs of votes and could be defeated if clearly aligned with a minority faction. The same applies to some lesser national officials, discussed below.

THE STATUS HIERARCHY

In 1960 there were 156 full-time officers in the Engineers, holding nine different job titles (see Table 9.2). It should be noted that eighty-three of the 263 district secretaries held full-time office. Supporting these there were 320 non-elected full-time staff, 59 per cent of whom worked at the head office. Approximately thirty of these were judged as having at least as much responsibility as a junior grade full-time officer, and several received higher salaries than the president. There were 6,300 members per full-time officer, and combining staff and full-time officers there were 1,900 members per full-time person (Clegg *et al.*, 1961: 104, 106–7, 216).

Included among the non-full-time officers were approximately 23,000 branch officers (about ten per branch), and a roughly comparable number of shop stewards. Branch officers are elected annually by a show of hands, with the exception of the branch secretary who must be elected by ballot if there are two or more nominees. It is often difficult to get people to accept nominations for branch office, as might be expected.

The average age at which full-time office was assumed was forty-five, as compared to the median of 40·6 for eighteen large and medium-sized unions studied by Clegg *et al.* (1961: 27, 47–8). Generally, British unions with a large proportion of skilled workers, and with entirely elective office, had a later age of entry into full-time officer status.

The salaries of the full-time officials were narrowly compressed between £950 and £1,300. By comparison, the minimum wage for skilled time-workers in the engineering trade in the same year was £507, which was no

TABLE 9.2   *Full-time officers of the Engineers, United Kingdom and Irish Republic, 1960[a] (by approximate levels)*

No. and Officers	Salary[b] (£)	Constituencies for Referendum
1 President	1,300	Entire membership, including overseas
1 General secretary	1,300	Entire membership, including overseas
7 Executive councillors	1,060	Memberships in 7 areas
2 Assistant general secretaries	1,030	Entire membership
3 National organisers	1,030	Entire membership
7 Regional officers	1,000	Memberships in 7 areas
26 Divisional organisers	1,000	Memberships in 26 divisions
26 Assistant divisional organisers (approx.)[d]	1,000	Memberships in 26 divisions
83 District secretaries	950[c]	Memberships in 83 districts

[a] Excluded are Commonwealth officers and minor officers in charge of employment and unemployment benefits.
[b] The salaries given here are for 1960, when there was an additional personal expense allowance of £100. In 1965, the private use of a union car was also offered. The most recent figures for salaries are: president and general secretary, £3,750; the seven executive councillors, £3,250; other senior full-time officials, £2,750 (*IRIS News*, December 1973: 2).
[c] £1,000 in districts of 20,000 or more members.
[d] Nineteen in 1965.
Sources: AEU *Rules*, 1960; and personal communication from AEU research department.

doubt often exceeded in practice, and university lecturers' salaries were raised to £1,100 in the autumn of 1960.[5]

From the point of view of the potential for electoral competition, what is probably most important is the large number of full-time officers at the second rank: the seven members of the executive council, and the two assistant general secretaries. The holders of these two approximately equal positions (the councillors may have a slight edge) have competed at times for either top post, but with only one exception since 1921 all vacant presidencies have been won by executive councillors and all secretaryships by assistant secretaries.[6] The exception occurred in 1933, when the two leading candidates were both divisional organisers. We will return shortly to the relative status of the top winners and their runners-up.

This situation with respect to potential competition among equals holds at all but the seventh and lowest full-time level: that of full-time district secretary. Every full-time position has its precise or approximate counterpart, where rank is concerned. This means that candidates usually compete against others of equal rank (plus others of lower rank), and that the two top officers can exert influence downwards in different directions.

Since all important full-time officials are elected (and must be re-elected periodically), there is no possibility for advancement excepting through competitive struggle. For example, each executive councillor has a personal assistant appointed by the general secretary; these are considered to be part of the technical staff and are ineligible for full-time officer status. The rules provide that candidates for full-time posts must have worked in the trade for twelve months prior to candidacy, or been unemployed. The struggle for top office is made fiercer by the fact that there is little time to waste – as in the Mineworkers, members who have reached the age of sixty-one are ineligible for a new full-time office (Clegg *et al.*, 1961: 47).

A fight against an incumbent at the next higher level is made easier in the Engineers by the fact that the seven levels of full-time positions rise with no dramatic jumps in job title or pay until just short of top office. While the pay for the top offices is remarkably low by American standards, and it could be argued that there might therefore be a less desperate resistance to being displaced, the importance of these posts is apparently more than enough to outweigh the small salary differential (see Lipset *et al.*, 1956: 213–14, 410, 415).

An important aspect of the status hierarchy is that no more than five of the 156 full-time officers are free for unrestricted assignment; the majority remain within the regions where they were elected.[7] This preserves their local base, and eliminates many of the possibilities either for harassment by higher officials or for assignments favourable to the enhancement of national reputations and the winning of higher office. It also means that the general secretary is in a position to favour one of the two assistant general secretaries as his eventual replacement, by giving one of them suitable field assignments while keeping the other in his office. The restriction also prevents 'raiding' elsewhere.

We shall return to some other features of the Engineers after demonstrating the effectiveness of opposition within the union.

ELECTIONS FOR TOP POSTS

The general secretaryship has been full-time since 1851, and the presidency since its creation in 1921. While the president is the senior officer, with responsibility in industrial matters, the secretary is responsible for the monthly journal and general-office staff, and acts as treasurer. Both may express their views at the executive council, but only the president may vote, and then only in the case of a tie. In no instance when the presidency has been vacant has the general secretary run for it – an indication of the importance of the secretaryship.

The results of all elections for new general secretaries and presidents since 1875 are shown in Table 9.3. Full-time officers had to stand for re-election every three years until 1958, and since then after their first three years in office and every five years thereafter. There was a further change several years ago exempting full-time officers over the age of sixty from standing for re-election, if already re-elected once. Thus, under these new

TABLE 9.3 Referenda under the second-ballot system for new general secretaries and presidents of the British Engineers, 1875–1975[a]

Year	Post	No. of candidates	Votes for runner-up per 100 for winner	Reversal of initial standing[b]	Percentage voting[c]	Winner's defeat in previous elections[a]	Comments
1875	secretary	3	66·7	?	34·3		
1887	secretary	3?	91·4	?	36·7		
1891	secretary	3	94·8	(1 ballot)	50·5		
1896	secretary	7	52·0[e]	(1 ballot)	30·2	2nd, 1887	Runner-up was ex-secretary (removed).
1909	secretary	7	84·0[e]	reversal	31·2	2nd, 1895	
1913	secretary	6	84·2[f]	reversal	25·3		
1919	secretary	22	71·0	reversal	16·8	3rd, 1913; 2nd, 1891	Incumbent defeated.
1921	secretary	32	72·0	reversal	24·0		
1930	president	15	93·7	reversal	22·3	3rd, 1921	
1933	president	21	80·4		24·3		
1933	secretary	19	34·1		24·9		
1939	president	11	72·7		15·2	2nd, 1933	Runner-up was ex-president (removed).
1943	secretary	8	54·2	(1 ballot)	10·2		Runner-up was same ex-president.
1954	president	7	66·5		9·0	3rd, 1939	
1956	president	10	42·2	reversal	12·4		
1957	secretary	7	99·4	reversal	7·9	4th, 1956	
1964	secretary	4	77·2		7·9		
1967	president	11	90·7		11·6		
1975	secretary[a]	11	58·5		30·1[g]	2nd, 1967	

[a] Posts vacant except 1913. From 1892 the structure is judged to be sufficiently similar to that at present to warrant a comparison of election results.

[b] The winner did not receive the greatest number of votes on the initial ballot.

[c] Computed from the total final votes and the total membership at the close of the year in which the final ballot was conducted.

[d] Not necessarily complete. Most elections involving incumbents were neglected, as were some minor candidates in elections for vacant posts.

[e] Approximate.

[f] If the special formula for defeats were used, the runner-up percentage would be 115·8.

[g] The turn-out was relatively high due to the use of a postal ballot (see p. 276).

Sources: AEU Journal; ASE Journal (ex-Monthly Journal); AEU, Jubilee Souvenir (London, 1901); Jeffreys, 1945; AEU, Financial Report for the year ended 31st December, 1960 (London, 1961) for membership figures; and similar Report for 31 December 1967.

rules, a full-time officer re-elected at the age of fifty-six could remain at his post until retirement at sixty-five. These are the only significant retrogressions from democratic rules since 1921 of which we are aware.

An incumbent top officer has been defeated only once, in 1913. On the other hand, top and other high officers are usually opposed for re-election, and two top officers were removed, in 1895 and 1932, by the executive committee and the appeals court for neglect of duty and for intoxication. In each case there were no restrictions against running for top office, which was tried again within a year (see Jeffreys, 1945: 141–2; *AEU Journal*, September 1932: 6–7, 10–12). The former officers were less than typically successful as runners-up in vacant-post elections. In 1973 the general secretary, the late J. Conway, was re-elected although opposed by the assistant general secretary, E. Roberts, a 'left-winger', by 169,806 votes to 96,206.

The Closeness of Elections

The organisational factors affecting the closeness of elections have remained substantially the same since 1892, when the full-time executive council was instituted. There appears to have been no definite long-range trend in the closeness of elections to fill top vacancies since that date, although it would be more conservative to summarise the results from 1921 on, following the constitutional changes. The two highest runner-up percentages for top vacant-post elections since 1892 were 93·7 in 1930 and 99·4 in 1957; the two lowest were 34·1 in 1933 and 42·2 in 1956. The latter, the last of an election slump between 1943 and 1956, was exceptional and is discussed below. The median for the eleven top vacant-post elections since 1921 is 72·7 votes for the runner-up per 100 for the winner, and the mean is 71·2. There have been only four elections since 1921 with a runner-up percentage below 70.

During 1949–66 the Engineers held eight periodic elections for president or general secretary, with a mean of 43·2 votes for the runner-up per 100 for the winner. One election exceeded 80 per cent. It was shown earlier that only the Foundry Workers and the Electrical Workers had comparably close periodic elections for top office during 1949–66, among sixteen British unions with 15,000 or more members holding periodic elections. Indeed, seven of the sixteen had entirely-uncontested periodic elections.

Participation in Elections

Prior to 1913 the percentages voting approached or exceeded one-third of the membership. Since 1933 the percentage voting has fallen drastically from 24·9 to between 7·9 and 12·4 per cent for the six top vacant-post elections since 1943. According to *IRIS News* (Survey, February 1968: 9–10), the participation in elections for lower-level national officers was even less, especially for assistant general secretaries and national organisers: 'Second ballot results . . . for the [now seven] National Organisers have not reached 9% in 16 years, and last year's figure was about 5·1%.' Yet there seems to be no relationship between the percentages voting and the closeness of elections. A simplistic view of competition as being related to participation – at least in elections – is incorrect (see p. 144, n. 19).

Voting in the Engineers takes place at fortnightly branch meetings, in no circumstances for more than five continuous hours (Rule 2: 19). According to B. C. Roberts (1956: 95; see also 96–112), average branch attendances in the large British unions 'appear to fall within a range of from 3 to 15 per cent, with a concentration in between 4 and 7 per cent in the majority of cases'. The very high percentage voting in the Mineworkers is due to the location of the ballot boxes at the mines, and is not accompanied by a large average attendance at branch meetings – Roberts estimates this average as only 2 to 3 per cent in some Areas, and from our research it is doubtful that the overall figure could much exceed 5 per cent.

In any union a special occasion may encourage a much larger turnout, but in the Engineers an election would seldom be such an occasion: ballots for both full-time and lay officers and delegates were, until recently, held many times during the year, and first or run-off ballots were no numerous as to be 'almost a normal feature of a branch meeting' (B. C. Roberts, 1956: 229). Furthermore, 'It was usual for branches to be given two branch meetings, sometimes three, on which to hold particular ballots. The ballot had to be confined to one night . . ., thus unless members were regular attenders at branch meetings they would be unaware when ballots were to be held and which particular ballot was being held on any particular branch meeting night' (*IRIS News* Supplement, April 1973: 20–1). The reference to a 'particular ballot' is relevant because many branch secretaries would try to avoid holding a ballot for more than one office on any one night. Nevertheless, very well-publicised contests between right- and left-wingers for vacancies may have added a few percentage points to the voter turnout, as in the 1956 and 1967 presidential elections.

One reason for the decline in branch attendance has probably been the further development of workshop organisation, by which the Engineers' territorially-based branch has become an ever greater anachronism. However, the problem of poor branch attendance is international (see Van de Vall, 1970: 104), and would probably not be substantially eased in the Engineers by a change to factory-based branches unless branch meetings could be held at the workplace.

In the Engineers, the decrease in branch attendance and the percentage voting are probably related to: the greater size and heterogeneity of the membership; the greater proportion of less skilled and women workers, and the increased turnover in employment of such members; full employment; the lesser importance of the friendly benefit aspect of the union since national insurance; the increase in commuting to work; the greater prevalence of shift work; the greater number of holidays, and changes in the working year; and the greater competition from readily available entertainment, including television. One may also wonder whether some of the visible remnants of craft union organisation, including the existence of a skilled section with higher dues and benefits, may have repelled many less skilled workers. Finally, branch attendance may have fallen even more with the recent introduction of the dues check-off and paid collectors. B. C. Roberts (1956: 103) reports that, even in the 1950s, members often paid their contributions through shop stewards or other members willing to oblige them, although required to make payment in person at meetings.

While many of the foregoing are common trends in large organisations and in society itself, it would be an error to romanticise the past or to neglect the artefactual aspects of the decline in voting in the Engineers. As B. C. Roberts (1956: 98) pointed out in the 1950s, in the Engineers 'many members simply call in at the meeting . . . [to pay their contributions] and they may vote if a ballot happens to be in progress at the same time'. At any rate, it should be noted that the very first, poorly-administered, controversial postal ballot for full-time officials in the Engineers, in 1972, produced a 41 per cent return on the first ballot in a periodic election for general secretary, and a 32 per cent return on the run-off. The turnout on the final ballot for one of the divisional organiser elections reached 48 per cent (*IRIS News* Supplement, April 1973: 5–11).[8] We will have to await further postal ballot elections, but there is no doubt that the characteristic level of participation will be much higher than in the past.

Number of Candidates

There have been no uncontested elections for a *vacant* top office since the founding of the ASE. There have been fewer than six candidates only once since 1892. In the five elections between 1919 and 1933, the smallest number of candidates was nineteen. There appears to be little relationship between the initial number of candidates and the closeness of an election (see Table 9.3), no doubt because only three elections were settled on the first ballot.

There have usually been a number of candidates even in periodic top-post elections. For example, in each of the five such elections during 1949–60 there were no fewer than four candidates.

Previous Defeats for Top Office

The general secretary elected in 1957 had been defeated for president (fourth place) in 1956. At least six of the thirteen winners of vacant posts since 1892 were similarly defeated before finally being elected, and four of the eleven winners since 1921. The number of elections involving previously-defeated winners is probably underestimated since most re-elections were not surveyed and many minor candidates were neglected.

Leadership of Mixed Political Complexion
Between approximately 1945 and 1959 the Communist minority is reported to have had at least two supporters on the seven-person executive council (M. Harrison, 1960: 143). Between 1957 and 1964 the president and secretary supported relatively right and left tendencies respectively. A politically-mixed leadership at the level of the second-ranking full-time officials at least has been a consistent feature of the post-World War II life of the Engineers.

Offices Held Previously
While superficially the Engineers have generally followed the common trade union succession pattern of second-ranking officers taking over the top post, this has ordinarily been done over the opposition of other second-ranking officers.[9] Excluding the 1933 and 1939 elections in which a deposed president attempted but failed to regain a top office, there have been nine top vacancies since 1921. In six of these nine elections two or more next-to-top officers (executive councillors or assistant general secretaries) competed against each other, and in a seventh (in 1933) the winner and the runner-up were divisional organisers. In only two of the nine elections (in 1943 and 1954) did a second-ranking officer defeat only lower-ranking competitors. It is obviously the nature of the status hierarchy which makes possible such competition between equal full-time officers.

Reversals of the Standing on the First Ballot
In four of the eleven top vacant-post elections since 1921 (ten of which required second ballots), the candidates leading on the first ballot lost the election (see Table 9.3). This was also true in the single case where the incumbent was defeated. The 1956 presidency reversal was unusual in that it was associated with the relatively low runner-up percentage of 42.2. This may be explained by the fact that, after a Communist had led on the first ballot, the anti-Communists organised to get out the vote and did so, no doubt aided by the attention paid to this election by the mass media. The second ballot involved 119,000 voters, as compared to 77,000 on the first. The turnout on the second ballot was 12·4 per cent, as compared to 9 per cent in 1954 and 7·9 per cent in 1957. Under the second-ballot system particularly, elections of moderately low final closeness may on occasion be associated with a certain amount of excitement.

ELECTIONS OF LOWER-LEVEL FULL-TIME OFFICERS

The most outstanding fact about the Engineers' elections for second- and third-ranking full-time officials is their relative frequency of defeats: two executive councillors were defeated during 1949–60, as were two national organisers, in a total of twenty-two and nine periodic elections respectively. During 1949–66, the mean runner-up percentage for thirty-five periodic elections to second-ranking posts was 58·3, as compared to the mean of only 18·8 per cent for sixteen British unions holding periodic elections (see Table 6.1). On the other hand, elections to fill second-ranking vacancies were somewhat less close than those for top-post vacancies. Our information on elections for national organiser covers only 1949–60, but the median runner-up percentages are over 70 for both vacant-post and periodic elections.

The keenness of the competition for full-time posts is indicated by the ups and downs of some of the competitors. In 1955 two national organisers, L. J. Ambrose (a Communist) and W. Cockin, ran against each other for a vacant post on the executive council. Ambrose won, only to be defeated for re-election by Cockin in 1958. One of the three national organiserships then fell vacant, and in 1959 Ambrose was again elected as national organiser. Cockin lost his executive council post to H. Scanlon, the current president, in 1963, but he eventually achieved the post of assistant general secretary, only to be defeated in 1968 at the age of sixty-three by K. Brett (a Communist) by a vote of 34,010 to 33,882. This last election was unusual in that Cockin's lead of 11,000 votes on the first ballot was completely wiped out (*Morning Star*, 11 January 1968).

In 1949 R. G. Crane, an incumbent national organiser, was defeated for re-election by H. G. Barratt. Crane ran against Barratt in 1952 but was again defeated. He tried again in 1953 but failed against one of the national organisers: the incumbent Cockin. When a post fell vacant in 1956 Crane finally returned as national organiser, only to be defeated again in 1959 by J. Conway, who had run third against Crane in 1956.

Conway, in the meantime, had tried unsuccessfully for the assistant secretaryship in 1957 (second place), and for the executive council in 1958 (third place) in the same election in which Cockin defeated Ambrose. Conway was subsequently elected as assistant general secretary, and finally as general secretary in 1964, dying in an air-crash in 1974.

These examples of competition, although showing a more than typical number of defeats, demonstrate a lack of hesitation among full-time officials to run against not only their equals, but also their superiors.

Full-time District Secretaries

The Engineers have had the *least* effective opposition against incumbents at the *lowest* level of constitutionally-recognised full-time office: that of district secretary. The results of 143 miscellaneous vacant-post and periodic elections for full-time district secretary during 1950–60 (probably about three-quarters of them periodic) show that *almost half* (48 per cent) were uncontested. During this same period there were *only two* uncontested elections among the fifty-nine vacant-post and periodic elections for president, general secretary, executive councillor and national organiser. We do not have direct information on district secretary defeats, but there were probably very few; in the forty-seven elections in which district secretaries were returned to office over opposition, none of the runner-up percentages reached 80. *IRIS News* (Survey, February 1968: 10) has stated that 'more than 100' of 350 full-time district secretary elections (at least 29 per cent) since 1952 were uncontested.

We have not been able to isolate the closeness of the vacant-post district secretary elections, but at best these would have had a median runner-up percentage in the 60s, at least a little lower than that for top office. On the other hand, when there is opposition the percentage voting is considerably higher than in the national elections, rising from below 10 per cent to more than 30 per cent (*IRIS News* Survey, February 1968: 10).

Where periodic elections especially are concerned, the ineffectiveness of opposition to incumbent district secretaries is probably due largely to the absence of still lower full-time officials, and to the close contact which many district secretaries undoubtedly keep with both branches and workshops. This would allow the incumbent an opportunity to build a personal following and to campaign during an election. In addition, many members would be reluctant to dismiss someone known to them personally. The district secretary negotiates with employers when requested to do so by the district committee (Rule 13: 6). In addition to the status hierarchy, the relatively small number of branches in many districts, together with inequalities in branch voting strengths, tend to be reflected in unequal support for candidates. This is exacerbated by the fact that some large plants with extraordinarily large turnouts, or with members in many of a district's branches, may be able to dominate a district's elections.

Many branches with a substantial proportion of their members in a single factory have been able either to transfer the branch meeting into that factory or, failing that, to otherwise change the time and place of the meeting for convenience in voting. *IRIS News* has estimated that about one-fifth of the Engineers' branches have made such arrangements, and that about one-eighth of all branches have been able to organise a very high percentage vote, usually overwhelmingly for a single candidate.[10] In spite of the bias of the source, it does indeed appear to be true, from a casual inspection of branch voting in 1967, that large second-ballot votes for district secretary – e.g. 271 to five, 194 to one, 246 to one, or 236 to two – are not uncommon, even in districts where the total vote is well under 1,000. However, it is also the case that there are usually other branches within the same district which have large and similarly-biased votes for the opposing candidate. Thus, the net effect of such inequality in voting strength, *when there is opposition*, should not be overstated.

A PARTY SYSTEM?

It is obvious that the Engineers' close elections are *not* the result of a two-party system. There have usually been at least three candidates for top vacancies with more than nominal support; before the voting it must often have been unclear which two candidates would proceed to the second ballot. In the most extreme example of this, the 1933 presidential election, the third-strongest candidate received only one vote less than the second. Indeed, the votes for the *five* highest of the twenty-one candidates on the first ballot were 6,659, 5,226, 5,225, 4,984 and 3,984 respectively. The second-placed candidate then went to the second ballot, to lose in a fairly close election (the runner-up percentage was 80·4). In only four vacant-post elections since 1892 has the number of votes cast for the third-place candidate on the first ballot fallen below 60 per cent of those cast for the second-place candidate.[11]

Another indication of the absence of a two-party system, and probably of a party system of any kind, is given by the number of candidates for second-ranking posts and the rather low proportion of the total first ballot vote for the two leading candidates. For example, there were twenty-nine candidates for the vacant post of assistant general secretary in 1961, and twenty-two for a similar vacancy in 1964. The combined vote for the two leading candidates on the first ballot in 1964 was approximately 27,000, and on the run-off ballot 74,000, the difference being due overwhelmingly to the elimination of the minor candidates.

Political divisions have been important in the Engineers since at least the 1880s, and have usually been reflected in the results of important elections. Official Communists were the runners-up for the presidency in 1954 and 1956, and the president elected in 1967 was both left-Labour and the choice of a left-wing coalition (to be described). The well-organised Communist machine is often in the position of choosing between two leading candidates whom it had no role in selecting. The anti-Communists have also been in this position. In 1958, an incumbent Communist executive councillor was defeated after receiving 4,613 votes on the first ballot to votes of 2,930, 2,143, 1,966, 916 and 490 respectively for his opponents – on the final ballot the Communist lost by 9,008 to 8,150.

The Role of the Voting System
It is clear that the voting system, which includes ease of nomination and the second ballot, contributes greatly to the extent and nature of electoral opposition. The interest of union members in factions, issues or candidates often seems to be transient or variable from election to election. Even more than in government elections, personal qualifications and a record of service are given great weight. The second-ballot system, in selecting the two

leading candidates, is blind to the bases for their differences. When existing political tendencies are grossly unequal in strength, the two candidates who proceed to the second ballot may both represent the dominant view. When the voters consider ideological differences, industrial issues or factional divisions to be more important, these views will be reflected in the selection of the two finalists.

When there are numerous candidates, the second-ballot system (as well as the simple plurality system) favours organised minorities, with the voters perhaps then faced with the unhappy yet artificial choice of the lesser of two evils, e.g. in the Engineers the rather frequent confrontation of Communist and more than typically right-wing Labour candidates. This tendency is exaggerated by the mass media focusing attention on these two groups in the Engineers' elections. For example, a letter to *Tribune* (21 July 1961) complained that the British Broadcasting Corporation was hardly unbiased in giving a résumé of an approaching presidential election in the Engineers, mentioning only two out of the ten candidates, 'one, a Catholic, and the other, a Communist, and in the event that was how they finished'.

The Mineworkers' system of preferential voting, with later preferences coming into play as minor candidates are successively eliminated, does not have this tendency to lift weak but cohesive minorities to near the top of the poll. Nevertheless, if such a system were to be employed in the Engineers it would often be necessary first to reduce the candidates to a manageable number, e.g. no more than six, less for technical reasons than to focus the voters' attention on the leading candidates and their programmes. A preliminary ballot could be conducted at branch meetings, as was done before the recent introduction of the postal ballot, and then the six candidates with the most votes would proceed to the final, postal, preferential ballot.

Factional Background

There has been a direct line of development of left-wing factionalism dating back to the last century (cf. Martin: 1968, 1969). Much of it is exemplified by the life of Tom Mann:

'Tom Mann who had been, successively, a major leader in the new [general rather than craft] unionism of the 1890s, the socialist movements, and the syndicalist movement, became a founding member of the Communist Party in 1920, the same year that he was elected General Secretary of the union [the Engineers]. Retiring in 1922 on account of age, he remained a prominent figure in the CPGB until his death in 1941. At this time the Communist Party could accept Mann despite his continuing faith in syndicalist ideas . . . The National Minority Movement [NMM] which he presided over at its launching in 1924 [and which was sponsored by the Communist Party], ignored parliamentary politics and sought union structural changes [a general council to co-ordinate struggles for immediate demands].[12]

'Wal Hannington . . . was elected one of the three national organizers during World War II. . . . Like Mann, he was a founder member of the Communist Party' (Richter, 1973: 41–2).

Hannington also retained the view that direct action was the way to gain improvements and change the system. A former syndicalist, J. Tanner, gained the presidency in 1939 with the support of the left, and held it until 1954. Even in 1945, Tanner's periodic election address made no mention of either the Labour Party or the country's general election. Syndicalism had gradually lost its emphasis on social transformation, but the syndicalist element in the Engineers continued to support rank-and-file activity at shop level. According to Richter, the residue of syndicalism also helps to explain the neglect of politics in 1945 and, at a deeper level, even much later, long after a formally more positive turn to the Labour Party.

Tanner broke with the Communist faction in about 1949, and broke publicly with both the Communist Party and the left-Labour members of his union in 1951 at the time of his conversion to parliamentary socialism. For the first time, the Engineers called for massive support of the Labour Party in a general election. 'Now, in 1951, when the union and the [Labour] Party were both agreed that nationalization and other "socialist" programmes were not feasible, we find the union hotly embracing the Party' (Richter, 1973: 51).

During the inter-war years the Engineers' leadership was concerned about Communist influence, but the division was not as sharply drawn as it is today. The National Minority Movement dissolved in the early 1930s (see Martin, 1969), and during the middle and late 1930s the union supported a 'United Front' of working-class groups and the affiliation of the Communist Party to the Labour Party. With Russia's entry into World War II the relationship between the Communist and Labour forces improved considerably, and this state of affairs continued until about 1947. Disagreements in the union between Communists and members of the Labour Party have had an important effect on elections from about 1948 onwards. There was some decline in Communist influence between about 1957 and 1967, followed by a gain along with the growth of a broader coalition on the left, similar to that in the Mineworkers. The Communists remain very strong in certain areas, including London, N.W.

The history of post-World War II factional organisation in the Engineers is similar in many respects to that in the Mineworkers, due in part to the Engineers' even stricter prohibition on the circulation of campaign literature (apart from election addresses printed by the union) and – somewhat less so than in the NUM – to the political traditions which this represents. The left-wing eventually evolved into a broad coalition which utilises a publication affiliated with *Voice of the Unions*, while the right-wing organisation remains covert but utilises *IRIS News*, both publications having played a role in the politics of the Mineworkers also. However, factional organisation and publications play an even greater role in the Engineers because of the far greater number of nationally-elected posts and the fact that all full-time posts are subject to periodic elections. Thus the factional situation is more fluid in the Engineers, and explicitly factional organisations are therefore more useful and in more continuous operation. It should be added, however, that neither the Engineers nor the Mineworkers prohibits attendance at political meetings, or the circulation of general political literature which may include references to the union's elections. The election addresses are useful but inadequate for factional purposes. Candidates were permitted 750 words in 1960, including testimonials if desired, and in 1965 this allowance was raised to 1,000. However, in 1960 the branches were sent only twenty addresses per 100 members, and this dispatch was reduced to ten in 1965 (Rule 2: 9). There is no guarantee that the booklets containing the addresses will be distributed completely or in an unbiased way, and probably most members can receive them only at branch meetings. While election addresses are uncensored, pressure has occurred to delete remarks criticising incumbent officials. Finally, many election addresses say very little programmatically, and some are positively misleading in their implications (particularly in references to membership of the Labour Party) and would require the give-and-take of a campaign to smoke out their authors.

It was not until about 1952 that the anti-Communists began to organise seriously. The organisation publishing *IRIS News*, Industrial Research and Information Services, was founded in 1956 (as we have already seen) to protect the unions from Communists and 'fellow travellers', but in practice it opposed left-wingers of all varieties, including left-Labour. Tanner, the ex-president of the Engineers, served as an IRIS officer. By 1959 IRIS had the support of Hallett, who had been elected general secretary of the Engineers in 1957 with Communist support on the second ballot (against Boyd, who was apparently considered to be more right-wing). During 1959–61, when the left–right factional struggle centring on nuclear disarmament pervaded the entire British labour movement, Party and unions alike, IRIS cells were built in the Engineers under the leadership of Hallett and Pannell, an Engineers-sponsored Member of Parliament. Left-wing candidates were opposed, and the anti-nuclear stand of the national committee was overturned in a campaign also participated in by Catholic groups and the pro-nuclear Gaitskellite Campaign for Democratic Socialism.[13] IRIS was censured by the Trades Union Congress in 1960 for interfering in union elections, but this seems to have had little effect on its activities (Richter, 1973: 144–5, 160–1).

Factional organisation has been facilitated since 1946 by official annual meetings of all full-time union officers. An informed source writes:

'These meetings are not specifically covered by Rule and are arranged by Executive Council. The meetings are semi-secret in that no report is issued and very little if any publicity is given. Of course, as can be expected, on the eve of these meetings the right and left wing factions hold separate meetings . . .

'This year [1972] as we understand it was the intention of E.C. [Executive Council] to cancel the F.T.O. [full-time officer] meeting, but because of the situation with regard to the negotiations with the Engineering Employers' Federation the officials met for one day, but it was an important meeting to get the active support of officials in pushing E.C. line with regard to plant bargaining. I believe that E.C. would like to do away with these meetings – they could be a forum for criticism of E.C. . . .[14]

'. . . nearly all officials can be categorized into right- and left-wing groups, therefore there is always competition between the two groups to get the support of a new officer who may be elected. Of course this is a big advantage to the group which the particular Executive Councilman of the officer concerned belongs to, because of the "perks" [perquisities] a Councilman can give to a junior officer. Life can be difficult if you oppose the line of the Executive Councilman. It can be seen that there are considerable advantages to a Councilman if he can get the support of the District Secretaries in his E.C. Division, especially when he has to go for re-election. But more important, it reduces the effect of criticism of his actions and that of E.C. in particular . . .

'By this process E.C. develops into an oligarchy and the better the party machines are organized, the stronger the trend . . .[15]

'I understand about 100 officers attend the right-wing meetings and about 80 the left-wing meetings, but some of these are part-time District Secretaries so the number of full-time officers involved is slightly less, but it can be seen that the majority are involved.[16]

The 'broad left' coalition began its rise with the publication of *Voice of the Unions* in 1963, after the collapse in 1962 of the Communist Engineering Group (the Engineering and Allied Trades' Shop Stewards' National Council) and its paper, *The Metalworker*. The latter, or its fore-runner, had been published since 1936, and its disappearance is strange considering the degree of militancy in the engineering industry in the early part of the decade.[17] (*Voice* itself dates from the mid 1920s when it was an organ of a section of the Independent Labour Party.) Between 1959 and 1964 the number of engineering strikes per year was more than double the average for 1955–8. The relationship between the Engineers' top officials and the rank-and-file had been getting very tense. The leadership was becoming increasingly involved in union–government collaboration via the National EconomicDevelopment Council, and against this came a grass-roots call for closer unofficial organisation of shop stewards. The Communist group itself was deeply divided and could not provide the leadership for this movement.

The grass-roots discontent was still without effective leadership following the collapse of EATSSNC. There was much anxiety in the industry with mergers and takeovers, and it seems that the leadership of the union became identified with this. From 1963 onwards, however, *Voice of the Unions* channelled these feelings for a greater degree of workers' control into a demand for the reform of the engineering procedures agreement to provide for an equitable *status quo* clause (i.e. a clause specifying no changes in the conditions of employment without collective bargaining). This was now a gauntlet thrown down before management, and a challenge to their prerogative. The existing disputes procedure had originally been *imposed* on the union after the 'lock-out' in 1922. *Voice* conferences on workers' control were held during 1964 and 1965. Soon after, in 1965, a special *Voice* journal for the engineering industry appeared, called *Engineering Voice*. It was prominently associated with an assistant general secretary of the Engineers, Ernie Roberts, a Labour Party member expelled from the Communist Party in 1942 for leading a strike. This seemed to be a force for unity of the broad left in the engineering industry. *Engineering Voice* suspended issue in 1965, but re-appeared in 1966. It held separate conferences for workers in the automobile and aircraft sectors, and the union actually threatened its shop stewards with disciplinary action for attending these meetings. It helped to publicise Scanlon, who was elected president of the Engineers in 1967, and to rally the anti-Carron forces. The unity of the broad left was also assisted by the reaction against the three-year 'package deal' which Carron, the president, put forward, and against proposals for rule book changes made by Conway, the general secretary – all opposed by *Engineering Voice*.

However, the organisational strength of the broad' left prior to Scanlon's presidential victory should not be overestimated, nor should its unity. In an interview shortly before the final presidential ballot in 1967 (8 August) Scanlon told us that, due to a split in the left, only twenty had attended the full-time officials' meeting called by the left two months earlier, in contrast to the 100 officials attending the right's meeting. Scanlon was being opposed for the presidency by Reg Birch, a Maoist member of the union's executive council. We shall return to this presidential election after a further discussion of the more fundamental bases for opposition and democracy in the Engineers.

In conclusion, while relatively-organised factions developed in the

Engineers, there has not yet been the equivalent of an American-style legitimised factionalisation, or of a full-fledged party system. First of all, the restrictions remain against the free circulation of literature by candidates, or by their supporters *within* the union. In recent years, however, the local circulation of unsigned election flyers has not been uncommon, and usually nothing is done about this, unless the flyers can be traced to the candidates or their supporters in the union. The more determined attempt to circumvent this rule by utilising the publications of *outside* organisations is inevitably somewhat centralised and inflexible, and certainly not fully adaptable to effective campaigning. Second, the absence of explicit and open internal factions (cf. Martin, 1968) is also something of a handicap to organisation for performing the numerous practical tasks required for the effort effectively to penetrate and dominate all levels of organisation in a systematic way. Third, it appears that the role of independent candidates remains greater than one would expect in a party system, especially at lower levels of organisation. Fourth, the endorsement of candidacies after the fact, or in run-off elections, is indeed a party function, but typically that of a minor party. Furthermore, there are the specific characteristics of the right- and left-wing groups. The major right-wing organisation – that co-ordinated informally by leading full-time officials – remains covert. The left-wing organisation has developed into something closer to an openly-operating political party, but remains a coalition of competing and potentially hostile political tendencies and groups. However, it must be admitted that the distinction between a coalition and a party is somewhat artificial, and its significance is mostly a matter of future relationships between the Communist Party and other groups.

NATIONAL POWER CENTRES

The union has a separation of powers, as it explains in its literature to potential recruits and new members, between its three governing bodies: the national committee (legislative), the executive council (administrative), and the final appeals court (judicial). The national committee, which is a small working substitute for the American convention, meets at least annually, for ten days. It consists of fifty-two voting rank-and-file members, indirectly elected by and from the twenty-six divisional committees (which in turn are elected by the district committees), plus (during 1949–67) seven participating members elected by the annual women's conference. This system of indirect representation clearly resembles the early Russian soviet system, reportedly by design rather than coincidence.[18]

The national committee consists entirely of members supposedly working full-time at their trades. Actually, of course, they may usually be off the job on union business but, as Clegg suggests, 'most union business is the local affair of the lay members' own section of the union, so that their experience is different from that of their chief officers' (Clegg, 1959: 133).

The committee initiates policy, reviews agreement with employers, and instructs the executive council for the ensuing year. It can also call or suspend a general strike, if in its opinion there is insufficient time for a ballot of members (Rule 14: 8, 10, 15).[19] Every fifth year, it holds a rules revision conference – which no full-time officials apart from the president and secretary may attend. Regular meetings are attended by three executive councillors as well, but no officials may vote except the president in the case of a tie.

There have been many skirmishes between the national committee and executive council, on at least one occasion ending up in the union's appeals court for resolution (M. Harrison, 1960: 142–9). During the disagreement over the question of nuclear armament for Britain in 1961, president Carron claimed that the pro-nuclear stand of the executive was more representative of the wishes of the membership because it had been directly elected, and called for a referendum on the issue. The rules empower the executive council to take a postal ballot (Rule 2: 26). However, the majority of the executive council itself turned down the proposal, in spite of political agreement with the president. The industrial reporter of *Tribune* (28 April 1961) pointed out that only one-tenth of the membership had participated in the election of Carron (and, he might have added, of the executive council – voting was at branch meetings), and asked rhetorically, 'if the inert majority are important enough to be balloted on nuclear disarmament, they are certainly important enough to be called on to vote in an election [postal ballot] for their own president'.

In 1957 the national committee's agenda contained 361 resolutions, and 384 in 1958, plus a few from the women's and youth conferences. While this includes duplication, nearly half of such resolutions may remain undiscussed. The national executive may not remove a district's resolution from the agenda, and rarely submits its own resolutions. In addition, it may indicate to a divisional committee that a resolution before it belongs more properly to one of the trade or industrial conferencss.[20]

The mass media often give full coverage to important debates and decisions in both the national committee and the executive council, especially where policy for the Labour Party seems to hang in the balance. Speculation may begin in the media weeks before, and may conceivably affect the representatives as well as the public. Harrison's characterisation of the situation in the national committee and the executive has some merit, in spite of some over-emphasis on the role of the Communists (1960: 143; see also 142–9):

'In no large union is political policy-making more complicated by the struggle against the Communists. Since the war they have always held at least two seats on the Executive, and several times they have come within striking distance of winning control. The basic support for Communist or fellow-travelling motions in the National Committee varies between fifteen and eighteen, but most of the other delegates are either left-wing or feel bound to give that impression. The non-Communists on the Executive must constantly fight to deprive the Communists of the chance to claim they are the only authentic militants.'

Nevertheless, the union supported the Marshall plan, and went along with or moderated its opposition to orthodox Labour policy in other respects until Carron retired in 1967.

Some very important decisions of the national committee have been cliff-hangers, apart from those on general political questions. In 1968 the AUEW's national committee acted in favour of a strike of Britain's 3,500,000 engineering workers, in collaboration with a confederation of shipbuilding and engineering unions, by a vote of thirty-one to thirty (*Sunday Times*, 13 October 1968).[21]

At its regular rules revision meeting in May 1970, the national committee voted twenty-six to twenty-five, with one abstention, for a postal ballot for full-time officials, to go into effect in January 1972. (It was also decided that ballots would take place only twice a year, to reduce costs.) This division was primarily one between right and left, the latter being strongly opposed to the postal ballot, which it regarded as a means of diluting the left's strength in the union. In addition, the left in particular had always participated in the rather common cult of the active member, an elitist but understandable homage to those presumably more militant workers who attended meetings while everyone else stayed home (cf. Peck, 1963: 324–6). Furthermore, the right-wing leadership had always claimed, since the publication of *IRIS News* at least (mistakenly, as it developed),[22] that the disproportionate representation of the left would be diminished by greater membership participation. In spite of the decision of the rules revision meeting,

'. . . there was little support for the principle of a postal ballot on the Executive and virtually no support at all from the administrators who were to operate the scheme. So great was the opposition . . . that little or no preparatory work was undertaken pending the re-call of the Rules Revision Committee to rescind their decision.

'The re-called Rules Revision meeting [the executive council or the national committee itself may recall] took place in November 1971 . . . Once again, after a full debate, the decision to continue the postal ballot was endorsed. This time there were no abstentions and the vote was 27–25 in favour of maintaining the policy' (*IRIS News*, April 1973: 2).

Largely as a result of the inadequate preparation for the eleven ballots conducted in March 1972 (for example, as late as December 1971 there was no central record of members' addresses), there were complaints about many minor and some serious deficiencies in the balloting procedure, and the issue of the postal ballot is not yet resolved (see *Voice of the Unions*, February 1973: 3).

Carron's Law

It is one thing to make policy, but another to see that it is carried out, as the dispute over the postal ballot shows. A more serious and more pervasive loss of the national committee's policy-making powers to the president took place under Lord Carron's right-wing rule, and ended only with Scanlon's election in 1967. It was made conspicuously evident by Carron casting the Engineers' massive block vote at conferences of the Trades Union Congress and the Labour Party in defiance of decisions of the national committee, under what became known as Carron's Law. However, a similar conflict between the national committee and executive council began in 1955, the year before that of Carron's election as president, over the question of support for the left-Labour Aneurin Bevan's bid for office in the Labour Party. The decision of the primarily rank-and-file delegation (chosen by referenda) the Labour Party conference was over-ruled by the executive council, which was represented in the conference delegation and claimed the power of decision in such matters. The Engineers' rules permit the executive council to appoint representatives from among its members and, together with the president and general secretary, to call a meeting of the delegation prior to the conference (Rule 44: 1, 2), but we see no grounds for the council claiming decision-making powers. On the contrary, the rules state: 'All decisions of the National Committee shall be final and binding on the Executive Council' (Rule 14: 8). Later in 1955, a decision of the rank-and-file appeals court supported the majority of the conference delegation, but the entire sequence was repeated in 1956 when a new national committee decision to support Bevan was again defied by the executive council at the Labour Party conference (see M. Harrison, 1960: 147-8).

Such defiance of the national committee, the Labour Party, TUC delegations and the appeals court was repeated under Carron's reign as president, with differences only in detail:

'In 1965 the . . . National Committee carried a fervid motion pledging 100 per cent support for the Labour Government. What exactly constituted 100 per cent was not defined, but this difficulty did not embarrass Sir William. From now on, the AEU vote was forever to be stacked behind the Government . . .

'In the . . . [1966] Labour Party Conference . . . 100 per cent was still no less . . . Sir William put aside all plaints from the delegates that the union had, in fact, gone on record against the American intervention in Vietnam, and in favour of cuts in military expenditure. From the moment that the Conference opened, he kept firm control of the pad upon which the votes of the delegation are recorded, and remorselessly plonked the AEU's 768,000 votes . . . straight down the line for the platform' (*New Left Review*, 1971: 169–71).

The ridiculously mechanical nature of Carron's control at the conference is illustrated by what happened when he was called away on personal business: the pad for recording the delegation's block vote was passed to the most senior member, the left-Labour executive councillor Scanlon, who then proceeded to poll the delegation. The result was that the Labour Party conference did indeed pass resolutions for reducing military expenditure and against American intervention in Vietnam, with the support of the Engineers, a support which would have failed had Carron been present.

Post-Carron's Law.   While the tension between the legislative and executive branches may not be resolved for all time, president Scanlon – to whom the voting pad was passed in Carron's absence – has taken an explicit position against anything like Carron's Law. Prior to the 1973 national committee meeting of the combined (amalgamated) union, the TUC discussed wages and social security with the Conservative Government, with Scanlon's approval and actual or planned participation. The national committee voted, thirty-five to thirty-three with one abstention, to oppose not only any form of wage restraint, but also any dealing with the Government on prices and incomes policy. This was understandable in view of its additional instruction to the executive council to campaign for industrial action against the Government's policies of legal restrictions on the unions, against which the TUC itself had campaigned. *IRIS News* (July 1973: 5), regretting the binding of Scanlon's hands, reported the following interchange under the caption 'President's Dilemma':

'Fred Lee M.P. a former Cabinet Minister and one time delegate to the National Committee issued a statement "I cannot understand why Mr. Scanlon gave to the Conference the power to veto his appointment as a member of the TUC team to meet the Government.

'" No other president of the AEU has ever interpreted the powers of the National Committee in this way."

'Rejecting Fred Lee's advice, Hugh Scanlon is reported as saying "I won the presidential election on two main issues. Firstly, that policy decisions of the National Committee are binding on all members from the President up or down depending on your view. Secondly, the Final Appeal Court is the body to which they can go if they think these decisions are wrong."'

Some of Scanlon's personal troubles in his rise to top office, to be described below, no doubt account in part for this stand.

Carron's Law illustrates the fact that even fairly democratic organisations may expect occasional disputes over legitimacy, and abuse of executive power. However, it should be noted that the government of the modern Engineers has not been known for its 'strong' leadership, either before Carron (see B. C. Roberts, 1956: 204) or since. While the tendency towards abuse of power is inevitable, resignation towards it is particularly inappropriate in the Engineers, which generally takes its 200-page rule book seriously. Certainly, constitutional amendments in the Engineers could at least restrain its full-time officers from exercising the power of the union's block vote at important conferences of the Labour movement,[23] although much more basic reforms would be required for any important changes in power relationships.

An Evaluation of the National Committee
There is no doubt that the national committee has been free of domination by the national or any other full-time officers, and that it has sometimes acted as an important check on the administration. It has also been a forum for the free expression of views, undominated by any single political tendency, and the visibility afforded its members has often provided a stepping stone to the lower levels of full-time office. (The visibility afforded by membership of the even smaller appeals court serves the same function.)

The role of the districts.   The independence of the Engineers' national committee can be understood only in the light of the high level of autonomy and the extensive range of functions afforded to the districts. The district committees negotiate with employers, and the outcome of such negotiations, including possible district-wide strikes, may be binding on all members in a district. The executive council may disapprove district resolutions or refuse to grant permission for a strike ballot, but it is not permitted to complete an agreement unless the terms are first submitted to the district(s) concerned. A disagreement between the executive council and a district committee must be submitted to the national committee, which consists of district committee members who have also been elected to the divisional committees and, from there, to the national committee itself. As B. C. Roberts has remarked, 'Since the National Committee is composed of persons who are also members of district committees it is hardly likely that it would be pre-disposed to favour the executive council' (120). District autonomy, which includes control over local factory negotiations, has been particularly important because 'In the metalworking industry ... more than one-third of a worker's earnings – including piece-work incentives and bonus pay – are negotiated on the shop floor' (*Business Week*, 22 March 1969: 71). There is often inadequate contact between the district committee and the shopfloor, but shop stewards are represented on the district committees and the latter have authority to call factory strikes, subject to executive council approval.[24] This background, and the frustration of having to abide by a multi-level national disputes procedure for the engineering industry, helps to explain Richter's remark concerning the national committee: '... attacking the officers and the EC have ... helped assure re-election as "a militant" delegate ... In addition, baiting of the bureaucracy – where there was endemic hostility between lower levels and the Executive – was a surefire tactic for winning at least a minimum of locally oriented delegate support' (1973: 100).

The most cogent criticism of the national committee has also been made by Richter (1973: 98–9): namely, that its functional role is now minimal. It has only a vestigial role in wage negotiations, and most of its political resolutions are inoperable. Its role in monitoring the administration is less relevant because the latter has also suffered a loss of authority, due to the dispersal of economic power. The interpretation is then offered that the national committee's political activity (and to a certain extent the executive council's injection of politics into the national committee's meetings as well) is essentially compensatory and is for the purpose of strengthening its image (presumably unconsciously in the case of the national committee).

First of all, it is argued, the objective situation limits the committee's role in bargaining. National committees as such can play no role in local bargaining. In national bargaining, the Engineers are a large but not a controlling union in the confederation, which makes it especially necessary to allow the Engineers' negotiators great latitude. Second, the rules provide that the president shall prepare and present the union's case in negotiations with employers wherever possible (Rule 15: 2), and in a passing reference they seem to assume that the executive council will negotiate with the employers' federation (Rule 15: 17). When the rules are silent, the executive council has original jurisdiction. At any rate, while the national committee may make its views known, and veto a negotiated national agreement (ordinarily at a recalled meeting), its members neither participate in negotiations nor advise on negotiations in progress.

The importance of the national committee's role in collective bargaining depends somewhat on the times and also on the character of the top leadership. Richter devoted only an epilogue to events after 1967. However, since that time the record shows important national committee bargaining decisions: for a national strike in 1968, for a cessation of national bargaining and a struggle at district level in 1972 (*Tribune*, 21 April 1972),[25] and for a breaking off of negotiations with the government in 1973. Nevertheless, subcommittees of the national committee might very well participate in national bargaining and perhaps oversee the operations of the executive council, although other rank-and-file committees might play these roles as well. There are, for example, trades advisory councils, not specified by rule and having no authority, in a number of industries and large corporations.

From the perspective of our theory, the essential features of the national committee which are favourable to democracy are: its small size; its frequent meetings; the severe limitations on the national officials' power to intervene in its proceedings; the equal voting strengths assigned to the moderately large number of divisions (twenty-six), on the assumption that the seven executive council regions cannot control these divisions; the somewhat artificial nature of the divisions themselves; and the fairly high degree of autonomy of the districts, which ultimately send representatives to the national committee. Most of these features are important in facilitating opposition outside the scope of the functioning of the national committee itself.

There are two features of the committee which are not optimal for opposition, one of them potentially important. The system of indirect representation, with votes within first the district committees and then the divisional committees, largely removes the resolution of the issues and the electoral struggles from the public sphere, and creates a potential for oligarchic domination. Ballot votes for delegates would avoid this problem, by allowing for fifty-two separate contests (one for each delegate) rather that what in effect must usually be a fight for the control of twenty-six block votes (two from each division). However, it must be admitted that this doubly indirect system of representation[26] has not had any noticeable dampening effect on competition for full-time posts or on controversy within the national committee itself. We attribute this to a balance of left-right forces for other reasons, and to a geographic distribution of supporters which, fortuitously, has not seemed to create gross political inequities. However, there are great disparities in the sizes of the divisions, which have not had their boundaries changed since 1940. In December 1967 Birmingham had 102,000 members, Dundee and Plymouth each had 13,000, and there was a wide range of divisional sizes in between. As a result, some large industrial centres had no delegates at the 1967 national committee meeting, e.g. Manchester, with some 32,000 members (*IRIS News*, November 1968: 7, 10).

The impact of the entirely rank-and-file status of the delegates is more arguable. We hypothesised that 'The presence as delegates of a small-to-moderate proportion of locally- or regionally-controlled full-time officials is the optimum condition for close elections.' The absence of this condition in the Engineers means that the full-time district secretaries and divisional organisers do not have the opportunity to build reputations at national meetings, since they are ineligible to attend; nor do they have a substitute arena. If this is relatively unimportant as a detriment to close elections for top office, it is because no one political tendency has been able to dominate the executive council, for other reasons.[27]

SHOP STEWARDS

The possible contribution of informal aspects of organisation to union democracy was mentioned earlier, especially Lipset's interpretation that the occupational community of the printing craft nurtured and provided a haven for political opposition in the American Typographers. Since the Engineers still has a considerable proportion of craftsmen among its membership, and is known to have shop stewards operating'outside its formal structure, we will consider the possible contribution of these to electoral opposition in the union.

The union had 23,500 shop stewards in 1960, about one for every forty members (Clegg *et al.*, 1961: 153n.), 26,600 in 1965 (AEU, 1965: 16), and 34,000 in 1973. The shop stewards are elected in the shops, subject to approval by the district committee, but they are not mandatory. Each district committee convenes general meetings of its shop stewards at least quarterly, and at one of these meetings the stewards elect one or more representatives (usually one)[28] to the district committee itself (Rule 13). However, the union has stated that, in addition, probably most of the district committee members elected in the branches are shop stewards in their own right (AEU, 1965: 16).

There is no direct formal contact between shop stewards and branches, and the contact through the district committee is inadequate to integrate the operation of the stewards into the life of the union. Because the union does not have exclusive bargaining jurisdiction in most workplaces, the joint shop stewards' committee from several unions may become 'a nearly independent body – a union within a union – negotiating on a whole range of matters including wages above the national scale' (Galenson, 1961: 46). When allowed to organise, the shop stewards 'tend to act like a branch, and engage in policy making' (B. C. Roberts, 1956: 75). This applies not only to the Engineers, but also to other engineering unions as well.

Since 1946, the Engineers has been a member of the Confederation of Shipbuilding and Engineering Unions, which negotiates national agreements and operates locally through its own district committees (B. C. Roberts 1957: 10). The employers seem to recognise the Engineers' shop stewards as representatives, not of the union, but of multi-union or *ad hoc* local and national organisations. Thus, there has been a source of tension between the recognised national leaders of the Engineers and the shopfloor leaders. The latter have the incentive and opportunity to communicate with each other (and with members of other unions) outside the formal structure. They may then express their views and discontent in the higher councils of the union, through the district committees, but this does not integrate them into the life of the organisation. Some of the major problems, particularly under Carron's presidency, have been well summarised by the union itself:

'Difficulties have arisen at times in reconciling the actions of Shop Stewards' Committees with the policies of the Union. Mostly, the trouble has arisen because of the growth of multi-plant firms with a wide geographical spread. Naturally, shop stewards in the various plants have a great interest in the wages and conditions in other plants of the same firm in other parts of the country and friction has arisen as the various Shop Stewards' Committees have endeavoured to arrange meetings to discuss common problems.

'The A.E.U. have always been opposed to this type of unofficial meeting, although there is machinery in rule for such meetings under the auspices of the Executive Council.

'To a large extent the problem has been met by the establishment of separate negotiating procedures with the large multi-plant firms . . . Fords, Vauxhalls, I.C.I., Massey-Ferguson are four such firms – perhaps this type of negotiatory body may well be extended as the structure of industry changes. Separate negotiating procedures are also in operation with the various government departments' (AEU, 1965: 17).

The problem of integrating the shop stewards into the life of the union has not, by and large, been resolved, although in the post-Carron era the Engineers seem not to have denounced the wilfulness of stewards' committees as insurgency and the work of Communist agitators.

The image of the British shop steward as strike-prone is based largely on the automobile industry,[29] in which the Transport and General Workers and other unions as well as the Engineers have substantial memberships. A broad view of the automobile industry internationally indicates that a formalisation of relationships within and between unions, and between unions and management, would not solve many of the severe problems of industrial relations with which the British automobile industry is beset. Certainly, the official recognition of separate negotiating procedures with Fords, cited above, has apparently done little to defuse the situation there. It would appear likely that British shop stewards in the automobile industry would continue to participate in *ad hoc* shopfloor struggles, even if they could be placed in a tidier niche within their unions' formal structures (see Beynon, 1973).

There is no doubt that a good deal of the Engineers' internal life has centred on the shop steward 'problem', just as it has also centred on the relationship between district autonomy and attempts to co-ordinate national bargaining. However, the popular image of shop stewards as invariably militant and left-wing has now been shown to be largely mistaken (e.g. see Evans, 1973: 82). Many shop stewards have achieved a *modus vivendi* with management which makes their lives easier and provides a means for the adjustment of grievances, as the Donovan Report of 1968 clearly showed. As the union has put it, 'Most shop stewards spend (much) . . . time dealing with what are, generally, personnal functions of management, in smoothing the path of productive process that might otherwise be interrupted or slowed down by the non-settlement of the many problems that arise in the day-to-day operations of industry' (AEU, 1965: 16; see also McCarthy and Parker, 1968; Goodman and Whittingham, 1969; Evans, 1973).

More important, such tension as has existed between unruly shop stewards and the top officials has not fed directly into struggles over full-time posts: the two fields of contention have only partially overlapped. The shop stewards or their followers have not equated their industrial 'militancy' (independence) with a left-wing orientation, and/or they have not seen much relationship between their problems and the electoral struggles within the union. Furthermore, the contact between shop stewards at different locations has tended to be only loosely organised and sporadic. For example, if the local shop stewards believed that their members were underpaid, and wanted information on the rates for comparable jobs elsewhere, they might write to convenors in other factories and, in the automobile industry, might send a delegate to a national meeting of a semi-official organisation of shop stewards.[30] Money for the delegate's relatively small expenses would be collected on the shopfloor or come from a shop stewards' fund. The interplant organisation would tend to fold up after achieving its immediate objective, but might be resurrected if similar conditions arose again. We were told that both right- and left-wingers would participate without hesitation in emergency national meetings which did not wait upon the action of the national officials, e.g. when an important cut-back in production was in the offing.

The failure to integrate the shop stewards has probably provided some baseline below which electoral opposition would seldom have fallen, if indeed other factors had not kept opposition far above this level. But the general contribution of the shop stewards problem to the Engineers' typically much higher level of opposition has probably been modest.

If the shop stewards could now be integrated into the union more effectively, closely-contested elections for full-time offices would still be frequent so long as considerable district autonomy remained. An independent shop steward structure has not been essential to close elections. For more than forty years after the founding of the ASE, shop stewards were unknown outside Scotland and Belfast, and their functions in those places were 'limited to ensuring that members remained in benefit and that newcomers were Society men (Jefferys, 1945: 165).[31] The granting to shop stewards of representation on the district committees in 1921 seems to have had no visible effect on the closeness of elections.

CRAFT STATUS AND OCCUPATIONAL COMMUNITY

Lipset *et al.* (1956) has showed that printers associated with each other off the job because they identified strongly with their occupation and because they had the opportunity to do so through certain peculiarities of their conditions of employment (and unemployment). This in turn led to organisations and communication networks which existed independently of the union administration and provided a basis for effective opposition to incumbents. Other factors thought to determine the printers' occupational community were the lack of status differentiation among members (due to similar salaries and skills), the opportunity for informal social relations at work, and their educational and cultural background which was an asset in setting up and managing organisations (Lipset *et al.*, 1956: 69–140, 142–4, 154, 163, 414–17).

There were a number of factors in the early days of the Engineers which stimulated contact and solidarity.[32] Sons of members were given preference in apprenticeship. Foremen remained members and their pay did not greatly exceed that of the most highly-paid workers. Since these foremen preferred to hire union members, it was advisable for the unemployed to keep in contact with them. The union circulated lists of job opportunities to be followed up by members on their own initiative, and issued travel cards which entitled visiting members to a welcome by branch secretaries. With the growth of the Engineers, Mutual Aid Clubs were formed outside the union in all large towns for exchanging information on job opportunities. During the 1880s the union encouraged the growth of the Clubs so that some of the minor crafts would not complain that their interests were being neglected (Jefferys, 1945: 105).

On the other hand, certain industrial practices reduced employment stability. Workers were sometimes fired before they could share in a 'gang' bonus administered by a taskmaster to whom the work had been sub-contracted. In other instances, skilled men were dismissed in favour of boys after they had established the method for producing new machinery. Furthermore, working and living conditions were extremely poor, and engineers were left with little time or energy for leisure activities or technical education. The status of their occupation, unlike that of the printers', could hardly have been regarded as marginal to the middle class.[33]

By 1910 the means of obtaining employment had changed considerably. The travel scheme was little used because of the reservoirs of unemployed in the major centres, and government Labour Exchanges outmoded the union's function as an employment agency.[34]

The Engineers retains many craft features, although since the mid 1930s the skilled membership has been heterogeneous *and has constituted a declining proportion of the membership.* Skilled workers may pay larger contributions if they wish and receive higher benefits, the AEU *Journal* carries technical articles for craftsmen, and craftsmen are said to dominate the leadership.

A union rule requires members on unemployment benefit to sign a 'vacant book' each alternate weekday. Undoubtedly this rule stimulated social and union contact considerably at certain times, and perhaps encouraged voting at branch meetings. The number on unemployment benefit is very small now, but during the 1930s it reached a peak of 12·4 per cent per month (*Financial Report,* 1960: 109–11).

Engineers have probably not had anything approaching the printers' occupational community since 1910 or earlier, if then. At present, their pride in craft and union solidarity are probably surpassed in many genuine British craft unions.

ORGANISATIONAL HISTORY

The Typographical Union stumbled onto its two-party system, and any one of a number of developments might have brought a different result; indeed, even today 'union law in the ITU flatly and explicitly prohibits such organization' or any other attempt to influence union policy (Lipset *et al.,* 1956: 255, 393–400). The Engineers, on the other hand, has seemed concerned with democracy and been willing to experiment. For this reason it is fruitful to study how its constitutional structure developed.

If it is true that organisational factors are decisive for the success of opposition within the union, then things might very well have turned out differently. They did not because of: (*a*) the existence from the beginning (in 1851) of district autonomy and the second-ballot system; (*b*) the involved but often intractable membership; (*c*) broad militant rank-and-file movements preceding and supporting important revisions of rules, including those concerning increases in the full-time officer force; (*d*) the concern for democratic rules; (*e*) the prolonged period of discussion and experimentation on how the membership might best implement its formal control over the national organisation; (*f*) the particular constitution of another union which apparently served as a model for a rules revision; and (*g*) wise or fortunate decisions at crucial points in the rules revisions.

The Early Days

The ASE was formed through an amalgamation, but most of its expansion-minded leadership came from one union. The district committees, set up at the amalgamation, were a step towards centralisation, although they represented a compromise to balance the establishment of what was, for the times, a strong executive council.

The 1892 Changes

By the 1890s rapid technological changes seemed to outdate the decisions of the delegates' meeting shortly after they had been agreed upon. At the instigation of militant forces which almost succeeded in electing the well-known trade union and syndicalist propagandist, Tom Mann, to the presidency in 1891, the executive council was made full-time in 1892. The council was to be elected by referendum under the second-ballot system, as full-time officers had been from the beginning. Six regional officers similar to present divisional organisers were also added, to increase the overall number of full-time officers from four to seventeen. There had been two assistant secretaries as early as 1866.

A Model for Change?

The changes in rules in 1892 and again in 1921, both preceded by a resurgence of industrial and political militancy, were in line with the 1872 constitution of the Society of Railway Servants, which became the model for many unions. The Railway Servants' rules 'provided for an executive committee of thirteen, elected annually by ballot in thirteen equal electoral districts. . . . It was responsible directly to the members, but the supreme authority of the union was the annual assembly of sixty delegates elected in sixty equal electoral districts, who could hear appeals against the executive, alter rules and lay down the general policy of the union' (B. C. Roberts, 1956: 7).[35]

Conflict with the Executive Council

The establishment of a full-time executive council did not seem to inhibit membership parochialism or district strikes. A national agreement negotiated by the executive was rejected, first in practice and then by vote, in 1902. In 1903 all the four members of the executive running for re-election were defeated by comparative unknowns. District committees were suspended for failure to accept executive council policy in 1906 and 1908, and the general secretary resigned in 1908 in protest against local strikes. New leadership elected with the support of less conservative elements soon adopted a more centralised, cautious policy. During one period in the early 1900s a final appeals committee (which had broader veto powers than the present, strictly judicial, final appeals court) regularly vetoed 40 to 50 per cent of the executive's decisions. Thus, the executive was hamstrung, while consensus was not available through other means. Jefferys (1945: 168) mentions 'the long standing contradiction between the powers given to the local committees to make wage demands . . . and their complete dependence on the Executive, national in outlook and policy, for permission to carry the demands through to a conclusion.'

Experiments in National Control

Between 1860 and 1910 it was not clear how the membership might exercise control nationally. From the beginning a referendum was conducted annually on whether a delegate conference should be called, but it was usually rejected, on advice of the executive, as an expensive luxury. Such conferences were also found to be unwieldy when held. In 1864 a delegate meeting gave the provincial members of a 'general executive council' (which included the executive council) the power to arbitrate between branches and the executive council. From 1874 onwards this became, in effect, the appeals committee (although it was known as that only from 1901), with the addition of the right to hear appeals from individual members and of a requirement to meet regularly (every two or three years) rather than at the pleasure of the executive council.[36] However, it could not initiate policy. After a brief experiment in 1904 a 'representative meeting', which could submit suggestions for changes in rules to a referendum, was abandoned.

The Final Form

The 1921 amalgamation was largely the result of a movement from below which fused with the shop stewards' movement. The first clear-cut demand for an entirely new body to formulate policy, made in 1910 by the man who was to become the first president of the AEU, was taken up by ASE 'reform committees' (Jefferys, 1945: 169). The suggestion was supported by the 1912 delegate conference, but referred to the branches for further consideration. Local 'amalgamation committees', organised shortly before World War I, formed a 'national committee' in 1915, and in the next two years held six 'national conferences' of rank-and-file delegates to discuss amalgamation. Contact was undoubtedly facilitated by the existence of 'district joint engineering trades committees' on which the local officers served.

During World War I the leadership's no-strike pledge, granted in return for certain concessions from the government, was partly responsible for the growth of the unofficial shop stewards' movement. A 'national administrative council of shop stewards' was formed in 1917. At this point the shop stewards negotiated with employers, and the union officially demanded even greater recognition of their right to negotiate. There were wildcat strikes immediately after the war, and unprecedented national agreements were reached for a reduced workweek and guaranteed rates for piece-work. When rank-and-file militants accepted greater centralisation, a basis was laid for a solution to the union's critical organisational problems.

The national committee and the representation of shop stewards on district committees were added to the organisational structure at the time of the amalgamation. Significantly, both the 1892 and 1921 changes, essentially steps in the direction of centralisation, were taken under the auspices of militant rank-and-file movements. The amalgamation was dominated by one organisation (the ASE) and its leadership. But the auspices could probably not have determined the democratic outcome without the already democratic if inadequate rules, the democratic tradition of the union, and some self-consciously democratic leaders with organisational proposals. It might well be asked what held the union together during some of its crises. There is no available evidence that a split was ever likely, even when the legitimacy of the executive council was challenged in the courts (1912–14), or when the shop stewards were in opposition during 1914–18. During the latter period the union's membership grew from 174,000 to 229,000, and this has been attributed to the efforts of the shop stewards (Jefferys, 1945: 170–1, 191).

THE 1967 PRESIDENTIAL ELECTION

It may appear from our description of the political process in the Engineers thus far that the institution of electoral competition is fully secure, or at least an accepted fact of internal life. Relatively secure it is, but nevertheless it is subject to those stresses and strains of factional struggles for advantage which sometimes push beyond the bounds of a stable accommodation and require resolution in courts of law. Indeed, Hugh Scanlon achieved the presidency only through legal assistance and a political situation favourable enough to overcome lengthy and prominent attacks against him and his supporters in the AEU *Journal* and elsewhere. Thus, the Engineers has not been immune to *tendencies* towards the abuse of official power in the interests of its retention. The story of the 1967 presidential election and the events leading up to it conveys the factional atmosphere at the higher levels, and some unresolved problems arising from the typically British constitutional injunctions against free campaigning and from the more universal failure to adequately limit official power.

Scanlon's rise to the presidency is similar to Lawrence Daly's rise to top office in the Mineworkers. Each was a left-winger who was helped by the temper of the times and the decreasing popularity of orthodox Labour leadership both inside and outside his union. Each defeated candidates of equal status, and neither would have made it without challenging the legitimacy of a count or ruling which would have turned a victory at an earlier stage in his career into a defeat.

It is of special sociological significance that the four leading presidential candidates in the Engineers, of the eleven standing in 1967, were on the seven-member full-time regionally-elected executive council, and by virtue of this were second-ranking officers. These candidates were: Scanlon himself, a left-Labour ex-Communist who had broken with the Party over Korea; Boyd, the chairman of the Labour Party and Scanlon's principal opponent; Birch, a pro-Chinese Communist suspended (or expelled) from the Communist Party shortly before the election; and Edmondson, a moderate Labour supporter.

Scanlon's victory helped to throw the weight of the Engineers against the incomes policy of the Labour Government and its programme for the regulation of strikes and industrial relations. The Government's policy had been decided upon the previous year (1966) 'when the balance of payments was out of kilter and the pound was seriously threatened. Pledged to avoid deflation, the government decided to hold down wages and prices and, by taxation and other measures, to force industry to streamline and modernize' (*New York Times*, 3 September 1967: Section E, p. 3). The Trades Union Congress over-rode Wilson's advice in 1967 and adopted a resolution criticising his Government's economic policies by a vote of nearly 5 million to 3·5 million. The TUC 'deplored the deflationary measures that have been responsible for a sharp rise in unemployment' (*New York Times*, 7 September 1967: 1). The number of unemployed at the time was nearly 600,000, the highest summer figure for twenty-seven years.

Unfortunately for Boyd, he was on the wrong side at the TUC conference which rejected the Government's policies, and he personally held up the yellow card which represented the more than 1 million votes cast by the Engineers (*Morning Advertiser*, London, 7 September 1967). This took place only two days after a majority (twenty-six to eighteen) of the Engineers' TUC delegation had made a widely-reported protest against the latest imposition of Carron's Law, in this instance committing the union to support the Government (*Glasgow Herald*, 5 September 1967). Although Boyd was somewhat critical of Labour Party policy at the TUC conference (see *The Guardian*, 5 September 1967), which was held during the Engineers' presidential campaign, he told us in the final days of the campaign that he was hardly helped by his Labour Party chairmanship.

Scanlon, fifty-four years of age, was described as a 'quiet militant' by *The Times* (8 November 1967). His election address called for a 'social order which would be a socialist order', and made clear that he was 'an implacable opponent of both wage freeze and wage restraint and any interference by the State in our duty to obtain the best possible wages and conditions for our members'.

Scanlon's widowed mother brought him to Manchester from Australia when he was two.[37] As a youth, he worked first as an instrument-making apprentice at the Trafford Park factory of AEI. Soon he became an active member in the Engineers, and ultimately won a seat on the executive council in 1963. *En route* to his position he studied through the National Council of Labour Colleges, becoming a shop steward when he was twenty-three. He concentrated his activities in the Trafford Park factory, and became the secretary and ultimately chairman of its works committee. In 1947 he became a divisional organiser, which post he held for sixteen years (see *The Times*, 8 November 1967).

He first challenged the top men in the union in 1961, when he stood for election against Cockin, the incumbent executive councillor for the Midlands and North-West region. This region included Manchester, Birmingham, Coventry, Crewe and Wolverhampton. He considered himself likely to win this election, but the president, Lord Carron, and other senior officials declared the vote void because of letters soliciting votes on his behalf. Scanlon, persistent as ever, took the matter to court and pressed his case until it was discussed in the High Court. Another ballot was held, which in turn was voided by Lord Carron and his executive. On the third attempt Scanlon won, by 13,700 votes to 9,500. Understandably, relationships between him and Carron were cool ever after. When Scanlon won the presidency, the outgoing incumbent made no attempt to congratulate him.

The Press and the Union Journal
A demand for restrictions on statements to the press arose on the left in 1964, perhaps partly in retaliation against the events described above, but also quite in line with a view on this matter widely held in the trade union movement. After an exceptionally strong showing by the Communist Reg Birch against the incumbent president Carron, and prior to an election for the vacant general secretaryship in which the left-Labour Ernie Roberts was expected to be a candidate, William Tallon of the executive council gave an interview to the press. *The Times* (3 June 1964) reported that Tallon 'said it was imperative that every member should vote in every election . . . [against] a communist or someone with communist support who might profess to be a loyal member of the Labour Party but associated with proscribed organizations with communist aims'. The next day the Communist Party's *Daily Worker* reported, under the caption 'MEMBERS ARE AFTER TALLON', the charge by an unspecified 'number of A.E.U. members' that Tallon's press statement broke the rule 'which prohibits the printing of matter in support of any candidate'. The *Daily Worker* of 8 and

9 June reported similar protests in the form of branch resolutions, one of them demanding that the executive council discipline Tallon and adding: 'We will not allow McCarthyism and witch hunting to become part of our union.' One of the presidential candidates in 1967 told us that the three executive councillors who were not themselves candidates were reluctant to support publicly any one of the candidates because of their collective responsibility for the general conduct of the ballot. They may also have been influenced by the reaction to Tallon's statement.

There is no doubt that the tone of the British press was more anti-left in covering the Engineers' elections over 1964–67 than it was in covering the Mineworkers' elections between the late 1950s and the early 1970s. To a considerable extent this was reflected in the reporting of the some-what hysterical anti-Communist statements made by leading right-wing officials, who indeed had some basis for their fears of an important change in the balance of internal forces. For example, the Tallon statement cited above was captioned 'APATHY WARNING TO A.E.U. – COMMUNIST DANGER'.

With president Carron's retirement in 1967 in sight, the union establishment made an unprecedented attack on the left in the *AEU Journal* of July 1966. The front cover was devoted entirely to a letter from Carron, boldly captioned, 'MEMBERS – BE VIGILANT!', which exhorted the membership 'to reject these attempts to negate our Union's democracy and to resist the undoubted attempt to bring the Union under the kind of dominance which enslaved the [Communist-led] ETU for so long'. This was followed by a two-page report of a meeting called by supporters of *Engineering Voice* – one of a number of newspapers oriented towards specific industries and sponsored by *Voice of the Unions* – at which Scanlon was unanimously proposed as a candidate for the presidency of the Engineers. Among the approximately ninety people attending the meeting were non-members of the Engineers, some of them Communist officials from other unions. In calling attention to the report of this meeting, Carron's letter stated, 'Perusal of the report discloses that Officers and Members of the Union present at the meeting were not only prepared to subscribe to the erection of a kind of organisation within our Union but that persons outside our Union should be participants.' An article by Carron covering the same ground also appeared in the *Sunday Times* (3 July 1966), mentioning, more accurately than usual, 'a unique coalition of Communist, Trotskyist and left-wing Labour rebels'.

The then general secretary, Jim Conway, added in his own column in the *AEU Journal*, 'what is deplorable about such meetings is that they are influenced, and for all I know initiated, by people outside the *AEU*. They are, to be blunt, influenced and guided by a political party opposed to the Labour Government.' He added that 'it is not for me as General Secretary

. . . to say how any member should vote in elections for office in the *AEU*'. The presence of prominent outsiders at a meeting to choose candidates was probably regarded as a tactical blunder by the organisers of the meeting themselves, and further flagrant examples of this were probably avoided. However, an advertisement for the first open *Engineering Voice* meeting in Nottingham, held on 24 June 1967, stated, 'National speakers. . . . All engineers invited' (*Morning Star*, 22 June 1967). The speakers were, in fact, members of the Engineers.[38]

The *AEU Journal*'s report of the *Engineering Voice* meeting mentioned by name a number of attending officials of the Engineers, including assistant general secretary Ernie Roberts, executive councillor Hugh Scanlon, and two national organisers. One could only gain the impression that the opposition was very strong and well organised. The 'Be Vigilant!' strategy was based on the premise, explicitly stated time and again by Carron and his supporters (including *IRIS News*), that the left would be defeated if only the proportion of the membership voting was moderately larger, perhaps by as little as several per cent. The election results since the introduction of the postal ballot cast doubt upon this assumption.

Suspicions Concerning the 1967 Election
As the presidential election approached there was understandable speculation in the press that the ballots might be declared invalid. The impossibility of candidates preventing the issuance of unauthorised campaign literature on their behalf (now handwritten as well as printed) was noted, as were Scanlon's earlier troubles in winning his executive council seat. It was also noted that irregularities in the conduct of the ballot in the branches were difficult to eliminate completely, and that ballot rigging, or the disqualification of some branches' votes, might make a difference in a close election. *The Times* (17 February 1967) reported:

'Both sides are throwing all available resources into ensuring that any ballot-rigging attempts, not unknown in the past, are defeated.

'Union headquarters are investigating the latest case of alleged interference with voting in a recent election for an executive member in the north-west. The votes from three branches in the Liverpool area were disqualified after it was discovered that several signatures of members who had not voted were apparently forged on ballot sheets.

'Since the difference between the two candidates after these disqualifications was only 92 votes in more than 12,000, it is clear that if the forgeries had escaped notice the result could easily have read differently. . . .

'The suspicion which has fallen on some of the A.E.U.'s past elections – and which already threatens to smear the present campaign well ahead of the voting – can only be an embarrassment to the candidates, and a dis-service to the eventual winner.'

The *Voice of the Unions* (March 1967), in its comments on the election, stated that determined ballot-riggers could leave a Trojan horse in any branch:

'An unscrupulous member could line up in the scrum [scrimmage] around the ballot-box, show his card to the teller and *sign some other member's name on the ballot sheet* [*Voice*'s emphasis] – say Joe Smith.

'Then, after the votes are counted in the branch, and if the result is "unsatisfactory" a complaint of malpractice is sent to the Executive and an investigation is ordered. The signatures on the ballot paper are checked and Joe Smith swears an affidavit saying that he never voted. As a result, the Executive scrubs the whole ballot for that branch.[39] One hundred oppos-ing votes, perhaps, down the drain. Very neat! . . .

'It is odd that Sir William [Carron] should "welcome" the result with such alacrity [an item in the *Financial Times*, 6 January 1967, was quoted earlier]. The minutes of the secret "Officers Plot" meeting [printed in an earlier *Voice* issue] show that the Right Wing worked extremely hard against *both* [finalists] [*Voice*'s emphasis] . . . – either of whom will, in the opinion of this paper, make an excellent addition to the Executive Council. Was it hoped that, in the excitement of charge and counter-charge, the Right would be able to lure the eventual winner under its wing?'

As it turned out, the results of the presidential election were not challenged.

Interviews with the Candidates
In spite of the problems of legitimacy cited here, the general acceptability of opposition in the Engineers is illustrated by the lack of hesitation dis-played by the four leading presidential candidates in agreeing to interviews while the election campaign was in progress, as well as by their replies to our questions.

The Interview with John Boyd.[40]   Throughout the interview Boyd charac-terised his opponents as Communists, Trotskyists and fellow-travellers, including Scanlon himself. Yet, he gave no hint that it would be a good thing if the opposition did not run or was outlawed. There was no hint of illicit practices by the opposition except the involvement of non-members of the Engineers. He didn't think there was deliberate infiltration of the union by Communists from outside, but a Communist employed in engin-eering would seek to belong to the Engineers, rather than to the Transport

and General Workers or the General and Municipal Workers, since these
didn't offer the same scope for activities.

Asked about the actual mechanics of election campaigns in the Engineers,
Boyd said there was no rule against his or anybody's supporters organising
a campaign in the union. It was no secret that he was the uncrowned head
of the anti-left alliance in the union. In terms of organisations, there were
the groupings around IRIS, the Catholics, and the Industrial Church Mis-
sions (Church of England); Sheffield had a Church centre for shop stewards.
(Boyd himself was known to have been a member of the Salvation Army.)
Of the anti-Communist organisations, IRIS was the most effective, Common
Cause the worst.

His organisation within the union was essentially informal: it had no
formal office-holders and no *formal* meetings, and was based on his personal knowledge of the full-time officials of the union – whether they were
for him, were against him, or didn't want to commit themselves. He kept
in contact mainly by letter. He agreed that poor communications were the
worst of his problems.

Asked about the possibility of ballot rigging in branches, Boyd said that
he didn't think this was a serious problem; nor had he heard of anyone
manoeuvring a branch into a technical breach of the rules if the voting
went the wrong way.

'What would be the effect on union policy if Scanlon were elected – what
was the power of the president?' Boyd answered that policy making was
the job of the national committee (the convention). The dispute at the TUC
over the casting of the delegation's vote arose because the delegation
couldn't make policy, but only carry out that laid down by the national
committee. He contended that the way he cast the union's vote was always
in line with this rule. Part of the trouble came from the different compositions of the national committee and the delegations to the TUC and to the
Labour Party conference in any one year; there was a practice among
union activists of sharing the honours. With one or two exceptions,
national committee members don't run for the TUC or the Labour Party
delegations.

The importance of the presidency internally is in the ability of the president and executive council to sway the national committee. Asked what
would happen if the president and executive council were continually at
loggerheads, as might happen if Scanlon was elected, Boyd replied that he
didn't think this would cause a major constitutional crisis: the president
doesn't derive his power from the executive council, nor work under its
instructions anyway. The history of the presidency is that the post was set
up to police the bureaucratic executive on behalf of the members' interests;
the president is the only nationally-elected member of the executive council.
Also, the executive council cannot challenge the president's ruling in the

case of a procedural dispute. This position of the president extends down
to the level of the district.

Whatever the validity of Boyd's interpretation, it does appear that many
in the Engineers accept his point of view concerning the powers of the
president. Perhaps this helps to explain Carron's Law.

The interview with Reg Birch.[41]   As early as Birch's 1964 attempt to depose
Carron as president, it was reported that he was receiving only reluctant
support from the Communist Party (*Financial Times*, 5 February 1964).[42]
He was dropped from the Party's executive committee early in 1966 (*Daily
Mail*, 1 July 1966), and suspended from membership for three months in
January 1967 'for publicly circulating material which is opposed to the
policy of the Communist Party and . . . which attacks the CP in a hostile
manner' (*The Guardian*, 25 January 1967). He was suspended along with
other members of the editorial committee of *The Marxist*, the publication
in question. He was reportedly not invited to the *Engineering Voice* meeting at which Scanlon was chosen as candidate, and he was expelled from
the Communist Party before the election. Birch as a person has been
described as warm, enigmatic, iconoclastic and even perverse. At any rate,
there was no doubt about his Maoism and his belief that the Party was
opportunistic (see *The Guardian*, 28 January 1967).

Birch insisted that the basic conflict in the union was between the militant
rank-and-file and the full-time officials. The rank-and-file were basically
left-wing in their class attitude on industrial issues, but not in any political
sense.

The normal way to achieve full-time national office was to be an active
shop steward first and then to progress up the ladder of the officialdom.
However, this was not always the case: the final appeals court could make
a member known nationally; he himself had gone straight from the rank-
and-file to the post of divisional organiser. When he took Carron to two
ballots in 1956, for the vacant presidency, he was a lay member.[43] He had
had a base as a militant shop steward in London, and was a well-known
Communist Party member. He lost in 1956 mainly because of the voting
system (he had led on the first ballot). With the second-ballot system and
easy nomination, there were eight Labour Party supporters and two with
more leftist views. The right wing came together on the final ballot.

Birch said that the Communist Party and right-wing electoral machines
in the Engineers were highly overestimated, and that both were rusty and
inactive. The influence of the Communist Party, such as it was, was based
purely on one or two personalities and there was no ideological basis for it.
He had not tolerated its telling him how to work in the union, and had
kept it as an external influence out of the union. The ambitious member
had nothing to gain from Communist Party membership, but certainly had

from Labour Party membership. He thought that on occasion the Labour Party as such had quietly intervened in union elections, using its agents in the constituencies with their many contacts. The Roman Catholic machine was very effective, because the Roman Catholics believed in a certain ideology and worked harder than the others.

Ballot rigging in the union wasn't important – after all, a branch counted for only a few score of votes in a total of tens of thousands. In the end, the decision was a genuinely political one.

The Communist Party machine in the union was working harder for Scanlon – 'a renegade' – than it had ever done for himself. Its decision to support Scanlon was, he believed, a byproduct of the international polemic between the Russians and the Chinese. It was purely an opportunist decision, not taken on the basis of who would be the best official for the union. For some time he had been in a minority of one on the Communist Party executive, in supporting Mao.

In the present election there was little to choose between Scanlon and Carron – both were opportunists. He would advise members to vote for neither candidate.[44]

Birch achieved the third place on the first ballot, with 11,445 votes to 35,793 for Scanlon and 35,492 for Boyd. Edmondson, in fourth place, received 7,926.

The interview with Len Edmondson.[45]   Edmondson's election address emphasised his record as a negotiator, and included this statement of policy:

'As District Secretary I encouraged the District Committee to determine a policy and endeavoured to build up an effective and efficient Shop Stewards Movement capable of implementing the policies . . . I consider it is the duty of the Executive Council to give guidance and encouragement to District Committees to determine and implement District policies within the framework of the Constitution of our Union and agreements to which we may be parties. I also consider it to be the duty of any full time official . . . to advise members on the procedure to follow and the action to take to ensure they will have the full support of the Union if they take strike action.'

As none of the ten other candidates made similar statements, Edmondson was asked to explain the need for it. He stated that districts should not be allowed to go blindly along – they might violate an agreement or the rules of procedure. A course of action should be followed which would make *approval* possible. Full-time officials could follow a line where advisement is possible *before* action takes place. The members at times do not realise that they are acting in violation. Sometimes the procedure can be obtained in a short time. Occasionally the members couldn't possibly wait to go through the procedure – when an employer took provocative action.

He did not accept that the executive council was out of touch with the membership, but acknowledged that it had become increasingly difficult to keep up with the work. The union now had over thirty sets of national negotiating machinery; once there were five.

He had no organised machine working in this election. He knew he had supporters working for him, mostly inside his council region, but there were some outside as well. The machines were at work now for the two leading candidates, in this election more so than ever.

He imagined that most of his supporters would now (after the first ballot) be supporting Boyd. (This was true, as shown in the final ballot, but with great variation from branch to branch and only a moderate margin for Boyd on the whole.)[46] However, the left-wing newsletter, *The Week* (20 July 1967), stated, 'The supporters of Len Edmondson, despite the undeserved right-wing tag they have received, are essentially against the establishment.'

The net vote for Boyd among Edmondson's supporters could have turned the balance in only the closest of elections.

The interview with Hugh Scanlon.[47]   Concerning the path to high office, Scanlon knew of only one executive councillor who had come straight from the shop floor. From shop steward and district secretary the path is usually, but not always, through the post of divisional organiser. A divisional organiser is 'king' in his own area. The (apparently higher-status) regional officer is an assistant to his executive councillor. Regional officers are field staff. In his own case, he went from divisional organiser to executive councillor. He believed that there was currently only one councillor who had been a regional officer. Edmondson had come onto the council directly from his post as district secretary (which he had held since 1953). The remainder of the councillors had been divisional organisers. The executive councillors have higher standing than the assistant general secretaries – there is no doubt about that.

Scanlon's election address attacked 'the ridiculous suggestion of scrapping our Rule Book', and argued for the continued right of members to elect all officials. Jim Conway, the general secretary, had proposed a sweeping re-organisation of the union, including 'a drastic reduction in the union's 3,000 branches concentrating them where possible on individual factories with a full-time secretary operating within the works itself' (*The Guardian*, 10 October 1966). The 40,000 members in Manchester, for example, would be organised in ten branches rather than the current ninety-two. Other proposed changes included the check-off of dues, and postal ballots in branches with full-time secretaries. Scanlon charged that there were those on the executive council who favoured the *appointment* of *full-time* branch secretaries; indeed, the council has split three-to-three on this question, with Carron's casting vote as president carrying the resolution. (However, only a rules revision conference could make this possible.) He also stated that there was support for the replacement of the national committee by a grand convention to be held every three years. Union democracy was in danger. In general, he advocated no major changes in the rules at this time.

Scanlon complained that the left had been weak, and poorly organised, for the past ten years. Asked why, he replied, 'A fair question. If I knew the answer to that one, I'd be president.' One had the distinct impression, from the construction of the answer, that Scanlon expected to lose the election.

In the final result of the 1967 election, Scanlon won by 68,022 votes to Boyd's 62,008. The total poll was 130,030 out of a membership of 1,129,000. The vacancy on the executive council left by Scanlon moving to the top post was soon filled by another left-winger. Scanlon was re-elected in 1970, by 76,000 votes to 32,000 for Boyd. Boyd was elected to the general secretaryship in 1975 (see Table 9.3).

TODAY AND TOMORROW

The Amalgamated Union of Engineering Workers in the early 1970s could be regarded as essentially a federation which was probably moving towards a more integrated union with a trade group structure. At that time the four sections had no common elections of officers at any level. The Engineers, the Foundry Workers, the Draughtsmen and Allied Technicians, and the Constructional Engineers were all relatively autonomous sections of the AUEW, each retaining its own structure and officers (see *Tribune*, 14 April 1972).

The president and general secretary of the Engineers' section were the corresponding officers of the AUEW, by rule. The executive council of the AUEW consisted of: the council of the Engineers' section; plus two representatives from the Foundry section, one of whom could be its general secretary; plus, similarly, two representatives from the Draughtsmen and Allied Technicians' section; plus, finally, one representative from the Constructional section when its membership was less than 50,000, or two when this was over 50,000. There was also representation of the four sections in a combined national committee for the AUEW, with the Engineers' section contributing its usual fifty-two voting delegates and the other sections adding modest numbers to these. Serious discussions on a common rule book for the overall organisation began in 1973.

The prospects for opposition in the combined organisation appear good, at least in the short run. Two additions to the Engineers – the Foundry Workers, and the Draughtsmen – were themselves fairly democratic unions with electoral opposition and active internal factions. There is, of course, some danger associated with any radical revision of a constitution. Posts may be made permanent or appointive; elections may be held less frequently; conventions may be made substantially larger and less frequent; district autonomy may be weakened; the pattern of succession may be 'simplified' to single out logical-appearing heirs to the top offices, e.g. by establishing a vice-presidency – there is no end of things which could go wrong. Whether or not a major revamping of the rules causes any erosion of democracy depends largely on the auspices of the change: the desires, understanding and programme of those most immediately involved, and their susceptibility to the pressures of rank-and-file activists. In the Engineers this is likely to become a factional question, with perhaps some important nuances in formulation being neglected and left to those actually drafting the new rules.

Some rather murky short-range issues may or may not inject themselves into constitutional revisions on the immediate horizon. How can branch life be made more meaningful, useful and participative? To what extent should factory branches be established? Where factory branches are large, should they have full-time officers? Where factory branches are impractical, should other branches be consolidated into much larger units? If so, should these be staffed by full-time officials, granting that such officials are elected periodically? Can such officials serve a useful function for those in the workshops, given a continued lack of exclusive bargaining rights for the AUEW?

We would hazard the guess that nothing short of factory-based branches would do much to invigorate branch life or strengthen the members' bargaining power. Given large factory-based branches, full-time officials elected within such branches should be little threat to democracy, so long as these branches are as autonomous as the present districts, or the latter themselves remain autonomous. Such full-time branch officers might be in an excellent position to compete with each other for district or divisional offices, given enough branch officers of this type.[48]

On the other hand, even in large factory-based branches a convenor of shop stewards might serve almost the same purpose as a full-time branch secretary, while remaining closer to the members, given preponderant bargaining jurisdiction for the AUEW. The convenor, as a branch officer, might make an 'outside' full-time branch secretary unnecessary. In addition, as convenors are technically rank-and-filers, he would remain eligible to serve on the national committee and in other capacities reserved for rank-and-filers. On balance, it is safer to keep the number of outside full-time officials as low as is possible without substantial sacrifice of effectiveness – in spite of the fact that it is not unusual for a convenor in a large plant to remain in this virtually full-time post for ten or twenty years.

Previous research suggests that, while size is an asset to democracy in local unions, dispersion is not (Raphael, 1965). While elected full-time branch secretaries in large dispersed non-factory-based branches need not spell catastrophe for branch democracy, their net effect seems to be arguable. Since such branches might lack viable sub-units – contrary to the current situation in districts, which at least consist of distinct branches – it might be difficult to keep a full-time branch officer accountable and under control. If there is indeed a current unmet need to 'service' members in the workshops (education might be an alternative), an increase in the number of full-time district officers might be preferable to establishing full-time branch secretaries with large amorphous constituencies.

There are grounds for suspecting that those who advocate the consolidation of branches and the establishment of full-time branch secretaries are more concerned with controlling than with servicing the membership. The press report in 1966 of the proposal of general secretary Conway and his 'specialist staff' along these lines – concentrating the branch within the workplace where possible – stated: 'It is argued that this kind of closely-knit organisation would prevent any recurrence of the "workers' trial" [kangaroo courts for local workers] scandals which created such a stir during the general election campaign' (*The Guardian*, 10 October 1966).[49]

The more long-term threats to democracy in the AUEW concern such questions as giantism and general unionism, which the union might conceivably approach, and the role of unions generally in the future. These will be discussed in Chapter 11.

CONCLUSIONS

Thus far, two major British unions, the Mineworkers and the Engineers, have been shown to have effective opposition for important posts and to comply in most respects with the standards of formal representative democracy. The major deviation in this respect in the Mineworkers is in the election of permanent full-time posts, although this has not inhibited competition for such posts as vacancies have occurred. The major deviation in the Engineers was, until recently, in the very low participation in elections, but this has since been partially remedied by the introduction of postal ballots.[50] Both unions under-represent lower-status workers in their officialdom.[51] We have not encountered demands for representation and don't know how such under-representation has affected the economic interests of the groups concerned. A colleague, Stanley Weir, suggests that the geographic rather than shop basis for branch organisation in the Engineers may be relatively more attractive (or less unattractive) to skilled workers, whose wages and working conditions are less dependent upon shop organisation. This seems reasonable, but we doubt that a change to factory-based branches would in itself overcome the problem.

Before stating the elements common to these two unions – essentially, the core of the theory of opposition presented earlier - it will be useful to summarise their differences (see Table 9.1). The Mineworkers, but *not* the Engineers, has a membership concentrated in large workplaces, and virtually exclusive-bargaining jurisdiction and mandatory membership for blue collar workers. These make possible in the Mineworkers, but *not* in the Engineers, a clear place in the union structure for workplace representatives, and place-of-work balloting with a high degree of participation in elections of full-time officers.

In the Mineworkers, but *not* in the Engineers, full-time officials are permanent, and may (and do) attend the national conferences as voting delegates. The Mineworkers has consisted of no more than twenty major subdivisions, while the Engineers has had over 260 with a comparable distribution of power. The Mineworkers' basic structure existed from the beginning of the Federation, while the Engineers' developed only after its formation. Finally, the Mineworkers has a great deal of opportunity for contact both on and off the job, while the Engineers has comparatively little. These points of difference seem to be of only secondary importance for the maintenance of effective opposition, given the similarities between the unions, although their effects have not uniformly favoured either union and may have cancelled each other.

What the two unions have in common summarises fairly well the basic explanation for their oppositions: (*a*) a status hierarchy and path for advancement which stimulate competition among relatively equal full-time officers; (*b*) a regional substructure which does the same; (*c*) limitations on the powers of national officials through specific rules governing their conduct, local autonomy, and other significant power centres in existence; and (*d*) a voting system which facilitates the combination of minorities against leading contenders for office. To these should be added the memberships' support of electoral norms, tolerance of political differences, and attachment to the union as a defender of its immediate interests (although the latter is more widely found in the Mineworkers). The absence of a completely open and free American-style factionalism, as it often exists in the United States, is a noteworthy feature; its effects for a democratic internal life are probably problematic.

The ideological splits within the Mineworkers and the Engineers have contributed the content to their electoral opposition, and have added to the democratic processes a significance which they might otherwise have lacked. Nevertheless, basically it has been the formal system which has provided the avenue for the expression of factional differences and a favourable environment for factional growth. The level of success of electoral opposition has been relatively independent of the degree of factional organisation, and – we believe – would have been maintained, at least for vacancies, even with a less politicised active membership.

NOTES TO CHAPTER 9

1 Amalgamated Engineering Union, *Financial Report for the Year Ended 31st December, 1960,* 1961: 9, 11.
2 An executive councillor told us that there was rarely more than one nomination from a branch, since the branch members did not want to appear foolish in the eyes of others.
3 The total is 101 per cent because of rounding.
4 Organised anti-Communist Catholic groups are especially active in Scotland, with the Communists possibly capitalising to some extent on anti-Catholic sentiment.
5 George Aitken wrote to us that the average weekly earnings of all men (unskilled, semi-skilled and skilled) in October 1960 was £15·25. On an annual basis this would be £793. It is not clear whether the average weekly earnings take account of unemployment and illness.
6 Between 1915 and 1947 there was an assistant general secretary for the national insurance department, and another for the trade union department. The former was, in effect, outside the political hierarchy of the union. These distinct functions and separate titles have not existed since 1948. The national insurance department became unnecessary after the post-World War II reforms of the Labour Government. While both the assistant general secretary posts were subject to periodic elections, we found no references in the *AEU Journals* to periodic elections for the national insurance post prior to 1928.
7 The five included the assistant general secretaries, who are probably needed largely at head office, and the national organisers. The regional organisers may be assigned to the head office, by rule. If one includes an estimated 100 full-time or almost full-time shop stewards, the proportion of members to each full-time officer is 1,600 to one (Clegg *et al.,* p. 189). It could be argued that this high ratio helps to limit the powers of the officials, thereby preserving democracy. However, the ratio is secondary when other factors are favourable.
8 However, these percentages are based on only the 710,000 members (65 per cent) who were registered to vote by their branch secretaries. The union had not maintained a central registry, and since the postal ballot itself was a controversial issue (the left wing opposed this system), some branch secretaries are said to have refused to co-operate in registering their members. A much larger number of secretaries were simply inefficient. It appears that the new system is as favourable to close elections (and to the left wing) as the old, but as yet it has not gained general acceptance.
9 The winner in 1964 had to resign his post as assistant general secretary shortly before running for secretary because of the AEU's rule against running in concurrent elections. This was not usually necessary because elections were held at many different times during the year. With the recent introduction of the postal ballot, elections are being held only twice a year to cut down on expenses: perhaps there should be 'free' post legislation, to help this. The controversy over the postal ballot is still unsettled.

10 See *IRIS News* Supplements, February 1968, April 1973. The context for these estimates was the argument in favour of postal ballots.
11 The figures since 1892 are (per cent): 1909, 36·1; 1919, 97·5; 1921, 61·6; 1930, 69·7; 1933, 99·9; 1933, 67·6; 1939, 79·8; 1943, 16·9; 1954, 64·4; 1956, 71·6; 1957, 70·0; 1964, 25·3; and 1967, 32·3.
12 One important objective of the NMM was union affiliation with the Communist-controlled Red International of Labour Unions.
13 The United States Central Intelligence Agency apparently played some role, at least advisory, in the left–right struggle in the Labour movement (Richter, 1973: 151).
14 Hugh Scanlon told us (interview on 9 August 1967) that full-time official meetings were always political 'in one form or another' (which does not necessarily imply factional organisation). The left did not speak up very much at the meetings of officials during the 1960s, after the right-wing president Carron 'had asserted himself', in order to avoid invective but not – it was claimed – out of fear. Finally, it appears that the left may have omitted two or three meetings of its own during approximately 1964–6.
15 We disagree with this judgement, but appreciate the basis for it in the previous paragraph.
16 The differences between left and right may be bitter and even personal, to the extent that individuals may not talk to each other at social gatherings.
17 See Carew (1971). Carew supplied most of the information in this and the next two paragraphs (letter of 11 February 1972). The fore-runner of *The Metalworker*, which came into existence in 1947, was *The New Propellor*. The latter was mainly oriented towards the aircraft industry, where the Communist Party had its major strength.
18 The comment is based on an interview with J. T. Murphy by Walter Kendall. Murphy was the 'theoretician' of the shop stewards' movement during 1914–18 and a member of the Engineers. He also became a member of the executive committee of the Communist International, and a founder of the Red International of Labour Unions. Murphy stated that the Engineers' constitution was consciously modelled (by its advocates) on the Russian soviet system (note from Kendall, 18 July 1973; cf. Richter, 1973: 40).
19 References are to the 1960 *Rules*, unless otherwise stated. The 1965 *Rules* were different in only minor respects.
20 The executive council may remove a resolution on the ground that it is not national committee business, but endorsement of this lies with the standing-orders committee (elected from among the delegates), and eventually with the national committee on report of the standing-orders committee (communication from G. S. Aitken).
21 The size of the national committee had been increased somewhat after the amalgamation with the Foundry Workers. The vote and the apparent brink-manship associated with subsequent negotiations with the employers had been attributed to Scanlon's desire for re-election: he was fighting for his political life (Haworth, 1968: 12). (The NC was that of the total AUEW.)
22 *IRIS News* commented recently (May 1973): 'The Engineering Section of the AUEW appears to be coming more and more under the control and influence of the Communists and their supporters. Not only have they achieved some success in the recent postal ballots, but from all accounts they had a majority at the policy making meeting of the National Committee, held last month.'

23 The much-publicised flouting of the Labour Party conference's decisions by the leadership of the Parliamentary Labour Party may have helped to create, among orthodox Labour leaders, a disregard for conference decisions in general.

24 District committee members other than shop stewards are elected annually by referendum vote in the branches they represent, but they may be removed at any time. In addition, there is a triennial referendum for the district president and secretary. This president may vote only in the case of a tie, and the secretary not at all. The committee member may be shared alternately among two or more branches, by arrangement rather than rule (interview with George Aitken, 10 January 1961). Political heterogeneity on district committees may be fostered somewhat by Rule 13:9: 'The candidate second in the vote for District Committeeman shall attend . . . when the acting District Committeeman cannot attend, of which fact he must be informed by the acting District Committeeman.'

25 This decision was made by a vote of fifty to two, but there was little follow-through by the districts.

26 To the extent that shop stewards (as well as branch members) elect members of the district committees, the system is *triply* indirect.

27 The unusually small size of the Engineers' conference makes it impossible to invite all the divisional organisers to participate, without vote, without the danger of their dominating the meeting.

28 One shop steward for every 5,000 members or part thereof is elected. In addition, a district committee may authorise the women in any particular workplace to elect shop stewards. Such women stewards in a district are also entitled to representation on the district committee, on the same basis as the general stewards. The executive council convenes an annual conference of from twenty-six to fifty-two women district committee members, and this conference elects representatives to attend the national committee meeting (AEU *Rules*, Part 1a: 4, 5).

29 Strikes in even the strike-prone engineering industry have been very unequally distributed. For example, a survey of strikes in 432 engineering establishments during 1967 and 1968 showed that only three establishments accounted for 41 per cent of all reported strikes (see Silver, 1973: 77).

30 In 1964 the automobile industry shop stewards met the Minister of Defence, and handed a letter of protest to the Prime Minister.

31 Also, 'By 1909 some shop stewards had been elected in most of the major centres of the industry' (Jefferys, 1945: 165).

32 Most of the historical references which follow are based on Jefferys (1945: especially 27–33, 55, 60–7, 70–3, 91–2, 105, 108–13, 136–7, 167–71, 174–94, 207–8, 241, 246).

33 Printers did not wish to associate with manual workers (because of differences in cultural background and their desire to retain a superior status), but often did not have the opportunity to associate with middle-class persons (Lipset *et al.*, 1956: 108–11, 120–1). On the other hand, W. F. Cooke calls it to our attention that in 1904 Bertrand Russell described those attending his lecture to a London branch of the Engineers as '*very* respectable – indeed I shouldn't have guessed they were working men' (Russell, 1967: 259–60).

34 W. F. Cooke has also noted that in the late nineteenth and early twentieth centuries there were changes in the technology of engineering workshops which, together with the employment of unapprenticed workers, both

down-graded the craftmen's skills and threatened their social status. Such developments may have led to heightened militancy among engineers (see Brown, 1965: 91–2).

35 The annual general meeting of the National Union of Railwaymen, the descendant of the Railway Servants, today has about seventy-seven delegates, but these are not elected indirectly as in the case of the Engineers. Its executive council consists of lay members (B. C. Roberts, 1957: 134, 510).

36 The general executive council was abolished in 1892, and when re-created in 1896 it or its provincial section may have had still greater veto powers (Jefferys, 1945: 73, 91–2, 109, 137, 168).

37 We were told that Scanlon visited Australia some time before the election, where there were 80,000 members of the Engineers at the time. His net majority on the second ballot among the Australian members was approximately 600; his net majority in the entire union was 6,400.

38 W. F. Cooke attended the meeting as an observer, with permission.

39 It was also argued that, by rule, only the forged ballot papers should be disallowed, but as we interpret Rule 2: 21 (1965) the vote of the entire branch should be disallowed.

40 The interview was conducted by Cooke and Warner (26 October 1967), and reported by Cooke. In most places we have followed Cooke's wording quite closely, apart from editorial changes and omissions.

41 The interview was conducted and reported by W. F. Cooke (4 September 1967).

42 The vote was: Carron 44,599 to Birch 31,213 (*Daily Worker*, 22 April 1964).

43 Birch's 1956 election address shows a record which includes thirteen years on the national committee, six years on the final appeals court, twelve years as president of London District, N., and ten years as chairman of a divisional committee.

44 The second-ballot votes of those branches preferring Birch on the first ballot were quite variable, but on the whole Scanlon appears to have profited more than Boyd. For example, of the ten branches in which Birch had at least forty-eight votes and an absolute majority on the first ballot: five preferred Scanlon by a large majority on the second ballot; one similarly favoured Boyd; one was divided; and three had what were apparently heavy abstentions (although such variability in the number voting is not unusual in the Engineers).

45 The interview was conducted and reported by Edelstein (8 August 1967).

46 Of the fifty branches in which Edmondson had thirty or more votes and an absolute majority on the first ballot: twenty-four were fairly evenly divided between Boyd and Scanlon on the final ballot; sixteen were fairly strong for Boyd; and ten were fairly strong for Scanlon.

47 The interview was conducted and reported by Edelstein (9 August 1967).

48 It was shown earlier that opposition in the Engineers was least effective in the elections for full-time district secretaries.

49 This is not to suggest that the realistic-appearing preparations for hanging workers convicted of rate busting or other crimes are defensible, assuming these were correctly reported.

50 The matter is subject to review at the 1975 rules revision conference.

51 We have never heard of a highly placed woman full-time official in the Engineers, where female membership is sufficient to warrant such representation. There is *one* woman district-secretary official.

Chapter 10

Case–Study 3: Top-Level Defeats in Certain American Unions

The defeat of a top officer is usually accompanied by a deep membership dissatisfaction with wages and working conditions, or with the power and status of the union or occupation(s) in society. Perhaps defeats are more likely to occur when conditions are perceived as threatening or deteriorating, but opportunities for economic benefits or union growth which have been forgone may also provide a stimulus (see Weir, 1970; Barbash, 1967: 98). However, the defeat of a top officer is, with few exceptions, also accompanied by a political split among important full-time officials, one of whom usually becomes the standard-bearer for the opposition and the candidate who replaces the incumbent. Indeed, we have suggested that the availability of other highly-placed full-time officials with independent power is one of the most important structural characteristics which facilitates successful opposition. We are more concerned here with discussing the role of formal organisation, some common problems of fraud and legitimacy in elections involving defeats, and some general background on leadership styles and power in recent *critical cases* in American unions which puts the entire matter in context.

The United Mine Workers of America

At least one exception to the rule of defeats by full-time officials is the defeat of the president of the United Mine Workers of America *by a rank-and-filer* in 1973, but the circumstances were highly unusual. The previous opposition candidate (an important full-time official) and some members of his family were murdered shortly after his unsuccessful attempt to displace president Boyle in 1971. By the time of the 1973 election, various full-time officials in the administration had been convicted of the crime, and the United States Government had moved in to conduct the entire ballot. (It had refused to intervene in 1971, although called upon to do so.) Boyle was implicated in the murder at the time of the 1973 election, and attempted to commit suicide after his subsequent indictment. The victorious rank-and-file slate soon initiated a series of important democratic reforms, with the result that, for the time being at least, the Mine Workers seem to be perhaps the most democratic and least 'bureaucratised' of the relatively large unions. Boyle has since been convicted.

However, the critical role of the government in the defeat was less exceptional. The president of the International Union of Electrical Workers was ousted in 1965 only after the United States Department of Labor had impounded and recounted the ballots. The Communist leadership of the British Electrical Trades Union was overturned in 1961 only after a court ruling of carefully- and centrally-organised fraud. And the defeat of the president of the United Steelworkers of America in 1965 must be be-clouded by the suspicion that he might actually have won: his opponent, the secretary-treasurer, had had much greater control over the poorly-supervised electoral machinery.

The International Union of Electrical Workers

In America, defeated incumbents are often accused, by the secondary leadership as well as by rank-and-filers, of extreme egoism and arrogance and 'thinking they own the union', let alone loss of contact with the rank-and-file and insensitivity to its desires. It does appear that there is often much merit to these accusations; the constitutional powers of the president no doubt facilitate the development of such attitudes.

The conceit of autocratic leadership seems to have been a factor in the defeat in 1964 of James B. Carey, president of the International Union of Electrical Workers: 'Carey's defeat must . . . be attributed in large part to personal qualities. His ungovernable temper, contentiousness, and "vindictiveness" . . . were increasingly directed towards his union colleagues, most of them old comrades in the anti-communist wars' (Barbash, 1967: 97). A former member of the administration who remained somewhat sympathetic to Carey told us in 1968: 'Jim Carey would never allow the secondary leaders of the union to lead. He did not keep them informed. He consulted with a few of them that he felt closest to, but they never felt they were making more than a consultative contribution.' Nevertheless, Carey was apparently 'clean' and a political liberal; he was one of the founders of the Committee for Industrial Organization in the 1930s, at the age of twenty-five, and outside his union was not generally regarded as a labour czar.

Carey himself told us in an interview,[1] 'I never did attempt to build a machine in the IUE. I determined that the IUE was not going to be a series of duchies like the Operating Engineers. And I would never allow one to form if I could help it, but one did in District 3 [to be discussed later].' Here Carey hinted that, if a president builds a machine (apart from appointed staff, whom he took for granted), he must automatically give up some of his power to his subordinates, and that he (Carey) preferred to rule alone by mandate of the membership.

The IUE had only two nationally-elected officers: the president and secretary-treasurer. The latter could sign cheques only jointly with the president, under whose direction he served subject to the authority of the convention and the executive board (Article VII, Sections A and C). However, the executive board was required to meet only quarterly.

Carey had been president of the United Electrical Workers (UE) from 1936 until his defeat at its 1941 convention. He established the IUE in 1949 after an anti-Communist split which took most of the UE's membership. We asked Carey: 'Did you set up the IUE differently when you set it up in 1949?' He replied: 'I made damn sure there was no organisational director. The president held that job.' Carey hinted that in the IUE the job of organisational director was given to the president not only to eliminate the existence of a third elective national post, which had existed in the UE, but also because that job creates a power base for its holder. Carey had an *appointed* director of organisation at the time of his defeat.

Carey also stated, concerning the referendum in the IUE:

'If it were not for the referendum method . . . I would not have lost to Jennings. I had the support of a majority of delegates at the 1964 convention, as the Proceedings make clear . . .'

Question: 'Who was responsible for getting the referendum instituted in the IUE constitution?'

Carey: 'I was.'

Question: 'What were your reasons?'

Carey: 'Referendums are good because they are so seldom used.'

It may be that the referendum is more common in unions formed under the CIO partly because of similar miscalculations common to that period. Nominations for the offices of president and secretary-treasurer of the IUE require considerable support. They are made at the convention, by delegates from ten or more locals in three or more districts, representing no less than 15 per cent of the national membership (Article XXII, Section A).

In the events leading directly to Carey's defeat, Carey engineered the recall of secretary-treasurer Al Hartnett in 1963, after Hartnett had opposed him on a programme of internal union democracy. Hartnett had brought suit against Carey in the courts, asking that Carey be enjoined from further violations of the union's constitution. The alleged violations included the unauthorised dismissal of at least ten field representatives, interference with union record keeping, the alteration of executive board minutes, the issuing of cheques without Hartnett's approval, and interference with the prosecution of a union aide in Puerto Rico who had been charged with the misappropriation of $10,000 (*New York Times*, 31 July 1962). There had been at least two physical encounters at union meetings between the two leading officials (Carey was only five feet five inches tall, but had been an excellent boxer).

The previously-mentioned informant told us:

'Hartnett was a nobody without a strong power base. Carey picked him, groomed him, only to see Hartnett build an anti-Carey faction in alliance with District 3 [the largest] leaders. [According to another informant, District 1 leaders were even more deeply involved.] Carey had given him such a build-up that it was hard at first to oppose his factionalism. Thus, Carey paid a big price for his circumvention of the democratic election of union officials. The fight that Hartnett finally lost cost the union a great deal in energy and then became a liability to Carey.'

Hartnett was removed under an exceptionally democratic recall provision in the constitution which left the initiative and final decision for the recall of either the president or the secretary-treasurer entirely in the hands of the local unions (IUE–CIO *Constitution*, 1955: Article X, Section A). However, it was charged that Carey 'promoted' Hartnett's recall. The opening nomination of Jennings at the 1964 convention included a call for democracy and 'a new beginning against the disgusting infighting of the past few years that has paralyzed this Union. A new beginning – doing away with absolute control, coercion and threats' (IUE, *Proceedings*: 128). The closing nomination called for 'an end to purges . . . an end to recalls' (159).

After Jennings' nomination as presidential candidate at the convention, he attempted to introduce a resolution entitled, 'Providing Safeguards for the Conduct of a Free, Honest and Democratic Election', on the grounds that this was to be the first such contested election to be held in the IUE. Carey ruled Jennings out of order on the basis that the constitution specified the rules for the election (which it did, up to a point). Jennings pointed out that the constitution allowed the president to interpret the constitution only *between* conventions (which it did), and attempted to appeal against the decision of the chair. Carey refused to allow the appeal, and 'For the better part of a day, they [Jennings' supporters among the delegates] pounded the tables with their shoes [as did some of Carey's men] and shouted at Carey · · · Jennings stood at the floor mike all that day in a challenge of the chair's ruling; Carey, for his part, flipped a switch on the podium cutting off the microphone' (T. R. Brooks, 1964; see also IUE, *Proceedings*: 213–35). This demonstration could hardly have continued so long without organisation. In fact, the pro-Jennings leadership on the convention floor kept it going to display Jennings' support for democracy.

There was also a dispute at this 1964 convention over the method of electing the five trustees, whose duties included the supervision of the presidential election and, in particular, the ballot counting. The Carey-dominated executive board endorsed a complete slate of five candidates, while Jennings' supporters nominated only two. In a roll call vote for the election of trustees, Carey first recognised those locals which were known to support his slate. A list had been prepared at a caucus meeting at the convention (Jennings' supporters complained that a room had not been made available for them to do the same), and such locals voted for five candidates. When the pro-Jennings locals attempted to vote for fewer than five, 'bullet voting' for their slate (as was advisable for a minority under a winner-take-all system), Carey ruled that delegates must vote for *five* candidates. Block voting by locals was not required, and in some instances delegates voted separately. The IUE constitution is silent on the matter, and at the 1962 convention votes were permitted for fewer than five candidates. The chair finally stated, after inquiries, that votes for fewer than five would be 'recorded under protest' (IUE, *Proceedings*: 245), but refused to clarify whether such votes would be counted. Many pro-Jennings locals voted for five candidates, and when all the votes were finally counted, including those for fewer than five candidates, the leading Jennings candidate was seen to have lost by 1,043 votes to 1,541 for the lowest winner (326 votes for this candidate were from delegates who had voted for five candidates). It is not clear whether a Jennings candidate might have won if bullet voting had been clearly permissible, but the election of the five pro-Carey trustees was to undermine the validity of the count for the presidency.

Not long after the September 1964 convention, District 3, Jennings' base of support, was ordered by the executive board to submit its financial records since 1960 to an audit. No member of the District 3 council was to be allowed to participate in national executive board meetings until the audit was completed. On this basis Milton Weihrauch, who as president of District 3 was an *ex officio* member of the board, was excluded. A representative-at-large on the executive board from District 3 was also excluded, on other grounds. Finally, the pro-Jennings chairmen of two conference boards (councils to co-ordinate the collective bargaining of all local unions dealing with particular major corporations) had their salaries reduced, supposedly because of the small size of the conference boards in question (*IUE News*, 19 November 1964).[2] The exclusion of the District 3 representatives from the executive board made it more difficult for the opposition to affect or protest against the conduct of the election and the ballot counting.

At the count itself, Jennings was permitted only two watchers, although counting was proceeding at five stations under conditions which permitted close observation of none. (The ballots were in most cases laid face down, after handling.) The loud and frequent protests of Jennings' watchers during the count were not acted upon by the trustees, and their written challenges were ignored. Although only three of the five trustees were found to have themselves miscounted ballots, any one of them might have given consideration to the protests. Carey himself, although out of the country during the count, would not support any of Jennings' proposals for a recount (see *IUE News*, 15 April 1965). Finally, at its meeting of 16–17 February 1965, the Carey-dominated executive board voted to set up a committee, headed by a pro-Carey district president, to look into the vote protests. It was hardly reassuring that this committee was authorised to remove the ballots from the security warehouse in which they were stored. At this point the Secretary of Labor intervened.

Apart from the conduct of the 1973 election in the Mine Workers, cited earlier, the IUE recount is the only instance in which the Department of Labor has intervened in an election for top office by recounting the ballots. Herling, a most able labour journalist, comments (1972: 270): 'It is doubtful that the [Labor] department would have moved as it did without the assent, indeed the urging, of AFL–CIO President George Meany, no admirer of Carey's, who normally would not have encouraged government intervention.' Carey expressed a similar view in our interview with him.

On the basis of the recount of the ballots impounded by decision of the Secretary of Labor, Jennings won by 78,000 votes to 55,000 for Carey, a margin of 23,000, with over 53 per cent of the membership returning postal ballots. However, in the original count by the union trustees, Carey won by a margin of 2,193. (At the time of the election there were 271,000 members in 552 locals.)

The IUE executive board decided, in a split vote, to continue Carey's full salary for thirty-two months, and afterwards to pay him $12,500 per year until he obtained full-time employment or reached retirement age (*IUE News*, 15 April 1965). Carey became the Director of Labor Participation for the United Nations Association of the United States, retiring from that position several months before his death in 1973 at the age of sixty-two.

The campaign.   The IUE rules require that the membership should receive postal ballots within forty days after the close of the convention, and that these ballots should be returned with postmarks dated not more than ten days after the date they were mailed to the voters. Thus, a short and concentrated effort was required of both sides. The Jennings group had attempted to find a candidate for secretary-treasurer as running mate for him, but learned only at the convention itself that their single prospect outside District 3 had declined their offer.

The rules also require that one issue of the *IUE News* should provide equal space for statements by each nominee. A full page was indeed made available to each presidential candidate, with pictures of supporters and testimonials by them included. However, the general lay-out of Carey's page was markedly superior to that of Jennings', and the opposition profited in its claim of bias in favour of the incumbent. The *IUE News* was, in general, unabashedly pro-Carey and anti-Jennings. The issue immediately following the convention devoted only three short paragraphs to the nomination of Jennings, but a full page to endorsements of Carey for re-election, in violation of the Landrum-Griffin Act.

Both sides engaged in an extensive distribution of campaign literature. The Carey faction sent out two or three national mailings, undoubtedly using the same name-plates employed for the union's postal ballot. At any rate, the Jennings faction could not obtain equal access to the membership list (or, for that matter, to a list of locals declared ineligible to receive ballots), as required by law, so resorted to three plant-gate and in-plant distributions approaching national coverage. This required shipping literature to the localities by bus, and then, in many cases, distributors travelling into distant enemy or neutral territory. In addition to the centrally-organised coverage, many local officers on each side used their local mailing lists, and there was a great deal of in-plant distribution. There were at least two instances in which the Jennings forces provided their local people with material suitable for local photo-offset printing under their own name, thus strongly identifying them with the national campaign. The members of locals actively involved in the campaign were the object of between ten and twenty distributions in all, according to one informed estimate.

Although any expenditure of union funds in support of the candidates was illegal, a government report found:

'A large number of local unions made donations [to cover legal expenses to insure a fair election] to the IUE Committee for a Constitutional Election [the Jennings faction] by checks drawn upon local union checking accounts. In most, if not all instances, the disbursements were authorized by the local union membership . . . A large number of local unions also purchased space in a souvenir journal published by the [Paul Jennings] Testimonial Dinner Committee for distribution to dinner guests [apparently neither fund was ultimately found to have been illegal].

'A campaign fund was also established by Carey supporters, and it appears that the most substantial contributions to this fund were in the form of donations from officers and employees of the international union and from Carey himself . . . [There is] no evidence to indicate that union treasuries were the source of contributions to this particular fund which was administered by . . ., IUE Comptroller' (Labor–Management Services Administration, 1965: 12).

It may be imagined that many if not most of the approximately 150 nationally-appointed field staff, and the thirty assigned primarily to the head office, found it difficult to refuse requests for even sizeable donations to the Carey fund, although the thought that they might be fired by a new regime might in many cases have been incentive enough. In any event, the constitution gave the president the power to determine the salaries of appointed staff, with the consent of the executive board, so that the prospects for an eventual return (with dividends) of even sizeable donations might have appeared good. There was also the matter of expense accounts.

The government found that the staff and facilities of both the national union and District 3 had been used for partisan purposes, but (naturally) could not disentangle the money spent on the campaigns from that spent for legitimate union business. However, the staff available to the national administration was much larger; a Jennings supporter told us that only five or six nationally-appointed staff had been willing to work openly for Jennings. There were a very small number of instances where people really close to Jennings were transferred to isolated areas of the country. The remainder of the nationally-appointed staff reportedly worked for Carey, but, according to another informant, some appointed field staff of both persuasions managed to remain uninvolved where assigned to enemy territory.

Finally, a highly credible source told us that the Jennings campaign had received sizeable donations from the presidents of two important American unions – in one case, it was surmised, to build a machine of supporters within the AFL–CIO. Such donations were also allegedly given to the opposition in the case of the defeat of the president of another union in our American sample. It was also pointed out that the opposition in the United Mine Workers must have received sizeable donations from the liberal-labour community. In the latter case such funds were openly solicited. It was argued that, in the three unions cited, the infusion of outside campaign funds was a virtual necessity for defeating the incumbent presidents. This may well have been right.

In an unusual and puzzling sequel to the campaign, the District 3 president, Weihrauch, and secretary-treasurer (one of the two watchers for Jennings at the ballot counting) were recalled from office in September 1967 after a committee appointed by Jennings had found that they had misused $140,000 of the district's funds. The situation arose 'when the Labor Department, which had been investigating charges of financial irregularities in the Carey–Jennings race, found evidence of other financial troubles in District 3. When the Department subpoenaed the District's financial records, Jennings cooperated fully . . . Jennings emerged unscathed from the scandal' (Moritz (ed.), 1970: 225). The district was under trusteeship to the IUE at the time of the recall, by vote of the membership. We were told that Weihrauch had claimed, in union circles, to have acted only to cover funds expended in the Jennings campaign. Our pro-Jennings informants disputed this claim vigorously, citing Weihrauch's allegedly-known spendthrift habits, both personal and as a union officer, prior to the campaign. At any rate, both district officials were convicted of embezzlement in 1968 and given five years' suspended sentence and five years' probation.[3] Our pro-Carey informant suggested that perhaps Weihrauch had chosen Jennings, the third-ranking District 3 official, as presidential candidate because Jennings was 'clean'. When asked about this possibility, a participant in the Jennings campaign stated:

'Weihrauch was an East-coast Jew in an essentially Mid-west, non-Jewish membership. I think that Weihrauch believed that he didn't have a chance. There wasn't *anyone* with much of a chance, but the fight was necessary. The dues question [Carey's attempt at the 1964 convention to centralize the collection and distribution of dues] required a fight; also the attempt to centralize the leadership. So, number 1, there was no option; and, number 2, the rank-and-file [in District 3] were also *desperately* opposed to Carey.'

The consolidation of the new regime. Jennings was remarkably self-restrained in the use of his presidential powers of discharge and appointment. Disregarding the urgings of his supporters, there were no discharges of field staff, and at the IUE office only Carey's director of organisation was purged. Very few new people were brought onto the staff. In 1968, Fitzmaurice, formerly a staunch supporter of Carey, was named secretary-treasurer, succeeding Collins who resigned to become assistant to the president (*IUE News*, 11 July 1968). The *Wall Street Journal* (6 August 1969) commented that this move was generally interpreted as expanding the president's power base and facilitating the union's organisational drive which, according to an unidentified IUE official, had been damaged by the 1967 scandals. By 1973 we were told that the Mid-west was now Jennings' power base; there was no one left with Jennings of those who had been with him in the fight that made him president.

Did the members benefit from Carey's overturn? Stanley Weir (1970: 473–4) presents one view:

'In a very short time Jennings did more to improve wages than his predecessor, but he too neglected the fight for working conditions. Under his leadership the IUE engineered a united effort of eleven unions [including the UE, from which the IUE had split off] in the 1966 negotiations and subsequent strike against GE [General Electric]. . . . The IUE-led united front broke GE's . . . practice of making their first settlement offer their last settlement offer . . . It also broke President Johnson's 3·2 per cent wage guidelines . . . [but] after the contract was signed, major locals of all unions in the front . . . stayed out on strike. Jennings and the leaders of the other unions had failed to negotiate an improvement of grievance machinery and working conditions. A Taft–Hartley injunction was necessary to end the strike of those involved in defense production.'

Is the IUE now more democratic? It is probably less oppressive, because of the personal style of the president, but the basic powers of the president remain. Jennings' victory did, however, safeguard some pro-democratic organisational features (to be described) which Carey's victory would have endangered. Since 1965, such oppositional tendencies as have existed – and there have been some – have not manifested themselves in the quadrennial presidential elections. Such opposition is not undertaken lightly. Perhaps next time it is tried it will get a little better treatment inside the union. But a large appointed staff, especially one nationally appointed, is incompatible with union democracy. The system takes precedence over the leader who, as its prisoner and the beneficiary of its bias, almost never initiates action to change it.

Some democratic features of organisation.   The organisational basis for the Jennings victory was: the relative autonomy of the union's locals and districts; the election of district officials within the districts themselves; the formal recognition of seven semi-autonomous corporation-wide 'conference boards' of local union representatives, cutting across regional lines (for General Motors, General Electric, Westinghouse, Sperry Rand, RCA, Sylvania, and Radio and TV Parts); and the representation on the executive board of district presidents, district-at-large representatives, and the chairmen of the conference boards.[4]

The opposition to Carey in 1964 was based largely on this threat to local autonomy. Our pro-Carey informant commented that, at the 1964 convention, Carey 'scared the District and local leaders (especially those from larger and older locals) by proposing . . . a constitutional change . . . to send the check-off dues money directly to the International . . . They probably saw this as a move to eliminate their weapon over the International – the withholding of per capita if they disagreed with an International policy or power play.' The locals were in a position of strength, with respect to the right to strike; their only constitutional obligation was to permit the president of the IUE a prior 'effort to adjust the dispute' (Article XIV). The proposal for a constitutional change was defeated at the convention, in spite of the generally pro-Carey majority. At the time of the Carey–Jennings election, T. R. Brooks (1964) commented: 'Local factions are always threatening to run off to the Teamsters or to the IUE's rival . . ., the UE', although actual split-offs must have been very few, if any.

The conference boards, whose jurisdiction includes most of the member-ship, had these functions: '(a) to formulate collective bargaining demands . . . (b) to designate negotiating committees . . . (c) to determine whether or not proposed national agreements shall be accepted; (d) to co-ordinate the administration of . . . agreements . . . (e) to determine whether or not strikes shall be called . . .' (Article XXIV, Section E). Chairmen are elected by conference for biennial terms. The IUE office may only 'appoint a representative to a Conference Board to assist and advise it' (Section C). The Sperry Rand conference board published its own newspaper, which boosted Jennings before the 1964 election. But, of course, a successful battle with a major American corporation requires the support of the international union, especially since the rise of multi-national corporations in the field of electronics.

The Defeat in the United Steelworkers of America

The defeat of the president of the million-member Steelworkers in 1965 ousted an even more autocratic leader in a referendum election. Soon after his election in 1952, president David McDonald surrounded himself with subservient appointed staff:

'Such people usually had a title of some sort, with an office and secretaries. Generally they were required to be only the president's companions in waiting.

'A pattern of behavior evolved to match McDonald's exalted station. A dramatic entrance heralded his presence. Outriders, a flying wedge of bodyguards, and a squad of protective staff representatives surrounded him as he and his men strode through a hotel lobby or down a corridor, proudly and purposefully, looking neither to the left nor the right. Ordinary observers prudently pressed themselves against the walls to avoid being run over by the awesome aggregation' (Herling, 1972: 28).

Union dissidents had even greater reason for being impressed. In 1960, Rarick, the defeated rank-and-file candidate in the 1957 presidential elec-tion and leader of the Organization for Membership Rights, was knocked down without warning by a blow on the head in the lobby of the convention hall, and then beaten and kicked by 'a dozen superzealous McDonald followers'. A few days later:

'On Monday, Anthony Tomko, president of 6,000-member local 1408 . . . was beaten right on the floor of the convention when he tried to pass out his own election literature. On Tuesday evening, James Ashton, attorney for the OMR, a thin young man, was abused, insulted, and menaced in a hotel lobby by a character who now serves as a bodyguard to McDonald.

Ashton was escorted to safety by a newspaper reporter' (*New America*, 18 October 1960).

At the convention two years earlier, McDonald had demanded the expulsion of Rarick from the union. Rarick was brought to trial in his local, but was exonerated and subsequently elected local president. He had received 223,000 votes to McDonald's 404,000 in 1957, but in view of the unsupervised election may well have received many more – indeed, some think, even a majority.

In a report written for this study, Stanley Weir has summarised the background to McDonald's defeat (16 November 1967):

'Open unrest became visible . . . as far back as 1952, when Phil Murray was still president. That unrest has grown steadily and visibly, due in part to automation and its attendant feelings of insecurity and mental pressure, mandatory overtime, the general unrest in the population, and perhaps, as one interviewee suggested, to the large number of workers hired since World War II who were not used to being driven: ex-miners, ex-farmers, and Southern and mountain whites'.

After a series of long strikes – in 1946, 1949, 1952 and 1956 – conducted only reluctantly by the top leadership, president McDonald, adopting the stance of a labour statesman, announced the opening up of a 'whole new area of effective teamwork between union and management' (quoted in Herling, 1972: 96). This did not prevent a 116-day strike in basic steel in 1959, after which McDonald participated in the formation of a union–management 'human relations research committee'. The collective bargaining agreements reached in 1962 and 1963 were, according to both union critics and the *Wall Street Journal*, the cheapest to management of any post-World War II settlements, and discontent was expressed with the 'human relations' contracts on the executive board as well as among the membership. The rank-and-file was also discontented with last-minute bargaining and the pressure upon local unions to settle their local problems after the heat had been taken off employers by the signing of national agreements (Herling, 1972: 92–101). An informed critic notes:

'Starting in 1960 and particularly in 1962–63, membership unrest expressed itself in the defeat of a large number of local union presidents [usually full-time, in large locals] who had been in office for some time. This was especially true in Germano's district, and Germano himself found that he, as district director, had a competitor in the referendum election for the first time in years. Germano needed to create a more militant image and "clean himself up" in order to eliminate continuing competition and ultimately to save his job. For some time he had been warning the international officials that their policies were making it hard to stay in office. That unrest at the local level was giving the local officials hell and in turn he was getting challenged. Just as important, with local officials unable to stay in office for any length of time it was difficult for him to stabilize a machine. For some time also, he [and others elsewhere] had privately been using McDonald as a scapegoat for his own inability to produce better conditions and wages for the members in his district. Somewhere in 1963, the local officials called his bluff on this and told him to "put his money where his mouth is".' (Our informant has requested anonymity.)

Finally, a few district directors and others began to work on secretary-treasurer I. W. Abel to run against McDonald, and, after much deliberation, Abel made the decision in the autumn of 1964. McDonald was sixty-two at the time of the September 1964 convention, and if he had been willing to support a constitutional amendment for the retirement of officials at the age of sixty-five, as was demanded by numerous locals, probably no prominent official would have opposed him in early 1965.

The campaign and the election. The official campaign period began with 1,310 local union nominations for Abel and 904 for McDonald, but the experience of the Rarick campaign showed that the vote for an underdog could be vastly greater than might be judged from the nominations (see Edelstein, 1960). The story of the 1964 campaign and election as described by Herling is almost incredible, even to an American reader. It involved, in rough sequence:

1 Editorial praise for McDonald in the *New York Times*.
2 A struggle by both factions to determine which of two competing groups would bargain for the full-time field staff of the Steelworkers.
3 Anti-Abel 'inside stories' planted in a nationally-syndicated column.
4 Member sentiment gauged by a national polling organisation, paid for by the McDonald faction. The initial favourable results were released to the press (the first poll was based on 600 interviews).
5 Rumours of considerable funds from outside sources for both sides (and, later, the forgiving of a $100,000 loan to the McDonald faction).
6 A demand by McDonald, well in advance, that the American Arbitration Association should conduct the election (the elected tellers were pro-Abel).
7 Hundreds of local nominations for Abel as secretary-treasurer, rather than as president, engineered by the McDonald forces.
8 A plan to raise $100,000 initially, from pro-Abel staffers and district directors, by 'voluntary contributions'. Additional funds were to be raised locally.

9 The employment by the McDonald faction of attorneys and publicists who had participated in the campaigns, or post-campaign litigation, involving presidential defeats in the IUE and the State, County and Municipal Workers. (One attorney was advising Carey on the challenge to the ballot count.)

10 Editorials purchased by the McDonald group, through a regular 'service' which makes these available to local newspapers.

11 $45,000 or more worth of radio time, in the last ten days of the campaign, purchased by the McDonald group.

12 Convenient or inconvenient polling places designated by the local leaderships, depending upon whom they expected their members to favour (voting inside the plant was often possible).

13 Unnumbered ballot papers used, mailed by the printer to the locals with an excess supply to each.

14 Final estimate made of total campaign expenditure of from $500,000 to over $1 million.

15 Department of Labor representatives present as observers at the ballot counting and at the hearings on the vote protests (of which there were 188). However, the Department did not intervene.

Abel won the election by a vote of 309,000 to 299,000, with over 60 per cent of the membership voting. If it had not been for his majority of 10,000 in Canada, where only 35 per cent voted, Abel's margin would have been smaller than 600 votes.

McDonald did not contest the official figures, but he might well have. Questioned on the national television programme, 'Meet the Press' (on which McDonald also appeared, by agreement), Abel was asked about a letter to local officials from District 31, Germano's district, instructing them to mail their completed tally sheets to an office within the district rather than to the USA headquarters, as was constitutionally required. (Germano was Abel's campaign manager.) Abel did not repudiate the letter, stating that this procedure was based on 'past practice' (Herling, 1972: 261). The publicity must have thwarted this plan, but many of the protests from both sides alleged improperly-conducted voting locally.

After the defeat. According to Herling, 'Abel affected neither the airs of a liege lord nor the posture of a flamboyant bullyboy' (1972: 383); he returned the making of important decisions between conventions to the executive board; and he allowed greater participation by convention delegates, reportedly without threats of retaliation. According to Weir (1970: 472–3), writing in 1967, the negotiation process began to be democratised, and the human relations committee was discontinued.

However, at the 1968 convention nearly 40 per cent of the locals were represented by one or more paid union employees, which were enough to make it difficult to get a roll-call vote (Herling, 1972: 401). And complaints of election irregularities at the local and even district levels have not been infrequent. For example, in 1973 the Department of Labor upheld the complaint of an anti-administration candidate for the post of district director in Germano's old district, and ordered the election to be re-run. The insurgent had 'lost' by a vote of 21,606 to 23,394 (Benson, 1973).[5] Also in 1973, Abel ushered in an experimental programme under which arbitration was to substitute, indefinitely, for national strikes.

Some organisational features. There were contested elections against incumbent presidents in 1957, 1965 and 1969, the latter won by Abel with 258,000 votes to 181,000 for his opponent, a little-known attorney for the union at the time of his nomination. During the latter campaign the question of scrapping the referendum method of election in the future was raised seriously in the Abel camp (Herling, 1972: 375). It is evident that the use of the referendum, and the relative ease of nomination as compared to the IUE,[6] have been factors favouring opposition to the president and other international officers. Referenda have also been used for district directors: eleven of the twenty-five districts saw contested elections in 1973, with respectable votes for the independents in most cases. And, of course, the representation of the district directors on the executive board, and their power in their own districts especially, may be factors favouring opposition to the president. It should be recalled that most American unions elect their leading officers and their executive councils by vote of the convention as a whole.

A comment is in order on the government prohibition against expending union funds in support of candidates for union office; whatever the intention, this often (perhaps usually) seems to hamper the opposition more than the incumbent administration, which has the national machinery at its disposal. The same may apply to British unions' 'equalisation' of opportunity by either banning campaign literature or even providing single election addresses for all candidates. In the absence of adequate established channels, the autonomy of locals or other subdivisions to disburse funds for campaign purposes (perhaps up to a certain limit) may be a lesser evil.

Younger and Older American Unions
Although formal organisational factors were associated as expected with the closeness of top and next-to-top elections and with defeats for such offices, as shown earlier, it should be noted that the American unions with more effective electoral opposition included, disproportionately, those that were formed during or after the 1930s and affiliated to the Congress for

Industrial Organization. Furthermore, the most clearly craft or ex-craft unions were under-represented among them.

The sixteen unions in the American sample formed after 1930 (fourteen CIO affiliates and two AFL affiliates) contributed all five of the top-officer defeats during 1949–66, while the thirty-five unions formed earlier contributed none. The CIO unions with top defeats in this period were the International Woodworkers of America, the Steelworkers, and the International Union of Electrical Workers (IUE). The two AFL unions were the International Chemical Workers (with two defeats), and the State, County and Municipal Workers. In addition, in the Rubber Workers, another CIO union, the incumbent president withdrew his nomination under pressure in 1966 (see Weir, 1970: 474). The president was also defeated in the Oil and Chemical Workers (CIO), which was not in the sample (it was formed through a merger in 1955). And the Mine Workers, with a top defeat in 1973, was an older union instrumental in forming the CIO. The International Typographical Union, which has by far the closest periodic elections for top office in either the United States or Britain, has had no top defeats since 1944 nor a change in the political party holding the presidency.

Of the five unions in the sample with next-to-top defeats, three were CIO unions formed since the 1930s: the Rubber Workers (with two defeats), the Communications Workers, and the Furniture Workers. The remaining two were the Brewery Workers, an older union which affiliated to the CIO, and the Brotherhood of Railroad Trainmen. In the Trainmen and the Communications Workers the next-to-top officer ran for the top post at the convention, with a good showing, immediately before running for re-election and being defeated. In two of the other three unions the defeated next-to-top officer was also in conflict with the president. All the defeated next-to-top officers made either good or – for the American sample – relatively good showings. None of the unions with next-to-top defeats used the referendum, but it was used in the IUE, the Steelworkers, the Woodworkers, and the Mine Workers.

The most obvious formal differences between the ten unions with top or next-to-top defeats during 1949–66 and the remainder of the American sample were the former group's more frequent conventions and more frequent elections, both of which features are associated with defeats (biserial $r = \cdot38$ and $\cdot36$ respectively). The percentage of the executive council with subdivisionally-chosen rank-and-filers was also of some importance (biserial $r = \cdot29$; see also Table 5.3).

All the above organisational variables were similarly associated with the percentage of *top* periodic elections resulting in defeats, but the percentage of the executive council consisting of subdivisionally-chosen full-time officers was also useful (biserial $r = \cdot23$; the multiple R using both kinds of subdivisional representation simultaneously was $\cdot34$). Finally, a multiple regression analysis for the percentage of top defeats showed the association, in addition, of the absence of automatic succession, the electoral system for the top post, and the percentage of the convention required for a roll-call vote.

Relative youth, industrial unionism, and mass production industries, whatever their independent contributions (if any) to these results, are inextricably linked to the above (and many other) organisational characteristics. We can only point to our British findings, which seem to show that union age and industrial unionism are not relevant in themselves, or, taken at face value, are even opposite in effect to what they are in the United States.

THE LANDRUM-GRIFFIN ACT

Finally, while it is doubtful that the passing of the Landrum-Griffin Act 1959 substantially affected our findings on the closeness of elections, in the long run its provisions for fair elections and adequate and honest financial reporting may have noticeable, if minor, effects on union democracy in the United States. That it has not had an important general effect on elections to top and next-to-top posts is due largely to a reluctance of the Department of Labor and the courts to investigate complaints until *after* an election has been run, and even then ordinarily not before internal appeal procedures have been exhausted. 'When DOL finally does investigate, it often seeks out only election day violations . . . the DOL tries to settle out of court, usually by an agreement for Department supervision of the union's next regular election . . . The process of investigation and litigation is so protracted [usually one to two years] that the remedy . . . is often worthless to the complainant' (Pearlman, 1973). Furthermore, the effect of the Act on national elections was probably greatest, during 1959–66, on those unions most likely in any event to have had contested elections.

However, more recently the Department's intervention against grossly undemocratic practices in two unions, the Mine Workers and the National Maritime Union, has undoubtedly had important effects on the closeness of presidential elections (without success for the challenger, in the Maritime Union). And the number of cases in which election violations were found to have affected the results of elections (mostly local and regional) rose to 251 for the period from July 1965 to June 1970, as compared to only sixty-five for September 1959 to March 1963.

But during 1965–70 there were only seven cases in which violations were found to have affected the results of elections to *national* office (in two instances the unions were not truly national). In five of these cases the elections were re-run, and in three (with some overlap) the unions were required to make constitutional changes to conform to the law (Labor–Management Services Administration, 1972: 6–27).

The most striking effect of the Landrum-Griffin Act has been the 715 convictions in criminal actions between 1959 and June 1973, probably involving embezzlement by local union officers in most cases (Labor–Management Services Administration, 1974: 1). A large number of these occurred in unions without taint at the national level. It must be noted that there are over 50,000 financial reports filed under the Act each year, by local unions and higher union bodies. In a country where large numbers of bank officers are found to have embezzled funds each year (usually without prosecution), it is unlikely that the number of such offences in unions will decline drastically without major changes in the trade union movement.

In the concluding Chapter 11 we will discuss the future trends of trade unionism as they relate particularly to the applicability of our theory of union democracy.

NOTES TO CHAPTER 10

1 The interview was conducted by Stanley Weir (16 February 1968).
2 We are indebted to Robert A. Lorenz for research on these and related matters.
3 See Labor–Management Services Administration, 1969: 54, 78–9; and 1970: 69.
4 The only nationally-elected officers are the president, the secretary-treasurer and five part-time trustees (one of whom sits on the executive board).
5 E. Sadlowski, the insurgent, won by almost two-to-one in the re-run in 1974; with the support of civil libertarians, liberals, and radicals; and with 'nearly 300 Federal agents ... posted at steel plants during the balloting' (*New York Times*, 18 November, 1974).
6 The support of 125 out of approximately 3,000 locals is required – that of only forty was required in 1957.

Part Four

CONCLUSIONS

Chapter 11

The Future of Union Democracy

The future of unionism is inseparable from the future of organised society. Our discussion will focus first on the implications of our findings in terms of the theory of organisations, and then more extensively on the possible future for democracy in unions engaged in collective bargaining in a capitalist society of the welfare state variety. Finally, we shall also comment briefly on the possible place of unions under democratic socialism.

ORGANISATIONAL THEORY

Most social theory is better at explaining oligarchy in large-membership organisations than it is at explaining departures from it, as we mentioned earlier. Organisational theory, which should be especially appropriate, is for the most part slanted towards bureaucratic, or at least intrinsically undemocratic, organisations and is usually exasperating in its tangential relevance to organisational democracy, the essential components of which are seldom given more than peripheral recognition. Furthermore, traditional organisational theory has tended towards simplistic pessimistic biases concerning the effects of such variables as the age, size and complexity of organisations, and of trade unions in particular. It has also been apolitical and vaporously global in its approach to political processes, to the extent that such organisational specifics as voting systems and the rules governing succession have seldom been considered. Finally, the historical origins of such constitutional features, and their relative independence from their current environment, have not usually been adequately appreciated.

Our own approach has been to operate at three levels of abstraction in order to explain and predict various manifestations of the effectiveness of electoral opposition. Proceeding from the general notion that consistently effective opposition results from competition between equally powerful potential competitors and their supporters, we then dropped down to specific propositions concerning how such equality might be determined by the status hierarchy, the regional and occupational subdivisions, and the national power centres, and how inequality might be ameliorated by the voting systems. Most of the relevant specific features of large-membership organisations are classifiable under these headings, plus the additional heading of the civil rights of members. Furthermore, the notion of the equality or inequality of potential competitors is easily applicable directly to the effects of many specific features of organisation that we have not dealt with. Posing the question often suggests a reasonable answer. Detailed conclusions are presented at each chapter's end.

Organisational specifics are important, we maintained, because a high level of democracy may be blocked by any one of a number of obstacles: e.g. restrictive rules for nomination, a voting system which provides no representation for minorities at the national level, or a distribution of the membership which permits one or two large regions to dominate elections. These specific features are not simply *indicators* of the presence of some underlying variables – they are the actual operative variables. It might therefore be unfortunate if their unique effects were lost through summating their measures with those of other variables. (Indeed, some organisational procedures, e.g. certain electoral systems, are unique in that, once having been entered into, they mechanically grind out their inevitable result, barring fraud or error.)

We completed our research with the conviction that formal organisation contributes even more to democratic decision making than we have been able to show here. The organisational factors, which we considered systematically, could not do justice to the variety and subtlety of distinctions among the organisational forms we encountered. The variables were too many, the unions too few, and some of the organisational features too rare to make possible the manipulation of more data in a systematic and convincing way. Nevertheless, knowledge of the unions plus awareness of the relative crudeness of our own categories lead us to believe that we have underplayed, rather than overplayed, the contribution of formal organisation to union democracy. We also believe that the theory itself has considerable carry-over to other kinds of large-membership organisations, and to large, would-be democratic, work enterprises, so long as the normative and perhaps technical prerequisites for democracy exist. Given suitable preconditions and in less than ideal circumstances, we have no doubt that an approach in terms of fairly specific organisational forms and procedures would be worthwhile.

We have perhaps neglected the potential contribution to organisational democracy of comprehensive and advanced communications systems, and of some little-used or non-existent features of organisation (e.g. accountability, and the independence of the legislature) such as those advocated by Alice Cook (1963: 219) and Robert Dahl (1970: 149–53). While these seem unlikely to be achieved without the organisational basis suggested by our theory, a consideration of such possibilities could advance social theory and perhaps help us to understand and to change the present situation.

We eagerly await further developments in these fields of speculation, and their ultimate application, while for the moment passing on to look at prospective developments in union democracy.

SOME SOCIAL TRENDS

A basic precondition for union democracy is interest and participation in union affairs by rank-and-file activists. Another is a suitable formal organisation. Conceivably, these preconditions could be undermined by a centralisation of bargaining to the point where there was no longer any appreciable area for direct participation by the individual member, his shop organisation, or his local union. If workshop organisation atrophied, and if at the same time it appeared impossible for individual members to have any considerable input into national or international negotiations with employers or the state, participation by rank-and-filers would offer few material or psychological benefits.

A possible parallel development might be the loss of the national unions' autonomy to the national or international federation of unions. How could the individual worker influence a federation? One might also ask how the worker in a particular industry or trade could influence an enormous general union – something approaching a federation in itself. The results might be the same if workers became sufficiently privatised for other reasons, including further 'affluence', loss of interest in work, or alienation from organisations generally.

There are three major reasons why centralisation of bargaining, and accompanying changes in union structures or strategies, may possibly take place:

1　The continued growth and diversification of the major corporations, particularly in the form of conglomerates and multi-national corporations.
2　Attempts by the state to control wages centrally, ostensibly to avoid inflation and generally to regulate the economy. This would be accompanied by bargaining between the state, employers and unions collectively (see Kassalow, 1967: 137).
3　In a state beyond and more interventionist than the welfare state, a supposedly critical economic interdependence to the point where strikes were regarded as intolerable and the state itself determined what was produced and how it was distributed (see Günter, 1972; Kerr *et al.*, 1960). Bargaining would be even more centralised under this condition.

However, it has been argued that the most important reason for the (not extreme) degree of centralisation of bargaining in the United States, thus far, has been the insulation from local pressures which it provides for both union and management leaders (see G. W. Brooks, 1961: 137–8).

SOME COUNTER-TRENDS

Some of the trends towards centralisation of bargaining and state control have not expressed inexorable economic necessity – they have been at most political expressions of the perception of such necessity, and are reversible. This is not to discount political 'necessity', but once the problem has been removed from the realm of economics it appears more susceptible to different solutions. At any rate, the regulation of wages which took place under the (first) Wilson and Heath Governments in Britain, and under the Nixon Administration in the United States, lacked political viability. Such attempts may recur, but we are probably a long way from a permanent regulation of wages. Even if the officialdom of the union federation should wish to enter into a period of centrally-negotiated wage regulation, they could not control their national unions or their memberships indefinitely, at least in the United States or Britain. Pressures from the rank-and-file would ultimately manifest themselves in unsanctioned strikes and internal factionalism (see Van de Vall, 1970: 95–102). The British trade union left has gained in both influence and office since 1966 as a result of the collaboration of most of the unions in the Labour Government's incomes policy.

One antidote to a confident view of an administered future for industrial relations is the following:

'. . . it seems odd now to think that up till about 1960 specialists could confidently assert a "law of increasing tranquility" as strikes declined and trade union co-operation with governments increased, this optimism being based, to take Professor Roberts' list, "on the theory that the factors responsible for the decline in industrial conflict were: (1) the increasing social responsibility of governments; (2) the growing involvement of trade unions in processes of economic planning; (3) the maintenance of full employment; (4) the greater degree of social mobility; (5) the continuous rise in real wages; (6) the provision of economic and social security."

'In hindsight, the events of the last decade make these predictions look pretty silly' (International Confederation of Free Trade Unions, 1971: 17–18).

During 1968–70 there were wildcat strikes and spontaneous workers' movements in many countries, some of which have recurred since. Among the common denominators of the situation were: a shift in power to the shop floor; a decline in respect for traditional authority in the factory; a 'gap between today's relaxed personal behaviour standards and conventional factory discipline' (19); feelings of alienation; a desire to control working conditions (or for 'participation'); the failure of material rewards to keep up with even more rapidly-rising expectations; inflation; increased knowledge of wages and conditions for comparable work elsewhere; and dissatisfaction with poor communications from the unions concerning the progress of negotiations. American workers have also shown a greater concern over local working conditions and plant-level bargaining in recent years (see Weir, 1970), and it has been widely noted that younger workers have been unwilling to accept the discipline of the assembly line speed-up without absenteeism and more direct forms of protest. It is difficult to see how these trends can be reversed without work being made something other than it is today.

Some hope that the days of the assembly line and cruder kind of mass production are numbered, and that the new workers in automated industry, service work and government will have fewer discontents. Where so, and where they are organised, such workers will probably follow the trend shown in the United States and the Netherlands, and participate more in union affairs. This would apply even more to high-status professional and technical workers. Furthermore, Dutch government workers, both blue and white collar, have been shown to attend union meetings much more often than their counterparts in industry (see Van de Vall, 1970: 156–63; Spinrad, 1960). Government employees may also be expected to take a greater interest in politics (see Lipset, 1960a: 184–6), probably because they are better informed and have more directly at stake. This may make a philosophy of business unionism less likely.

One might think from the foregoing that the changes in such technology might make the working class perhaps as willing to sustain a steady participation in union life, but less willing to engage in unauthorised strikes, and hence less of an explosive force in oligarchic unions. It would seem to make a difference *what* changes occur – e.g. a continuous process such as may be found in the chemical industry, or automation. Workers in continuous process industries seem to be under less pressure than mass production workers, and to like their jobs better (Blauner, 1967: 135–42), but one view suggests new occupational hazards under automation:

'. . . automation tends to generate its own peculiar pathology. The strains engendered in an automated plant or office may differ from those of the older, more conventional factory, but they exist nevertheless. Workers who must continually match panels and lights develop fatigue just as much as does the auto worker, although it is fatigue of another type, a neurotic fatigue apt to end in gastric ulcers. The World Health Organization reported. . . . that 40 per cent of the employees in automated offices were irritable, suffered from insomnia and headaches, and were likely candidates for coronary attacks. Even such optimistic researchers as Floyd

Mann and L. R. Hoffman discovered a higher incidence of tension in an automated power plant, compared with that in a traditional installation. Automation . . . also requires shift and night work, as the machines must operate continuously to be economic. In fact, the sense of loneliness in computerized plants has led some British unions to ask for "lonesome" premiums. Automated work can be utterly boring' (Seligman, 1970: 276).

The labour–management relations in automated offices tend to resemble those in a factory, with the office becoming a 'paper-processing factory, with workers tied to the machine' (278).

Most of the advanced countries seem to face an indefinite period of economic dislocation due to technological change and the reorganisation of the market. Van de Vall states that 'The indications are that labor force displacement is becoming a semi-permanent trend in advanced industrial society' (1970: 206). British workers have seemed especially unwilling to accept redundancy passively, and where their leaderships seem unwilling to take preventive or adequate ameliorative action this may contribute to opposition. Collective bargaining would have to concern itself with the length of the workweek, the introduction or application of plant-wide seniority systems, severance pay, intra-plant or company transfers, the timing of re-conversions or shut-downs, and conceivably with whether the latter should be permitted at all. Plant takeovers by the workers may occur, e.g. as in the Clyde-side shipyards in Scotland, and calls for government assistance or nationalisation may express further demands for workers' control. It is inconceivable that most of the above can be accomplished without a detailed knowledge of local conditions and deep local involvement, so that the major role of national bargaining would be supportive. Thus, in a highly-organised country technological change is likely to result more in expressions of local militancy and a broader politicisation than in demoralisation. Both these results should contribute to union opposition and democracy.

It would be simplistic to view technological change as an abstraction, separate from the regional and international flow of capital to maximise profits. Gorz (1967: 137–90) has argued that, in the Common Market, the investment of public capital in co-operation with autonomous regional bodies will probably be insufficient to prevent an aggravation of regional imbalances with repercussions for their respective economies. And, apart from the Common Market, there is every sign that international competition will continue to threaten the employment and wages of workers in certain countries (e.g. those in the steel, electronics and textile industries in the United States).

In spite of what we have said above about a possible long-term erosion of membership participation at the local union level, at present the trend in Britain and continental Europe is probably in the other direction. On the Continent, the unions have been weakened by the membership of workers in weak plant-level 'workers' councils', not infrequently used by the employers against the unions. As a result, many unions have tried to make their presence in the plant felt through achieving representation of union supporters on this council (see Sturmthal, 1964). More important, in the post-World War II period (and probably before) the western European unions have been weak in workshop organisation and plant-level bargaining (see Sturmthal, 1972: 203; Reynaud, 1967: 40), and have been trying to make up for this by obtaining legal rights for unions within the workshops – e.g. in France, an 'information hour' for in-plant discussion on company time (see *Trade Union News from the European Community*, winter 1970/71: 25).

In Britain, the concept of formal rather than unofficial workshop bargaining has gained the acceptance of both the state and most employers, as well as the unions. The Report of the Royal Commission on Trade Unions and Employers' Associations (1968: 262) stated:

'The central defect in British industrial relations is the disorder in factory and workshop relations and pay structures promoted by the conflict between the formal and the informal systems . . . Factory-wide agreements can however provide the remedy. Factory agreements (with company agreements as an alternative in multi-plant companies) can regulate actual pay, constitute a factory negotiating committee and grievance procedures which suit the circumstances, deal with such subjects as redundancy and discipline and cover the rights and obligations of shop stewards.'

Some British unions have stated the objective of moving towards factory-based rather than geographic branches for conducting local bargaining, and have looked towards amalgamation with other unions as one step in this direction.

Furthermore, the British Commission on Industrial Relations suggested in 1971 that workplace union representatives, including shop stewards, be provided with paid leave from their jobs, meeting places, a telephone and other office services, and that typing and duplicating be provided depending on the steward's duties and the plant's size. It was further suggested that the numbers, areas of representation and responsibilities of shop stewards be considered at the level of the industry, and that all of the foregoing be embodied in a written agreement between unions and employers (see *OEF Newsletter*, 10 June 1971).

346 Comparative Union Democracy

THE 'AMERICANISATION' OF BRITISH BARGAINING?

Some would like a movement of British industrial relations towards a rather different and perhaps Americanised system – one whose potential for worker participation and union democracy depends considerably upon how it is finally worked out. The dangers lie in the potential for written formal agreements to *limit* workshop organisation and to prohibit strikes, particularly in large multi-plant corporations. For example, the United Automobile Workers has a ratio of bargaining shop stewards to workers in most automobile plants of only one to 250, while the ratio of foremen to workers is one to fifteen, making it 'physically impossible to provide adequate representation' (Weir, 1970: 500).

Most collective bargaining contracts in the United States ban strikes for any reason during the life of the agreement, which commonly runs for three years. Instead, there are usually provisions for the ultimate arbitration of local or other disputes during the term of the agreement. When union–management relations are poor, the large number of cases arbitrated (usually after delay and often with expense to the local union) and their negative outcomes (which may depend upon the precise wording in the contract) may become intolerable to many members. The problems associated with written contracts may be magnified when the National Labor Relations Board insists that all the plants of a given corporation be combined into a single bargaining unit (see Ulman, 1962: 10).[1] Discontent with such contracts may eventually lead to revolt, but a long time may pass before this is reflected in the formal union channels. One suggested solution to such problems appeared in a resolution passed by the District 29 (covering Michigan and Toledo) Conference of the United Steelworkers in 1970: '. . . that the right to strike over health and safety, over job classification (both new and revised), over incentives, and over breakdowns in the grievance procedure be written into the contracts' (*Labor Today*, March–April 1970: 8). This demand was made almost thirty years after the local unions lost such rights.

The basic problem has been stated well by Stanley Weir (1970: 495):

'It is absolutely necessary and proper that American workers permit the top leaders of their international unions more centralized power. There is no other way to challenge growing corporate power during the negotiation of master collective bargaining agreements. At the same time, the ranks want to determine the goals of these negotiations and to use their power in the workplace to increase their control over the nature of work. How to simultaneously centralize labor's total power on the one hand and decentralize it on the other is a decisive issue of the [recent union] revolts.' Union members can live with this problem more easily while the right to strike remains.

MERGERS AND GENERAL UNIONISM

In both Britain and the United States, there have been mergers of national unions since 1966 which have substantially increased the size of the largest unions, moved some of them in the direction of general unionism, and – in Britain – strengthened the existing general unions. There have also been mergers in both countries which have created industrial or near-industrial unions. The motivations have been primarily to achieve an increased bargaining power against the now even larger and more diversified employers, and to reduce the mounting costs of operating a headquarters, organising, negotiating, lobbying, research and education. Small and medium-sized unions especially have found it hard to meet such costs. Many British mergers have been facilitated by a 1963 law which made possible a 'transfer of engagements' – something short of a complete merger – under which one union could become a section of another, retaining its own officers (and procedures for electing them) as a section of the combined organisation.

In the short run, in the context of the current militancy of the British labour movement, the increased strength and efficiency are likely to lead to a revitalisation of the unions, more participation and internal turbulence, and hence more democratic functioning. Even the General and Municipal Workers has been affected.[2] In the longer run, the growth of general unionism would seem to present a problem for democracy in both countries because of the nature of organisation inherent in unionism of this type, and, in Britain, also because the two largest general unions have important non-democratic features, including the appointive nature of so many of their full-time posts, as has been shown.[3]

General Unionism

The United Steelworkers of America moved somewhat in the direction of general unionism in 1971 when, with 1,200,000 members, it merged with the 170,000-member District 50 of the Allied and Technical Workers, itself a general union formerly affiliated to the Mine Workers. District 50 brought to the Steelworkers 81,000 members in 'manufacturing and other industries', and 60,000 in 'chemical and related'. The Steelworkers had had previous mergers: with the Stone and Allied Products Workers (20,000 members, in 1970), the Mine, Mill and Smelter Workers (40,000, in 1967), and the Aluminum Workers (45,000, in 1946) (see *Steel Labor*, September 1972). Furthermore, the basic membership of the Steelworkers includes workers in the fabrication of metal products.

Nevertheless, the heterogeneity of the Steelworkers is no match for that of the British Transport and General Workers, with its fifteen national trade groups. Most of the latter do not have exclusive bargaining jurisdiction within their spheres, so they cannot act as industrial unions in themselves. As early as 1950 the T & GWU was represented on the negotiating bodies or wage-fixing authorities of 200 industries, and conducting negotiations in fifty-nine (B. C. Roberts, 1956: 523). In 1972 the T & GWU absorbed the 80,000-member Vehicle Builders (in our sample) into its vehicle building and automotive trade group. It had 1,747,000 members in 1973.

Some of the problems of communication within the T & GWU are illustrated in this letter to *Tribune* (7 April 1972):

'Some time ago, Jack Jones [the general secretary] wrote an article for *Tribune* about democracy and participation within the Transport and General Workers' Union which our general executive council reproduced as a leaflet for distribution to our members.

'The fate of that leaflet in our local section of the union is a good illustration of how progressive national policy is being frustrated by obstructionist elements down the line. That particular leaflet, and many other previously published items, was not distributed in the local sugar beet factory. Nor was it, as far as I know, distributed anywhere else in the Bury St. Edmunds area.

'How can the very much changed attitude of our general executive council be communicated to our members when we have such a difficult distribution problem?

'In my 20 years of membership of the union I have not known such emphasis on the rights of the rank and file members as under the leadership of Jack Jones. Yet they cannot respond to his call for participation if they do not know that he has said: "What we have sought to do is to get the decision-making within the hands of those whose working lives are affected – and involve not only the shop stewards but also the membership in negotiations."

'Mr. Jones also said: "The larger the union has grown, however, the more it has become obvious and necessary to centre union activity at the place of work." That policy was initially defeated in our factory by the efforts of people who should have known better. It has taken exactly one year to get a meeting within the factory to discuss a wages policy. That would not have come about had it not been for the advent of a new district officer.

'The general secretary's article also said: "Lessons learned in one group can be developed in another. Experience and information gained can be put to wider use." But when we tried to apply that policy we were further obstructed by people who should have known better. We tried to communicate our resolution to the other 16 factories within the Sugar Corporation. We were attacked as being "unofficial".

'Our opposition does not seem to be aware that it is the policy of the GEC "to make the TGWU the most democratic union in the country". What is more democratic than trying to win the support of other workers in other factories?

'Fortunately, it is not just Jack Jones who can appreciate his statement: "To face them with a number of separate industrial unions would be merely to divide the workers' strength, with the obvious result." Representatives of the majority of the Corporation's factories [not just TGWU] met early in March and decided on a wages policy. The opinions of that meeting and the opinions of the Bury St. Edmunds Sugar Beet workers have been unacknowledged and ignored by our national negotiators.

'A wage claim has been lodged on our behalf which is so inadequate that it is obvious that our National Food Officials are not aware that the GEC has said: "The days of the remote national agreement, with sometimes a few officers determining the wages and conditions of 100,000 members, are over."

'If our general executive council cannot solve the problem of directly communicating with the rank-and-file members, their task of radicalising and modernising the union will fail!
Bury St. Edmunds.'   Frank Dunne

Even a more democratic form of giant general unionism, which in Britain might very well include as many as 3 million members, would present some problems for democracy. The top officer might seem distant or irrelevant to the occupationally conscious membership, but nevertheless detract national attention from potential competitors at the heads of the numerous industrial sections. The second-ranking sectional officers might be virtually faceless and lack the ability to compete effectively for the top sectional posts. It would be impossible to represent most sections by more than one or two representatives on an executive council of reasonable size, which would in effect deprive political minorities within sections of representation. Competition within sections might be reduced further by solidarity against other sections, especially if the union reached comprehensive agreements with the government or with employers collectively. Free communications across sectional lines would be inherently difficult, and no doubt often be intentionally obstructed by jurisdictionally jealous or threatened office-holders. The national office could easily become a bottleneck for the flow of work or communications. It might be burdened with the conduct of numerous referenda, for elections or on other issues, and so press for less frequent elections or for decisions by committees or conferences. The size as well as the heterogeneity of the union would require a greater full-time staff at head office, probably including a larger proportion of specialists (see Kasarda, 1974), some perhaps with officer status.

Attempts to avoid or de-emphasise sectional organisation would be impractical for conducting the business of the general union, and lead to the alienation and non-participation of lower-status members and the smaller occupational groups (see Van de Vall, 1970: 159–60). Nevertheless, one may conceive of many ameliorating democratic features, e.g. a president and general secretary of equal status, and a number of regionally-elected second-ranking national officers between the top officers and sectional heads. Branches might be represented in both geographic and industrial subdivisions, as in fact they are in the T & GWU. But while a reasonably democratic general union of massive size remains a possibility, general unionism as such would seem to handicap democracy – at least so long as the major functioning of unionism is collective bargaining.

A 'federation' as centralised as the Swedish type would seem to present similar difficulties for union democracy, especially in a large country. It is significant that in the Swedish Trade Union Federation (the LO, for non-salaried workers), which had 1,734,000 members in 1973, 'the final decision in matters concerning collective agreements must rest with the executives of its constituent unions, not with the membership as a whole' (Fulcher, 1973: 50).

Constitutional Changes in Amalgamation
The constitution of an amalgamated organisation typically involves departures from the rules of the separate organisations involved, especially when these are of comparable size. Since the new rules must constitute a coherent whole, and since a rejection of some portion of them would ordinarily delay the amalgamation and perhaps upset the result of prolonged and delicate negotiations, the members no doubt tend to view the proposed rules as a package and to accept or reject them as a whole. Thus, the top leaderships of the separate unions necessarily play a critical role in drawing up the rules for a new organisation, and an amalgamation may be an opportunity for retrogression from democracy under the auspices of oligarchic leaders. On the other hand, with a strong push for unity from below, there is also the opportunity for democratisation, as the history of the Engineers before the 1921 amalgamation shows. The future of union democracy may be determined for some time, in either case.

Recently, the British Woodworkers, the Painters, and the Building Trade Workers (all in our sample), together with the small Association of Building Technicians, amalgamated in a move towards an industrial union in the construction industry. The amalgamated union had 271,000 members in 1973, and with over 1 million workers employed in construction its potential for growth is large. (Woodworkers are also employed in shipbuilding and elsewhere, and bricklayers in the iron and steel industry.) In a referendum within the amalgamated Woodworkers and Painters on a constitution for a further amalgamation with the Building Trade Workers, fifty-six proposed revisions in rules were approved by overwhelming majorities, with the least popular proposal – pertaining to rates of contribution – passed by a vote of 19,000 to 7,000 in a 12 per cent ballot (*Woodworkers and Painters Journal*, April 1971). No overall oligarchic trend was apparent in these changes, but many of them were important.

Other post-1966 mergers in Britain included: the Electricians, and the Plumbers (both in the sample); and the Furniture Trade Operatives (in the sample), and the Woodcutting Machinists. Mergers not yet mentioned in the United States include: the Bookbinders (in the sample), and the Lithographers and Photoengravers; the Pulp, Sulphite and Paper Mill Workers (in the sample), and the Papermakers and Paperworkers; the Brewery Workers, and the Teamsters (both in the sample); and the mergers of five postal unions, and of five railway unions.

Amalgamations of unions in related fields will undoubtedly continue. Our research shows little reason to expect substantial changes in electoral opposition due to an increase in size alone, and the increased opportunities for growth and collective-bargaining gains may very well generate opposition centring on whether such opportunities are being adequately exploited (see Warner, 1969). The greater size and heterogeneity of union membership may ultimately detract somewhat from cohesiveness and participation in union affairs (the size and composition of the local union are of greater importance), but a predominant focus on a single industry provides a basis for identification with the union and sets limits to heterogeneity.

THE ROLE OF FULL-TIME OFFICERS

Given the opportunity, some British leaders of manual unions would undoubtedly move towards 'professionalising' the full-time officer staff, requiring higher educational and technical qualifications and permitting recruitment from outside the union into permanent appointive posts. Some American leaders might welcome a greater opportunity to do this informally. Since the most successful opponents of top officers are likely to be other full-time officers, any promotion path which put appointed officials in line for the top elective posts would be a major set-back for union democracy. The top post itself could become appointive, as it has in so many British white collar unions. Trade union administration, of course, requires specialised knowledge and skills in law, engineering, economics, statistics, office management and other fields (see Wilensky, 1956: 244), but how these requirements are incorporated into an organisation's structure is a matter more of ideology and problem solving than of necessity. Nevertheless, the technocratic approach to trade union government has some superficial logic to it, and there is a danger that it will prevail in the long run. Something akin to it exists in the collegial oligarchies (see Chapter 2) of Dutch trade unions, which preserve the formality of periodic elections:

'Most vacancies in union office arise at the customary entry level to the union hierarchy, the district representative . . . the union recruits candidates through advertisements in its journal, scrutiny of local activists, and a review of recent graduates of the federation's officer schools. Usually, a formal application must be submitted. As a rule, applicants . . . should preferably be members of a union affiliated with the proper federation. A subcommittee of the national executive council or executive board, sometimes acting in consultation with a committee of active rank-and-file members, then establishes a "short list" for psychological (aptitude and character) tests and interviews with union officers. The successful candidate receives a one-year probationary appointment to a district of his own or as assistant to a senior district representative. Toward the end of the year . . . the national officers hold informal hearings with local unions in the district . . . If the overall judgment is favorable, the officers place a recommendation to that effect before the general council where it will be voted on in a process called an election but more properly designated as a ratification' (Windmuller, 1969: 213–14).

Furthermore, in the Netherlands there has been an increased recruitment of 'elected' officials with a university education, some of whom even bypass the hierarchy and enter as important federation officials (218–19).

Most of the machinery exists now for the implementation of a policy of external recruitment of graduates in the British General and Municipal Workers (and, technically, in the T & GWU), as a recent instance shows. John Edmonds, twenty-nine years old, is one of eleven 'elected' national industrial officers:

'On his graduation (from Oriel College, Oxford) in 1965, Edmonds took a job in the research department of the General and Municipal Workers Union. . . . He specialized in the local government sector . . . and took an active part in the 1969 and 1970 local government manual worker strikes. Edmonds made a highly favourable impression on the GMWU bosses, so he was brought out of the research department and given a post as trade union officer in the southern region of the union. After two years, under the union rules, Edmonds faced election by the members. He won handsomely. Not long afterwards he returned to [headquarters] . . . to become national officer for the GMWU's 42,000 gas-workers' (Taylor, 1973: 688).

In the GMWU, 'Only candidates [for national office] who have satisfied the National Executive Committee as to their fitness and qualifications shall be submitted to election,' subject in principle to the over-riding authority of the general council (Rule 19). In these circumstances the question of external versus internal recruitment is secondary. Nevertheless, the argument for external recruitment, if accepted, could easily lead to similar procedures being accepted elsewhere.

There is certainly room for speculation as to how people with highly-specialised skills might be integrated into unions without detriment, or as an asset to union democracy. At least these general principle whould seem necessary for the maintenance of democracy: (*a*) the elected generalists in the organisation should remain in charge, at all levels; (*b*) the specialist positions should carry no general authority over members of the organisation; and (*c*) the specialists (and all appointed staff) should have their own career ladder, and should in general be ineligible for elective positions with authority over the membership. Some specialist positions might very well be elective, e.g. a miners' compensation agent or safety officer, or even those advisory positions whose occupants tend to assume a key role in negotiations, thus determining policy. Finally, apart from the above, outside professionals might be encouraged to contribute their skills voluntarily, and conceivably to participate in executive council or other meetings on a regular basis. In the latter case their contributions would undoubtedly be political, and such positions might be formalised and made elective in order to avoid indirect influence by the top officers.

NEW FUNCTIONS FOR TRADE UNIONS?

The almost universally-low routine participation of members in formal trade union meetings or decision making is a reflection of the union's role in their lives and in society. Probably much could be accomplished by the provision of time and facilities for union meetings at the workplace, to consider bargaining issues and other union business, but beyond a certain limited level increased participation would depend upon expanded functions for the union. These might include participation in the running of industry, perhaps with links to the community and political decision-makers, and in the administration of social welfare and vocational education programmes now usually run by the state. Ideally, patterns of work and residence should remove many of the barriers of time and space which impede the regular participation of all but the hardy and highly-motivated few. Short of that, participation can be furthered by the provision of resources: time off from work, secretarial services, means of communication, and travelling expenses.

Workers' Councils and Co-management

It was pointed out earlier that workers' (factory) councils in Europe have usually been organised apart from the trade unions, and have often been co-opted by the employer and used against the union (see also Dahrendorf, 1959: 261–7). In Britain, where the questions of factory councils and workers on company boards are currently under discussion, the TUC and the Labour Party have taken the position that the vehicle for such representation should be the trade unions. As early as 1967, a Labour Party working-party report on industrial democracy (Labour Party, 1967: 7), which was eventually adopted, stated:

'So far as forms of participation are concerned our conclusion is that we must develop industrial democracy on the basis of A SINGLE CHANNEL OF REPRESENTATION. Although the single channel may involve specialist committees (e.g. on safety matters), it will not hinge on any distinction between subjects appropriate for bargaining and those appropriate for consultation.'

At the first level, representation would be by shop stewards or, where the branch and workplace were closely identified, by lay branch officers. Workplace facilities would be provided for the conduct of union meetings and ballots, and training would be made available to workers' representatives under union control. Electoral arrangements for the selection of representatives would not be imposed upon the union from the outside. The union might have unilateral control over such areas as promotions and the distribution of overtime, and there would be room to experiment in extending direct worker responsibility over the division of labour and the allocation of work and rewards. Eventually, there would be 'a striking extension of the functions and range of specialist services provided unilaterally by the unions' (Labour Party, 1967: 40), e.g. in the field of safety, with financial support from the state.

In 1973 (and again in 1974), the TUC reacted thus to a scheme, proposed by the European Economic Community Commission, for workers' representatives on company boards:

'In this country, worker appointments to supervisory boards would need to be made through trade union machinery at company level – not as in Germany, through workers' councils . . . Moreover, it would be essential for these representatives to remain responsible to trade union members rather than to shareholders [as British company law now requires].

'A proposal from the EEC is that workers should have a third of the places on the supervisory boards. The TUC General Council argue that workers should have half of the representatives, and they should have the right to appoint or veto some members of the second tier management board – the personnel manager, for example.

'Another improvement sought by the TUC is to make the scheme apply to all companies with over 200 workers, rather than just to those with over 500, as now proposed' (TUC, *Industrial News*, no. 3, 11 April 1973).

The TUC took a similar view on proposals for multi-national companies that might choose to be incorporated under EEC law, and for European Works Councils 'designed to provide some common trade union control over recruitment and terms and conditions of employment in the European multi-nationals'. The TUC position on representation is in part a reflection of the ideology of left–Labour union leaders, e.g. the presidents of the Engineers and the T & GWU, but more broadly it may reflect a dissatisfaction among union members:

'. . . dissatisfaction particularly with the traditional "balance of power," which gives union members only a crude and unpopular power of veto, depending ultimately on systematic sulking (like working to rule) or striking. Nationalization, a well-established nostrum, has also proved unsatisfying for the workers in the industries concerned because they are "managed" like everyone else. . . . The Scandinavians have been through the same experience. Five years ago it would have been hard to find a Swedish trade union official who was in favour of worker-directors. Now the law requires them, as a direct result of a reversal of policy by the equivalent of the TUC' (*Management Today*, 19 March 1974: 36).

While the effects of works councils and representation on company boards have been quite limited in western Europe and have probably been perceived as such by the average unionist, in a number of countries the unions' reaction has been to demand greater representation and increased powers. The advances since 1971 in West Germany, the Netherlands, Sweden and Norway have generally been made over employer opposition, and the demand for full parity with employers has either been raised or appears, logically, to be not far off. Co-determination 'is increasing in popularity as an experiment, and seems to have established expectations leading to demands for more extensive forms of worker participation in management' (Garson, 1974: 9). Some of the gains at the level of the works councils are significant in themselves. For example, in West Germany in 1971 the councils were given 'greater power over unjustified transfers, regroupings, and dismissals' (Garson, 1974: 7; see also Kendall, 1973).

In spite of the above, we have no reason to believe that a moderate increase in participation, even through the unions, would *in itself* have any major effect in democratising the life of the national union and, especially, in increasing electoral opposition at that level. On the other hand, such formal participation would increase local autonomy to some extent, and – more important – perhaps create semi-autonomous company-wide bodies, thus weakening the chain of command of the national officers. Further-more, it might furnish the impetus for trade union reform by *raising* the political aspirations of the membership and highlighting the contradiction between democratic rhetoric and organisational practice. Finally, discussions at the level of the European Community (or other supra-national bodies) might introduce political controversy from outside the particular national unions.

DEMOCRATIC SOCIALISM

The very discussion of workers' councils and co-determination has called into question the role of the private corporation, and suggested the possibility of democratic socialism. In discussing the European labour movement, Garson (1974: 39) has stated that 'one may only speculate on whether labor will seek to move from a parity position compatible with capitalism toward a majority position involving major structural changes creating self-management. If this seems utopian today, present developments seemed utopian a decade ago.' This is relevant here primarily because some of the problems of democracy in self-managed enterprises or industries, or in a society based on these, seem to be similar to those in large national trade unions. Second, one may question the role of the trade union in a society run largely through workers' organisations. The elimination of the private corporation might place the union in the anomalous position of bargaining for workers while simultaneously acting as 'management'.

Unions

There is an apparent paradox in that practical steps towards workers' control under capitalism seem to be best taken through trade union organisation, while the achievement of full workers' control in a society would seem to warrant a separate organisation which would bargain effectively for the workers as employees. For example, if the workgroup or factory council fires an employee, to whom is he to turn if he claims an injustice? If unskilled workers in a factory, an industry or the society feel exploited or abused, to whom are they to turn? It clearly cannot be assumed that workers' control will occur only under conditions of ultimate affluence, equality or justice. Thus, to represent their interests as employees, workers would require organisations independent from those concerned primarily or largely with the production of goods or services. Industrial democracy would still require the right to strike. The problem for *union democracy* is not how one might answer the common query, 'Why should the workers strike against themselves?', but rather what, if anything, might be done to ensure that stable organisations with bargaining functions remain important enough to warrant adequate participation and political enough to sustain internal opposition? Collective bargaining might become only an occasional or residual function in a much more affluent and genuinely participative society. Thus, any stable form of 'union' democracy might require the assumption of social service or professional/ occupational functions, which ordinarily put bargaining in second place.

Workers' Control

In a giant enterprise under workers' control, many of the dangers to democracy might flow, as in the case of the national union, from an absence of important autonomous subassociations, from an apparent homogeneity, and from a precedence of administration over ideology or interest-group politics. These in turn might flow, as in the case of the national union, from the isolation, specialisation and relatively simple hierarchical authority structure of the organisation – and all that these imply. The issues could appear to be too inconsequential to stir regular and effective competition for leading posts, and decision making might be left largely to bureaucrats and technocrats. The greater resources of large work enterprises under workers' control, and their links to the larger society (including perhaps representatives of the public on governing bodies: see Edelstein, 1972), might facilitate a greater penetration of political controversy than in the national union, but this cannot be taken for granted. It is safer to assume that democracy in a giant work organisation will have to depend largely on its internal formal organisation, as in the unions' case: on a structure and procedures which produce relatively equal potential contenders for the top posts; on relatively equal substructures which may support different contenders; on ground rules for electoral struggle which reduce rather than exaggerate inequalities; and on potentially counter-balancing significant power centres near the top. The right to organise an opposition is, of course, assumed, preferably one with the free use of the communications channels which an advanced technology could provide.[4] More broadly, the extension of democracy in the modern world may partly depend on whether important decisions are viewed as political rather than administrative, and therefore as proper subjects for public debate. However, there is a reciprocal relationship between formal organisation and what is viewed as properly political. An organisation's overall system of authority may imply (and impose) either a political or an administrative context for decision making. Both politics and formal organisation converge at the point where we ask what the nature of the latter should be.

The period of social flux and crises into which we are entering will not leave trade union organisation untouched. Union constitutions will be revamped, occasionally under pressure from internal reform movements. We must not under-estimate the degree to which such changes will be made self-consciously, in some cases after years of struggle and debate.

In recent years union democracy as an idea, and even a slogan, has been surprisingly widespread in the United States and Britain, kept alive more often than not by unknown and beleagured members. Where changes are made for the better, they will be primarily to their credit. They will often need all the help they can get. Most of all, they need a climate in which organisational and social democracy are elevated to a higher level of concern.

NOTES TO CHAPTER 11

1 See Ulman (1962: 3–39) for an excellent account of resistance to the loss of autonomy in bargaining in the Steel Workers, during approximately 1937–42.
2 Under the GMWU's plurality system, Basnett was elected general secretary in 1972 with 208,000 votes to 146,000 for Donnett, 133,000 for Derek Gladwin, 102,000 for Eccles, 71,000 for Jim Mason and 54,000 for Cyril Unwin (*IRIS News*, December 1972: 4). The runner-up percentage was 70, as compared to 68 per cent in filling the previous vacancy. The general secretaryship, with a salary estimated as certainly over £7,000 in 1972, has been described as one of the most lucrative union positions in Britain. Although the winner and the runner-up were both right-wing (orthodox Labour), Basnett was regarded as the more radical industrially, and some on the left regarded him as the least objectionable of the leading candidates and possibly willing to entertain some suggestions for the reform of the union.
3 Whatever the significance of its 1972 election, the GMWU may be regarded as essentially a cross between a collegial and a federal oligarchy, with top vacancies filled after legitimate, if restrained, competition between clans. It had been one of the most undemocratic unions in Britain, but among unions of its type its moderately close elections are exceptional. The opposition manifest in elections for the top post is only the tip of the iceberg, in most unions. But even in the GMWU, with a primary role for appointment along the promotion path towards the top, such opposition may at times be of more than cosmetic significance.
4 Questions of communication, and press, freedom are clearly linked to the problem of both union democracy and opposition in the wider political context. They are mutually supportive, for the most part.

Epilogue to the Revised Edition

'The study of succession—of the passage from an old to a new leader—is as old as history. Indeed, much of history *is* the study of succession.... Succession is so important that the forms of government themselves may actually be defined, at least partly, by the kinds of succession they employ. "Democracy" itself can be thought of as a form of succession to the highest office in which the choice is made by popular selection, with guaranteed rights and protection to those replaced, and with the changeover occuring in a more or less peaceful and orderly manner.' (Alvin Gouldner)

However partial the above conception of democracy, the emphasis on high office in government and large organizations is appropriate and is likely to remain so for some time. As the initial draft of this epilogue was being written, an important election campaign for the presidency of the American Steelworkers was in progress. In some respects, the election was a replay of the Steelworkers' defeat of an incumbent president in 1965, described in chapter 10. A consideration of this election and of recent elections in the British Engineers (see chapter 9)—in two of the largest national unions in the world—will point out more sharply some of the problems for democracy in running elections of this scope under less than ideal conditions. This book has emphasized organizational structure and electoral systems, but more should be said about the conduct of the ballot itself and the role of the mass media once the more basic organizational features are conducive to close contests for top offices. However some of the immediate issues in these two unions may be resolved, their situations illustrate some general problems of democracy in both countries.

Voting in the 1.4 million-member Steelworkers took place in 5,400 local unions (at over 5,700 locations) on the United States mainland, in Puerto Rico and the Virgin Islands, and in Canada, often some distance away from the place of work and during more than one shift. The turnout was only 41 percent with 578,000 valid ballots, due in part to large-scale layoffs during the severe winter.

Over 30 percent of the 1.1 million Engineers (in the Engineering Section of the AUEW) voted in recent postal ballots, which generally require two separate mailings and two ballot counts for each election, since a runoff is usually required to secure an absolute majority. There have been problems in keeping the mailing list up to date,[1] and the large number of national and regional elections each year (some simultaneous with those for president or general secretary) have been costly and no doubt an administrative burden.

Clearly, the logistics of the voting in the Steelworkers and the Engineers are more complex than those in some major cities. In addition, there have been self-serving disagreements concerning the rules of the game; a potential for fraud, especially in the Steelworkers; some less than democratic rules and practices; and unequal access to union periodicals and the mass media, although some of these have varied with the particular election.

In the Steelworkers' 1977 election, both the 'establishment's' candidate, Lloyd McBride, and the 'rebel,' Ed Sadlowski (they accepted their respective designations) were district directors. Each of the union's 25 districts elects a director, by referendum, who sits on the international executive board. The presidency, the secretary- and treasurerships (just become separated), and the two vice-presidents (one new) were vacant or only temporarily filled, and each of the two presidential candidates ran as the leader of a full slate for these offices. There was also competition for 15 of the 25 district directorships and for the national director for Canada, with candidates associated with the two slates in many instances.

The Steelworkers, formed from the top down as an organizing committee in the 1930s, 'centralized in haste and became legitimate at leisure' (Ulman, 1962, p. 3). However, the independent political base of each of the district directors was established at the first constitutional convention in 1942, at least partly as a concession to the opposition, which objected to the presidential appointment of field staff (see Ulman, 1962, p. 122). Sadlowski's district, with about 120,000 members, is the largest in the union.

Sadlowski originally lost his try for district director in 1973, but his charge of election fraud was upheld by the Department of Labor, and he won a rerun, monitored by almost 300 Department of Labor agents in 1974, by almost two-to-one. His request, and officially the union's, for a similar monitoring of the 1977 national election was refused, but the Department of Labor did agree to offer technical advice and to total the sheets returned by the locals. The locals were not required to send their ballot papers to a central location. There was ample reason for the election to have been run, in its entirety, by an outside organization. As it turned out, the Sadlowski forces managed to monitor the polling at only 800 locals of the 5,400 participating in the election.

The union estimated that the election involved 20,000 local union officers, tellers, observers, and other officials (*Steel Labor*, February 1977). The large majority of the local officers must have been McBride supporters, since McBride was nominated by 2,901 locals as compared to 521 nominating Sadlowski.

The Sadlowski caucus, Steelworkers Fight Back, attacked the 'tuxedo unionism' of the administration and advocated the restoration of the right to strike, rather than the arbitration required by the Experimental Negotiating Agreement, and the ratification of collective bargaining agreements by direct vote of the members. Sadlowski himself often sounded like a populist and was attacked by his opponent for being 'in bed with left-wingers.'

Sadlowski had the political and financial support of such nationally-known liberals as Ralph Nader and John Kenneth Galbraith, and of some wealthy businessmen who had supported liberal causes in the past. The Sadlowski caucus raised $150,000 from 2,000 contributions by approximately January 10, including $30,000 from outside the union (*New York Times*, January 17, 1977), but—one month before the election—the caucus was about $87,000 in debt. The McBride caucus had received $180,000, including relatively modest contributions from the secretary-treasurer of the AFL-CIO and the presidents of some large national unions. Each side finally spent an estimated $300,000.

The McBride forces attempted to sue Sadlowski for receiving contributions from employers, in violation of the union constitution. (On national television, McBride claimed that Xerox Data Corporation contributed $2,000 to Sadlowski's campaign.) Sadlowski filed a motion to dismiss, arguing that the rules were too broadly drawn—'employer' could include almost anyone. He also instituted a libel suit for five million dollars against McBride for saying, on four occasions, that he (Sadlowski) had accepted contributions from a major official of a corporation that had been cited for unfair labor practices. In addition, he instituted suits against McBride for coercing union staff members to make contributions, and for accepting the services of a public relations firm, which worked for the union, at less than its usual rate.

Finally, Sadlowski initiated suit against the union for unequal coverage of his campaign—its 16-to-20 page monthly tabloid included no explicit campaign material from either side—but dropped it when the union agreed to a mailing of four-page campaign statements to its 1.4 million members. It has also been charged, undoubtedly with good reason, that Sadlowski's 20 campaign 'organizers'—all but a few Steelworkers on layoff or vacation—were no match for the union's 800 appointed full-time field staff.

Sadlowski lost the election by a four-to-three margin—the count, before the intervention of the Department of Labor, was 328,861 to 249,281. He presented a lengthy election protest to the tellers, but after 40 days of hearings in 25 cities throughout the United States and Canada, the tellers denied each and every charge by Sadlowski—not a single vote was changed (*Steel Labor*, May 1977). H.W. Benson commented that 'they [the tellers] were originally elected on Abel's official family slate, *the very same tellers who had whitewashed the District 31 election of 1973 when Sadlowski had been counted out in the illegal election later challenged by the Labor Department*' (*Dissent*, Fall 1977: 458; emphasis in the original). Sadlowski's appeal to the international executive board (council), the next step under the union's constitution, produced an identical result. Benson added: 'There his charges were reviewed by the same men whose candidates he tried to defeat, who contributed money to elect McBride against him, who circulated the opinion that he is a tool of outside enemies of the working class' (ibid.).

Under the union's constitution, an appeal had to be submitted to the tellers within ten days after the election, the same grace period allowed locals for the transmission of their tallies to the tellers. Sadlowski could not possibly have known, for example, that over 420 locals, with over 10,000 total votes cast, recorded not a single vote for him (only 21 showed unanimous votes for Sadlowski.) Instead, he noted in his appeal that 95 locals had recorded near zero or zero votes for him.

Having exhausted his internal remedies, Sadlowski could now appeal to the Department of Labor, which he did along with other members of his slate on June 17. The Labor Department's investigation included 712 locals representing 25 per cent of the union's membership, and 30 per cent of the votes cast in the United States. Its November 11 report[2] found that violations of the Landrum-Griffin Act did occur, but not to an extent which affected the result of the election. The department reduced McBride's margin of victory in the United States by 15,000 votes—from approximately 42,000 to only 27,000—on the basis of findings of fraud and various disallowable practices. For example, violations were found in over 50 locals with unanimous votes for McBride, resulting in a reduction of his margin by approximately 1,100 votes. McBride's margin was reduced most by findings of a failure to give proper notice of the election (2,708 votes); ballot-box stuffing (2,346); a failure to ensure that all eligible voters, and only such, could vote (1,972); the use of union facilities for campaign operations (1,606); campaigning at the polls (1,571); the support of candidates by local union publications (1,090); and the lack of a secret ballot (at least 1,000).

The Labor Department had no authority to conduct an investigation in Canada, where McBride had a margin of 37,000 votes in the 827 Canadian locals. However, arrangements were made through the Canadian Labor Minister for the appointment of an Industrial Inquiry Commissioner to conduct an investigation. Again, the violations found were judged to be insufficient to have affected the outcome of the election.

Sadlowski charged that the election had been "stolen" in Canada, where he had been beaten by almost three to one.

Sadlowski's lawyers went much further. In a June 30, 1977 letter to the Secretary of Labor (*Union Democracy Review*, September 1977) they charged that there was a 'long-standing alliance between the Department and the incumbent Official family establishment'; that the union administration was engaged in a massive coverup; and that the '250-person investigative force cannot possibly investigate the Steelworkers union . . . without a set of questionnaires requiring answers under oath.' In its final report, the department gave various reasons for not following the latter suggestion, including the impossiblity of completing the investigation and evaluating the results within the 60 days permitted by law. It did conduct 5,422 'interviews' with members and employees of the union.

One of Sadlowski's allegations was: "On November 4, 1976, a letter from Mr. Abel and an expensive brochure, both heaping unrestrained praise on ENA [Experimental Negotiating Agreement] (the number one issue in the campaign), were sent to hundreds of thousands of members of the USWA for the purpose of influencing their vote against the Sadlowski slate' (p. 28). The Department of Labor's report stated in response: 'There was no evidence disclosed to substantiate the allegation that the literature was sent to the members for the purpose of influencing their vote against the Sadlowski team, and, although ENA was an issue in the campaign, there is nothing in the brochure to indicate that it was in the nature of campaign propoganda . . . . The business of a union must continue even during heated election campaigns' (p. 28). Whatever issues of law may be involved, there are clearly some issues of union democracy, especially where the union periodical allows no room for a reply.

One of the most serious of Sadlowski's allegations was: 'The election in many parts of the country was permeated by violence and intimidation' (p. 37). Concerning one of the more serious incidents, at the ARMCO plant in Texas on July 22, 1976, the department's report states: 'The verbal threat and physical attack of individuals handing out literature in support of Sadlowski [a distributor was hit four times and knocked to the ground] by the principal officer of the [local] union and two staff representatives appears to have been a concerted effort to try to intimidate and abuse those who supported Sadlowski. Stories of these incidents were reported in the Houston papers and received wide publicity. As this was an isolated incident during the nomination period, long before the actual election campaign, it did not appear that it could have affected the outcome of the election' (p. 38).

A shooting took place four days later in Houston, and involved three distributors who were present at the previous incident. The department's report stated: 'Ben Corum and others were handing out literature for Sadlowski at the Hughes Tool Company gate. One of the people was informed that there was going to be trouble. A few minutes later Corum was shot in the neck [one-half inch from his spinal column, it was reported elsewhere] by someone in the back of a car that sped by. No identification was made and there is no evidence that the union or any union officials was responsible for the shooting. David Julian was interviewed and did not substantiate the allegation that he was intimidated by the incident' (pp. 38-39). Sadlowski supporters claimed that the 'police refused to undertake a serious investigation . . . even refusing to take statements from eyewitnesses' (*Labor Today*, September 1976). The above-mentioned David Julian is not known to us, but we are inclined to suspect that someone was intimidated.

The electoral struggle seems to have pushed the international administration into a more aggressive bargaining stance. The ENA banned industry-wide walkouts, permitting only individual locals to strike over local issues. Nevertheless, the union demanded a 65 cents an hour bonus for 15,000 workers in 21 iron-ore mining and processing locals, in violation of the ENA (which permitted only local strikes) according to industry officials, who attempted to stop a walkout by a court-ordered injunction. A strike that was to last 17 weeks began on August 1, with support from the international leadership (*Wall Street Journal*, July 19, 1977). The agreement was negotiated by Lloyd McBride. On the Minnesota Iron Range, where many of the strikers were concentrated, the vote for Sadlowski had been overwhelming (*In These Times*, January 4-10, 1978). It should be obvious, from this and many earlier examples, that the resolution of disputes over policy is often intimately related to the outcome of union elections, even when the proponents of a new policy lose.

Steelworkers Fight Back retained control over Sadlowski's large district, won a few more district directorships and many more local posts, and gained a majority of the votes in the basic steel sector of the union. The faction states that it has a long-term orientation, and intends to maintain its organization. We were told in January 1978 that Sadlowski was about to carry his case to the federal courts.

The problems of elections in the British Engineers are related to those in the Steelworkers in that outsiders—in this case the national press— have recently begun to play a much more important role, and in that the union itself has failed to provide adequate channels of communication for the candidates. Indeed, the latter has magnified the effects of the former.

There have also been problems of legitimacy, with recourse to the courts.

A narrowly-carried constitutional revision in 1970, almost reversed in 1971, required postal ballots for the election of the Engineers' officials, rather than voting at local union meetings. The leading representatives of the "broad left" opposed the postal ballot, which they regarded as a threat to their electoral strength in the union and—especially since 1967—to their strong representation on the full-time national executive council. Postal balloting began in 1972, raising the usual level of participation from under 10 per cent to over 30 per cent, but was almost ended at the next rules revision conference in 1975 after two pro-postal ballot delegates were disqualified. The latter appealed to the courts, which reversed the disqualification, and the postal ballot was retained, although it remained an issue within the union. In addition, in 1975, the Conservative Party pledged itself to facilitate (require?) postal ballots in unions generally, and Michael Foot, in the Labour cabinet, said that the government would consider paying the bill if requested to do so by the Trades Union Congress (which has not acted on the matter).

The broad left coalition continued to increase its representation in the early elections under the postal ballot. However, after the Labour Party had won the two general elections in 1974, the left in the Engineers became an internal problem for the 'moderate' leadership of the party from within (since the unions are affiliated with it) and an external problem as well in the form of resistance to the Labour government's control over wages. The British press began a massive campaign against the left in the Engineers' elections, and a whole series of left-wing candidates went down to defeat. This chain of events was finally broken in 1976, for no apparent reason, with the decisive victory of the left-wing Bob Wright in an election for assistant general secretary. He had earlier lost his post on the executive council. Wright recently received almost as many votes as the leading, right-wing candidate in the first ballot for the presidency—Scanlon, the incumbent, is retiring.

The American national press preferred to titillate its readers with reports of Sadlowski's colorful public personality and the rebellion in the ranks. This probably worked to his advantage, perhaps even over-coming the many hostile editorials in the localities where union members were concentrated. But eventually, if rank-and-file movements generally begin to have a greater impact, the dangers of radicalism may become an important theme.

The Engineers have always published candidates' campaign statements and made them available to voters at local meetings. However, with the constitutional change to the postal ballot in 1970, no provisions were made to accompany the ballots by campaign statements. Furthermore, the union rules have long *banned* the circulation of campaign literature by candidates or their supporters in the union, although they do not bar the general secretary, who controls the monthly journal, from editorial attacks on (left-wing) candidates (see pp. 304-5). While the periodicals of outside organizations may be sold or distributed, these cannot compete with the British press, or substitute for candidates' statements accompanying the ballots, or replace the now unconstitutional initiative of local members in publishing campaign literature at will. Neither the left nor the right has demanded these.

With the fall 1977 presidential election in view, some leaders of the 'broad left' asked it to accept the postal ballot as a fact of life, and to see to it that as many left-wing supporters as possible registered their current addresses with the union. Indeed, some of the defeats of the left may have been due to their opposition to the postal ballot, and to their well-publicized self-discrediting tactics against proponents of the postal ballot in the higher councils of the union. Such tactics were reminiscent of those of the right wing before the left won the presidency in 1967 (see p. 303).[3]

Place-of-work voting is not feasible in the Engineers, since the membership is too scattered. The 8 per cent voting for general secretary in 1957 and 1964 is indefensible, given the alternative of the postal ballot, which yielded a 39 per cent participation for the same office in 1975. The defeat of the incumbent president of the American International Union of Electrical Workers, described earlier (pp. 320-29), took place through a postal ballot with 53 per cent voting.[4] Short of a suitable reorganization of the Engineers' local branches (see pp. 310 - 13), which may not be feasible without a change in the British industrial relations system, the postal ballot would seem to be the best vehicle for an expression of membership opinion in a national election. A transferable vote system, as in the British Mineworkers (see pp. 214ff.), with preliminary voting in the branches to reduce the number of candidates to six, would lighten much of the administrative burden and expense, while eliminating the tendency of the second ballot system to lift weak but cohesive minorities to near the top of the poll (and onto the second ballot).

Most of the requirements for a really democratic election in a large union are fairly obvious, and implicit in the foregoing, and we will not belabor them. Where there is any possibility of fraud in the preparation, casting, or counting of the ballots, an outside organization should be brought into the picture. Normally, this should be arranged well in advance, and indeed, incorporated into the regular procedure. Any such organization should be as competent and neutral as possible; it should certainly not have a conflict of interest, which means that politicians who deal with the labor leadership should have no say over its operations or personnel. Running a large-scale operation of this sort is expensive, and public funds should be provided, not only for the outside organization but for the mailings, and perhaps use of the mass media which effective communication to (and from) the membership would require. The civil rights of members and candidates should be secure, and the right to campaign should be virtually unrestricted, in the workplace as well as outside. This implies rights for the union, and union members, which they do not generally enjoy (for example, the right to hold union meetings at the workplace). The usual monthly union periodical should have a full page, or more, set aside for a discussion of the campaign for at least six issues before the election. Considering how early the campaigns begin in the Steelworkers and the Engineers, even this may not be enough. While this is not the place to raise again the entire question of organizational structure, we must point out that, unfortunately, the existence of a large, nationally-appointed field staff can usually vitiate all of the foregoing; their activities cannot be regulated to any degree.

It is legitimate and often necessary for 'outsiders' to lend their moral and material support to trade union reformers. In addition to structural and procedural reforms, a greater politicization of trade unions and their increased permeability to national politics is desirable for democracy and progressive social change. We would say the same for life within large work organizations, and for daily life generally: democracy, if genuine, cannot remain narrow in scope. But to return to the harsh reality of much of trade union life today, we quote Joseph L. Rauh, Jr., attorney without fee to Sadlowski: 'Tony Boyle would be president of the United Mine Workers today, instead of a lifelong resident of a Pennsylvania prison, if the public—what Boyle and [leaders of other unions] . . . call "outsiders"—had not rallied to the support of the reform group' (*New York Times*, January 17, 1977).[5]

NOTES TO EPILOGUE

1 A source favorable to the right-wing Labour general secretary quoted him as saying, 'To have an up-to-date record of 863,968 addresses, out of a paying membership of 1,100,000, is a wonderful achievement' (*IRS News*, January 1977).
2 See the news release of the Labor-Management Services Administration, USDL—77-992, November 11, 1977. The report is in the form of a letter to Sadlowski, the union, and others involved. It was made available to the press.
3 At the 1977 TUC Congress, President Scanlon of the Engineers refused to let the unions' delegation decide how the union's block vote was to be cast on the question of a return to free collective bargaining, at the end of the second stage of the 'social contract' with the government. He personally made the decision to accede to the government's wishes. It is ironic, and was widely

noted, that he had won the presidency in part because of his opposition to his predecessor's similar behavior (see 'Carron's Law,' pp. 289-91; *Labour Leader*, October 1977)).

4 On the retirement of the incumbent IUE president in 1976, a postal ballot took place in which the more militant candidate received approximately 80 per cent of the vote cast for the administration-backed candidate. The per cent voting was lower than previously (*Syracuse Post-Standard*, December 21, 1976).

5 Boyle, now over 75, was recently released from prison pending a retrial. There is virtually no chance of his regaining the presidency. (See pp. 319-20.)

Bibliography

Adams, John Clarke (1955) 'Italy' in Walter Galenson (ed.), *Comparative Labor Movements* (New York: Prentice-Hall) pp. 410–79.

Allen, V. L. (1954) *Power in Trade Unions* (London, New York and Toronto: Longmans, Green and Co.).

Allen, V. L. (1957) *Trade Union Leadership* (London, New York and Toronto: Longmans, Green and Co.).

Almond, Gabriel A. and Verba, Sidney (1963) *The Civic Culture: Political Attitudes and Democracy in Five Nations* (Princeton: Princeton University Press).

Amalgamated Engineering Union (1965) 'Trade Unions and the Contemporary Scene', submitted to the Royal Commission on Trade Unions and Employers' Organisations, London.

Aristotle (1962) *The Politics*, book IV, trans. T. A. Sinclair (Harmondsworth, Middlesex: Penguin Books).

Arnot, R. Page (1949) *The Miners* (London: George Allen & Unwin).

Arnot, R. Page (1953) *The Miners: Years of Struggle* (London: George Allen & Unwin).

Arnot, R. Page (1955) *A History of the Scottish Miners* (London: George Allen & Unwin).

Arnot, R. Page (1961) *The Miners in Crisis and War* (London: George Allen & Unwin).

Bain, George Sayers (1970) *The Growth of White-Collar Unionism* (Oxford: The Clarendon Press).

Bambrick Jr, James J. and Haas, George H. (1955) *Handbook of Union Government, Structure and Procedure* (New York: National Industrial Conference Board).

Banks, Robert F. (1971) 'British collective bargaining: the challenges of the 1970's', *Relations Industrielles*, vol. 26, no. 4 (November) pp. 642–91.

Barbash, Jack (1967) *American Unions: Structures, Government and Politics* (New York: Random House).

Barber, Bernard (1950) 'Participation and Mass Apathy in Associations' in Alvin W. Gouldner (ed.), *Studies in Leadership* (New York: Harper) pp. 477–504.

Benson, H. W. (1972) 'Apathy and other axioms: expelling the union dissenter from history', *Dissent*, vol. 19, no. 1 (Winter).

Benson, H. W. (1973) 'Election challenges in two unions', *Union Democracy Review*, no. 5 (Fall) pp. 1–6.

Beynon, Huw (1973) *Working for Ford* (Harmondsworth, Middlesex: Penguin Books).

Blauner, Robert (1967) *Alienation and Freedom* (Chicago: Phoenix Books, University of Chicago Press).

British Information Services (1958) *Parliamentary Elections in Britain*, I.D. 1314 (September) (New York, Washington, etc.).

Brody, David (1964) *The Butcher Workmen* (Cambridge, Massachusetts: Harvard University Press).

Brooks, George W. (1961) 'Unions and the Structure of Collective Bargaining' in Arnold R. Weber (ed.), *The Structure of Collective Bargaining: Problems and Perspectives* (New York: Free Press of Glencoe) pp. 123–41.

Brooks, Thomas R. (1964) 'Uneasiness in labor's ranks, and the leadership shake-up', *New America* (16 November) p. 3.

Brown, E. H. Phelps (1965) *The Growth of British Industrial Relations* (London: Macmillan and Co.).

Bureau of Labor Statistics (1966) *Directory of National and International Labor Unions in the United States, 1965*, Bulletin no. 1493 (Washington, D.C.: United States Department of Labor).

Bureau of the Census (1971) *The American Almanac* (New York: Grosset and Dunlap).

Callahan, Raymond E. (1966) 'The History of the Fight to Control Policy in Public Education' in Frank W. Lutz and Joseph J. Assarelli (eds), *Struggle for Power in Education* (New York: Center for Applied Research in Education) pp. 16–34.

Caplow, Theodore (1957) 'Organizational size', *Administrative Science Quarterly*, no. 1, vol. 1 (March) pp. 484–505.

Carew, Anthony (1971) 'Rank and File Movements and Workers' Control in British Engineering, 1850–1969', M.Phil. thesis, University of Sussex.

Child, John, Loveridge, Ray and Warner, Malcolm (1973) 'Towards an organizational study of trade unions', *Sociology*, vol. 7, no. 1 (January) pp. 71–91.

Clegg, Hugh A. (1959) 'The Rights of British Trade Union Members' in Michael Harrington and Paul Jacobs (eds), *Labor in a Free Society* (Berkeley and Los Angeles: University of California Press) pp. 119–38.

Clegg, Hugh A., Killick, A. J. and Adams, Rex (1961) *Trade Union Officers* (Oxford: Basil Blackwell).

Coben, Philip (1953) 'Democracy under socialism', *Labor Action* (4 May) p. 8.

Cohany, Harry P. and Phillips, Irving P. (1958) *Election and Tenure of National and International Union Officers*, Bulletin no. 1239 (Washington, D.C.: Bureau of Labor Statistics, United States Department of Labor).

Cohany, Harry P. and Phillips, Irving P. (1959) *Union Constitution Provisions: Trusteeship*, Bulletin no. 1263 (Washington, D.C.: Bureau of Labor Statistics, United States Department of Labor).

Cohen, Sanford (1970) *Labor in the United States* (Columbus, Ohio: Charles E. Merrill Publishing).

Coleman, James S. (1970) 'Reply to Cain and Watts', *American Sociological Review*, vol. 35, no. 2 (April) pp. 242–9.

Cook, Alice H. (1963) *Union Democracy: Practice and Ideal* (Ithaca, New York: Cornell University Press).

Cook, Philip J. (1971) 'Robert Michels's political parties in perspective', *Journal of Politics*, vol. 33, no. 4, (October) pp. 773–96.

Coser, Lewis A. (1964) 'The Functions of Social Conflict' in Lewis A. Coser and Bernard Rosenberg (eds), *Sociological Theory* (New York: MacMillan) pp. 206–8.

Cox, Archibald (1959) 'The Role of Law in Preserving Union Democracy' in Michael Harrington and Paul Jacobs (eds), *Labor in a Free Society* (Berkeley and Los Angeles: University of California Press) pp. 45–87.

Craig, John G. and Gross, Edward (1970) 'The forum theory of organizational democracy: structured guarantees as time-related variables', *American Sociological Review*, vol. 35, no. 1 (February) pp. 19–33.

Dahl, Robert A. (1970) *After the Revolution?* (New Haven: Yale University Press).

Dahrendorf, Ralf (1959) *Class and Class Conflict in Industrial Society* (Stanford, California: Stanford University Press).

Davies, Ioan (1966) *African Trade Unions* (Harmondsworth, Middlesex: Penguin Books).

Derber, Milton (1968) 'Collective bargaining in Britain and the United States', *Quarterly Rev. of Economics and Business*, vol. 8, no. 4, (October), pp. 55–65.

Donaldson, Lex and Warner, Malcolm (1972) 'Organizational structure of occupational interest associations', working paper, London Graduate School of Business Studies.

Donaldson, Lex and Warner, Malcolm (1974) 'Elections and bureaucratic control in occupational interest association', *Sociology*, vol. 8, no. 1 (January) pp. 47–58.

Downs, Anthony (1957) *An Economic Theory of Democracy* (New York: Harper).

Duverger, Maurice (1963) *Political Parties* (New York: John Wiley and Sons).

Edelstein, J. David (1960) 'The election of international union officers', *Political Research: Organization and Design*, vol. 3, no. 5 (January) pp. 30–2.

Edelstein, J. David (1972) '"Consumer" Representation on Corporate Boards: The Structure of Representation' in Eugen Pusic (ed.), *Participation and Self-Management*, vol. 2, First International Sociological Conference on Participation and Self-Management, 13–17 December 1972 (Zagreb: Institute for Social Research, University of Zagreb) pp. 73–81.

Edelstein, J. David and Ruppel Jr, Howard J. (1970) 'Convention frequency and oligarchic degeneration in British and American unions', *Administrative Science Quarterly*, vol. 15, no. 1 (March) pp. 47–56.

Edelstein, J. David and Warner, Malcolm (1971) 'On measuring and explaining union democracy: A reply to Dr Martin's critique', *Sociology*, vol. 5, No. 3, (September) pp. 398–400.

Editors of the *Yale Law Journal* (1966) 'The American Medical Association' in William A. Glaser and David L. Sills (eds), *The Government of Associations* (Totowa, New Jersey: Bedminster Press) pp. 227–30.

Etzioni, Amitai (1961) *A Comparative Analysis of Complex Organizations* (New York: Free Press of Glencoe).

Etzioni, Amitai (1964) *Modern Organizations* (Englewood Cliffs, New Jersey: Prentice-Hall).

Evans, Edward Owen (1973) 'Cheap at Twice the Price? Shop Stewards and Working Relations in Engineering' in Malcolm Warner (ed.), *The Sociology of the Work-place* (London: George Allen & Unwin) pp. 82–115.

Ezekiel, Mordecai and Fox, Karl A. (1959) *Methods of Correlation and Regression Analysis* (New York: John Wiley and Sons).

Faunce, William A. (1962) 'Size of locals and union democracy', *American Journal of Sociology*, vol. 68, No. 3 (November) pp. 291–8.

Fisher, Lloyd and McConnell, Grant (1954) 'Internal Conflict and Labor-Union Solidarity' in Arthur Kornhauser, Robert Dubin and Arthur M. Ross (eds), *Industrial Conflict* (New York: McGraw-Hill) pp. 132–43.

Fletcher, Richard (1970) 'Trade Union Democracy: Structural Factors', in Ken Coates, Tony Topham and Michael Barrett Brown, *The Trade Union Register* (London: Merlin Press).

372   *Comparative Union Democracy*

Foner, Philip (1964) *History of the Labor Movement in the United States*, vol. 3 (New York: International Publishers).

Foot, Paul (1967) 'The Seamen's Struggle' in Robin Blackburn and Alexander Cockburn (eds), *The Incompatibles: Trade Union Militancy and Consensus* (Harmondsworth, Middlesex: Penguin Books) pp. 169–209.

Fore, Mark (1970) *G.M.W.U.: Scab Union*, Pamphlet no. 32 (London: Solidarity).

Freeman, Michael (1973) 'Social science and democratic theory', *Political Studies*, vol. 21, No. 1 (February) pp. 70–4.

Friedman, Abraham (1969) 'The Leaders of International and National Labor Unions', unpublished Doctoral dissertation, Graduate School of Business, University of Chicago.

Friedrich, Carl Joachim (1930) 'Oligarchy', *Encyclopedia of the Social Sciences*, vol. 11 (New York: Macmillan) pp. 462–4.

Fulcher, James (1973) 'Class conflict in Sweden', *Sociology*, vol. 7, no. 1 (January) pp. 49–70.

Galenson, Walter (1955) 'Scandinavia' in Walter Galenson (ed.), *Comparative Labor Movements* (New York: Prentice-Hall) pp. 104–72.

Galenson, Walter (1961) *Trade Union Democracy in Western Europe* (Berkeley and Los Angeles: University of California Press).

Garbarino, Joseph W. (1970) 'British and American labor market trends: a case of convergence?', *Scottish Journal of Political Economy*, vol. 17, no. 2 (June) p. 319–36.

Garson, G. David (1974) 'Recent Developments in Workers' Participation in Europe', paper delivered at the First National Conference of People for Self-Management, Cambridge, Massachusetts, 12–13 January 1974.

Goldstein, Joseph (1952) *The Government of British Trade Unions* (London: George Allen & Unwin).

Goldthorpe, John H. (1960) 'Status and Conflict in Industry: A Critique of Two Aspects of the Personnel Policy of the National Coal Board', paper read to the British Sociological Association, Industrial Sociology Group, 26 November 1960.

Goodman, J. F. B. and Whittingham, T. G. (1969) *Shop Stewards in British Industry* (London: McGraw-Hill).

Gorz, André (1967) *Strategy for Labor* (Boston: Beacon Press).

Gorz, André (1973) *Socialism and Revolution* (Garden City, New York: Anchor Press/Doubleday; preceded by Anchor Books).

Gouldner, Alvin (1971) *The Coming Crisis of Western Sociology* (New York: Avon).

Guildford, J. P. (1954) *Psychometric Methods* (New York, McGraw-Hill).

Günter, Hans (1972) 'Social Policy and the Post-Industrial Society', *Bulletin* no. 10 (Geneva: International Institute for Labour Studies).

Hagood, Margaret J. (1973) 'The Notion of a Hypothetical Universe' in Denton E. Morrison and Ramon E. Henkel (eds), *The Significance Test Controversy* (Chicago: Aldine Publishing) pp. 65–78.

Hall, Richard H. (1972) *Organizations: Structure and Process* (Englewood Cliffs, New Jersey: Prentice-Hall).

Hall, Stuart, Williams, Raymond and Thompson, Edward (1968) 'A Socialist Policy for the Unions' in Ken Coates and Anthony Topham (eds), *Industrial Democracy in Great Britain* (London, Fakenham and Reading: MacGibbon and Kee).

Harrington, Michael (1962) *The Retail Clerks* (New York: John Wiley and Sons).

Harrison, Martin (1960) *Trade Unions and the Labour Party Since 1945* (London: George Allen & Unwin).
Harrison, Paul M. (1959) *Authority and Power in the Free Church Tradition* (Princeton: Princeton University Press).
Haworth, David (1968) 'Strike Britain cannot afford', *The Observer* (13 October) p. 12.
Hayes, Paul (1973) *Fascism* (London: George Allen & Unwin).
Herling, John (1972) *Right to Challenge: People and Power in the Steelworkers Union* (New York: Harper and Row).
Horowitz, Morris A. (1962) *The Structure and Government of the Carpenters' Union* (New York: John Wiley and Sons).
Howe, Irving and Widdick, B. J. (1949) *The UAW and Walter Reuther* (New York: Random House).
Hughes, John (1960-1) 'The rise of the militants', *Trade Union Affairs*, no. 1 (Winter) pp. 45-57.
Hughes, John (1964) *Change in the Trade Unions*, Fabian Research Series 244 (London: Fabian Society).
Industrial Relations Unit, Warwick (*c.* 1971) 'The Training Needs of Full-Time Trade Union Officers: First Report', mimeographed undated report (Warwick University, England).
International Confederation of Free Trade Unions (1971) 'Crisis in European industrial relations?', *Free Labour World*, no. 251 (May) pp. 17-21.
Jefferys, James B. (1945) *The Story of the Engineers* (London: Amalgamated Engineering Union).
Jencks, Clinton E. (1966) 'British coal: labor relations since nationalization', *Industrial Relations*, vol. 6, no. 1, (October), pp. 95-110.
Jenkin, Thomas P. (1968) 'Oligarchy', in David L. Sills (ed.), *International Encyclopedia of the Social Sciences*, vol. 11 (New York: Free Press, Macmillan Co.) pp. 281-3.
Jenkins, Clive (1964) 'The Common Cause', *Tribune* (25 September).
Jenkins, Roy (1960) 'Not really a rebel', *The Observer* (18 December).
Karson, Marc (1958) *American Labor Unions and Politics, 1900-1918* (Carbondale, Illinois: Southern Illinois University Press).
Kasarda, John D. (1974) 'The structural implications of social system size: a three-level analysis', *American Sociological Review*, vol. 39 (February) pp. 19-28.
Kassalow, E. M. (1967) 'National Wage Policies: Lessons to Date, Europe and the U.S.A.', *Proceedings of the Nineteenth Annual Winter Meeting (1966)* (Madison, Wisconsin: Industrial Relations Research Association) pp. 125-38.
Katz, Daniel and Kahn, Robert L. (1966) *The Social Psychology of Organizations* (New York: John Wiley and Sons).
Kendall, Walter (1973) 'Industrial democracy in Western Europe', *Free Labour World* (July-August).
Kerr, Clark, Dunlop, John, Harbison, Frederick and Meyers, Charles A. (1960) *Industrial Man* (Cambridge, Massachusetts: Harvard University Press).
Labor-Management Services Administration (1965) *Interim Report on Election of National President of International Union of Electrical, Radio and Machine Workers (IUE)* (5 April) (Washington, D.C.: Office of Labor-Management and Welfare-Pension Reports, United States Department of Labor, Government Printing Office).

Labor–Management Services Administration (1966) *Summary of Operations, 1965, Labor–Management Reporting and Disclosure Act* (publisher as above).

Labor–Management Services Administration (1967) *Summary of Operations, 1966, Labor–Management Reporting and Disclosure Act* (publisher as above).

Labor–Management Services Administration (1969) *Compliance, Enforcement and Reporting in 1968 Under the Labor–Management Reporting and Disclosure Act* (publisher as above).

Labor–Management Services Administration (1970) *Compliance, Enforcement and Reporting in 1969 Under the Labor–Management Reporting and Disclosure Act* (publisher as above).

Labor–Management Services Administration (1972) *Union Election Cases Under the Labor–Management Reporting and Disclosure Act, 1966–1970* (publisher as above).

Labor–Management Services Administration (1974) *News Bulletin to Professionals* (publisher as above).

Labour Party (1967) *Report of the Labour Party Working Party on Industrial Democracy* (London: Labour Party).

Lakeman, Enid and Lambert, James D. (1959) *Voting in Democracies* (London: Faber and Faber).

Lazarsfeld, P. F. (1973) *Main Trends in Sociology* (London: George Allen & Unwin).

Leiserson, William M. (1961) *American Trade Union Democracy* (New York: Columbia University Press).

Lenin, V. I. (1932) *State and Revolution* (New York: International Publishers).

Lipset, Seymour Martin, Trow, Martin A. and Coleman, James S. (1956) *Union Democracy* (Glencoe, Illinois: Free Press).

Lipset, Seymour Martin (1959) 'Political Sociology' in Leonard Broom and Leonard S. Cottrell Jr (eds), *Sociology Today: Problems and Prospects* (New York: Basic Books) pp. 81–114.

Lipset, Seymour Martin (1960a) *Political Man* (Garden City, New York: Doubleday and Co.).

Lipset, Seymour Martin (1960b) 'The Political Process in Trade Unions: A Theoretical Statement' in Walter Galenson and SeymourMartin Lipset (eds), *Labor and Trade Unionism* (New York: John Wiley and Sons) pp. 239–41.

Lipset, Seymour Martin (1962a) 'Trade Unions and Social Structure: I', *Industrial Relations*, vol. 1, no. 1, (October) pp. 75–89.

Lipset, Seymour Martin (1962b) 'Trade Unions and Social Structure: II', *Industrial Relations*, vol. 1, no. 2 (February) pp. 98–110.

Lipset, Seymour Martin (1962c) 'Introduction to Robert Michels', *Political Parties* (New York: Collier Books).

Lipset, Seymour Martin (1964) 'The Biography of a Research Project: Union Democracy' in P. E. Hammond (ed.), *Sociologists at Work* (New York: Basic Books) pp. 96–120.

Lipset, Seymour Martin (1967) *The First New Nation* (Garden City, New York: Anchor Books, Doubleday and Co.).

Lipset, Seymour Martin and Solari, Aldo (1967) (eds), *Elites in Latin America* (New York: Oxford University Press).

Lord, F. M. (1963) *Elementary Models for Measuring Change* (Madison, Wisconsin: University of Wisconsin Press) pp. 21–38.

Lorwin, Val R. (1954) *The French Labor Movement* (Cambridge, Massachusetts: Harvard University Press).

Lorwin, Val R. (1955) 'France' in Walter Galenson (ed.), *Comparative Labor Movements* (New York: Prentice-Hall) pp. 313–409.

MacIver, R. M. (1965) *The Web of Government* (New York: Free Press of Glencoe).

Madison, James (1961) 'No. 58: Madison' in Alexander Hamilton, James Madison and John Jay, *The Federalist Papers* (New York: Mentor Books, The New American Library of World Literature).

Magrath, C. Peter (1959) 'Democracy in overalls: the futile quest for union democracy', *Industrial and Labour Relations Review*, vol. 12, no. 2 (July) pp. 503–25.

Mann, Michael (1970) 'The social cohesion of liberal democracy', *American Sociological Review*, vol. 35, no. 3 (June), pp. 423–39.

Marcus, Philip M. (1962) 'Trade Union Structure: A Study in Formal Organization', Doctoral dissertation, University of Chicago.

Marcus, Philip M. (1966) 'Union conventions and executive boards: a formal analysis of organizational structure', *American Sociological Review*, vol. 31, no. 1 (February) pp. 61–70.

Martin, Roderick (1968) 'Union democracy: an explanatory framework', *Sociology*, vol. 2, no. 2 (May) pp. 205–20.

Martin, Roderick (1969) *Communism and British Trade Unions, 1924–1933: A Study of the National Minority Movement* (Oxford: Clarendon Press).

Marx, Karl (1940) *The Civil War in France* (New York: International Publishers).

May, John D. (1965) 'Democracy, oligarchy, Michels', *American Political Science Review*, vol. 59, no. 2 (June) pp. 417–29.

McCarthy, W. E. J. and Parker, S. R. (1968) *Shop Stewards and Workshop Relations*, Research Paper No. 10, Royal Commision on Trade Unions and Employers' Associations (London: HMSO).

McNemar, Quinn (1949) *Psychological Statistics* (New York: John Wiley and Sons).

Meyers, Frederic (1961) *European Coal Mining Unions: Structure and Function* (Los Angeles: Institute of Industrial Relations, University of California).

Michels, Robert (1962) *Political Parties* (New York: Collier Books): publ., 1911.

Moffat, Abe (1965) *My Life with the Miners* (London: Lawrence and Wishart).

Moran, James (1964) *NATSOPA, Seventy-Five Years: A History of the National Society of Operative Printers and Assistants (1889–1964)* (London: National Society of Operative Printers and Assistants).

Murphy, J. T. (1919) Report of the discussion of a paper by J. T. Murphy read at Ruskin College in Council of Ruskin College (eds), *The Trade Unions: Organization and Action*, no. 5 of a series on 'The Reorganization of Industry'; reprinted in Ken Coates and Anthony Topham (eds) (1968), *Industrial Democracy in Great Britain* (London, Fakenham and Reading: MacGibbon and Kee) pp. 81–5.

Moritz, Charles (ed.) (1970) 'Jennings, Paul (Joseph)', in *Current Biography Yearbook 1969* (New York: H. W. Wilson Co.), pp. 223–5.

Muste, A. J. (1928) 'Factional Fights in Labor Unions', in J. B. S. Hardman (ed.), *American Labor Dynamics* (New York: Harcourt Brace).

New Left Review (1971) 'The State of the AEU' in Ken Coates (ed.), *The Crisis of British Socialism* (London: Spokesman Books) pp. 167–74.

Newman, J. R. (1960) *The N.A.O.P. Heritage* (Wembley, Middlesex: National Association of Operative Plasterers).

Ozanne, Robert W. (1954) 'The Effects of Communist Leadership on American Trade Unions', unpublished Ph.D. dissertation, University of Wisconsin.

Panitch, Leo V. (1971) 'Ideology and integration: the case of the British Labour Party', *Political Studies*, vol. 19, no. 2 (June) pp. 184–200.

Parker, Stanley (1973) 'Research into Workplace Industrial Relations: Progress and Prospects' in Malcolm Warner (ed.), *The Sociology of the Work-Place* (London: George Allen & Unwin) pp. 19–35.

Parry, G. (1969) *Political Elites* (London: George Allen & Unwin).

Pateman, Carole (1970) *Participation and Democratic Theory* (Cambridge: Cambridge University Press).

Paterson, Peter (1972) 'All in the family', *New Statesman*, vol. 84, no. 2158 (28 July) p. 116.

Pearlman, Daniel (1973) 'A review: union elections under LMRDA', *Union Democracy Review*, no. 2 (winter) p. 7 – a review of 'Union elections and the LMRDA: thirteen years of use and abuse', *Yale Law Journal* (January 1972) pp. 407–574.

Pearlin, Leonard I. and Richards, Henry E. (1960) 'Equity: A Study of Union Democracy' in Walter Galenson and Seymour Martin Lipset (eds), *Labor and Trade Unionism* (New York: John Wiley and Sons) pp. 265–81.

Pease, John, Form, William H. and Rytina, Joan Huber (1970) 'Ideological currents in American social stratification literature', *American Sociologist*, vol. 5, no. 2 (May) p. 131.

Peck, Sidney M. (1963) *The Rank-and-File Leader* (New Haven, Connecticut: College and University Press).

Pelling, Henry (1958) *The British Communist Party* (London: Black).

Perlman, Selig (1958) 'Foreword' to Marc Karson, *American Labor Unions and Politics* (Carbondale, Illinois: Southern Illinois University Press) pp. v–vii.

Peters, C. C. and Van Voorhis, W. R. (1940) *Statistical Procedures and Their Mathematical Bases* (New York: McGraw-Hill).

Ranney, Austin and Kendall, Willmoore (1969) 'Basic Principles for a Model of Democracy' in Charles F. Cnudde and Deane E. Neubauer (eds), *Empirical Democratic Theory* (Chicago: Markham Publishing) pp. 41–63.

Raphael, Edna (1965) 'Power structure and membership dispersion in unions', *American Journal of Sociology*, vol. 71, no. 3 (November) pp. 274–83.

Renshaw, Patrick (1968) *The Wobblies: The Story of Syndicalism in the United States* (Garden City, New York: Anchor Books, Doubleday and Co.).

Reynaud, Jean Daniel (1967) 'The Role of Trade Unions in National Political Economies (Developed Countries of Europe)' in Solomon Barkin, William Dymond, Everett M. Kassalow, Frederic Meyers and Charles A. Myers (eds), *International Labor* (New York: Harper and Row) pp. 33–61.

Reynolds, Lloyd G. (1951) *Labor Economics and Labor Relations* (New York: Prentice-Hall).

Richter, Irving (1973) *Political Purpose in Trade Unions* (London: George Allen & Unwin).

Roberts, B. C. (1956) *Trade Union Government and Administration in Great Britain* (London: G. Bell and Sons).

Roberts, B. C. (1959) *Unions in America: A British View* (Princeton, New Jersey: Industrial Relations Section, Department of Economics and Sociology, Princeton University).

Roberts, E. (1973) *Workers' Control* (London: George Allen & Unwin).

Romer, Sam (1962) *The International Brotherhood of Teamsters* (New York: John Wiley and Sons).

Rose, Richard (1964) *Politics in England* (Boston: Little, Brown and Co.).

Rousseau, J. J. (1962) 'The Social Contract' in *Social Contract: Essays by Locke, Hume, and Rousseau*, with an introduction by Sir Ernest Barker (New York: Oxford University Press) pp. 169–307: publ., 1762 originally.

Royal Commission on Trade Unions and Employers' Associations, 1965–68 (1968) *Report Presented to Parliament by Command of Her Majesty*, cmnd. 3623 (London: HMSO).

Russell, Bertrand (1967) *The Autobiography of Bertrand Russell, 1872–1914* (Boston: Little, Brown and Co.).

Sartori, Giovanni (1965) *Democratic Theory* (New York: Praeger).

Sayles, Leonard R. and Strauss, George (1967) *The Local Union* (New York: Harcourt, Brace and World).

Schlesinger, Joseph A. (1965) 'Political Party Organization' in James G. March (ed.), *Handbook of Organizations* (Chicago: Rand McNally) pp. 764–801.

Seidman, J., Karsh, B. and Tagliacozzo, D. L. (1958) *The Worker Views His Union* (Chicago: University of Chicago Press).

Seligman, Ben B. (1970) 'The Impact of Automation on White Collar Workers' in Simon Mareson (ed.), *Automation, Alienation, and Anomie* (New York, Harper and Row) pp. 270–8.

Siegenthaler, Jurg K. (1970) 'Decision-making in Swiss Labor Unions', *Proceedings of the Twenty-Second Annual Winter Meeting (1969)* (Madison, Wisconsin: Industrial Relations Research Association).

Silver, Michael (1973) 'Recent British strike trends: a factual analysis', *British Journal of Industrial Relations*, vol. 11, no. 1 (March), pp. 66–104.

Solomon, Benjamin and Burns, Robert K. (1963) 'Unionization of white-collar employees: extent, potential, and implications', *Journal of Business of the University of Chicago*, vol. 36, no. 2 (April) pp. 141–65.

Spinrad, William (1960) 'Correlates of trade union participation', *American Sociological Review*, vol. 25, no. 1 (February) pp. 237–44.

Spinrad, William (1970) *Civil Liberties* (Chicago: Quadrangle Books).

Stieber, Jack (1962) *Governing the UAW* (New York: John Wiley and Sons).

Stieber, Jack (1968) 'Unauthorized strikes under the American and British industrial relations systems', *British Journal of Industrial Relations*, vol. 6, no. 2 (July) pp. 232–8.

Stinchcombe, Arthur L. (1965) 'Social Structure and Organizations' in James G. March (ed.), *Handbook of Organizations* (Chicago: Rand McNally) pp. 142–93.

Stinchcombe, Arthur L. (1973) 'Formal Organizations' in Neil J. Smelser (ed.), *Sociology: An Introduction* (New York: John Wiley and Sons) pp. 23–65.

Sturmthal, Adolf (1964) *Workers Councils: A Study of Workplace Organization on Both Sides of the Iron Curtain* (Cambridge, Massachusetts: Harvard University Press).

Sturmthal, Adolf (1972) 'Discussion', *Proceedings of the Twenty-Fourth Annual Winter Meeting, 1971* (Madison, Wisconsin: Industrial Relations Research Association).

Taft, Philip (1948) 'The Constitutional Power of the Chief Officer in American Labor Unions', *Quarterly Journal of Economics*, vol. 62, no. 3 (October) pp. 459–71.

Taft, Philip (1954) *Structure and Government of Labor Unions* (Cambridge, Massachusetts: Harvard University Press).

Taylor, Robert (1973) 'Officer class', *New Society*, no. 547 (29 March) pp. 688–9.

Theil, Henri (1971) *Principles of Econometrics* (New York, London, John Wiley and Sons).

Thompson, James D. (1966) 'Common Elements in Administration' in William A. Glaser and David L. Sills (eds), *The Government of Associations* (Totawa, New Jersey: Bedminster Press).

Trades Union Congress (1948a) *Defend Democracy: Communist Activities Examined* (London).

Trades Union Congress (1948b) *The Tactics of Disruption: Communist Methods Exposed* (London).

Turner, H. A. (1962) *Trade Union Growth, Structure and Policy* (London: George Allen & Unwin).

Udy, Stanley H. (1965) 'The Comparative Analysis of Organizations' in James G. March (ed.), *Handbook of Organizations* (Chicago: Rand McNally).

Ulman, Lloyd (1962) *The Government of the Steel Workers' Union* (New York: John Wiley and Sons).

Ulman, Lloyd (1968) *The Rise of the National Union* (Cambridge, Massachusetts: Harvard University Press).

Van de Vall, Mark (1970) *Labor Organizations* (Cambridge: Cambridge University Press).

Vanek, Jan (1972) *The Economics of Workers' Management: A Yugoslav Case Study* (London: George Allen & Unwin).

Warner, Malcolm (1969) 'The big trade unions: militancy or maturity?', *New Society* No. 376 (11 December), pp. 938–9.

Warner, Malcolm (1970a) 'Unions Integration & Society', *Industrial Relations Journal*, vol. 1, no. 1 (May), pp. 43–53.

Warner, Malcolm (1970b) 'Organizational Background and Union Parliamentarianism', *The Journal of Industrial Relations*, vol. 12, no. 2 (July), pp. 205–17.

Warner, Malcolm (1972a) 'Trade Unions and Organizational Theory', *The Journal of Industrial Relations*, vol. 14, no. 1 (March) pp. 47–62.

Warner, Malcolm (1972b) 'Organizational Profile of the Small Trade Union' *Industrial Relations Journal*, (Winter) vol. 3, no. 4 pp. 51–64.

Webb, Sidney, and Webb, Beatrice (1901), *Industrial Democracy* (London: Longmans).

Webb, Sidney and Webb, Beatrice (1965) *The History of Trade Unionism* (Clifton, New Jersey: Augustus M. Kelley): publ., 1894 originally.

Weir, Stanley (1970) 'U.S.A.: The Labor Revolt' in Maurice Zeitlin (ed.), *American Society, Inc.* (Chicago: Markham Publishing) pp. 466–501.

Widdick, B. J. (1964) *Labor Today: The Triumphs and Failures of Unionism in the United States* (Boston: Houghton Mifflin).

Wilensky, Harold L. (1956) *Intellectuals in Trade Unions* (Glencoe, Illinois: Free Press).

Wilensky, Harold L. (1966) 'Class, Class Consciousness, and American Workers' in William Haber (ed.), *Labor in a Changing America* (New York: Basic Books) pp. 12–44.

Windmuller, John P. (1969) *Labor Relations in the Netherlands* (Ithaca, New York: Cornell University Press).

Won, George Y. M. (1962) 'Democratic Sentiments in Unionism: A Case Study of the UAW Convention', unpublished Ph.D. dissertation, Michigan State University.

Wootton, Graham (1961) 'Parties in union government: the AESD', *Political Studies*, vol. 9, no. 2 (June) pp. 141–56.
Yinger, Michael J. (1960) 'Contra-culture or sub-culture', *American Sociological Review*, vol. 25, no. 5 (October) pp. 625–35.
Yorkshire Area, National Union of Mineworkers (1959) *Report of the Yorkshire Miners' Delegation to the People's Republic of China* (Barnsley).

Acknowledgements

We are grateful to the Editors of the Journals cited below (and conference convenors in question) for permission to reproduce material as parts of several chapters, which originally appeared as earlier versions, later revised and expanded (in chronological order):
J. David Edelstein (1965), 'Democracy in a National Union: The British AEU', *Industrial Relations*, (University of California), vol. 4, no. 3 (May), pp. 105–25.
J. David Edelstein (1967), 'An Organizational Theory of Union Democracy', *American Sociological Review*, vol. 32, no. 1 (February), pp. 19–31.
J. David Edelstein (1968), 'Countervailing Powers and the Political Process in the British Mineworkers' Union', *International Journal of Comparative Sociology*, vol. 9, nos. 3–4 (September and December), pp. 255–88.
J. David Edelstein and Malcolm Warner, with W. F. Cooke (1970), 'The Pattern of Opposition in British and American Unions', *Sociology*, vol. 4, no. 2 (May), pp. 145–163.
Malcolm Warner and J. David Edelstein (1973), 'Factions in British and American Trade-Union Organizations:—A Comparative Structural Approach', *Relations Industrielles* (Université Laval, Quebec), vol. 28, no. 1 (March), pp. 166–202.
J. David Edelstein and Malcolm Warner (1974), 'Models of Oligarchy in Large Trade Unions', a paper presented at the VIII World Congress of Sociology, 19–24 August, Toronto, Canada.
J. David Edelstein and Malcolm Warner (1974), 'Organizational Size and Complexity as Related to Opposition in British and American National Unions', a paper presented at the annual meeting of the American Sociological Association, Montreal, Canada, 25–29 August 1974.
Malcolm Warner and J. David Edelstein (1974), 'The Future of Union Democracy', a paper presented to the Nuffield Foundation sponsored conference on Industrial Democracy, London, December 16–18.

List of Tables

2.1   The logical and hypothesised practical compatibility of the dominant
      characteristics of the models of oligarchy.   *page* 37
2.2   The place of the models on some dimensions of oligarchy.   40
4.1   British unions included in the study.   88
4.2   American unions included in the study.   89
4.3   The means of the American and British independent (predictor) variables
      (and correlations with number of members).   100
5.1   Principal axes factor analysis of American independent variables, varimax
      rotation (51 unions).   120
5.2   Predicting the mean closeness of periodic elections for the top posts of
      fifty-one American unions, 1949–66: regression analysis trying thirty-one
      predictors.   126
5.3   The simple correlations for the American unions of the independent
      variables with six measures of effectiveness of opposition (and equivalent
      British correlations where available), based on 1949–66.   136
6.1   The mean closeness of elections in British unions electing top and next-to-
      top officers periodically, 1949–66 (votes for the runner-up per 100 for the
      winner).   154
6.2   The mean closeness of elections in British unions electing top officers per-
      manently, 1949–66 (votes for the runner-up per 100 for the winner). 155
6.3   The composition of executive councils among the British unions electing
      periodically to top and next-to-top posts, as related to the closeness of
      elections.   163
6.4   Intercorrelations for permanent-post unions among organisational com-
      plexity variables, size and closeness of elections (N=15).   170
6.5   Intercorrelations for unions electing periodically among organisational
      complexity variables, size and closeness of eelctions (N=16).   171
8.1   The membership of areas and percentages voting in the May 1960 NUM
      presidential election.   212
8.2   Referenda by preferential ballot (transferable votes) for full-time permanent
      general secretaries and presidents of the British Mineworkers' Union,
      1918–74.   217
8.3   The May 1960 presidential election: first preferences and the deciding
      count.   220
8.4   Percentage of the initial count for nominees and leading candidates within
      the twenty Areas of the NUM in three national referenda for top post, 1959–
      1960.   223
9.1   Summary of differences between the Engineers and the Mineworkers. 268
9.2   Full-time officers of the Engineers, United Kingdom and Irish Republic,
      1960 (by approximate levels).   271
9.3   Referenda under the second-ballot system for new general secretaries and
      presidents of the British Engineers, 1875–1975.   273

Index

Abel, I. W. 331-1
administration of American unions 13-14, 21
affiliations, political 23-7
age of union, and opposition 151, 333ff
Aitken, G. S. 265, 315, 317
Allan, W. 9
Allen, V. L. 46, 87, 91-2, 105, 181, 186, 190, 201-3, 205, 215, 235, 259
Alliance for Labor Action 24
Almond, G. A. 199
alternative votes *see* transferable votes
Amalgamated Engineering Union *see* Amalgamated Union of Engineering and Foundry Workers
Amalgamated Meat Cutters 15
Amalgamated Society of Engineers 9, 263ff, Ch. 9 *passim*
Amalgamated Society of Woodworkers 105, 160, 165-6, 168, 195, 202, 205
Amalgamated Union of Building Trade Workers 164, 195
Amalgamated Union of Engineering and Foundry Workers 69, 105, 158, 164-5, 175, 192, 201-3, Ch. 9 *passim*: candidates for elections 276, 306-11; comparison with National Union of Mineworkers 266-70; craft status and occupational community 297-8; elections 301-11; executive council 267-8, 287, 299-300, 316; history 263-4, 298-301; membership 264-5; National Committee 291-4; national power centres 286-94; postal ballots 288-9; press and the Union Journal 303-5; shop stewards 294-7, 300-1, 316-17,; structure 265-6; voting in elections 274-6
Amalgamated Union of Foundry Workers *see* Amalgamated Union of Engineering and Foundry Workers
Amalgamated Union of Operative Bakers 151
Ambrose, L. J. 278
American Communications Association 13
American Federation of Labor 8, 12, 23, 25; *see also* Congress of Industrial Organizations
American Federation of State, County and Municipal Employees 334
American Federation of Teachers 15, 50, 53, 76-7
American Medical Association 48

American National Educational Association 48, 53
'Americanisation' of collective bargaining 346
appeals 110-11, 119-20, 126, 132-3, 137, 143, 145, 157-60, 186-7, 268
Arnot, R. P. 209, 211, 229, 259
Ashton, J. 329-30
Associated Society of Locomotive Engineers and Firemen 162, 173, 203
Association for Union Democracy 205
Aston research 112; *see also* Donaldson; Warner; size of unions
authority of officials 5ff
autocracy of top officials 320ff

Bain, G. S. 91
ballot-rigging 242, 305-7, 318; *see also* irregularities in elections
ballots, postal 288-9, 315
ballots, secret 106-7
Bambrick, J. J., Jr 107
Barbash, J. 13, 19, 45, 103-4, 196, 319
bargaining *see* collective bargaining
Barratt, H. G. 278
Battle, R. 197
Beck, D. 45
Benson, H. W. 197, 333
Beynon, H. 5, 18, 295
Birch, R. 285, 302-3, 308-9, 318
'blanket clauses' 109, 128, 130, 133, 135, 142, 147
Blauner, R. 343
Boyd, J. 250, 269-70, 283, 302, 306-11, 318
branch *v.* district representation at conventions 177-8
Brett, K. 278
Briginshaw, Lord 154
British Association of Colliery Workers 210
Brody, D. 15
Brooks, G. W. 342
Brooks, T. R. 322, 328
Brotherhood of Railroad Trainmen 334
bureaucratisation, Weberian 7
Burns, R. K. 91
business enterprises compared with unions 4-6

Callahan, R. E. 48
campaign literature 243-4, 325; prohibition of 193-4, 333

democracy: organisational theory of, in United States Ch. 5 *passim*: contingent variables 117–18; factor analyses 118–124; predictors in combination 124–34; relationships of explanatory variables 116–17; simple correlations 134–43
democracy: organisational theory of; relevance to societies 82, 339ff
Derber, M. 7–8, 19
discipline and appeals 109–11, 128, 130, 132–3, 135,137, 142–3,145, 147,157–60, 186–7, 240–1, 268
district *v.* branch representation at conventions 177–8
Donaldson, L. 5, 27, 112, 174
Donovan Report 296; *see* Royal Commission on Trade Unions and Employers' Federations
Downs, A. 73
Dunne, F. 349
Duverger, M. 65

Edelstein, J. D. 84, 98, 105, 177, 357
Edmonds, J. 352
Edmondson, L. 302, 309–10, 318
elected levels 69, 111, 121, 126–7, 130, 132, 139, 142, 145
election to leadership 33, 41, 46–7, 50–1, 63ff, Chs 4–7 *passim*: case studies Chs 8–10 *passim*; closeness of elections 66ff, 95–100, 123–47, 154–75, 177–85, 187, 218, 257, 274, 333, 335, electoral models 73–4; equality of candidates in 66–9, 92–4, 215; frequency of elections 105, 122–4, 126, 128, 139, 143, 145, 156–7, 334; irregularities in 242, 323–4, 326, 333, 335; long-term trend in opposition 98–9; periodic elections 79, 96–7, 105–6, 123ff, 150–68, 171, 173–82, 184–8, 193–196, 201–4, 256; permanent posts 151–8, 160, 162, 164–70, 172–3, 175–82, 184–7, 193–5, 201–5, 256; regional substructures 70–2; size of union and closeness of election 97–8; voting systems 72–80, 106–8,115, 119,122, 131, 160–2, 214–15, 280–1
elections: AUEW 301–11; NUM 215ff; United States unions Ch. 10 *passim*; voting in 274–6
electoral competition *see* election to leadership
electoral models 73–4
electoral monopoly 50–1
Electoral Reform Society 242, 259
electoral systems *see* voting systems
Electrical Trades Union 80, 164, 202–3
Engels, F. 56

Engineering Employers' Federation 264
Engineering Voice 304–5; *see Voice of the Unions*
Engineers (Union) *see* Amalgamated Society of Engineers
equality of candidates 66–9, 92–4, 102–3, 215
Etzioni, A. 34, 190
Evans, E. O. 18, 296
executive councils 107–8, 118, 128, 130–2, 138–43, 145–6, 151, 157, 162–4, 178, 236ff, 240, 267–8, 287, 299–300, 316, 321, 323ff
externally appointed oligarchy 49
externally appointed one-party system 49–50
Ezekiel, M. 117

factions: Great Britain 188–96, 198–205, 251–2, 258, 267, 281–6, 316, 333; United States 55, 188–9, 196–201, 328ff
factor analyses 116–24, 148
Faunce, W. 75
Feather, Lord 202
federal oligarchy 44–5, 358
Fire Brigades Union 167, 177, 195
Fisher, L. 33–4
Fitzsimmons, F. 14
Fletcher, R. 59
Foner, P. 17
Fore, M. 57, 192
formal organisation 4–6, 27, 60–2, 340
fraud 320–2, 326–7, 336; *see also* corruption; racketeering
frequency of elections 105, 122–4, 126, 128, 139, 143, 145, 156–7, 334
Friedman, A. 101, 103
Friedrich, C. J. 32
Fulcher, J. 350

Galenson, W. 294
Garson, D. G. 355–6
general unionism 347ff; constitution changes 350–1
geographic hierarchy 111, 129–30, 133, 138, 142–3, 146–7, 152, 170–6
Glass Bottle Blowers' Association 109
Goldstein, J. 3, 54
Goldthorpe, J. H. 258
Goodman, J. F. B. 296
Gormley, J. 249–51, 269
Gorz, A. 57–8, 344
Gouldner, A. 29
governing oligarchy 38
Gross, E. 189
Guilford, J. P. 119
Günter, H. 341